# Rock & Roll Review
## A Guide to Good Rock on CD

D1446996

# A Guide to Good Rock on CD

## Bill Shapiro

# Andrews and McMeel

A Universal Press Syndicate Company • Kansas City

ISBN: 0-8362-6217-4

Library of Congress Cataloging-in-Publication Data

Shapiro, Bill.
    Rock & roll review : a guide to good rock on CD / by Bill Shapiro.
        p.   cm.
    Includes bibliographical references.
    ISBN 0-8362-6217-4
    1. Rock music—Discography.  2. Compact discs—Reviews.
    I. Title. II. Title: Rock and roll review.
ML156.4.R6S43    1991
016.78166'026'6—dc20                                    91-16060
                                                            CIP
                                                            MN

TO CARIN AND TONY
WITH LOVE, AGAIN

TO THE MEMORY OF MARION KEISKER,
WITHOUT WHOM, WHO KNOWS?

Rock & roll is a stance, an attitude—more so than a discernible musical form. Born out of the great schism of youth from their elders that began in the fifties and flowered unrepentantly in the sixties, it has had a profound impact on the nature of our world for the last thirty-plus years.

# CONTENTS

# INTRODUCTION TO THE SECOND EDITION

For reasons that, a half a century after the fact still remain a mystery, in the early 1940s at the tender age of four or five I became an avid and passionate fan of popular music. That passion has remained paramount in my life ever since. In the fall of 1978, I was afforded the opportunity to express that passion in the form of a weekly one-hour radio program called "Cyprus Avenue," which began airing on the public radio affiliate in my home town, Kansas City, Missouri, KCUR-FM. In the intervening years, the concept behind that program: i.e., to provide an intelligent, hopefully insightful look into the vastly influential and often underappreciated world of pop music, has proved to be sustaining. At this date "Cyprus Avenue" airs on approximately forty-five public radio stations across the United States uplinked through the National Public Radio Satellite System.

In early 1987, I was contacted by a local fan of the show, Donna Martin, who also happened to be editorial director of Andrews and McMeel. Through Donna's initiative and able assistance, in the spring of 1988 Andrews and McMeel published *The CD Rock & Roll Library: 30 Years of Rock & Roll on Compact Disc,* my attempt to provide an historic overview of the most vital music of our times with an insight into the newest technology available for its reproduction.

In all honesty, Andrews and McMeel and I were probably a little anticipatory. The CD revolution was just beginning to take hold in this country, and I vividly recall during the promotional tour for the book innumerable questions regarding the potential longevity of CDs and concerns about another newer technology following rapidly on its heels, which would make these new, shiny little discs obsolete. Given what has occurred in the three short years since *The CD Rock & Roll Library* was published, it seems clear that issues of longevity are no longer relevant. The market has not only embraced them, CDs have proven to be an economic godsend to a recording industry sadly lacking in new product of sufficient quality to generate substantial consumer interest.

Reflecting on the impact of the digitization of popular music, which is now less than a decade old, it strikes me that as is so often the case, the hardware is secondary to the impact generated by the software. While progress continues to be made in the quality of compact disc recordings and players, what may be the real revolution arising out of the advent of the CD era is the curatorial perspective it has brought to the music. Commencing with Columbia's 1985 release of the three-disc Bob Dylan compilation, *Biograph,* the record companies have discovered and exploited a major appetite in the rock listening public for historical assemblies of classic as well as rare work by the artists and aggregations that have shaped the sounds of the last thirty-five years. From the masters in the Chess vaults, which include the work of Chuck Berry, Muddy Waters, and Bo Diddley, through Eric Clapton, the Allman Brothers, Elton John, Led Zeppelin, James Brown, The Byrds, Little Richard, Jerry Lee Lewis, Rod Stewart, The Rolling Stones, the entire Stax/Volt singles catalog, and Robert Johnson, to the 1991 release of Dylan's *The Bootleg Series, Vols. 1–3,* the recording industry has discovered the enduring value of the recorded legacy long stored away. The end result has been a series of boxed-set recordings that not only provide comprehensive musical coverage of artistic careers, but are generally augmented by informative, detailed booklets that codify both the history and influences that have shaped much of the great pop product that has, in turn, shaped the textures of our lives. From the esoteric to the essential, the laser beam that now conveys the musical message also illuminates the context out of which it was born as well as the growth that has caused it to thrive.

To those who would discount the glorious noise of rock & roll as just one of the more obnoxious examples of adolescent hormones and rebelliousness, I would respectfully suggest that the most important cultural/political event of the last half of the twentieth century—the decline and fall of world communism—was precipitated as much by blue jeans and rock & roll as it was by ICBMs and nuclear submarines.

# PART I
# Rock & Roll on CD

# THE
# MUSIC

The one cultural beachhead that the youth rebellion of the sixties took, and held, was in the realm of pop music. Before the onslaught of rock & roll, popular music was just another "adults only" province of what has come to be called popular culture.

The rock music that became the soundtrack for the madly turbulent sixties had its roots in the early/mid-fifties. It was then that the unlikely progenitors of the "devil's music" first stalked the AM airways, mounting a populist wave of rebellion against a staid, but ripe, society. A gay black dishwasher from Macon, Georgia; an enigmatic black hairdresser with a criminal record from St. Louis; and a white truck driver from Tupelo, Mississippi, who oozed defiance from every beautiful pore, merged the energy of hard-assed Saturday nights with the fervor of Gospel Sunday mornings to create the most exuberant art form of the century.

It is important to remember that before the world had heard the sounds of Little Richard, Chuck Berry, and Elvis, the pop music that emanated from the car radios and jukeboxes of postwar America was, for the most part, written by one or often two individuals (composer and lyricist) and performed by a totally unrelated singer or group. Thus, in the late forties and fifties it was not uncommon to have more than a dozen recordings of the same hit song covered by a dozen different artists. This music, which was primarily created on Broadway and Tin Pan Alley, was performed by artists whose roots were, for the most part, in the big bands that brought the swing era to America in the thirties and forties.

The true revolution of rock & roll was the merger of the creator and the performer into a single artistic entity.

With that merger, popular music became an art with as much cultural legitimacy as film, fiction, or any other form of musical or poetic expression. In the process rock & roll attracted some of the brightest, weirdest, and most creative minds of a highly precocious generation as their preferred medium for expression.

It is equally important to remember the spark that ignited it all. That was: first, foremost, and always, rebellion against the status quo—whatever it might be or become, from time to time. To this day, one of the major elements that separates the real thing from the pale corporate-controlled imitations that smother our commercial airwaves is how effectively a given recording or performance captures that primal spirit of rebellion. It is when the music feeds on, as well as passes on, its dark swamp spirit that it has the power to truly shape the moment. And what moments they can be! There can be few people under fifty in the Western world who cannot recall some vivid time in their lives that wasn't partly shaped by the music of Elvis, the Beatles, the Stones, or Dylan.

In retrospect, it's obvious that the original energy that propelled rock & roll into nearly universal popular acceptance in the fifties and sixties also spawned its most enduring moments. The punk rebellion of the seventies was founded on a sound respect for the original scripture—kick out the jams. But the punk's demise was clearly self-inflicted. The casualties that were sustained by the originators of the fifties and sixties were too often the result of wounds inflicted by the other side. While Jim Morrison's death may have been the inevitable end result of self-indulgence to the extreme, those of Janis and Jimi could be traced, in part, to their association with an outcast form of expression. The critical blows dealt to the careers of Jerry Lee Lewis and Phil Spector were the results of conspiratorial attempts from within and without the music community to suppress the influence of the big beat and all that it stood for.

Americans who became teenagers in the early to mid-fifties were exposed to a shattering, completely novel experience that Saturday night in January of 1956 when an unknown kid out of Memphis, with the unlikely name of Elvis Presley, thrust his youthful sexuality and obvious disregard for prevailing social conventions into millions of living rooms across the country. Not that Elvis was some spontaneously generated mutant—his intellectual forebears were the Beats, who were fomenting a similar, but literary, spirit of rebellion against the staid prosperity of a nation whose global might and apparent supremacy had been established a scant decade before. He had popular counterparts suggested in certain screen portrayals of James Dean and Marlon Brando. Yet Elvis was different—more immediate somehow, more directly personal. Perhaps it was because he was the first to violate the sanctity of the home itself, through what was to become the most incursive technological icon of the postwar world—the medium of television. But more probably it was his choice of audience that established his vital role as the prime progenitor of the youth rebellion that quite literally defined many of the mores of the next decade. Here was a teenager expressing heretofore suppressed feelings of adolescent frustration with all the energy of youth to an audience strictly composed of his peers. An audience that was just beginning to find its private arena and one that then failed to perceive that its arena would soon be the biggest venue around. That didn't come until some years later when it was dubbed the baby boom generation. It was the confluence of their vast numbers combined with a general affluence not previously the province of the young that forged the stage on which rock & roll found its gloriously profane voice.

The teenagers of the fifties failed to sense immediately the full implications of the primally compelling new sounds that crept through their radios into the record stores. Hell, it just sounded great. It would take a few more years before youth came to accept and revel in their new potent role. But the institutions of the establishment sensed the challenge immediately, instinctively. It was decried as the voice of the devil from pulpits across the land. It was censured in the press and intimidated by governmental agencies at all levels. It was also inevitable and unstoppable. How long could a nation that had just severely bled for world freedom countenance the burning of records and general suppression of individual expression?

The opposition, of course, still has its agenda. In the mid-eighties, some thirty-plus years after the fact, there were still those in the Washington establishment who would attempt to suppress the music in the name of patently unconstitutional censorship. By the end of the decade these would-be abridgers of freedom of expression had taken their case to state legislatures and into the courts and had obtained labeling support from the marketers who run the modern recording industry. That the youth rebellion marching to rock's compelling beat has failed to eradicate this muddy thinking from the common consciousness is sad, but not unexpected. That the energy of rock in the eighties and early nineties has been so drained of its original intent that it has not risen up out of its own grooves to smite down this latest manifestation of institutionalized ignorance may be the closest thing yet encountered to its true epitaph.

But within its relatively brief life span, this sometimes violent, often moving, frequently genuinely creative art form has both formed and reflected much of our recent history.

As the times have changed, so has the music. Yet it remains the most popularly accepted of all the arts—the rock artist speaks to the largest, most impressionable of all audiences.

Today's rock critics accurately bemoan the fact that it's been almost forty years since Elvis, and almost twenty-five since the Beatles literally changed the world, or, at least its popular culture. In part, that is the result of the fact that the surviving founders and their surviving audience have both grown into middle age. In part, it is the natural outgrowth of rock's phenomenal commercial acceptance with resultant economic success and excess. And, in large part, it is the result of the overall homogenization of Western culture brought to us largely by the same medium that helped spawn Elvis—television. All of which has led to a canonization of sixties culture that will not die, and, thus, continues to impede new creativity and expression.

In the fertile fifties and sixties much of the energy that nurtured the creativity manifest in the best of rock & roll came from the clash of cultures and the music indigenous to those cultures. The seventies and eighties brought us the golden arches and shopping malls with their inherent message of standardization. While diminishing our differences they have drained our vitality. But perhaps all is not lost, if the line between black and white (R&B and pop) in America has become indistinct, then the music may well find renewed vitality in the juxtaposition of world cultures, as evidenced by Paul Simon's *Graceland* in 1986, the continued vitality of reggae, and the impact of World Beat upon much of current commercial product.

The flame still burns, perhaps with less heat and noise, but burn it does. Thirty-plus years after Elvis jolted the pulpits of America, his spiritual descendants rock for Amnesty International and Africa's starving millions. Rock & roll . . .

Within its best lyrics is the poetry of our time.

Within its rhythms are roots to the inexplicably mystical powers of true voodoo.

Within its music are the sounds of all music—the synthesis of all our joyous noise!

# THE
# TECHNOLOGY

The moment the recording process begins, when the sound is first captured by the microphone, it is changed from a "live" experience, and that change is changed again in myriad ways in each step of the recording and reproduction process. For that matter, even the "live" listening experience changes from room to room, row to row. Thus, any form of sound reproduction is exactly that—a technological effort to re-create in the listener's home or car what the ear perceives to be an accurate restatement of a variable original source.

While the eighties failed to deliver a revolution in pop music similar to those which occurred in the 1950s and 1960s, a revolution did occur in the technology that delivers the recorded rock product to its audience.

It is probably coincidental that the formative years of rock & roll (the early 1950s) coincided with technological advances in the recording medium when the 45 rpm single and 33$^1/_3$ rpm LP both became consumer products. There can be little doubt that a factor in the reinvigoration of the form in the mid 1980s was very much attributable to the advent of the compact disc. As recent years have brought a wave of rock nostalgia, the amplitude of that wave has been magnified by the development and phenomenal consumer acceptance of CDs as the preferred form of listening.

In 1984, the first full year in which CDs were marketed, their U.S. gross sales at retail totaled $113.4 million—a small fraction of the multibillion-dollar market for recorded music. In six short years, by the end of the decade, CDs had essentially replaced the LP and the 45—the industry staples for more than thirty years.

Because it is easier to market the known or the familiar (and because the rock artists of the fifties, sixties, and seventies generally had less restrictive contracts with their labels), CDs have brought forth new compilations of the work of those earlier artists who established or substantially enhanced rock & roll. Thus, while one of the major objections to the new medium has been the high cost of discs, the problem is now rapidly moving toward extinction. Value line releases of older material, greater market competition, and larger volume sales are all working toward price reduction. And it has always been the case that some compilation discs (providing upwards of an hour of music) could give the music collector a comprehensive package of major work for a very fair cost. Stated more simply, for less than fifteen dollars one could purchase the CD *Buddy Holly From the Original Master Tapes*, with twenty selections—everything most Holly fans would want in their music library. In addition, the Holly selections are presented in sound quality unheard of before—arguably better than the original.

While this book is primarily about the music, it is about the music as packaged for and heard from the compact disc.

**6**

Many advantages of the disc format are obvious and appropriately heralded by the manufacturers, but other attributes are less well known to the listening public. What follows are some of the well-publicized features that account for the amazingly rapid public acceptance of compact discs as the preferred form of listening:

1. **Permanence.** Unlike its fragile predecessor, the LP, the sound of a CD is not readily affected by handling, although care always makes sense. Pops, clicks, and scratches, the bane of any serious audiophile, for all intents and purposes, have been totally eliminated. The LP was an inherently perishable medium—the quality of sound reproduction diminished, albeit infinitesimally, with each repeated playing; in theory, a CD should sound exactly the same on the first and one-thousandth listenings.

2. **Facility.** Most CD players utilize an elementary computer chip to perform simple, but rewarding, tasks. Specifically, these machines allow the user to program, in advance, the order of selection of cuts to be heard, eliminating the undesired and programming the remainder in any sequence. (Some units even "remember" the user's program on a predetermined number of CDs.) In an age when the record industry would have us believe that the threat to the well-being of society second only to nuclear demolition is home taping, this facility represents a major step forward in that banned activity, not to mention generally enhanced listening.

3. **Enhanced Sound.** CDs provide a dramatically increased dynamic range in sound reproduction. This term, usually found in manufacturers' specifications, defines the difference between the intensity of the loudest and softest sounds on a recording. Because the sounds from an LP are the result of the tracings by a stylus of a V-shaped groove that varies in surface and width, it is necessary, when converting the "live" sound to LP sound, to reduce the intensity of the loudest passages and, correspondingly, to increase the intensity of the softest to meet the physical limitations of the stylus. Since loud or intense sounds require more stylus movement, thus wider grooves, at some point, the width of one groove can become so great that its walls affect the adjacent grooves. Very quiet passages, on the other hand, require minimal stylus movement, and at some point the groove becomes too small for the stylus to trace, so the engineer brings up the loudness to traceable levels. The end result of all this messing around is that the degree of difference between the loudest and softest sounds perceived by the listener is substantially greater in live performance than it is coming from an LP. The CD essentially eliminates this problem because the grooves that carry the sound, concurrent with their inherent mechanical limitations, are also eliminated, being replaced by billions of bits of digital information conveyed in numerical form. Thus, the sound from the CD is more lifelike. This lifelike quality is further enhanced by the medium's elimination of actual contact between the source of the musical information and the device which converts it into hearable sounds. In a CD player, that information is transferred from disc to sound system by a beam of laser light. No surface contact with the information source totally eliminates any surface noise—when there is no sound coming from the disc, there is no sound coming from the stereo system and when music is heard, that is *all* that is heard.

It is principally for these reasons that a CD player has represented to the component stereo buyer the most sound-efficient investment available in the last several years. The $100 it takes to purchase a reasonable compact disc player today will provide the component buyer with more pop for his or her sound dollar than any other similarly priced addition to a home stereo system. And the market has responded accordingly, making CD players the most successful product ever introduced by the home electronics industry.

But there are other, less apparent, reasons why compact discs have so rapidly caught the fancy of the listening audience. These less obvious, but equally appealing, attributes arise out of the nature of the actual technology utilized.

To understand that technology, think of a photograph, highly magnified so that its component parts are visible to the naked eye. As the magnification becomes greater, ultimately all that the eye sees are series of dots of different intensity of light or dark. Those dots are the representative expression of an instant of light in time captured on photographic film, generally 1/60th to 1/125th of a second in duration. Now imagine, if you will, a picture of sound taken at an interval of 1/44,000th of a second. That is precisely the basis for compact disc technology. A computer bisects each second of a musical sound into 44,000 infinitesimal slices and makes a picture of each slice which is recorded not in dots (like the photograph), but in a numerical equation expressed in the binary language of computers. In other words, each of the sound photographs is expressed as a highly complex incredibly lengthy mathematical formula. The amount of numerical information on a seventy-minute compact disc, if converted to printed text, would produce 270,000 pages. Thus, each compact disc is nothing more than a package of formulas handed to the disc player that turns those formulas into 44,000 sound pictures which are reproduced in the speakers each second. Just as the eye blends the individual dots of a photograph to see a cohesive whole, so the ear blends these multiple pictures into a continuous sound of music.

Since the information medium is a numeric formula, it is totally variable. This is a key element in the unique quality of CD recorded sound that is sometimes overlooked by the public. The infinite variability of the numbers in the equation translates into total malleability in the nature of the sound which these equations describe. Therefore, a talented engineer working from strong basic equations (a first-quality original sound source) supported by a record company willing to spend the money for experimentation, can quite literally produce a compact disc that sounds better than the original recording made one or more decades ago by simply manipulating the "numbers" in the formula.

To return to the analogy between a sound "picture" and a photograph, the digital mixing engineer is, in many ways, the equivalent of the photo lab technician who employs manipulative printing processes like "cropping," "dodging," or "burning in" to reframe the picture and heighten or lessen contrast, all intended to produce a final image with more impact that what was originally recorded on the film.

Unfortunately, not all discs are created equal, and not all engineers have the ears or financial support necessary to consistently provide top-quality conversion of original material into the digital format. One of the goals of this book is to provide a guide to some of the true gems that are to be found in the early catalog of compact disc releases and also to alert you to some of the real bummers that lurk out there.

Inevitably, this totally new concept in sound reproduction has bred misconceptions.

One is that "all CD players sound the same." At first glance, a theoretical argument can be made to support this invalid claim. After all, if we're talking about a device that simply reads numbers, then shouldn't all the answers come out the same and, thus, all the sounds be the same? If that were the whole story, then the claim would be true. However, just as in the recording process the engineer must convert the audio or sound information into numbers, so in the receiving process the CD player must convert those numbers back into sounds.

The methods and theories for dealing with this second conversion are as varied as the myriad minds that propel this technological era. Different engineering theories and different electronic components play a critically discernible role in the quality of sound reproduction. This is best evidenced by the fact that in the current audio market, the consumer is faced with a selection of CD players varying in price from under $100 to over $12,000.

A second misconception that seems popular among both the media and the general public is that the technology that has brought us the compact discs will be rapidly outmoded by the next generation of electronic creativity. This is a questionable premise. The compact disc player represents the leading edge of today's technology applied to the reproduction of recorded sound. Its predecessor, the LP, provided the most cost-efficient form of home entertainment for over three and a half decades. At the time of this writing, there is little reason to assume that the LP's successor in the eighties will not provide a listening life of substantial duration.

In reality, the disc is wonderfully designed to accommodate its users. Its portability makes it accessible to the "walkperson," and it has already made a strong inroad into the automobile audio market.

On average, in 75 percent to 80 percent of the conversions, the CD version of a recording is sonically superior to its LP or tape version, with the percentage being higher in the case of most newer material and lower in the case of original recordings made in the fifties and sixties. But when the sound engineering on a disc is right, the LP and cassette simply aren't in the same league. Unfortunately, particularly with older material, often the original sound source or the ear or competency of the person making the digital conversion is too limited to result in a disc that justifies its purchase price. In other instances, the digital remix may contain excessive tape hiss, muddy the mix, or overly emphasize the upper midrange to the point of harshness; not to mention pure audio glitches like dropout or shifting imaging, any one of which can result in a product inferior to its vinyl predecessor.

But the bottom line is that when the new medium's sonic benefits are maximized, digital has the clearly demonstrable ability to add a whole new vitality, an enhanced "lifelikeness," that establishes CDs as the preferred form of listening for those who seek the best form of sound reproduction.

# THE
# RATINGS, ETC.

Because CDs represent a relatively new technology that, like all new audio technologies, was commercially midwifed by the audiophile community, many reviewers provide a dual rating approach: one for sound and a second for musical content. While the reviews that follow reference both attributes of the material, the discs are each assigned a single rating that considers both. Thus, an "A"-rated CD is one that combines first-rate musical content with high-quality sound reproduction, while a "D"-rated disc might contain quality music mutilated by poor sound quality or vice-versa. The ratings appear in bold face following the technical data listed for each disc reviewed. The ratings used are:

A—A first-quality recording, both musically and sonically

B—Generally first-rate material, perhaps less than ideally reproduced or containing a little too much filler

C—OK, but little of sustaining value

D—Either the engineer or the artist (or both) managed to screw things up

F—Unforgivable

As you read this book, you will note that I sometimes review the same disc but released on different labels. The differences between the two can be subtle or substantial, depending on the engineering, remixing, or mastering. It is my suggestion that you compare these reviews carefully to make your selection.

## Some Comments on Coverage

I would hope that it would be obvious that no one listener/critic is able to cover the totality of the pop music catalog on compact disc, which literally numbers in the tens of thousands of titles. Opinions shared throughout this book owe substantially to other critics whose reviews and work I copiously read, and who are not infrequently quoted in the review sections that follow. Yet the final distillation of point of view, and more importantly, the final determination of what will and will not be included, must all be clearly laid at my door.

On the opinion side, it is, obviously, just that. You will either agree or disagree as is your wont, but it is my hope that I have maintained a voice of some consistency, thereby allowing those of you who find that your tastes coincide with my own to utilize this book as the reference tool for which it is in large part intended.

As to what is included or omitted, that is entirely a different matter. Since the inclusions speak for themselves, let me address those items that are not included. Some of this is conscious and some unconscious. As to the latter, there is probably a substantial amount of quality material out there that has never crossed my ears. This is the case even though I have been an ardent popular music collector for over forty-five years, and a serious student of the form for close to thirty years. But we live in an age where there is a plethora of product filtered through a very narrow funnel that principally remains radio, now sadly augmented by MTV. As a resident of the Midwest I am afflicted by one of the more heinous ills of our homogenized society—basically, programmed/formatted radio. Thus, I hereby confess that commercial FM/AM programming is a minimal source of new recorded material for me. Rather, I rely on local live music featuring new bands and, to a greater extent, the critical columns and music periodicals to alert me to material of interest. Of course, all of this is built upon a long history with the form and therefore many recordings and artists have been located through research and the information provided by knowledgeable friends.

Lest you get the idea that the exclusion of Black Sabbath, Bon Jovi, or, for that matter, Billy Joel and Neil Diamond, is the result of ignorance on my part, please don't be misled. In the case of Black Sabbath, Bon Jovi, and other of the heavy metal/glam bands, I simply view them as cartoons that are mildly entertaining before the main feature arrives. Thus, while I abhor current attempts to censor them, I am also not willing to clutter what follows with their inclusion.

As to groups such as Billy Joel, Journey, Neil Diamond, et al., I find my personal distaste for what I perceive to be their intellectually and emotionally fraudulent music to be too great for me to write an even-handed review. Therefore, rather than indulge in gory orgies of critical flagellation, pleasant as that may be, I have decided to save my dollars, not to listen, and thus, not to review.

What I have attempted to include is a fair cross-section of those groups and artists whose work provides historical or personal meaning sufficient to suggest some degree of longevity in what is, by nature, an ephemeral form. Thus, in the cases of artists like the Beatles, Bob Dylan, and the Rolling Stones, all of whom are of acknowledged stature, I have attempted to provide complete or essentially complete discographies of all material available currently on CD through normal commercial channels. In the case of other artists whose stature may be more cult-like, such as Van Morrison and David Bowie, again I have attempted to provide essentially complete discographies, in the former case because of my deep personal feelings for the artist's output, and in the latter, because of his historic importance during the seventies and eighties.

As long as we are in a confessional mode, let me also confess that I am no longer sure what constitutes "rock & roll," because of the form's pervasiveness, diversity, and general co-option by the forces of mass marketing.

The artistic bankruptcy of the record market of the latter half of the 1980s was definitely established by the disclosure, late in 1990, that Grammy Award–winning pop group Milli Vanilli—which had enjoyed multimillion album sales and the heretofore prestigious Best New Artist award—included no singing by the group members.

These two pop poseurs merely lip-synched songs performed by some other nameless, faceless artists. The package became the product and the public got suckered, big time, once again. If this weren't bad enough, deception has reached a level where more than one state legislature is considering enactment of bills requiring that where performers lip-synch to prerecorded music, this information must be disclosed on ticket and promotional information before these tactics can be utilized in "live" performance. However, in a time where pop music is dominated by MTV, what do you bet that, disclosure or not, the appearance of the music carries more cachet with the buying audience than its substance? We seem to be living in an age where it is necessary to prove the obvious once again—legislation and art, particularly when the former is aimed at "protection," have just about as much compatibility as Iraq and Kuwait.

# A BRIEF
# HISTORY

As the times change, so does the popular music that echoes through the days and nights in which those changes are manifest. Obviously the division of any history into specific decades is arbitrary and often erroneous, but milestones are milestones and decades are convenient dividers, so here's an encapsulated overview of four of them.

## The Fifties

"... Beware of change to a strange form of music."
—Socrates

In a very real, physical sense, the war that this nation fought during the first half of the 1940s impacted Americans in ways that the electronic reproductions of the wars we fought in the sixties and eighties simply could not replicate. The lives of the country's youth in the forties were directly affected by food and gas rationing and by the fact that Detroit was making no new automobiles. The lifestyle of this generation was partially measured by periodic paper and scrap drives generally conducted on school yards anchored by red, white, and blue grease boxes where drippings from Mom's kitchen were salvaged in tin cans to be returned to Uncle Sam for some sinister but, obviously, patriotic effort.

America's backyards were partitioned into victory gardens, where urban kids learned the tasks of weeding and harvesting and the satisfaction of fresh, hand-picked produce.

All across the nation, the young saw their fathers and brothers don uniforms and disappear to places far away, while their mothers left the primacy of home to fill the void in the work force created by Dad's departure. Thus, teenage self-involvement placed a distant second to the war that was pervasive. These were the children who first heard the words "Hiroshima" and "Nagasaki"; who first faced the inexplicable horror of the Bomb.

The fathers and brothers, some of them anyway, returned home around 1945; more sophisticated and anxious to build homes and raise families in the world to which they had given so dearly to make free. The products of these desires began to come of age in the mid-to-late 1950s and with them came the glorious roar of rock & roll.

The energy behind that roar was tindered by the friction inherent in the juxtaposition of divergent cultures within the boundaries of a "single" society. While America's black and white children, particularly in the South, generally attended separate schools (serving separate neighborhoods), their very separate forms of popular music could be heard on radio or record by anyone adventurous enough to simply "change the station."

From the blues to rhythm and blues, it was a relatively small step to rock & roll.

Because of the diversity of the music's "founding fathers" and pervasiveness of their varying influences, the exact moment of the birth of the music and place of its creation are impossible to specify. This much is clear: its home territory is the American South. Historically this country's richest cultural region, where the voodoo-rooted musical expressions of a black population hummed through tepid nights. It is also equally obvious that this was, at least initially, the music of the "have-nots" of America's polyglot society.

If one must seek a starting point, probably the Sun Studio in Memphis, Tennessee, in 1955 is as likely a candidate as any. It was here that Sam Phillips, one of many independent record producers operating outside pop music's bicoastal "establishment," supposedly tracked his legendary Bigfoot—a white man who could sing like a black. Phillips had been perceptive enough to realize that white kids, at least in the South, were naturally drawn to the rhythm and power inherent in black music—music which still belonged "at the back of the bus" as far as the mainstream white pop music industry was concerned. Known then as race music, it was separately charted by the trade press and was as alien to "The Hit Parade" as blacks in a Mississippi voting booth.

Of course, Phillips found his man or, if legends are true, Elvis Presley found Sam Phillips. And, in Elvis, Phillips found much more than just a white man who could sing like a black; he found a charismatic performer possessed of the style of youthful rebellion, gently interwoven with the straitlaced principles then common to white God-fearing Southern youth.

For America's teenagers in the mid-fifties, Elvis Aron Presley personified all that was unspoken and unspeakable between the worlds of youth and adult. He was the incarnation of the youth revolution, the barbarian to vault the barricades. In all probability, of the many attributes uniquely possessed by Presley which enabled him to ascend to the throne of rock & roll, the one that probably served him best was his unique sense of his time and place in American history. He not only saw the brass ring and grabbed it the first time around; he seemed to be totally aware of the act while it was taking place.

The rock critic, Greil Marcus, has said that with the exception of Presley's earliest "Sun sides" and perhaps the live footage done before an audience for the 1968 TV special, Presley always had the ability to stand outside of himself and not get caught up in the hysteria he spawned. This attribute alone probably kept him sane for as long as he was able to manage survival in the absurd role in which he cast himself.

In retrospect, it is easy to see that Presley established many of the music's basic attributes. The original Presley group, selected by Phillips and made up of Scottie Moore on guitar and Bill Black on bass (later augmented by drummer D.J. Fontana), laid down the basic rock or rockabilly sound that remains the authentic underpinning of much of what is still produced in the name of rock & roll today. Elvis also introduced rock & roll to the first visible specter of commerce, in the somewhat sinister form of former carny barker Col. Tom Parker. The vast commercial potential of this pure teen product was first intuited and then exploited by this shadowy showman. It would only take five years or so before the full commercial potential of the music exploded with an impact not even Parker could have foreseen. It would only take another five to ten years before rock's commercial aspects became preeminent, much to the detriment of the product itself.

But mostly, Presley brought the attitude—an attitude of rebellion combined with the belief that one could make music for an audience of youth and prosper in a world of adults.

As Marcus also aptly pointed out, perhaps the most intriguing and disturbing aspect of the phenomena that was Elvis Presley is that he was the truest personification of the American dream. Born in nearly abject poverty, Presley achieved fame and fortune unprecedented in the history of pop culture. Yet, it all ended so terribly badly. On August 16, 1977, the King died bloated, a sad personification of the "stature" to which his creation had fallen.

During those formative years, when Elvis was claiming his kingdom, there were others who defined the original parameters of the realm.

Chuck Berry survives to this day, a habitué of occasional oldies forays on television and a charter member of the Rock & Roll Hall of Fame. If any single individual can validly be credited with being the architect of the musical form that expressed the voice of youth in the fifties and the decades to follow, that man is Chuck Berry. As a writer/performer, he was among the first, if not *the* first, to direct his lyrical messages specifically to the teenage audience. And, oh, what lyrics. More than one rock critic has compared the verse contained in Berry's lyrics to that of perhaps America's greatest poet, Walt Whitman, a comparison that can withstand scrutiny. To these words he added a vocabulary of basic rhythm guitar licks which loudly echo through the music to this very day and established the electric guitar as the music's primary musical voice. He combined all this with duck-walking showmanship that defined the rock musician's stage persona.

Perhaps the aspect of Berry's impact which is most impressive is that he popularized and established the role of the rock star as both creator and performer. Rock & roll thus became a medium of total expression, the performer/writer providing his or her audience with potentially a very singular and unique vision. True, this tradition is readily traceable to folk music; and, in a very real sense, rock & roll is the electronically amplified folk music of the technological age.

The concept of totality of individual expression in the rock format was greatly advanced by another of the fifties pioneers, Buddy Holly. Holly's fleetingly brief recording career left an indelible mark on what followed. Holly took the idea of total artistic creativity further than any of his predecessors in that he realized that the recording process was as integral to the creative act as the writing or the playing. By his nerdy appearance he further proclaimed the everyman roots of the rock star; and, through his tours of Britain, spread those roots to where they would flower in the next decade.

And then, there was Little Richard!!!! The man who codified the music's first password: "awopbopaloobopawopbamboom." Little Richard's music was the truest generational litmus test—one's reaction to his recordings quickly established which side the listener was on. More clearly than anyone else, Little Richard enunciated a basic truth of rock & roll: If the parents can't stand it, the kids are definitely going to buy it.

One of the elements that sets rock above mere aural wallpaper and makes the best of it sustain is its concern with the eternal confrontation between the forces of darkness and light. The voodoo power of the music's sound finds its heart in this conflict, as did much of the original (and continuing) reaction of society. The personification of this conflict survives in the form of "The Killer," Jerry Lee Lewis, the spirit of rock & roll incarnate. Called by his producer at Sun Studios the greatest natural talent he had ever seen, Lewis's life and career pulse with the energy that still fuels the best of the music.

Rock was more than a change in the sound of music: it was the first truly populist call to a change in the values of the listening society. It was rebellion pure and simple. Like all rebellions, the establishment rose up to resist it, and not without success. The Army took Elvis, the press took care of Jerry Lee, the penitentiary took Chuck Berry; and the church got Little Richard.

# The Sixties

"—Seen at times thru dark sunglasses and other forms of psychic explosion, a song is anything that can walk by itself . . ."

—Bob Dylan. Liner notes from
*Bringing it All Back Home* © 1985

J.F.K. . . . Jack Paar . . . beatniks . . . Khrushchev's shoe . . . Casey Stengel . . . sit-ins . . . Gary Powers . . . The Wall . . . the twist . . . Peace Corps . . . Bay of Pigs . . . John Glenn . . . James Meredith . . . Cuban missile crisis . . . Lee Harvey Oswald/Jack Ruby . . . L.B.J. . . . Billy Sol Estes . . . Christine Keeler . . . *Hello, Dolly* . . . Tonkin Bay . . . discotheques . . . topless swimsuits . . . Vietnam . . . peace marches . . . peace symbols . . . Selma . . . Martin Luther King . . . Montgomery . . . Great Society . . . Watts . . . Black Power . . . big blackout . . . Richard Speck/Charles Whitman . . . Medicare . . . *Valley of the Dolls* . . . Miranda . . . miniskirts . . . hair . . . Twiggy . . . hippies . . . Haight-Ashbury . . . LSD . . . Timothy Leary/Owsley Stanley . . . Berkeley . . . Muhammed Ali . . . Dr. Spock . . . *Bonnie & Clyde* . . . Christiaan Barnard . . . Cape Kennedy . . . Robert Kennedy . . . Jackie Kennedy . . . Tiny Tim . . . U.S.S. *Pueblo* . . . Nehru jackets . . . airline hijackings . . . "Laugh-In" . . . Neil Armstrong . . . moon walk . . . Chappaquiddick . . . Broadway Joe . . . the Pill . . . Aquarian Age . . . My Lai . . . the sixties, pure rock & roll.

From grimy Liverpool to enlightened San Francisco, the pulse of this century's most tumultuous decade was rock & roll. The soundtrack for unique times. Times when everything was moving, changing, shining, and melting—usually all at once. Rock music defined style in an age when style was essential. Rock music defined rebellion in a time of immense social and political upheaval.

The musicians who created this soundtrack, in many instances, have become cultural icons, revered and influential beyond anyone's wildest dreams. Their involvements became the involvements of their fans to a degree that rock stars' endorsements were sought by the political establishment.

The Beatles, the truly transitional group that turned the fifties rock & roll into sixties rock, achieved a musical world union not experienced since. At one point in the sixties, eight of the Top Ten hits were Beatles' songs—eight of the Top Ten: a feat never approximated before and not repeated since. In June of 1967, the radios of the entire Western world became the *Sgt. Pepper's Lonely Hearts Club Band* chorale—the music was everywhere; the music mattered.

The yin to the Fab Four's yang, the Rolling Stones, carried forth the tradition of Jerry Lee Lewis on the sounds of Chuck Berry. One of the most complex, influential, and essential bands the music has yet produced—their cynical view has proved to be sadly prophetic.

Meanwhile, back in the U.S.A., the Beach Boys, rock's only choir, created the most effective advertisement for a lifestyle and region yet witnessed in these commercially saturated times. In the process, they laundered the form to create an extraordinarily durable sound. The Beach Boys made rock & roll acceptable in venues previously deemed outside its influence; but then, how threatening is a tanned, smiling blond kid whose sole stated desire is to romp on the beach?

While the British were co-opting, repackaging, and selling America's pop musical heritage back to its homeland, San Francisco was announcing the dubious joys of modern (and ancient) chemistry to a newly potent, blindly optimistic generation; and psychedelia was added to the mix.

Across the continent in Greenwich Village coffee houses, Bob Dylan, rock's towering intellect/poet, brought political currency to the medium. In terms of the form of the music, Dylan and Chuck Berry stand as rock & roll's two greatest individual contributors—it was Dylan who turned on the light so that everyone could see. During his conversion from folk hero to the creator of folk rock, Dylan's genius became incandescent and the classic recordings of that time not only still crackle with the energy of pure creativity, they stand with total authority several decades after the fact.

Then there was Detroit's other major contribution to the good times of the fun-seeking youth of the era: Motown.

In a very real sense, Motown, the most financially successful black business venture in American history, was a vindication—the full realization of the commercial potential of the black music that had been co-opted and exploited in white rock & roll. By mixing the joyous energy born of the black church gospel choir with lyrics aimed at the youth experience and serving it in brilliantly produced two-to-three minute doses, Berry Gordy found a formula that yielded some of the most perfect pop sounds yet experienced. The market, black and white, responded by acclamation—the Supremes alone had a dozen No. 1 hits between 1964 and the end of the decade, and Smokey Robinson and the Miracles, the Temptations, Marvin Gaye, the Four Tops, plus numerous other Motown acts were frequent contributors to the Top Ten.

But Motown was only a part of a black musical resurrection which, in its way, was every bit as potent and pervasive as that which was revolutionizing the bleached "Hit Parade." In the fifties, Ray Charles had begun to combine gospel and blues forms to create what has been dubbed "soul" music, which, in the sixties, flowered through the efforts of an extraordinarily talented group of performers who were principally nurtured by Atlantic Records. Otis Redding, Aretha Franklin, Wilson Pickett, Ray Charles, the Coasters, and the Drifters were making music of broad enough appeal to escape the boundaries of color—music that, combined with Motown's output, insured that this was the golden decade for both black and white pop sounds.

This was also a time of maturation, and inevitable self-awareness—with attendant self-conciousness. It was the decade in which the rock press came into being. *Craw-daddy* and *Rolling Stone* in the U.S., and *Creem* in England, began to define and identify the music's community, ultimately an invaluable tool in its inevitable commercialization.

Obviously, a press is composed of words, and the authors of those words, at least the best of them, became an integral part of the rock establishment in the latter half of the decade. Critics like Greil Marcus, Lester Bangs, Robert Christgau, John Landau, Jonathan Cott, Peter Guralnick, Dave Marsh, Ed Ward, Nick Tosches, and Paul Williams created a body of commentary, not only covering the music itself, but also the milieu from which it arose. Their influence on their readers ultimately became an influence over the product itself. Today, Marcus has veered off in search of the fundamental attitude, an admirable but currently unrewarding venture; Marsh is either the wisest or dumbest man in the world, take your choice; and John Landau saw "the future of rock & roll" and became a prophet in his own time.

This was the age of free-form radio, when the airwaves had personality and commitment to something more than the sale of another motorcycle or acne preparation, at least that was the case on the FM side of the dial. Until the sixties, AM radio was the dominant broadcast form in America and musically it was devoted to a Top 40 or Top 100 format, composed of frequently played hit singles, generally two to three minutes in duration.

FM, because of its better sound capabilities and, ultimately, its stereo broadcast capability, was reserved for classical music or simulcast of the "sister" station's AM programming. But in the sixties, the Federal Communications Commission intervened, requiring a majority of FM station owners who held both AM and FM licenses to provide different programming on each format. Thus, however unwittingly, Uncle Sam played a major role in the spread and development of rock music. With so many hours of air time to fill, and a predilection toward "popular music," it was inevitable that the FM stations in America would turn to populist rock & roll.

Since early FM radio was clearly the outcast form of broadcasting, various station managers employed disc jockeys to just fill the time. This gave birth to free-form radio, which programmed extended album cuts in lieu of heavily promoted singles, and mixed artists, forms, and musical history with creative abandon. Ultimately, this meant the death knell for the standard two- to three-minute pop song because within the album format, rock musicians were extending the boundaries of their compositions to whatever length was appropriate to express an idea. Probably, Bob Dylan's "Like a Rolling Stone," which clocks in at six minutes playing time, was the song that broke through from FM programming to Top 40 radio, thereby shattering the time limitations along with countless other restrictions on pop songs forevermore.

This was the decade of the second, and to date, last, great cultural revolution fomented basically by teenagers with plugged-in guitars and personas.

It was the best of times. It couldn't last. It didn't. It left a heritage of gloriously moving sounds and a fair share of physical and emotional casualties. But there is always a price to be paid when the balance of power shifts—even slightly. The best rock music of this decade throbs with the energy of pure, innocent creativity; energy that still rejuvenates—still resonates.

It was a cornucopia of promises—it was a river of wretched excess; Woodstock and

Altamont. Ultimately, the sixties proved to be times of involvement, times of community; and those were the richest of times.

# The Seventies

*"You're the man who squats behind the man who works the soft machine."*
—Mick Jagger and Keith Richards

Like the third month, the third decade of rock & roll came in like the proverbial lion and left like the proverbial lamb.

The early seventies, for the most part, marked a continuation of the great musical creativity that had exploded from the mid-sixties forward. But all was far from perfect in paradise.

The very success of rock and its acceptance by vast numbers of the affluent culture of the western world began to nurture the seeds of destruction, or, at least, substantial diminution.

Popular acceptance in a commercially oriented world means material excess for the accepted. By the mid-seventies, the gross revenues from the sales of direct recorded product (LPs, 45s, and cassettes) were approximating $4 billion a year. In addition to those revenues, the industry was earning substantial amounts from the sale of concert tickets, T-shirts and related memorabilia, as well as vast sums from the publishing rights that reflected the domination of rock music over national radio.

As was inevitable with the American economy, that kind of meteoric financial success attracted the business establishment, which, during the seventies, was marching to its own drummer: conglomeratization. The end result of this unholy alliance was a transfer of control over the creation, promotion, and distribution of the rock product from artists whose principal concern was the product, to executives and accountants whose principal concern was the bottom line.

To suggest that commercialization alone was responsible for the decline in the quality of the music would be unfair. Both the adulation and the excess of success took their toll on the performers who had made the sixties a magic musical decade. The early seventies brought the drug-related deaths of many; and, in the case of too many of the survivors, it brought a preoccupation with the lifestyle as opposed to a continued commitment to art. This result was inevitable. For rock & roll to have retained its purity in the face of such massive monetary seduction would have been an event unique in the annals of human economic history.

It also must be remembered that these "rock stars" were generally young, in their late teens or early twenties, whose commitment to their music had often consumed their short lives. Usually the children of middle- to lower-middle-class backgrounds, these youthful phenoms had no preparation for stardom. How does someone who is an unknown in Port Arthur, Texas, or Los Angeles, for that matter, become a world-renowned celebrity showered with adulation and wealth almost overnight and remain unchanged by the experience? Would you?

Since artists generally draw upon their life experience as a fount for their creativity, when that life experience is exploded with the potency of stardom, it inevitably affects the creative process. This can be illustrated by comparing the quality of an artist's or group's first and second recordings. Generally, debut records are stronger than second releases. In part, this is because debut material is culled from the trial and error of the road and the dues paid to make the record in the first place; frequently, in part, it is because the success which allowed the second recording to be made also severed the artist from his original creative roots. Of course, sometimes the transitions themselves become stimuli for renewed creativity, but that's what frequently separates the stars from the lesser luminaries.

While the audience that had enshrined those sixties icons who survived and continued to perform in the seventies seemed content to age with its heroes, the youth (at least some of it) of this era accurately perceived that the torchbearers of yesterday held little relevance to their present. And thus, the mid-seventies brought youth's response, decorated with safety pins, rendings of flesh and fabric and accompanied by technologically abbetted abrasive "noise." Punk. It was, and, it is wonderful—the wild essence of the music once again roaring its subversive call.

Perhaps because the audience was too comfortable or too emotionally spent from the dislocations of the mad sixties, whatever the reason, punk proved to be more theoretical than tangible in its ultimate impact. The failure of the new wave of seventies music to revolutionize the rock establishment was also attributable to its failure to produce any creative personalities with both the charisma and talent to attract a mass audience. But then, that may be just another case of the chicken/egg debate.

The Ramones in New York's then-fertile East Village scene and, more potently, the Sex Pistols in Malcolm McLaren's London first sounded the clarion call of change. But the really sustaining artists to rise from this short-lived movement were Talking Heads in New York and Elvis Costello in England—both performers who perceived and capitalized on the intellectual nature of their respective enterprises. Both are fine artists whose work has been illuminating and sometimes challenging, but this wasn't any third revolution—that is yet to come.

Perhaps the biggest obstacle to continued real creativity (in the sense of originality) was the homogenization of the music's audience during the so-called "me" decade. Increased communication (McCluhan's "global village"), with its attendant commercialization, homogenized the audience, blunting the cultural edges that had previously sparked the artistic impulse.

Actually, the most interesting advent of the decade may have been the development of a world audience for the rhythm and revolution of Jamaica's principal cultural export to the modern world: reggae. A fascinating synthesis of New Orleans-based rock/soul sounds with Rastafarian ritual and belief overlaid on the same voodoo roots that started it all in the first place; it extended rock's central message to a Third World population most responsive to its siren call.

The seventies were the decade that saw the music's focus move from Dylan to disco, while radio changed from free form to format, and honesty of expression gave way to commercial complacency.

# The Eighties

"In the eighties rock & roll went to work for corporations and got up at 6 A.M. to go jogging."

—Bono

If the seventies marked the beginning of the decline in pop/rock music, then, the eighties certainly produced little to reverse that direction, the dominant themes of the decade being marketing and technology.

However, all is not without hope. The same artists who have come to realize the power of their communicative abilities (through their obvious commercial rewards), have, in some cases, chosen to exercise those awesome powers to advance humane causes and needs. It should never be forgotten that this most often vilified form of popular culture has not only been at the forefront, but has also been the most potent, of all the arts in the advancement of the human condition. Whether it be the starving millions in famine-plagued Africa or a heroic few men and women deprived of basic human rights, rock & roll performers have taken up the gauntlet while others in the arts have too often merely chosen to observe.

Apart from that more elevated preoccupation, on an artistic level technology dominated the rock music industry in the eighties. The synthesizer, which literally put almost all known, as well as some previously unknown, sounds at the fingertips of a keyboard player, along with the ability to modulate or modify those sounds at whim, replaced the electric guitar as the principal instrumental voice of much of the decade's pop product. Added to this was the now almost ubiquitous drum machine: the computerized metronome that guarantees perfect time. Hell, it guarantees the best recorded licks of the great drummers of rock's past. Then came the Digitizer. This electronic wonder allows those hidden souls in the techno end to "borrow" a sound, a phrase, or any other recorded effect from anyone, anywhere, and add it to the sound of current recorded product.

It may be entertainment; it sure ain't rock & roll. It's more like a game of Pavlonian chess played among the hidden stars of the eighties' mostly mediocre pop music business: the producers and engineers ably assisted by the radio programmers, demographers, and marketing experts who all account to the finance department of their respective conglomerates.

Probably, the ultimate perversion of it all is reflected in the merger of audio/video technology manifest in MTV: the bastard merger of video technology and the popular recording arts.

MTV, which has promoted mostly recycled, synthesized Motown in video-perfect packages, was principally responsible for the elevation of eighties "stars" who were more notable for their physical attractiveness than their musical abilities. But the real price of the decade's more dazzling, diverting entertainment was the loss of the capacity of imagination, perhaps humanity's most precious part.

In an age when the anti-heroes of yesterday's pop culture (or at least their contemporary successors) have embraced marketing/commercialization to a shocking degree with various and sundry commercial tie-ins between bands and products becoming the unfortunate norm, the music itself has not been particularly notable.

The decade saw the rise of Michael Jackson, whose *Thriller* is the runaway bestseller of all time, proof that Jackson represents the perfect eighties synthesis rock star—his appeal being as much visual as aural.

The era's other major superstar—like Jackson, a man whose musical beginnings preceded the decade—Bruce Springsteen established the canonization of blue-collar American rock. Springsteen managed to attain almost heroic stature in the Reagan-resurrected eighties' reenactment of the Eisenhower fifties with his monster mega-seller, *Born in the U.S.A.*

Prince probably provided the most innovative and creative music of the decade, although his skin color and performance affectations and attitudes have prevented him from attaining truly mass commercial acceptance. (They have not, however, prevented nearly everyone else in the industry from mining his creative genius.) His motion picture debut, *Purple Rain*, may well be the definitive rock movie.

But another seventies group, Talking Heads, may represent the ultimate incarnation of the rock group that best personified the spirit of a generally uneventful decade.

# The Nineties

"It's not music, it's a disease."
—Mitch Miller on rock & roll

At the date of this writing the last decade of the twentieth century is less than eighteen months old. Yet it is already clear that the attitudes of the greed-driven eighties are being rejected in favor of more traditional values and the promise of a true world community emphasizing greater social and environmental responsibilities.

Additionally, it appears that America, through its wildly successful prosecution of the Gulf War, may have finally shed the mantle of self-doubt that the assassination of JFK and defeat at the hands of the Viet Cong draped over the world's most vital nation.

Ah, but that the same promise appeared in the world of popular music—but that is not yet the case. To the contrary, the outlook from here ain't much to get worked up about. The business bias of the record industry has become more pronounced as the last significant major independents, Geffen and Island, have been consumed by international entertainment conglomerates resulting in essentially all major recorded product being created, distributed, and marketed by six globe-straddling music companies. To date, none of them has given any inkling that real creativity is a requirement for recording. In fact, a credible argument can be made that the current music market is about as mundane and predictable as it was thirty-five years ago when rock & roll ignited a revolution.

The industry's profits come principally from the vacuous pandering of heavy metal's pretty boys for whom appearance and decibel level are the coin of the realm. Their other major source of financial prosperity is the subject of this volume—the CD revolution has revitalized the classic catalog of rock & roll. Stoked by commercial radio, which sadly continues to feed America's apparently insatiable appetite for sixties/early seventies rock product, the work of the original rock revolutionaries and their progenitors has been repackaged and resold with startling success. For the music historian, this has proved a bonanza. For those who believe in the power of rock & roll to incite and illuminate, it is anything *but*.

All is not bleak, however. With the avent of rap's ascendancy, the element of real danger has returned to the form—and it has been notably absent for too long. Unfortunately, the very colloquial, nonmusical nature of rap raises serious questions about its ultimate durability and impact. Yet in a very real sense it is both musically and socially the most vital new sound to be heard since the short-lived punk explosion of the mid-seventies.

Lest we forget, there's also the virulent strain of censorship, which greeted the musical revolution of the fifties, and has sadly reemerged with born-again vengeance. Perhaps it should be reassuring that some things never change. Perhaps what rock artists need is something to again rebel against. Perhaps the current generation will awaken to forge their own culture and values. Perhaps.

Don't assume that the glorious river of sound begun in Memphis over thirty-five years ago has run aground. There is still good music, rock & roll music, being made today. There's just less of it, making it harder to find. But what does come through loud and clear is the fact that it has now been over two decades since anyone added anything major to the mix.

The music obviously has, and will, continue to change. Yet, the spirit that sparked it in the first place is a recognizable constant in the best of it all, whether made in Memphis in 1955 or in Minneapolis in 1985.

In the end, it's probably wise to remember that real understanding and evaluation can only come from the perspective of time passed, even for a medium whose principal currency is currency.

# PART II
# CD Reviews

## King Sunny Ade and His African Beats (Sunday Adeniyi)

b. 1946—Oshogbo, Nigeria

The son of church organist whose musical career began as a teenager. Formed his first band, The Green Spots, in 1966.

### JuJu Music (1982)

Mango CCD9712 (43:07)  **[A]**

JuJu is the name given to the "popular" music of Nigeria which is based upon Yoruba tribal roots. Ade, or Chairman King Sunny Ade as he is locally known, builds his intricate sounds upon the classic call and response approach (in this case between singers and African talking drums), employing modern sounds and technology (electric guitars, synthesizers, and even Hawaiian slack-string guitars) to achieve what he accurately calls "a very rich music." Sinuous, elegant, and compellingly rhythmic, it's not difficult to understand how the King and his large band could have made over forty albums (with average sales of a couple hundred thousand per release). The CD's sound is wonderful, precise, spacious, instrumentally defined, clean, warm, and all supported by dynamic percussion.

## Aerosmith

Formed 1970—New Hampshire

**Greatest Hits (1973–1980)**

Columbia CK 36865 (37:30)  **[B–]**

Sure, it's warmed-over Stones (they never pretended to be much else), and only "Dream On" and "Walk This Way" cracked the Top Ten. But maybe because they've triumphed in the face of living the rock & roll life to extremes, or because they obviously worked so hard, Aerosmith somehow manages to rise above most of the other early-to-mid-seventies hard rock smashers. That's not to say this is anything special, but if you're already a fan. . . . Soundwise, it's pretty clean, but also somewhat muddy and compressed at times, excessively bright at others.

## The Alarm

Formed 1981—South Wales

**Declaration (1984)**

IRS CD70608 (46:14)  **[C–]**

Empty sloganeering by another of the guitar-driven eighties rock revolutionaries. Anthems devoid of meaning other than as an opportunistic location to hang the hooks. The sound is relatively clean and dynamic, but with a marked tendency to shrill overbrightness.

# Allman Brothers Band
Formed 1968—Macon, Georgia
The first and most successful of the
Southern rock bands. Featuring the
brothers Duane and Gregg Allman, the
band also included dual drummers and
a raft of fine blues-oriented musicians.
During the early seventies, they were
one of the biggest draws on the rock circuit—they headlined the huge (600,000
persons) Watkins Glen Festival held July
28, 1973. The band seemed to have
been subject to a cruel curse (Duane
Allman and bass player Berry Oakley
were both killed in motorcycle accidents; Greg turned state's evidence in
the drug conviction of Scooter Herring,
his manager). But before those problems
hit, they reached the pinnacle of success. Subsequently, the group disbanded
and re-formed on several different occa-
sions, unfortunately, always with diminishing quality.

### At the Fillmore East (1972)
Polydor 823 273-2 (78:36—two discs)   [A]
The band's forte was live performance
and the extended instrumental jams that
the freedom of such performance abetted. On this classic release, it all works,
each sound contributing to the intent
behind the music. Duane's guitar work
easily verifies his stature as one of rock's
best-ever guitarists, and the rhythm section drives like a moonshiner on a moon-
less night. Given the fact that this was a
live recording done over eighteen years
ago, the CD's sound is all that one can
reasonably expect; in fact, it's pretty
damn good.

### Brothers and Sisters (1973)
Polydor 825 092-2 (38:02)   [D]
Released in 1973, this recording contains Dickie Betts's "Ramblin' Man" and
the then-popular instrumental "Jessica."
While Gregg's vocals remain the high
point, it's obvious that the band's fire
had gone out several years before. The
sound is, at best, adequate, like that of a
clean LP.

### Dreams (1966–1988)
Polygram 839417-2 (301:51—four discs)   [A–]
Producer Bill Levinson, who captured
the varied career of Eric Clapton on his
1988 five-CD package *Crossroads*,
brings the same thoroughness and
obvious personal involvement to
*Dreams*, a retrospective of the Allman
Brothers Band that begins with the mid-
sixties Allman Joys and ends with the
Dickie Betts Band. Filled out with previously unreleased material, *Dreams*
nonetheless includes almost all of the
classics and properly emphasizes the
1969 to 1973 zenith of a group Levinson
believes to be one of the truly original,
great American road bands. He makes
a convincing case. The twin-guitar
double-drum attack celebrates the myth
and mystery of the American South, seasoned with a bit of Miles Davis and
western swing, and reverberates with
moving power and thrust. Before drugs,
motorcycles, and death demolished
these Southern rockers, they made
some enduring music, most of which is
right here, with its antecedents and its
remnants intact. With certain limited
exceptions, the sound, overall, is better
than decent, certainly more revealing
than its vinyl predecessors. The accompanying booklet is readable, informative, and beautifully produced.

# Gregg Allman
b. December 8, 1947—Nashville
**Laid Back (1973)**
Polygram 831 941-2 Y-1 (35:45)  **[B]**
Wracked by tragedy and treachery, the
Allman Brothers Band disintegrated in
the early seventies. This was Gregg's first
recording following that break-up. It's an
excellent southern rock/blues album,
which rightfully focuses on Allman's
laid-back but affecting vocals. While the
overall quality of the material is pretty
good, the standouts, "Midnight Rider,"
Jackson Browne's "These Days," and
"Multi-Colored Lady," are exceptional.
The CD's sound is very clean, with nice
vocal definition and placement, and is a
clear improvement over the LP.

# The Amos Garrett, Doug Sahm, Gene Taylor Band
Formed 1989
One of those fortuitous "one shot"
gatherings, this time by some seasoned
Texas blues/rock road warriors.

### The Return of the Formerly Brothers (1989)
Rykodisc RCD 10127 (44:06)  **[A–]**
The flavor is Texas (and everything that
connotes), the mood is party, and the
musicianship is what you would expect
from seasoned pros, including Queen
Ida. Sahm's plaintive voice has never
sounded better than on "Teardrops on
Your Letter" and on Bob Dylan's "Just
Like a Woman." These are people who
make music because it's something they
just have to do, and they do it with an
ease that belies their true artistry. If a
cold one in a smoky roadhouse is your
idea of a good time, this one's for you.
Ryko's sound clearly captures the appropriate ambience.

# Eric Andersen
b. February 14, 1943—Pittsburgh
One of the early sixties folkies who
worked the Boston, New York, San Francisco scenes and who adopted the lifestyle, if not the electrification, of the
seminal folk/rockers.

### Blue River (1972)
Columbia CK31062 (39:35)  **[C–]**
Recorded in Nashville with some of the
best country studio pros providing simple, sympathetic backing, *Blue River* was
deemed a minor classic of the singer/
songwriter school from an artist whose
roots go back to the founding days of
folk rock. Reminiscent of James Taylor, a
bit too wide-eyed, pretty, and mawkish
to sustain the test of time—or even the
moment—it delivers a resonant, pleas-
ing sound, but little of substance (e.g.,
"to give my foot another chance to try
another shoe"). The best of the bunch
is "Sheila," and it's been done better a
number of times by a number of others.
On the other hand, the sound is excellent—warm, open, and clean.

### Ghosts Upon the Road (1989)
Gold Castle D2 71327 (50:20)  **[A]**
A long overdue gem from an artist
whose talent has never been acknowledged by the mass audience. Cursed
with the recurrent "New Dylan" label
when his folk-oriented recording career
commenced in 1965, he has labored in
relative obscurity ever since, the sole
exception, perhaps, being his 1973
release, *Blue River. Ghosts* features
Andersen's basically acoustic sound,
fine melodic sense, and lyrics that seem
more lived-in than sung. The title song
is a stunning ten-minute-plus autobiography that transcends its well-drawn
details to achieve almost epic proportions. Other highlights include "Spanish

Steps" and "Too Many Times (I Will Try),"
but each vignette rings with place and
truth, resulting in a first-rate release by
one of the few sixties artists working
today who still has something to say
and knows how to say it. Beautifully
recorded.

# Laurie Anderson
b. 1947—Chicago
Conceptual musician/artist who has
succeeded in effectively merging contemporary music and theater for a
broader than normal audience for this
genre.

### Big Science (1982)
Warner Bros. 3674-2 (38:58) **[B + ]**
The debut recording from the eighties'
most fascinating and successful performance artist. *Big Science* is a partial
soundtrack from her multilevel, techno-
live presentation, "United States I–IV,"
featuring the cut "O Superman," which
garnered some commercial recognition,
particularly in Europe. Her keen sense
of observation, genuine wit, and ear for
sonic texture combine to produce an
arresting listening experience—how sustaining it may be is another matter. The
recording manages to remain vital apart
from the theatrical presentation, but it's
still a soundtrack, an integral component of a more complex statement; as a
result, it fails to be fully satisfying. Interesting, at times wonderfully entertaining, but not fully satisfying. The voicings
are mostly synthesized and subjected to
electronic modulation, but the desired
sound is delivered cleanly, with shimmering clarity.

### Mister Heartbreak (1983)
Warner Bros. 9 25077-2 (40:18) **[A]**
Ms. Anderson has obviously set her
sights more clearly on the songtrack
aspect of her art, and *Trouser Press*
accurately described the result as a
"blinding, studio-perfect maelstrom of
oddity." The humor is less a factor, and
what there is tends to be more oblique,
less topical. Along with the inventive,
provocative musical/sonic textures, this
results in a unique, effective recording.
It may not be everyone's cup of tea, but
considering her adventurous concepts,
it is remarkably accessible. Anderson
obviously has a wonderful ear for sound,
its texture and the space it occupies, and
this CD delivers it all with marvelous
dynamics and clarity.

### Home of the Brave (1986)
Warner Bros. 9 25400-2 (34:53) **[B + ]**
It may not be rock & roll music, but in a
way, Laurie's work is defined by a rock &
roll sensibility. This is the soundtrack to
her concert film and is a trip into techno-,
electro-, voice-modulated eighties multi-
media expression. Ideally suited to the
digital medium, this all-digital recording
is nothing less than a pure sonic delight.
Experimental, yes, but witty and ultimately compelling listening.

### Strange Angels (1989)
Warner Bros. 25900-2 (46:06) **[A]**
The most musical performance yet by
America's premiere performance artist—
weird, wonderful, humorous, and
timely, Anderson's impressive talent
illuminates every track. Though her
work provides joyous audio/video one-
woman theater, this soundtrack stands
firmly on its own. This is no transient
talent; although the topicality of some of
her work may eventually date it, so far,
so good. Anderson is a different, easy,
yet rewarding experience. This is her

most accessible release—and maybe her best. The mostly electronic sound is full, rich, and the slightest bit otherwise—just as it should be.

# The Animals
Formed 1960—New Castle, England
**The Best of the Animals (1964–1965)**
abko CD43242 (46:27)   **[B + ]**
Back in the late seventies and early eighties, when Midwestern radio stations would take listener surveys of the greatest rock single of all time, the Animals' "House of the Rising Sun," their first and only No. 1 hit (it charted for eleven weeks in 1964 amidst formidable competition), topped those surveys more often than might be expected. One of the strongest of the third-tier British Invasion bands, the Animals are probably best known for Eric Burdon's rough, earthy blues voice, and for their affiliation with roots rock/blues and R&B material. Like the rest of the Invasion, they were simply unearthing American black musical culture for white, middle-class teens. Their principal weakness was as writers, but their strength was in creative, quality musicianship—particularly Alan Price on keyboards, whose band, the Alan Price Combo, became the Animals when Burdon became lead singer. This compilation fairly well covers Price's years with the band (he left in late 1965), which encompassed its best work: "House of the Rising Sun," "Don't Let Me Be Misunderstood," "We Gotta Get Out of This Place," "It's My Life," "The Story of Bo Diddley," and "I'm Crying," among the fifteen tracks. The balance includes lesser "hits" from Chuck Berry, John Lee Hooker, and Sam Cook, the last being a pale piece of work. The sound is pretty impressive—

big, bright, and punchy. There is some tape hiss on certain cuts, and an overall tendency toward harshness in the vocals and instrumental upper mid-range, but still vastly superior to the vinyl. The liner notes are an added plus.

# Joan Armatrading
b. December 9, 1950—St. Kitts, West Indies (raised in England)
One of the best female writers and performers to debut in the seventies, her sensitive, intelligent, complex music which draws on a number of source strains has always enjoyed better critical than audience response.

**Classics Vol. 21 (1973–1985)**
A&M DC2519 (68:36)   **[B]**
Joan's sophisticated music is more pop than rock and evidences a strong jazz/folk/funk/reggae orientation. Possessed of a large, expressive voice and first-rate guitar technique, Armatrading's performances extract maximum impact out of her compositions which lack the musical hooks necessary to achieve popularity. Her self-confessional lyrics are never maudlin, rather, they reflect the toughness expected of the post-feminist modern woman. The eighteen cuts sample her recorded output from 1973's "Whatever's For Us," to 1985's "Temptation" with most of the highlights in between adequately represented. Over her recording career, Joan has consistently worked with name producers, and the sound of this disc reflects their above-average production values; clean, bright, spacious, and appropriately punchy. The only sonic criticism is a tendency to over-brightness, which sometimes results in vocal harshness.

## David Baerwald
**Bedtime Stories (1990)**
A&M 75021 52892 (55:26)  **[B]**
In 1986, David Baerwald, along with David Ricketts, released a vision of L.A. that was tense, taut, and accurate: David + David's *Boomtown* is one of the better recordings of the decade. 1990 saw one-half of David + David produce a worthy successor, but two Davids prove better than one. The sensibility is the same, but the songs are more personal, with less bite and resonance. Still, *Bedtime Stories* makes for sometimes-compelling listening; its sound and production values are first-rate.

## Joan Baez
b. January 9, 1941—Staten Island, New York
One of the antecedents of the flowering of rock & roll in the sixties was the concurrent folk music revival which gained its primary footing on the college campuses of America. Baez was the queen of this revival and its perfect symbol, embodying the achingly pure voice of the classic female balladeer with a social conscience directly traceable to the principles of Woody Guthrie.

**Any Day Now (1968)**
Vanguard VCD 79306/7 (68:42)  **[C+]**
Beautiful readings of classic songs, but the strength of Dylan (and these are all Dylan compositions) has to do with an edge of honesty, an intensity which Joan's interpretation sadly lacks—it's an empty package. She sounds so concerned with the music, she's ignored its meaning. The sound is like that of a perfectly surfaced LP and it beautifully showcases one of the finest female folk voices around; but, there is little detail or spatial enhancement from the CD version.

**Greatest Hits (1973)**
Vanguard 811 667-2 (53:58)  **[B+]**
These songs span a period from 1960 to the early 1970s, but a preponderance of the material is drawn from the sixties, which is the only time the folk queen was related at all to rock & roll—and that by virtue of the close Dylan association. She was very much a part of the turbulent sixties' New York, Dylan-centered, creation of "folk rock," but Joan has remained true to her roots, sometimes treating rock lyrics like the folk material they very much are. This is a lovely collection that sounds bright yet rarely harsh, and clean but thin.

## Anita Baker
b. December 20, 1957—Memphis
Sang lead with Chapter 8 from mid-seventies to mid-eighties. Big sales, small soul.

**Rapture (1986)**
Elektra 9 60444-2 (37:35)   [C + ]
A major '86 soul/jazz/pop hit from an artist with one of the loveliest, most supple and expressive voices currently around. The weakness in the song selection and sameness of the slick, lush production ultimately drain the life from a fine vocal effort. The sound is eighties clean, albeit with a slight tendency toward edgy brightness.

## Hank Ballard

b. November 18, 1936—Detroit
Ballard, a Johnny Otis discovery, joined the vocal group the Midnighters as lead, producing what has been referred to by some as "the first Motown sound." They garnered six Top Ten R&B hits between 1954 and 1956 and scored two pop hits with "Finger Popping Time" and "Let's Go, Let's Go, Let's Go," both in 1960. The Midnighters were originally known as the Royals and included in their first line-up Levi Stubbs (who ultimately gained fame with the Four Tops). Ballard scored his biggest success in 1954 by employing sexually explicit lyrics over raw, traditional-based gospel music ("Work With Me Annie").

**What You Get When the Gettin's Good (1954–1961)**
C.D. Charly 29 (41:42)   [C + ]
The sixteen selections on this disc cover most of the group's better known efforts and provide a good overview of the mid-fifties black pop sound that attracted white listeners, opening the door to rock & roll. The sound quality varies all over the place, and some of it is pretty bad; but given the age of the masters, none of this is unexpected. You purchase this disc for its historical value and some good, but dated, party music, but it isn't one you're going to use to show off your

CD player. Ballard, by the way, is the guy who wrote "The Twist," but it was Chubby Checker who scored with it.

## The Band

Formed 1967, Woodstock, New York
This five-man group (four of whom were Canadian) first gained notice working behind Ronnie Hawkins, and then achieved fame backing Bob Dylan. They captured, in rough, rustic, and real terms, America's rich southern-frontier cultural heritage better than any other group, and in the process made enduring music. One of the truly great rock bands

**Music From Big Pink (1968)**
Capitol CDP7 46069 2 (42:05)   [A]
This, their first recording, was based upon Robbie Robertson's vision of American mythology as the foundation for the sixties' rock & roll. At first listening it had the feel of "classic" about it and that has not diminished. The timelessness of its themes, honesty of its voicings, and artistic interplay of its instrumentation mark it as a recording of sustaining value. The CD's sound is clear, clean, and dynamic. Garth Hudson's imaginative organ work becomes even more impressive through the enhanced clarity of the digital mix.

**Music From Big Pink (1968)**
Mobile Fidelity UDCD 527 (42:03)   [A + ]
Mobile Fidelity's gold ultradiscs are expensive, but the added cost is justified in their audibly enhanced sound. *Music From Big Pink* is simply among the best sounding in the series to date, making it a "must own" for any serious audiophile with a love of classic rock.

**The Band (1969)**
Capitol CDP7 46493-2 (43:57)   [A +]
Ralph J. Gleason called it "lean and
dusty." *Rolling Stone* selected it nine-
teenth among the top 100 rock albums
of the 1967–1987 period and called it "a
masterpiece of electric folklore." One
basic element of the sixties youth "revolution" embodied a return to the simpler
countrified values and truths of America's potent history—its rural frontiers-
men and agrarian pioneers. Many bands
worked this rich vein as source material,
but The Band truly represented its living
incarnation. *The Band* was recorded in
Sammy Davis, Jr.'s, pool house in Los
Angeles, California, in the winter of
1968, and the somewhat boxy sound of
that "studio" is retained on the CD, but
it's part of it, this is the way it was meant
to sound. It's clean and clear with a couple of glitches here and there, and the
openings and closings of selections are
clipped, but these are minor complaints.
The digital conversion highlights the
shadings in the plain vocals and harmonies, which adds significantly to the
listening experience.

**Rock of Ages (1972)**
Capitol CDP7 46617 2 (71:59)   [B–]
Released in 1972, this live double record
(slightly edited to fill one CD) covers sixteen live selections recorded at the New
York Academy of Music on New Year's
Eve, 1971/72. Arguably, it is the group's
last real quality release, with a possible
exception of its 1978 reprise, *The Last
Waltz*, which officially marked The
Band's final appearance. When you get
right down to it, there really isn't much
new involved here. Three of the songs
had never been previously released, and
the basic musical unit is augmented with
a fine horn section arranged by New
Orleans's resident musical genius Allen
Toussaint, which adds coloration, if not

structure, to the material. The musicianship is consistently first rate, the end
result is appealing, but certainly nothing
extraordinary. The CD's sound is clear
and relatively clean for a live effort, but
overall, the lows are weak and the
sound is excessively bright, sometimes
bordering on harshness.

**In Concert—Rock of Ages (1972)**
Capitol CDP7 93596/7-2
(79:50—two discs)   [B]
For some reason Capitol decided to
reissue this recording on two CDs and
add eight minutes of Garth Hudson's
wondrous organ workout on "Genetic
Method," including everything from the
original vinyl. If they'd only edited out
some of the excessive crowd apprecia-
tion or waited for the technology to
advance, they could have gotten the
whole thing on a single disc. They have
been good enough to include Greil Marcus's essay on the reissue, and while he's
right about "Rag Mama Rag" being the
highlight, I can only conclude, regarding
his overall enthusiasm, that you had to
have been there. The sound quality is
identical to that of the prior release.

**Moondog Matinee (1973)**
Capitol CDP97 935922 (36:01)   [B]
Given their many roadhouse years
pounding it out in the raucous early
decades of rock & roll, the idea of an
oldies collection by these masters seems
like a natural. Their eclectic choice of
material: "Mystery Train," "Ain't Got No
Home," "The Promised Land," "The
Great Pretender," "A Change is Gonna
Come," and "The Third Men Theme"
just heightens the interest. Yet, somehow, it never quite achieves its promise,
because of a prevailing sense of restraint
rather than the pure kick-ass rock & roll
the material demands (and which, during
their tumultuous early days, they had

the chops and inclination to play). It closes stronger than it begins, and if preconception can be set aside, *Moondog Matinee* is a decent addition to the abbreviated catalog of one of rock's truly great, original bands. Soundwise, the CD may be a slight improvement over the vinyl, but the obvious compression and lack of spatial clarity are disappointing.

### Northern Lights—Southern Cross (1975)
Capitol CDP7 935942 (41:06)  **[B]**
While they continue to create sepia toned Southern countrified rock, this release reveals a shift in The Band's sound—away from the string-driven earlier work toward Garth Hudson's reedy keyboards. Hudson creates some refreshing multileveled melodies, but the lyrics (with the exception of "Acadian Driftwood") barely merit the effort. Their best music was already behind them. The CD sound is better than the LP, but not nearly what it should be.

### Islands (1977)
Capitol CDP7 935912 (35:15)  **[C–]**
Their last studio album—it's really one too many. The resonance is gone, replaced with an empty slickness—a disservice to the rest of their fine catalog. Ah, contract obligations. The sound is adequate, compressed and afflicted with audible tape hiss.

### The Last Waltz (1978)
Warner Bros. 3146-2 (129:46—two discs)  **[A–]**
On Thanksgiving night in 1976 at San Francisco's famed Winterland—where The Band had given its first concert nine years earlier—The Band invited Bob Dylan, Neil Young, Van Morrison, Joni Mitchell, Dr. John, Muddy Waters, Ringo Starr, Eric Clapton, Paul Butterfield, the Staple Singers, Bobby Charles, Emmylou Harris, Ron Wood, Ronnie

Hawkins, and Neil Diamond, and a fine horn section arranged by Allen Toussaint, to memorialize the end of their performance career. Martin Scorsese filmed the concert, and a couple of years later this soundtrack was released. It contains thirty songs, including many of their classics, generally performed with fire and enthusiasm. The fascinating guest artists provide highlights (Young, Clapton, Dylan, and Morrison) and lowlights (Diamond). Given the numbers and magnitude of the assembled talent, it was inevitable that reality would fall short of expectation, but on the whole, this was a major concert recording, and on its own terms is generally successful. It contains some new material from The Band, but nothing that makes you question their decision to call it quits. For the most part the studio renditions of the group's classics remain definitive—still, you'll wish you'd been there. Given the time that obviously went into this production, the sound quality, particularly of the live concert portion, is far from ideal, with a boxiness and unpleasant vocal edges to most of the performances. The seven studio tracks completing the package have much better sonic quality, but even they are a bit edgy in the vocals.

### To Kingdom Come (The Definitive Collection) (1968–1978)
Capitol CDP 92170/71
(134:08—two discs)  **[A +]**
All The Band's classics are included here, along with samples from each of their career phases, and three previously unreleased cuts, "Back to Memphis," "Loving You is Sweeter Than Ever," and "Endless Highway." Unless you own all the original albums, no collection of classic rock & roll should be without *To Kingdom Come*. Because of the diversity of the source material, the sound quality varies; overall, it's well

above average, providing enhanced clarity and dynamics that surpass the vinyl original.

A convincing argument can be made that this mostly Canadian aggregation was North America's single greatest rock band, after Creedence Clearwater Revival, with which The Band shared a certain natural, traditional sensibility. Perhaps because they spent so many years in the backwater of Canadian and U.S. roadhouse rock & roll behind Ronnie Hawkins, perhaps because they lived almost communally for much of their decade-long career, the members blended blues, country, and folk that to this day resonates with passionate integrity. Robbie Robertson had a hand in compiling these selections, overseen by Rob Bowman, who provides the informative liner notes.

When it comes to the reissue of classic back catalog, Capitol was late to the party, but the overall quality of their late-eighties CD reissues has compensated somewhat. Clearly, The Band was one of the most important and enduring of the sixties acts. Their best performances seem chiseled in basic American sensibility—music of extreme instrumental and vocal complexity, that is ultimately music of the most direct emotional simplicity.

# Bangles
Formed 1981—Los Angeles
A major label push, some fine harmonics and novelty all brought brief stardom. Egos ended it.

### Different Light (1986)
Columbia CK40039 (38:48) **[C + ]**
In an earlier part of the decade, the Go-Gos achieved brief stardom, the first all-woman rock band to do so. The Bangles, who have followed the same path,

achieved justifiable success in the mid-1980s through bright vocal harmonies, strong song selection, and an energetic guitar-based sound. It's not memorable, but it's sure listenable, light rock/pop. Clear with excellent separation, the sound mix tends toward the bright, thin side.

# Lou Ann Barton
b. Fort Worth, Texas
A fixture in the fine Austin scene, involved with the founding of Stevie Ray Vaughan's Triple Threat Revue and early versions of The Fabulous Thunderbirds.

### Read My Lips (1989)
Antones ANT0009 CD (50:05) **[C]**
Anyone who listened to the rave reviews for Barton's 1982 release *Old Enough* and acquired that R&B-drenched roadhouse recording must still be asking what happened. The answer is one bad EP, and a lot of nights working the fabled Texas R&B circuit. At first glance, *Read My Lips* appears to be the perfect panacea for too many years of relative obscurity—the songs all fit the formula for a shit-kicking Saturday night. Lou Ann is backed by seasoned veterans of this raucous scene—Jimmie Vaughan and Kim Wilson from the Fabulous Thunderbirds and David "Fathead" Newman. Yet, somehow, it just misses, and what it misses is Jerry Wexler's production sense that captured her on *Old Enough* "with the mud between her toes." It's listenable, but lacks magic. The sound is bright and crisp.

# The Beach Boys
Formed 1961—Hawthorne, California
Building on Chuck Berry's foundations and Phil Spector's grandiose aural concepts, all enhanced by Brian Wilson's

pure pop production genius, the Beach Boys were a uniquely innovative American rock group. It has been known for some time that relatives are able to sing better harmony than nonrelatives, and four of the five original members of this band (the brothers Wilson and cousin Mike Love) were related. This group has probably never been given its due in popularizing rock & roll with mainstream America, at least in the critical press.

### Surfin' U.S.A. and Surfer Girl (1963)
Mobile Fidelity UDCD521 (49:57)   [A]
This gold ultradisc pairing of their second and third (first stereo) albums yields absolutely stunning sound, markedly superior even to Capitol's standard two-fer remasterings.

### Surfin' Safari and Surfin' U.S.A. (1962–1963)
Capitol CDP793691-2 (55:57)   [B]
By now everyone in the civilized world has probably been exposed to these surf chestnuts. Lord knows the surviving Boys have been mining this musical lode for decades—sadly to the point of general embarrassment. Most CD fans also know that the Beach Boys' label, Capitol, has proven to be the most recalcitrant to reissue classic catalog in digital form. In 1990 Capitol belatedly redeemed itself—repackaging the Beach Boys' early sixties albums as two-fers, offering bonus tracks, informative liner notes, and state-of-the-art sonic remastering, thereby finally preserving one of rock's greatest and most listenable band's enduring legacy in a manner befitting its content—a little doo-wop, a lot of Chuck Berry, and a healthy splash of Southern California beachfront sunshine. The liner notes to their debut album, *Surfin' Safari*, included a definition of surfing: "A water sport in which

the participant stands on a floating slab of wood resembling an ironing board and attempts to remain perpendicular while being hurled toward the shore at a rather frightening rate of speed on the crest of a huge wave." Now *that* puts it all into perspective. The CD boasts twenty-seven cuts, three of which are bonus tracks (two previously unreleased—"Cindy, Oh Cindy" and "The Baker Men"), and the rare "Land Ahoy." Their earliest work yields a few classics, "409," "Surfin'," "Shut Down," and "Surfin' U.S.A." It also includes "The Lonely Sea," a forerunner to their great ballad harmonizing, unfortunately marred by a spoken bridge, as well as several Dick Dale–derived surf instrumentals ("Moon Dawg," "Misirlou," and a modified "Honky Tonk"), and a lot of novelty throwaways. The CD includes an excellent liner book, as do all the Beach Boys two-fers, but *this* one has current comments from Brian Wilson. *Surfin' Safari* and two of the bonus tracks are in mono, and *Surfin' U.S.A.* was their first stereo release. While a bit compressed, the sound is clean and impressive.

### Little Deuce Coupe and All Summer Long (1962–1964)
Capitol CDP7 936932 (59:30)   [B + ]
The second in the Beach Boys excellent two-fer reissue series focuses on the alma mater and automotive aspects of their sunny early-sixties "perfect wave" lives. It yields the title track, "Be True to Your School" (the album version and a very different single version), "409," "I Get Around," and a pallid cover of the Hondells' "Little Honda." The total twenty-eight tracks include bonus cuts, alternate takes, the previously unreleased "All Dressed Up for School," and some lesser gems—"Wendy," "Girls on the Beach," and "Hushabye." The rarer

ballads are more interesting because of the truly gorgeous harmonies, but the upbeat material suffers from a sameness in their Chuck Berry–borrowed primal rock. The sound quality is generally first-rate, although it varies from session to session, and exhibits some expected compression.

### Surfer Girl and Shut Down Vol. 2 (1963–1964)
Capitol CDP7 93692 2 (59:56)   [A–]
*Surfer Girl* was the group's third album released in 1963, the same year as *Surfin' U.S.A.*, and *Shut Down Vol. 2* followed in 1964. Included among their combined twenty-seven tracks are "Little Deuce Coupe," "Catch a Wave," "In My Room," "Fun, Fun, Fun," "The Warmth of the Sun," and "Don't Worry Baby." But the lesser-known, supporting tracks yield more pleasant moments—"The Surfer Moon," and a beachy version of "Louie, Louie." The single version of "Fun, Fun, Fun," "In My Room" performed in German, and the rare "I Do," make interesting, if not revelatory, additions to the CD. The essentially all-stereo sound is great, and since sound was the Beach Boys' (Brian Wilson's) preoccupation, it makes these reissues special. Capitol has gone the full nine yards by including extensive, informative liner notes in a twenty-three-page booklet by Wilson's biographer, David Leaf—adding up to one hell of a package. This is the way classic catalog should be handled.

### Today and Summer Days and Summer Nights (1964–1965)
Capitol CDP7 936942 (67:21)   [B]
By 1965 when most of this material was recorded, Brian Wilson's musical genius was preoccupied with studio and production manipulations that would color his sonics. And although the techniques he employed were often unimaginably

primitive (check the use of fade in "Help Me, Rhonda"), he was expanding the scope and scale of sound, and adding innovative textures. Their strengths and weaknesses are, once again, clearly on display. While there are fewer Beach Boys hits on this two-fer, and the lyrics overall are generally less successful, there is a sense of anticipation about this work, and some lush, rich ballads that are too often overlooked. As is the case with all these Capitol two-fer reissues, this disc includes dubious studio repartee. Phil Spector and the Beatles waft through most of the twenty-nine tracks, five bonus, including the original and a fascinating alternate version of "Dance, Dance, Dance," and "California Girls." The sound varies from luminous a cappella to overproduced, compressed, occasionally distorted examples. Still, probably the best sonic quality ever afforded this material.

### Pet Sounds (1966)
Capitol CDP7 48421 2 (43:00)   [A]
This one's so good, even Capitol realized it was too strong to pair up with anything else. Besides that, no true Beach Boys fan or, for that matter, no true fan of rock's mid-sixties gilded era, would require any bonus incentive to buy this genuine classic. Actually, that's a bit harsh when one considers what an exemplary job Capitol has done on its belatedly-released Beach Boys Compact Classic Discs, of which this is an integral part. With *Pet Sounds*, one of the most impressive, influential albums in rock history, you get a comprehensive booklet with current comments from Brian Wilson, liner notes on each of the sixteen tracks, details of the recording attitudes and processes, as well an over-enthusiastic essay from David Leaf. The meaning behind it all, of course, resides in the grooves—some of this immensely

popular band's best known songs
("Wouldn't it Be Nice," "Sloop John B,"
"God Only Knows," "Caroline No") fitting seamlessly into the sonic tour de
force. Wilson acknowledges in the notes,
as he has previously, that *Pet Sounds*
was a direct reaction to the Beatles' *Rubber Soul.* He's also quoted as saying, "I
believe that music is God's voice," and
what he sought on *Pet Sounds* was "a
white spiritual sound." Sonically, it
always has ranked as a benchmark
recording. The CD effectively captures
the potent bottom and echoing spaciousness of the production, but also
suffers from some surprisingly thin,
compressed, occasionally edgy vocals.
*Pet Sounds* wasn't a giant commercial
success by the Beach Boys' high standards, but it foreshadowed major aspects
of *Sgt. Pepper.*

### Smiley Smile and Wild Honey (1967)
Capitol CDP7 96396 2 (74:25)   **[B]**
A fascinating pairing of two below-aver-
age Beach Boys albums that chronicle a
major shift in Brian Wilson's sometimes
magic music. *Smiley Smile* was the end
of his homage to consuming studio production control (this was the year of *Sgt.
Pepper*). It was a confusing, strained,
ultimately unsuccessful end, although it
did yield some amazing and beautiful
pop music: "Good Vibrations," "Heroes
and Villains," and "With Me Tonight."
With *Wild Honey* Wilson abandoned
overwrought studio sheen for a return to
raw rock & roll. The juxtaposition is dis-
quieting—*Wild Honey* is notable for its
exuberance, but it lacks any memorable
songs. The six bonus cuts include insightful, early takes on "Heroes and Villains"
and "Good Vibrations." The sound on
*Smiley Smile* is impressive, particularly
given the amount of studio wizardry;
*Wild Honey* tends to be overbright,
revealing occasional marginal tape hiss.

### Made in the U.S.A. (1962–1981)
Capitol CDP7 46324 2 (64:17)   **[A–]**

### Endless Summer (1962–1966)
Capitol CDP7 46467 2 (50:39)   **[A]**
The Beach Boys, or at least those who
still survive, have been living off the
music contained on these two discs for
over a quarter of a century, and hearing
these CDs clearly explains why. The two
contain forty-six cuts, thirty-six different
songs. Buy both, and you've got ninety
percent of a major sixties rock band's
best work. The sound quality is generally good on both discs; however, there
is some unevenness among the selections, as would be expected given the
divergency of recorded source material.

### Friends and 20/20 (1966–1969)
Capitol CDP7 93697 2 (67:11)   **[B–]**
Both of these albums were basically singles compilations made up of less-than-
memorable material. There's still plenty
of impressive singing and production,
but the material simply isn't notable, the
one exception being the wonderful
throwback, "Do it Again." Five of the
twenty-nine tracks are bonus additions.
The sound is generally dynamic and
spacious, but is marred from time to
time by clearly audible tape hiss.

# The Beatles
Formed 1959—Liverpool, England
The event that the compact disc world
had been anticipating since the first CDs
were released in 1983 finally occurred
on February 26, 1987: Capitol Records
released *Please, Please Me, With the
Beatles, Beatles For Sale,* and *A Hard
Day's Night* on compact discs. Over a
million copies were originally shipped.
The media covered this release as a
major news story.
     Was all this hype justified by the prod-

uct? The answer is a resounding "Yes!" Not so much because of technological advances in the digital conversions (which are notable and positive), but because the availability of Beatles' material on disc caused music lovers to once again listen to what may be the one truly great group in the growing history of rock & roll.

The Beatles were the bridge between the music's somewhat primitive beginnings in the fifties and its ultimate flowering as a complex art form in the sixties. Their roots and experience commenced with the raw sounds and spirit of rock's first decade and their ultimate product simply defined its second.

The amazing pervasiveness of Beatlemania, which encompassed vast numbers and cut through diverse age and social groups, created an international musical bond not duplicated since. If you lived through it, this music is probably an essential element in your personal history. If you didn't, it is still probably totally familiar because its popularity has been unparalleled in the annals of the form.

In a sense, this was more than just rock music. It was the essence of its moment in time.

These releases, listed below, constitute all the "official" Beatles recorded output and have been issued on CD in their original English configurations, which means that the selections (on the discs up to *Sgt. Pepper*) vary from their U.S. counterparts with which most U.S. listeners will be familiar. It should also be noted that the first four recordings were released in mono, much to the chagrin of many critics, but this is really a bit of a tempest in a teapot—the CDs simply sound better than the stereo versions of the LPs. In fact, the fifth and following releases in the series, which are in stereo, tend to suffer somewhat from the extremity of the separation employed.

### Live in Hamburg '62
K-Tel CD1473 (46:30)   [C+]
Yeah, it sounds like the master tape was made on a cheapie portable recorder by someone wandering aimlessly through the audience with a low-grade, handheld mike—but have you heard the LP version? As an historic icon of the rough early roots of the most remarkable group in pop history, this recording ties the band and their music to the American counterparts which inspired it. Generally the poor sound quality and miserable mix overwhelm the material, but every now and again the Beatles' uniqueness and their compelling energy slip through the noise level and the future seems inevitable.

### Please, Please Me (1963)
Parlophone CDP7 46435 2 (32:48)   [A–]
The first album statement—simply indispensable.

### With The Beatles (1963)
Parlophone CDP7 46436 2 (33:26)   [A]
Released the same year as *Please, Please Me*, it's essentially more of the wonderful same with a couple more original Lennon/McCartney compositions and perhaps their single strongest rock & roll statement—John Lennon's reading of "Money."

### Beatles for Sale (1964)
Parlophone CDP7 46438 2 (34:15)   [A–]
Released in 1964, this recording shows the Beatles moving somewhat away from their original roots material (and recorded cover versions thereof) and Lennon/McCartney's expansion of the actual form of pop song. A little of the influence of Bob Dylan is clearly felt in

the content of the lyrics as well as the nuances of the lead vocals.

### A Hard Day's Night (1964)
Parlophone CDP7 46437 2 (30:32)  **[A]**
The first recording made up of exclusively Lennon/McCartney compositions, not to mention its relevance to a certain film of the same name. Probably the best-sounding of the first seven Beatles "original" releases.

**Help!, Rubber Soul,** and **Revolver** are three of the most important recordings in the history of rock & roll. Originally recorded and released in 1965 and 1966, this was the material that established Beatlemania, and forever changed the shape of the pop music that followed. It was within these grooves that the Beatles' amazing eclecticism, their nonpareil melodic power, and complete reshuffling of the conventions that had previously constricted rock music, were given free rein.

### Help! (1965)
Parlophone CDP7 46439 2 (34:23)  **[A]**
Another soundtrack, but this may well be the best soundtrack recording ever released.

### Rubber Soul (1965)
Parlophone CDP7 46440 (35:50)  **[A + ]**
While the argument about which is the best album of this seminal group's ten-year recording career will probably last as long as the music is heard, *Rubber Soul* is clearly a strong candidate for that designation.

### Revolver (1966)
Parlophone CDP7 46441 (35:01)  **[A]**
Psychedelia meets Beatlemania, and the world of pop music is unalterably changed again. In retrospect, this recording, released in 1966, sounds the most dated of any of this group's work to that time, but it's still essential.

### Sgt. Pepper's Lonely Hearts Club Band (1967)
Parlophone CDP7 46442 (39:52)  **[A + ]**
On June 1, 1987, twenty years to the day after the original English release, *Sgt. Pepper's Lonely Hearts Club Band* made its digital debut. According to a consensus of rock critics assembled by Paul Gambaccini for his "Critic's Choice—The Top 100 Rock & Roll Albums Of All Time," *Sgt. Pepper* is the greatest rock recording. *Rolling Stone* in its August 27, 1987, issue devoted to "The 100 Best Albums Of The Last Twenty Years (1967–1987)" accords it the same distinction. Whether that is musically the case or not is difficult to pinpoint; however, it changed the rules of the game, and that's hard to do. It is rare when a single release so clearly and specifically is the cause of so much change. This classic responds to digital reproduction awesomely. Sure, you can hear the tape hiss. But the boys and George Martin (their producer, sometimes referred to as the fifth Beatle) created this madness by overdubbing with only three-track-capacity recording equipment (sixty-four tracks or more are commonplace in the modern studio). The clarity of CD allows you to hear more of how it was all put together in the first place, for better or worse. The spatial and dynamic potential of the disc gives the sound a punch which adds a whole new level to the listening experience. From the breadth of its lyrical subject matter to the sophistication of that sound, *Sgt. Pepper* declared rock & roll to be the equal of any contemporary form of artistic expression.

## Magical Mystery Tour (1967)
Parlophone CDP7 48062-2 (36:52)   [A]
The Beatles released two albums in
1967, the first being *Sgt. Pepper,* generally conceded to be rock's single most
important release, and *Magical Mystery
Tour,* generally undervalued because the
film for which it provided the soundtrack was probably the Fab Four's first
commercial disappointment (and justifiably so). *Rolling Stone's* review of this
release in 1967 simply took the form of
the following quote from John Lennon:
"There are only about a hundred people
in the world who understand our
music." Viewed from the perspective of
twenty years, *Magical Mystery Tour*
(which is the brief soundtrack plus an
assembly of excellent Beatles' singles
releases) is very much of a piece with its
illustrious predecessor, evidencing the
same contagious, bizarre studio antics
and showcasing more great pop songs:
"The Fool on the Hill," "I Am the Wal-
rus," "Hello, Goodbye," "Strawberry
Fields Forever," "Penny Lane," "Baby,
You're a Rich Man," and "All You Need Is
Love." 'Nuff said? The sound is clean,
crisp, clear, and open. However, its compression betrays analog sources, and it
evidences a slight tendency to thin overbrightness.

## The Beatles (The White Album) (1968)
Parlophone CDP46443-2 (Disc 1)
CDP46444-2 (Disc 2) (93:40)   [A]
It was 1968, the movement and the
music had peaked in '67 (the Summer
of Love), and while the "high" was still
stratospheric, the signs of decline were
perceptible. *The Beatles* is, historically,
the group's most fascinating and naked
recording. The individual personas
begin to eclipse the group—the obvious
first harbingers of the end which would
come within the next couple of years.
The tensions, however, energized much

of the music, making this one of their
stellar releases; although it doesn't
require particularly close listening to
perceive the fractionalization within the
group. The sound is bright and punchy
yet afflicted with telltale traces of its era;
tape hiss is occasionally audible, and
while the spatial attributes and detailing
are both noticeably enhanced, there
often remains an overall awareness of
compression. On balance, the CD's
sound is an improvement over that of
the original LPs.

## Abbey Road (1969)
Parlophone CDP7 464462 (47:26)   [A+]
Simply put, if you own only one rock
CD, this should be the one. From the
magical, mystical opening chords of
John Lennon's "Come Together" (which
*Rolling Stone* aptly described as his
"word salad song"), to the momentous
summation of it all (the Beatles, the sixties—you name it) "The End," this is the
essential Beatles album, and thus the
essential rock & roll album. Occasional
tape hiss notwithstanding, the CD
version materially expands what was
an endless vision, highlighting Paul
McCartney's extraordinary bass work
and searing vocal on "Oh Darling," as
well as Lennon's perfectly acid guitar.
A triumph.

## Past Masters, Volume One
Parlophone CDP7-90043-2 (42:30)   [A–]

## Past Masters, Volume Two
Parlophone CDP7-90044-2 (51:03)   [A+]
It took much longer than early CD collectors wanted to wait, but with these
two discs released late in 1988, all of the
Beatles' official recordings were available in the digital format. The thirty-
three selections contained here pick up
EP material, A and B singles, and more
offbeat tracks (German versions of "I

Want to Hold Your Hand" and "She Loves You"). Together with the previously released thirteen English albums, they comprise the single greatest body of work in pop/rock history. Both *Past Masters* discs are accompanied by informative liner notes detailing the history and source of each cut. *Volume One* has the more offbeat material: a rare Ringo lead vocal on the rockabilly classic "Matchbox" and a scorching McCartney cover of "Long Tall Sally." It also offers indispensable early material: "Love Me Do," "From Me to You," "She Loves You," "I Want to Hold Your Hand," and "This Boy," covering their career from 1962 into mid-1965. *Volume Two* opens with the 1965 single "Day Tripper"/"We Can Work it Out," and works its way through one classic after another, including "Paperback Writer," "Lady Madonna," "Hey Jude," "Revolution," "Get Back," "Don't Let Me Down," "The Ballad of John and Yoko," closing with their last single release (March 6, 1970), the A side of which was "Let it Be." Need anyone say more? As must be expected, the sound on *Past Masters* varies with their many sources, and the first volume continues the controversy surrounding the decision to digitize the mono versions of their earliest material (eight of the thirty-three of these cuts are in mono), but on the whole the material represents a substantial sonic improvement over the original releases.

**Ultra Rare Trax Vol. 1 (1962–1967)**
Swinging Pig TSP-CD-001 (33:10)   **[A–]**

**Ultra Rare Trax Vol. 2 (1963–1967)**
Swinging Pig TSP-CD-002 (26:53)   **[A–]**
Back in the legendary sixties—"when the music really mattered"—rabid fans and compulsive record collectors gave rise to a bootleg recording market—live performances taped from hidden mikes, or better yet, the concert soundboard; radio broadcasts; or the occasionally purloined alternate or unreleased studio master tapes. Some of the better ones took on mythic stature and price among collectors, some eventually forced commercial release—e.g., Bob Dylan and The Band's classic *Basement Tapes*. Obviously, the ethic (or lack thereof) behind these releases is indefensible: The artist and the record company are both deprived of their rightful profit. But even worse is the artistic rape inherent in the practice, the theft of the performer's discretion as to what he or she feels is appropriate for release. An unexpected side effect of the CD revolution has been the resurgence of bootleg market, particularly in Europe, where the laws of some nations are lax compared with those of most industrialized countries. Bootleg CDs brought into the U.S. are subject to seizure. *Ultra Rare Trax* Volumes 1 and 2 are perhaps the two most famous bootleg CDs ever released— all tracks are supposedly from the original masters.

Included are alternate versions of classics like "I Saw Her Standing There," "Can't Buy Me Love," "Penny Lane," "Paperback Writer," "Strawberry Fields Forever," "A Hard Day's Night," "Norwegian Wood," and "Day Tripper," along with previously unreleased material, and several heretofore unknown Lennon/McCartney originals. This is generally first-rate, fascinating, and insightful material that illuminates the Beatles' musical mastery and rock roots, and reconfirms their genius. Bits of studio banter, acknowledged flubs, and some skeletal arrangements add the appeal of an intimate, stolen glance into the recording of rock's most influential band. Brief but detailed liner information tells the date and source of each track and, in some cases, its relationship to the commercially released version. The sound quality on these discs is extraordinary, often surpassing that of the officially released material. There have been another half-dozen recordings issued in this illicit series.

# Bell & Shore
### L-Ranko Motel (1989)
ROM 26008 (42:25)  **[B + ]**
Nathan Bell and Susan Shore write and perform material that their record company has chosen to dub "rock & country." It's a poor attempt to bring what is pretty much a pure country sound to a broader market. These two talents don't need labels, they just deserve exposure. The liner notes accurately describe their work as "a blend of offbeat literary storytelling and gritty realism," but should have gone on to describe their music's knowing detail and incisive humor; e.g., "The widow wore black velvet/The mistress drank the same." Bell and Shore both sing and play guitar, and are backed by a very complementary group of countrified sidemen. Shore's beautiful voice, reminiscent of Joan Baez, blends effortlessly with Bell, a vocal chameleon who sounds sometimes like Willie Nelson and sometimes like Jimmy Buffett. It's their material that sets Bell & Shore apart, and on *L-Ranko Motel* they do it justice. Soundwise, this release is a gem—clear, open, natural, and warm.

# The Belmonts
Formed 1957—Bronx, New York
Arguably, the greatest white doo-wop group, or at least right up there with Frankie Valli and The Four Seasons, they achieved fame with Dion's lead, but survived his 1960 departure.

### Cigars, A Cappella, Candy (1972)
Elektra 60989-2 (35:35)  **[A−]**
With Dion singing lead in 1957 the Belmonts recorded some of the finest white doo-wop ever committed to vinyl. For fifteen years after the fateful "I Wonder Why," they sold out, missed out, and generally fell victim to the dark shadows just outside the spotlight. But in 1972, without Mr. DiMucci, they got it together for the record—the glorious *Cigars, A Cappella, Candy*, which features nine time-stopping workouts from prerock pop to covers of late-sixties hits. As Greil Marcus states in his liner notes, the Belmonts deliver "Teenage music claimed as a birthright by adults." Street-corner harmonizing has principally been the province of the enthusiastic amateur—and that directly emotive sound is what ultimately makes *Cigars, A Cappella, Candy* such a wonderful listen. There's hardly a bad cut in the bunch, but "That's My Desire," "Rock and Roll Lullaby," and "Street Corner Symphony" are the highlights. Soundwise, the disc is bright, dynamic, and intimate—but it has an unfortunate tendency toward harshness in sections.

# Chuck Berry (Charles Edward Anderson)
b. October 18, 1926—St. Louis
In July of 1955, "Maybellene" took to the roads of America on car radios across the land and Berry, who at the time was trying to determine whether his career should be in hairdressing, photography, or music, found the light! Chuck had the audacity to identify and write for a youthful white audience, and to be embraced by that audience. For this mid-fifties heresy he paid his dues in a federal penitentiary (more than once). Aptly described by more than one critic

as the Walt Whitman of rock & roll, this is the one pioneer whose contributions to the musical form simply cannot be overrated.

### Greatest Hits (1955–1964)
C.D. Chess 21 (56:47) **[A]**
In many senses, the original testament of rock & roll. Almost all the essential cuts are included among its twenty-three selections; unfortunately, the quality of the sound reproduced does not begin to equal the quality of the material which gives rise to that sound. But then, the audio fidelity of the 45s on which this material was originally released was nothing to write home about either. Let's face it, the Chess Brothers who first gave Chuck studio time were just trying to make a buck, not history. As is often the case with compilation collections, the sound varies from recording to recording depending upon which sessions happened to produce each of these classics. While many of the selections are far from clean, let alone dynamically enhanced, the recording is generally clear and provides almost an hour of classic Berry on compact disc, which makes it a must (just don't discard your old 45s or 33s).

### The Great 28 (1955–1964)
MCACHD92500 (69:58) **[A+]**
Musically probably the best and most comprehensive of the Chuck Berry Chess collections. The sound quality varies substantially from cut to cut, some of the better-known material being pretty weak sonically. But on the whole, and once again considering the age of the masters, it's the best reproduction you're going to hear. Among the several Chuck Berry collections available in CD, this is the first choice. The breadth of the collection also provides insights into Berry's blues roots.

### More Rock'N'Roll Rarities (From the Golden Era of Chess Records) (1956–1965)
Chess MCA CHD-9190 (30:56) **[B]**
These twelve cuts (recorded between 1956 and 1965) are mostly alternate takes of better-known material ("Brown-eyed Handsome Man"), stereo remixes ("I'm Talking About You"), or demo recordings ("Sweet Little Sixteen"). Since Berry's music is simplicity itself, these selections don't sound that different from the more established versions, except that they lack that certain "finish" and spark which make Chuck's classic two-minute rock singles truly timeless. Berry's stature is such that there is legitimate interest in any recorded material available, but this is one for those whose interest goes beyond the casual—this is pretty esoterically primitive stuff. The sound is equivalent to a clean 78 (if you can imagine such a thing); respectable, but not particularly special, and the liner notes are minimally factual.

### Rock'N'Roll Rarities (1957–1964)
Chess CHD 92521 JVC-473 (52:00) **[A–]**
The sound quality on this disc is generally better than on the above-referenced *Greatest Hits* recording. It provides a wonderful supplement to that disc, including alternate takes on some of the classic material ("Sweet Little Sixteen," "Little Queenie," and "Johnny B. Goode") which stand in quality with the original releases included on the *Greatest Hits* collection. In addition, this CD covers numerous "lesser," but nonetheless wonderful, selections in the Berry repertoire, e.g., the Christmas classic, "Run Rudolph Run."

**20 Greatest Hits (1955–1964)**
Spectrum Stereo Speck 85004 (52:51)  **[F]**
God only knows where the "masters" for
this French import came from, but its a
shame they were ever found. A rip-off.

**Two Dozen Berrys (1955–1964)**
Vogue VG 651 6000085 (60:07)  **[B +]**
This French import provides the best
sound quality of any of the CD collections currently available of Berry's work.
Included are some interesting off-beat
cuts as well as "other" or cover versions
of some of the classic material. Certainly
a valid addition to the library of anyone
who seeks comprehensive coverage on
this founding father; but the lesser musical quality of much of the material pre-
vents it from being a first-rate offering.

**The Chess Box (1955–1973)**
Chess MCA CHD30-80,001
(201:56—three discs)  **[A +]**
Everybody (except Little Richard) knows
that Elvis was the King of rock & roll,
and everybody *should* know that Chuck
Berry was the architect. For the doubters
out there, *The Chess Box*'s seventy-one
cuts lay out all the blueprints with perfect clarity—his blues roots, driving
rhythms, classic lyrical excursions, and
the most enduring guitar licks in rock
history all are on ample display. If
there ever was an enduring musical
legacy, this has to be it. It's all right here,
along with a thirty-four-page booklet
containing a fine career overview by
Billy Altman, a conversation with the
reluctant Berry, a compilation of Berry's
twenty-seven *Billboard* Top 100 hits,
album discography, detailed personnel
and recording information, with vintage
photos thrown in for good measure.
While some of the tracks aurally betray
their vintage, on the whole the digital
remastering is first-rate, resulting in the

best-sounding versions currently available of this important material. Hats off
to MCA for an indispensable, rocking,
revealing package. This collection is
simply a must in any comprehensive
rock library.

**Hail! Hail! Rock 'N' Roll (1987)**
MCA MCAD6217 (42:04)  **[C +]**
Lord knows the man is entitled—he *is*
the architect of rock & roll. The fact that
this soundtrack recording celebrates his
sixtieth birthday says a lot about Chuck
Berry and the music. With foremost
exponent Keith Richards leading the all-
star backup band, the ingredients were
all here for a momentous musical
moment. Unfortunately, while *Hail!
Hail! Rock 'N' Roll* is a listenable concert
outing that includes most of Berry's original rock & roll testament, ultimately it
plays like an oldies show—maybe he's
just done it all too often to still find any
true inspiration. There are contributions
from myriad guest artists: Linda
Ronstadt gets closer to rock & roll than
she's been in years on "Back in the
U.S.A." and Etta James cooks "Rock and
Roll Music" until it sizzles; there are
numerous tasty instrumental solos from
the assembled all-stars, but the real
highlight is Berry's impromptu reading
of Bing Crosby's 1931 hit, "I'm Through
With Love," which rather incongruously
closes the recording. The sound betrays
its concert, analog roots with a certain
flatness, but it's not all that bad.

# B-52s

Formed 1976—Athens, Georgia
Parlayed a party sense, off beat guitar
leads, and a lyrical preoccupation with
horror movies and food into some of the
most meaningless, danceable music of
the eighties.

## Cosmic Thing (1989)

Reprise 25854-2 (47:19)   [B + ]

It had been three years since these party rockers released a new album. During that time they suffered the loss of Rick Wilson, the founding member of the B-52s whose weird guitar tunings were as much a part of their sound as bouffant hairdos are a part of their look. The remaining members returned to their rollicking roots, added a strong bass line to underpin the bouncy beat, and came up with the party record of the year. There's still the manic weirdness that distinguished their earliest successes like "Rock Lobster," and the lyrics still lean to the upbeat, funny side of life, but they also reflect more realism and maturity. A guaranteed good time for dancing feet and party minds, with sound that is bright and open.

# Big Brother and the Holding Company

Formed 1965—California

This is the band which, in 1967, at the Monterey Pop Festival, brought the pride of Port Arthur, Texas, Janis Joplin, to the attention of a national audience.

## Cheap Thrills (1968)

Columbia CK9700 (37:13)   [A]

This is a rough, raw, blues-drenched live outing that remains easily the best recorded work Janis Joplin ever put down. For reasons that in retrospect seem highly suspect, after this release Janis abandoned Big Brother and the Holding Company (her "advisors" said that she was the real talent in the group and the band was holding her back) and never found as compatible a backup during the remainder of her sadly brief career. The sound is definitely "live," and somewhat limited, but it is a marked improvement over its LP predecessor.

# Blondie

Formed 1975—New York City

Disco/punk from N.Y.'s hot/CBGB mid-seventies downtown club scene.

## The Best of Blondie (1977–1981)

Chrysalis VK41337 (44:12)   [B]

Bleached, bouncy, ultimately insulated American New Wave by a late seventies/early eighties band that managed to ride that New Wave to a pop crest with "Heart of Glass" in the spring of 1979. Drawing on a broad pastiche of sixties and seventies strains and supported by Clem Burk's power drumming, the group achieved more recognition than most of the bands who attempted to bring the "new sound of the seventies" to the charts. This album presents a fair overview of their slick, but not sustaining product (note that the mixes have been changed in some of the hits included here). The sound is clean, generally well-defined, and punchy, but it suffers from some hiss and that brittle, overbright radio mix.

# Luka Bloom

b. Ireland

## Riverside (1990)

Reprise 260092-2 (44:33)   [B]

The tradition of the balladeer is not far removed from the root music of rock & roll, which may be why the Irish, from Van Morrison to U2, have shown a natural proclivity for America's second great popular music contribution (after jazz). I suspect it has more to do with soul than with history, and Luka has his fair share of soul, filtering through the mature words and simple instrumentation. It all seems very real and important somehow, though Bloom's themes focus on the commonplace. Like his brother, Barry Moore (Bloom's stage name derives from Suzanne Vega and James Joyce), he is a musician of distinction who succeeds on this fine debut more often than he fails—more wellspring than mainstream, his songs, like the best of all folk music, sound ageless on first listen. The CD's sonics effectively emphasize the warm, amplified acoustic guitar and human voice in a highly complimentary way.

# The Blue Nile

Formed early eighties—Scotland
Moody, evocative technopop, from trio influenced by both John Cale and Joni Mitchell.

## A Walk Across Rooftops (1983)

Linn Records LKHCD1 (38:11)   [A–]
Minimalist, techno-rock from a band notable for its intelligence and restraint. As *Melody Maker* accurately said of *A Walk Across Rooftops,* "nostalgia, romance, elation, and reflection are woven into the fabric with gossamer delicacy." Music for contemplation, it is recorded with beautiful spaciousness, precision, and clarity resulting in a premier example of CD sound.

## Hats (1990)

A&M 5284 (38:58)   [C–]
Atmosphere is one thing, lack of focus is something else. The Blue Nile's followup to their wonderfully strange *A Walk Across Rooftops* suffers from a fragmentary repetition of music and lyric. While this technique can be effective, as Philip Glass has proven, that's the exception rather than the rule. Try as it might, *Hats* doesn't break any new ground, and therein lies its problem. The band's ethereal, echoed vocals and synthesizer-heavy sound are compelling—just the thing for hip New Age Sunday mornings. "Saturday Night" manages to

capture the somewhat mystical feeling of their prior work. The overall sound is wide and sumptuous, although there is a bit of compression in the midrange.

# The BoDeans

Formed early eighties—Waukesha, Wisconsin
Unpretentious retro-rock highlighted by offbeat vocal voicings.

## Love & Hope & Sex & Dreams (1986)

Slash/Warner Bros 9 25103 2 (41:54)   [B]
The '86 debut by a Wisconsin-based retro-rock band whose music echoes with the classic strains of Dylan and the Band. Heightened by T-Bone Burnett's simple, clean production values, The BoDeans don't break new ground, but amply illustrate proficiency in making known elements insinuatingly memorable. The CD sounds very clean, defined, and dynamic.

## Outside Looking In (1987)

Reprise/Slash 25629-2 (48:56)   [B–]
A lot has changed for this promising young group from Waukesha, Wisconsin, between their 1986 debut release and this, their second recording. The original quartet is now a trio (albeit one abetted by a number of guest artists on this release) and production has moved from T-Bone Burnett to Jerry Harrison, Talking Heads' keyboard player. The result is another slice of eighties heartland retro-rock, although this time around the sound is a bit more atmospheric and dense. Highly listenable, but lacking in any real outstanding specific selections and somewhat weak lyrically. The all-digital sound is excellent.

# Gary U.S. Bonds
# (Gary Anderson)

b. June 6, 1939—Jacksonville, Florida
First charted in 1960 with the party
voice, party atmosphere of "New
Orleans" that influenced Bruce Springsteen.

### The Best of Gary U.S. Bonds (1960–1966)

Rhino R270971 (52:30)  **[C]**
Gary U.S. Bonds, who had three Top Ten
R&B hits between 1960 and 1962, may
be best known today because of his
acknowledged influence on Bruce
Springsteen, who was responsible for
Bond's credible 1981 comeback, *Dedica-
tion.* The oldies crowd will remember
him for the great party anthem "Quarter
to Three." Like the girl groups of those
musical times, Bonds was very much a
producer's creation. Frank Guida created
the man, the music, and the mayhem.
Today this material retains a certain marvelously contrived innocence and some
historical cachet. Except on "Quarter
to Three," the excessive overdubs,
repetitive formula, and party racket
obscure much of the original energy.
That tendency toward overdubbing
makes this material sound better on the
original 45s—where mud was part of the
aural magic—than it does on CD. This
eighteen-song package delivers all the
sixties chart hits.

# Booker T and the MG's

Formed 1962—Memphis
Made up of Booker T. Jones (organ),
Steve Cropper (guitar), Donald "Duck"
Dunn (bass), and Al Jackson (drums):
the ultimate sixties studio band.

### The Best of Booker T & the MG's
### (1962–1971)

Stax FCD-60-004 (63:12)  **[C+]**
Booker T (Jones) and the MG's (Memphis
Group) began as the Monkeys, the
house band for Stax Records during that
studio's sixties golden soul era. Countless black artists (Otis Redding, Wilson
Pickett, and Sam & Dave among them)
first caught commercial fire with the
sympathetic backing of Booker T & the
MG's' definitive groove. The group also
enjoyed hit status on their own, particularly with "Green Onions" (not included
here). This collection of seventeen cuts
(all instrumentals except for Booker T's
vocal on "Johnny, I Love You") highlights their simple, easy, yet tight way
with a variety of material, from originals
to such chestnuts as "Eleanor Rigby"
and "Mrs. Robinson." John Fogerty has
said they may be the best rock band of
all time—perhaps an overstatement, but
this quartet did have its thing together.
The sound quality is essentially comparable to that of a slightly used LP and
suffers from very audible hiss on several
cuts.

# David Bowie
# (David Robert Jones)

b. Jaunary 8, 1947—London, England
A musical gadfly—the man of a thousand personas. An artist whose mastery
of media manipulation was as much an
attribute of his extraordinary popular
success as his true musical creativity.
But Bowie has proved to be an accurate
mirror of his changing times and has
enjoyed immense popular success
throughout his multi-faced career.

### Space Oddity (1969)

Rykodisc RCD 10131 (56:55)  **[C+]**
Bowie's pretentious but promising debut
features the knock-out title cut that still

echoes from oldies playlists. Primarily acoustic, *Space Oddity* displays the erratic self-indulgence that rapidly became this ephemeral artist's career credo—but the intelligence, sense of self-image, and astute awareness of the changing complexion of pop success are also on display. Overall, the album presumes more than it delivers, but the single, "Space Oddity," in its own weird way, is a classic of the era and, thanks to Ryko's remastering, has never sounded better. In fact the sound, with a few minor exceptions, is startlingly clean, clear, and dynamic. Ryko has also enhanced things by providing the 1970 version of the single "Memory of a Free Festival Parts 1 and 2" ("the first appearance of Mick Ronson on a David Bowie record"), the last track on the original album, and "Conversation Piece," as bonus tracks.

### Hunky Dory (1971)

Rykodisc RCD 10133 (57:16)  **[B + ]**
The Thin White Duke as accessible pop star with influences obvious. The Beatles echo through "Oh! You Pretty Thing," Lou Reed in "Queen Bitch," and Bob Dylan (including precise vocal mannerisms) on "Song for Bob Dylan." Best of all is the early seventies teen anthem "Changes," which opens the album with a nod to the Who. Pop music for the seminally weird. In the words of Robert Christgau, "This ambitious, brainy, imaginative singer/composer has created an album that rewards the concentration it demands instead of making you wish you'd gone on with the vacuuming." *Hunky Dory* foreshadows Bowie's sci-fi world and total image reconstructions that were to frame some of the more interesting music of a generally uninteresting decade. This fine-sounding CD also includes four strong bonus tracks, the

best of which is the previously unreleased "Bombers."

### The Rise and Fall of Ziggy Stardust and the Spiders from Mars (1972)

Rykodisc RCD 10134 (56:09)  **[A–]**
The ultimate rock poseur steps forward to announce a brave new apocalypse as seen through a male/female eye. *Ziggy Stardust* is one of Bowie's stronger releases, the material is concerned with stardom, rock, and the general state of a confused world predicted to follow. He paints his picture with wit and insight, and frames it with strong production values—astro glam/jam, but with arresting lyrics: "Like tigers on vaseline," and "That weren't no D.J., that was hazy cosmic jive." The CD contains five bonus tracks—a previously unreleased mix of "John, I'm Only Dancing," "Velvet Goldmine," the previously unreleased "Sweet Head," and the acoustic demo versions of "Ziggy Stardust" and "Lady Stardust," which are interesting because of the focus on the vocals. He's at his best when the sometimes heavy-handed musical accompaniment doesn't overwhelm his lyrical nuance, as in "Rock'n'Roll Suicide." Ryko's digital remastering is extraordinary, resulting in a clean, bright, dynamic sound.

### Pin-Ups (1973)

Rykodisc RCD 10136 (40:50)  **[C + ]**
It's a noble conceit, rerecording some mostly obscure creations from the groups who made London the center of the pop music world in the mid-sixties. His choices are interesting, ranging from the well-known—Pink Floyd, the Who, Them, the Kinks, and the Yardbirds, to the marginal—Mojos, Pretty Things, and the Merseys. It's just that Bowie's versions really add nothing to the originals, other than attention, which isn't all bad—it's quality material. The CD

includes two bonus tracks from entirely different sources: a previously unreleased Bruce Springsteen cover, and a B-side Jacques Brel cover. The sound quality is very good, but not quite up to some of the other Ryko Bowie reissues, in that it displays a bit of compression.

### Aladdin Sane (1973)
Rykodisc RCD 10135 (41:35)   **[A–]**
Dissonant, panoramic, sexual confusion from cover to contents. With the exception of the ill-advised inclusion of an abbreviated version of the Stones' "Let's Spend the Night Together," there's an undeniable power in the songs and the production—tinkling piano notwithstanding. It ain't a pretty picture—it's a barren, vacuous world of sensation without feeling, sex without lust, contact without connection. But Bowie, always the litmus of current attitudes, hit the nail on the head with *Aladdin Sane,* which went a long way toward burnishing his legend. Again, Ryko's remastering results in a splendid sounding recording, effectively conveying the power and energy in the original grooves.

### Diamond Dogs (1974)
Rykodisc RCD 10137 (46:28)   **[C]**
Mick Ronson and his stinging guitar were gone, as was Bowie's inspiration. Pompous and drenched in doom, it was time for a change, and thankfully, Bowie knew it. The sorry thing is that he still felt it necessary to verify it with the release of this posturing, ill-conceived, and unnecessary album. That said, fairness dictates that the inclusion of "Rebel, Rebel," one of his best songs, be mentioned, and the title track is not without its merits. There are two bonus cuts: a previously unreleased 1973 track, "Dodo," and the demo version of "Candidate," which is superior to the overproduced vinyl version. The

original recording suffered from poor production values, so while the CD's sound is a major improvement, it is still limited by its source. As an added plus, the CD reproduces the original putrid album cover.

### David Live (1974)
Rykodisc RCD 10138/39
(90:28—two discs)   **[C–]**
On one hand, there may be merit in Ryko's reissuing the *entire* Bowie catalog on CD, on the other hand, Bowie probably insisted on it when the deal was cut. Whatever the reason, a dog is a dog is a dog—and this one has a hoarse bark. The recording was done at the Philadelphia stop of the *Diamond Dogs* tour, and also includes tracks from *Aladdin Sane* and *Ziggy Stardust,* as well as the previously unreleased "All the Young Dudes" and Eddie Floyd's aged "Knock on Wood." Bowie's performances on those two songs are mediocre, and the rest of the disc is a mess. This CD includes three "bonus" tracks: Bowie's nine-second introduction of the band (no kidding), "Here Today, Gone Tomorrow," and "Time." Ryko is to be complimented on the sound quality, which is first-rate for concert material—certainly of a higher quality than the performance.

### ChangesOneBowie
### (1976—compilation release date)
RCA PCD1-1732 (46:40)   **[C]**

### Fame and Fashion
### (1984—compilation release date)
RCA PCD1-4919 (55:03)   **[C]**
Within these two greatest hits collections are Bowie's best-known selections from 1972 forward. Like MTV without the video, this is music for faddish mass consumption, a triumph of form over substance, all surface surrounding an empty shell. The sound, while nothing

extraordinary, is clean and serviceable, not much different from the LP versions.

**Sound + Vision (1969–1980)**
Rykodisc RCD90120/21/22; RCDV 1018
(190:54—four discs)  **[A]**
In terms of the total packaging concept, Ryko's debut release from the much desired Bowie catalog, *Sound + Vision* easily sets the standard by which all other boxed retrospectives must be measured. The design and graphics of the silkscreened box, the individual covers of the four CDs, as well as the fifty-two-page booklet, are all appropriate to the content and are executed with remarkable style and class. And if you are possessed of the right equipment—which few seem to be—you also get a CDV of the "Ashes to Ashes" video. Musically, there are fifty tracks, seven of which were previously unreleased—an excellent representation of the multiple personas and styles that made Bowie one of the monster acts of the vapid seventies. Everyone will have some criticisms of content, personally, I would have dropped the three tracks from the dreadful *David Live* and substituted "Queen Bitch," "Suffragette City," and "The Jean Genie." Also omitted are his two Top Ten hits "Fame" and "Golden Years." These complaints aside, this is a masterful presentation, and a must for any hard-core Bowie fan—unless, of course, you already own all of the albums, in which case you're enough of a fanatic that the rarities still make *Sound + Vision* an absolute must. While there is the inevitable variation in sound quality, Ryko, which has established its market niche based on the sound of its digital remasterings, lives up to its fine reputation, with overall excellent sonics, consistently superior to the vinyl originals. The Kurt Loder essay, which, along with detailed recording information on each track, is a bit overzealous, but genuinely informative.

**Changesbowie (1969–1990)**
Rykodisc RCD 20171 (74:38)  **[A]**
The essential single-disc Bowie collection. Ryko has taken the original compilation, *ChangesOneBowie*, and added "Ashes to Ashes," "China Girl," "Fashion," "Heroes," "Let's Dance," "Modern Love," and a killer remix of "Fame" ("Fame '90") to provide an all-hit overview of a varied and various career. As has been the case with all the Ryko Bowie CD remasters, the sound is audibly enhanced.

# The Box Tops
Formed 1966—Memphis
**Ultimate Box Tops (1967–1969)**
Warner Special Products 9-27611-2
(51:10)  **[B + ]**
One of the many sixties high school bands that managed to crack the national charts; in the Box Tops' case, they succeeded more than once and quite effectively with "The Letter" (8/12/67) and "Cry Like A Baby" (3/2/68). What set this band apart was its lead singer, Alex Chilton, who has one of those raw, rough voices that seems almost indigenous to rock & roll and which was perfect for the blue-eyed soul that was the Box Tops' stock and trade. There is a quality to this music, limited though it might be, which has held a core group of fans for twenty years. The compilation covers all the charted hits plus some obscure, but strong cover versions of other groups' contemporary material. The sound on this CD is a pleasant revelation—the masters must have been pristine, because the digital transfer cuts the original recordings by a wide margin—a fine sounding collection.

# James Brown

b. May 3, 1928, Macon, Georgia
Born into true southern black poverty
of the Depression era, Brown literally
picked cotton, danced in the streets, and
eventually stole to survive in a less than
hospitable world. His thefts resulted in
his incarceration for three years; and,
upon release, Brown tried his hand at
prizefighting and baseball before returning to his gospel church roots with a
group originally known as the
Sewanees, which James rapidly converted into the Famous Blue Flames. He
remains the single preeminent figure in
black popular music of the last thirty
years, the inventor of funk, the predecessor of rap, the godfather of soul.

### Live at the Apollo (1962)
Polydor 843-479-2 (31:36)   [A + ]
In addition to securing his overworked
appellations "Godfather of Soul" and
"The Hardest Working Man in Show
Business," this seminal live recording
confirms that Brown had a clear picture
of his destiny and the steps needed to
realize it. Brown essentially forced his
recalcitrant record company to record
this performance at Harlem's soul music
mecca; he claims to have paid the original recording costs. But Brown knew the
power of his live performance and
rightly believed a record of the Famous
Flames and Soul Brother No. 1 doing
their very special thing would find an
audience. Right on, JB—this may well
be the best live rock/soul recording
ever. The moment and the excitement
still burn with Brown's awesome intensity. The liner notes, both original and
current, are an excellent addition to this
historic package. The LP covered the
same excitement but was sonically defi-
cient; the sound of the CD (particularly
for an almost thirty-year-old live record-

ing) is a dramatic improvement in
clarity, spaciousness, and range. A winner in every way!

### The CD Of JB (Sex Machine and Other Soul Classics) (1956–1974)
Polydor 825714-2 (56:09)   [A + ]
These eighteen selections cover "Soul
Brother No. 1's" pop output from his
original "Please, Please, Please" to his
mid-seventies hits. The sound quality is
simply wonderful, making this historic
collection of the roots of funk a must disc
in any comprehensive collection of
American popular music of the last
thirty years.

### James Brown Live at the Apollo (1968)
Polygram 823 001-2 (73:34)   [A–]
First off, this isn't the classic *Live at the
Apollo* recording done in October of
1962. This recording was made in 1967,
and while it lacks the pure animal fury
that makes the '62 concert a legitimate
candidate for the best live recording of
all time, it's still Soul Brother No. 1, it's
still the Famous Flames, it's still the
Apollo and it still pulsates as only the
man can. The sound is sharp and generally clean. While there may have been
more energy five years earlier, he still
laid down a legitimate claim to being
"the hardest working man in show
business."

### In the Jungle Groove (1970–1972)
Polydor 829 624-2 (63:45)   [B + ]
This compilation of early seventies
efforts by the Godfather of Soul and his
famous funksters, the "J.B.s," includes
some previously unissued material,
some remixes and some classics, "Soul
Power" and "Hot Pants (She Got to Use
What She Got to Get What She Wants)."
From start to finish the Hardest Working
Man in Show Business and the J.B.s
cook. The sound varies, evidencing

occasional hiss and some compression, but overall, it is amazingly clean, tight and dynamic.

### Gravity (1986)
Scotti Bros. ZK40380 (39:44)   **[B]**
Producer (and soul singer) Dan Hartman brings Mr. Dynamite's sound into the eighties, which means that the funk is programmed as well as played, with mixed results. It did produce Brown's first major hit of the decade, "Living in America," which featured Stevie Ray Vaughan on lead guitar; while it's great to hear James's driving sounds in a current context, the whole enterprise has a bit of the feel of current convenience packaging. Yet, Soul Brother No. 1 still has his moments, thirty years into one of the most influential careers in pop music history. While the mix has a slightly overbright edge to it, it also leaps off the disc with dynamic intensity.

# Jackson Browne
b. October 9, 1948—Heidelberg, West Germany
Very much a part of the commercially successful L.A. singer/songwriter coterie that achieved pop dominance in the early to mid-seventies, Browne's strength has been his writing—his singing voice being charitably described, at best, as serviceable. His early to mid-seventies work involved romantic insights into interpersonal relationships. With the passing of time, and personal tragedy (the suicide of his wife), his vision broadened, resulting in a strong political preoccupation that now dominates his lyrics.

### Saturate Before Using (1972)
Asylum SD50551-2 (41:15)   **[B + ]**
One of the better lyricists of the last thirty years of pop, Browne's finely crafted words and occasionally inspired melodies reflect a serious artist who has consistently attempted to grapple with the current state of the human condition. There is an unevenness in both the content and performance on the ten selections which comprise this debut release; but, at its best—"A Song For Adam," "Doctor My Eyes," and "Rock Me on the Water"—it represents the benchmark by which other seventies singer/songwriters can be measured. The sound is clean and surprisingly spacious, although little detail enhancement is noticeable.

### For Everyman (1973)
Asylum SD 5067-2 (41:09)   **[B–]**
Browne was a premiere member of the early seventies singer/songwriter school—in his case, the emphasis is on the songwriter side. *For Everyman* includes some fine examples of his lyrical skills: "These Days," "Redneck Friend," "Ready Or Not," and the title cut being the most notable examples. As usual, he is backed with sympathetic, professional arrangements, but the CD's sound is nothing special: it's murky, with limited dynamic enhancement and some tape hiss.

### The Pretender (1976)
Asylum 6E 107-2 (35:30)   **[A]**
The perfect culmination of the first phase of Browne's career (1972–1976). Produced by Jon Landau, *The Pretender* is the artist's final statement on the role of everyman in contemporary society. In this instance, Browne's always outstanding lyrics are set to melodies and production values which provide a perfect accompaniment. Perhaps because of Landau's positive influence, this is more pure rock & roll than the pop/ballad form which had previously dominated Browne's work. The LP had first-rate sound when it was released, and the

sound is enhanced with a greater spatial quality that fits the material to a tee.

**Running On Empty (1978)**
Asylum 6E 11302 (42:30)   **[A]**
Audio verité—one of the most conceptually fascinating recordings in the history of rock & roll. With *Running On Empty,* Browne attempted to capture the experience of a rock & roller's life on the road. To achieve the desired result, the selections (most of which were not written by Browne) were recorded both on and behind the stage, on the tour bus, and in motel rooms: the milieu of the rock tour. As must be expected with an undertaking of this type, there is variation in the quality of the recordings, but not as extreme as one might expect. The CD sound is full and open, consistent with the entire enterprise, even to the extent of providing background details inaudible in prior releases.

# Buckwheat Zydeco (Stanley Dural)

Accordionist and successor/popularizer of the contagious musical form created by Clifton Chenier.

**On a Night Like This (1988)**
Island 7 90622-2 (35:16)   **[B]**
Described by David Browne in *Rolling Stone* as "the dance hall music of French-speaking Louisiana blacks," zydeco is designed for one thing—a good time, party-down from the region that earns its keep, keepin' on. The central elements to the zydeco sound are the accordion, rub boards (breastplates ribbed like metal washboards and played with finger thimbles), and absolutely contagious dance rhythms. Dural seasons his musical mix with electric guitars, synthesizers, and horns. It's a good time

in French and English (strong covers of the Blasters' "Marie" and Dylan's "On a Night Like This). The sound is clean, clear, and dynamic, but retains some compression and tape hiss.

# Buffalo Springfield
Formed 1966—Los Angeles
The lineup included Neil Young, Stephen Stills, Ritchie Furay, Dewey Martin, and Bruce Palmer. Named after a piece of farm equipment, one of the seminal country rock bands. Mercurial personalities doomed longevity, but together and separately they proved to be among the most influential musicians of the era.

**Buffalo Springfield (1967)**
Atco 33-200-2 (33:02)   **[A–]**
The debut release of an immensely talented, influential, but short-lived pioneering country/rock band that leads off with one of the anthems of a great decade, "For What it's Worth." While every member of the original Buffalo Springfield moved on to even greater popularity, it was Stephen Stills and Neil Young (not necessarily in that order) who were showcased in this first release. Fascinating for all of the obvious reasons, this high-energy, sometimes rough recording still sounds impressive almost a quarter century after its groundbreaking release. Highlights among the tracks include the above-mentioned Stills opus, plus "Sit Down I Think I Love You," and Young's naked "Out of My Mind." The overall quality is everything you'd expect from artists of this caliber. The sound quality is superior to the LP in its clarity and separation, but compression and tape hiss date the disc.

### Buffalo Springfield Again (1967)
Atco 33-226-2 (33:56)   [A +]
The clear standout of this band's three albums, *Again* is a classic—it opens with "Mr. Soul" and closes with "Broken Arrow," two great Neil Young songs, and includes Stephen Stills's "Bluebird" and "Rock & Roll Woman" which, according to the estimable Dave Marsh, "are the finest songs he's ever written." Everything came together on this one—great songs, powerful, imaginative production values, and kick-ass playing—a standout album from rock's classic decade. The sound is an added plus—natural, spacious, and much cleaner than the vinyl. Buffalo Springfield was one of America's truly great, original rock bands, and *Again* is their crowning achievement.

### The Best of the Buffalo Springfield/ Retrospective (1969)
Atco 38105 (40:17)   [A–]
It's hard to fault *Retrospective*'s twelve selections, mostly from the first two albums (the third album, *Last Time Around,* lived up to its name—the band had disbanded before its release). Since all the expected classics are included, it would have been nice, given its relatively short playing time for a compilation, if they had included the extended version of "Bluebird," with the four-and-a-half-minute instrumental jam that appeared on the double LP 1976 "best of" release, *Buffalo Springfield.* For that matter it would have been nicer if that compilation (even in slightly edited form) had been released as the group's "best of" CD. Still, given what's currently available, if you want only one Springfield CD with all the familiar sides, this is the way to go, but I'd recommend picking up *Buffalo Springfield* and *Buffalo Springfield Again.* The sound on this disc varies depending on the recording session; when it's good, it's very good, and when it's not, it's not awful.

# Jimmy Buffett
b. December 25, 1946—Mobile, Alabama
"I like the life I love, I love the life I live."

### Songs You Know By Heart (Jimmy Buffett's Greatest Hits) (1973–1979)
MCA MCAD 5633 (42:28)   [B–]
Caribbean country by the man who invented the form; and, as a result, has managed to live the life that he sings about. This is highly listenable music—party songs for the laid-back crowd. Included among the thirteen songs are some, but far from all, of Jimmy's better efforts: "A Pirate Looks at 40" and his *piéce de résistance,* "Margaritaville." Actually, Buffett, beach-bum persona notwithstanding, is an intelligent lyricist possessed of a genuine comic flair. It's too bad that this collection doesn't do a better job of underlining that fact. The sound varies with the divergent sources, but is generally clean, well-detailed (particularly in the lead vocals) with a nice openness, but occasionally it succumbs to an overly bright mid-range.

# Solomon Burke
b. 1936—Philadelphia
Preacher and soul music pioneer, purveyor of "rock & roll soul music," his first R&B hits date back to the early sixties.

### A Change is Gonna Come (1986)
Rounder CD2053 (42:41)   [B +]
At the half-century mark, Burke can still preach a lyric with heartfelt fervor and one big voice. This set of smooth soulful sounds was recorded in New Orleans in 1984 and it doesn't disappoint. Highlighted by Paul Kelly's "Love Buys Love" and Sam Cooke's "A Change Is Gonna Come" (a definitive contemporary version), the sound is spacious, clean, well-

defined, and only slightly occasionally compressed. The surface may be smooth, but the roots are still there.

# T-Bone Burnett
# (J. Henry)

b. St. Louis; raised in Texas

This lanky, laconic reborn classic/country rocker first achieved notice as a part of Dylan's Rolling Thunder Review and then as a part of the short-lived Alpha Band. In the eighties he has enjoyed limited success with a few recordings of his well-written contemporary parables, but his star has ascended in recent years as a sought-after record producer.

## Truth Decay (1980)

Takoma TAKCD7080 (43:08)   [C+]

Straight-ahead rock propels these twelve compositions, notable for their pithy, yet trenchant vocal observations and the monotonal voice in which T-Bone delivers them. The initial release of one of the brighter minor luminaries to arrive on the American music scene in the last half of the seventies, this recording of what Dave Marsh labeled, "mythic Christian blues" is loose, but somehow tired. The sound is OK, occasionally overbright and occasionally subject to hiss; however, it is more dynamic and defined than on the LP.

## T-Bone Burnett (1986)

MCA MCAD5809 (44:33)   [A]

Over four days in the early summer of 1986, Burnett gathered a half-dozen "country" oriented musicians (including David Hidalgo, Byron Berline, and Billy Swan) in a digitally equipped studio, where they laid down these thirteen tracks on this "live" studio recording with obvious feeling and affection. This is a contemporary country sound that lies close to its roots and the artists'

hearts with a resultant timeless sound. A gentle but deeply moving effort that feels almost like eavesdropping on the private ruminations of people playing for the love of a music that is integral to their being. The all-digital sound is a revelation: quiet and clean with beautifully defined shadings.

# The Byrds

Formed 1964—Los Angeles

One of the least acknowledged, highly innovative, and immensely influential of America's sixties rock bands. Folk rock, country rock, and the psychedelic sound can all be traced to this highly transitory group.

## Mr. Tambourine Man (1965)

Columbia/CBS CK 9172 (30:45)   [A+]

The irresistible, influential debut of L.A.'s premiere folk/country/rock band, led by Roger McGuinn, focused on the then-current folk/rock sound, with Gene Clark and McGuinn adding their own worthy compositions. As good as the music is, it's the Byrds' sound—the jangling twelve-string guitar and glorious vocal harmonies driven by a strong bottom—that make it all so special. This sound echoes shamelessly through the work of the Eagles, R.E.M., and countless others. Measured by current standards, this disc's sound leaves a lot to be desired; it is compressed, at times edgy and muddy. Yet the original strong production values prevail, and a classic is a classic is a classic. The inclusion of the original liner notes in this budget disc is a nice addition that lends a certain innocence to it all.

## Turn! Turn! Turn! (1966)

Columbia/CBS CK 9254 (30:05)   [A]

*Mr. Tambourine Man, Volume 2,* just about sums it up, but why mess with a good thing? The Byrds were smart enough not to, so again we have a first-rate recording highlighted by three Dylan covers. Arguably, the material is a shade weaker this time out (maybe the group actually played and sang everything this time) but the difference certainly doesn't represent any meaningful dropoff, which means that the comments about *Mr. Tambourine Man* apply here. The sound quality is essentially equivalent to its predecessor.

### Fifth Dimension (1966)
Columbia CK 9349 (29:17)   [A–]
Less than two years after their landmark debut, *Mr. Tambourine Man*, the exodus had begun—Gene Clark being the first to fly the coop. But eighty percent proved to be enough. The chemistry of the era was beginning to seep into the repertoire, for example, "Mr. Spaceman," the truly classic "Eight Miles High," and the lesser-known "I See You," but roots reverence remains, with sensitive readings of "Wild Mountain Thyme" and "John Riley." Throughout, the tight harmonics and chiming guitars lead this adventurous band through a thoroughly creative and satisfying outing. The sound of this disc is nothing to write home about—edgy, compressed, and suffering from some vocal distortions—it impairs an otherwise quality effort.

### Younger than Yesterday (1967)
Columbia CK 9442 (28:17)   [A]
Opening with the prescient, ironic "So You Want to Be a Rock & Roll Star," and including another fine Dylan cover, "My Back Pages," *Younger than Yesterday* reflects most of this great American band's folk, country, and psychedelic influences. It is also the last great recording the original band, before Crosby and

Clark continued a round of departures. (The Byrds would make the classic *Sweetheart of the Rodeo* the next year, but that was a very different band and sound.) They were headed toward country music, as Hillman's four contributions to *Younger* clearly foreshadow. The band may have been in personal turmoil, but their creativity was apparently sparked by it, because this is a classic. The sound quality of this CD is generally impressive.

### Sweetheart of the Rodeo (1968)
Edsel EDCD234 (32:14)   [A+]
The musical focus of this highly influential L.A.-based band shifted with the musicians who officially and unofficially held membership over the years. From pioneering folk/rock to country/rock with occasional large doses of psychedelia, their trademark chiming guitar sound still reverberates. In 1968, Roger McGuinn and company ventured to Nashville with newest member Gram Parsons, one of the least acknowledged but most influential musicians of the era, and recorded *Sweetheart of the Rodeo*, a true rock classic. Generally conceded to be the seminal country/rock album, it helped spawn the Eagles and much of the L.A.-based ersatz country/rock sounds that ultimately influenced much of the early- to mid-seventies FM rock radio. Parsons was a true country musician, whose haunting voice and musical vision honestly reflected longstanding American musical heritage. From Bob Dylan's "You Ain't Going Nowhere" to Parsons's "Hickory Wind," the sounds of *Sweetheart of the Rodeo* were at once new and familiar—traditional and innovative. The CD brings exciting clarity to this classic. There's a bit of hiss, a little softness in the bottom, but the voicings and picking have amazing presence and separation on disc.

This import CD will make you forget the LP after one listening.

## The Notorious Byrd Brothers (1968)
Columbia/CBS CK 9575 (28:39)  [B + ]
Dylan's been replaced by Carole King (the album's highlight, "Goin' Back") and Roger's difficult ways have resulted in a wholesale turnover in talent. David Crosby left in the middle of these sessions. Some countrified sounds and Beatlesque psychedelia now compete with the jangling twelve-strings, but a unity of vision prevails, and the Byrds continued to make exemplary music in a time when greatness was often the norm. The sound quality is a little better than that on the first two Byrds releases, but still has a few dropouts and other problems.

## The Byrds Collection (1965–1973)
Castle CCSCD151 (52:58)  [C + ]
The Byrds popularized Bob Dylan, laid down the foundations of what became country rock with their seminal *Sweetheart of the Rodeo,* and included a brief sojourn as space cowboys in the middle of it all. This compilation covers all aspects of the band's relatively brief, but very influential, career. Their chiming guitar trademark sound has been resuscitated by many young eighties bands, most notably R.E.M. Unfortunately, their fine music is shackled with muddy, thick sound and by too edgy highs. It's listenable, but certainly nothing to write home about.

## Never Before (1965–1968)
Murray Hill D22808 (45:54)  [A]
Californian Jim Dickson, who worked as an A&R man in the jazz and folk fields, is generally credited as the catalyst behind the creation of the Byrds. This 1989 release, defined in its excellent liner notes as "the great lost Byrds singles" and "the Byrds' stereo debut," is a fascinating compilation of seventeen previously unreleased tracks and alternate stereo remixes of classic work from this ultimately transient band's classic period—when the five founding members were still working together. The new stereo remixes of their best known work ("Mr. Tambourine Man," "Eight Miles High") are revelatory, and a number of the previously unreleased items ("She Has a Way," "I Know My Rider," and "Moog Raga") are worthy additions to their early catalog. For hardcore Byrds fans this album is a must, and anyone who has an ear for one of America's truly original, creative rock bands will not be disappointed. It's obvious that great care was taken in the digital remixes (the aforementioned Dickson being involved in ten of the tracks and Roger McGuinn in seven), and the bright, open sound is outstanding.

## Untitled (1970)
Columbia CGK 30127 (71:15)  [C–]
This double album is made up of half live cuts and half studio material. The former are more effective than the latter. Of course, by this point, Roger McGuinn was the only member left from the original group. The live material contains some classics, "So You Want to Be a Rock & Roll Star," "Mr. Tambourine Man," and "Eight Miles High," but the mix reveals heavy, muddy bass and bottom. The comparatively weak singing leaves you longing for the originals. The studio material starts promisingly enough, with McGuinn's "Chestnut Mare" and Little Feat's "Truck Stop Girl," but after that, it goes rapidly downhill, so the fact that the studio tracks are a notable sonic improvement doesn't matter. Like Roger said, he should have called it quits in 1968.

### The Byrds (1965–1990)
Columbia Legacy 46773
(266:33—four discs) **[A + ]**
If you ever had any question about how a band that was almost as famous for the instability of its personnel as it was for the mere sixteen songs it charted between 1965 and 1970 (only two of which, "Mr. Tambourine Man" and "Turn! Turn! Turn!," made it to the Top Ten—both reached No. 1 in 1965) could have been as influential as the Byrds, set aside four hours and immerse yourself in this meticulously detailed, beautifully produced boxed set. Tom Petty, one of their many disciples, puts it this way in the comprehensive accompanying booklet: "The Byrds, to my mind, created one of the handful of *original* sounds in all of rock & roll history. Like Elvis Presley, the Who, Chuck Berry, and later Led Zeppelin or the Ramones, the Byrds created something that would influence most of the pop and rock that followed." From Dylan to space cowboys, these country/rock pioneers with their chiming guitars and haunting harmonies identified a uniquely American sound that still reverberates with a special energy and integrity.

This twenty-fifth anniversary compilation is exhaustive. In addition to four CDs, it includes a fifty-five-page booklet complete with a family tree tracing the rapidly changing personnel who inhabited this groundbreaking band with meticulously detailed source information on each of the ninety tracks, twenty-two of which were previously unreleased or alternate takes. For those other than the hopelessly devoted, there's probably more dross than is really necessary—McGuinn has been quoted that he should have disbanded the group in 1968, and the post-1970 material suffers from both weaker writing and singing—but there is fine pickin'

throughout. It was 1965's *Mr. Tambourine Man* that ignited the folk/rock movement and helped make Bob Dylan accessible to a mass audience. Their space cowboy experiments (1966's "Eight Miles High") and 1968's Gram Parsons–inspired *Sweetheart of the Rodeo* secured their rightful place in the Rock & Roll Hall of Fame. What this exhaustive retrospective ultimately conveys is the far-ranging musical curiosity and imagination that fueled their creativity. Their backgrounds were in the popular folk scene, but their influences extended from John Coltrane and Hugh Masakela to Byron Berline and "Sneaky" Pete Kleinow. The newly released material includes a couple of Gram Parsons leads on "Reputation" and "Lazy Days," alternate takes on "The Christian Life," "One Hundred Years From Now," and "You Don't Miss Your Water." There are also two live selections from the 1990 *Tribute to Roy Orbison,* "Turn! Turn! Turn!" and a ragged and rowdy version of "Mr. Tambourine Man" with a guest appearance from Bob Dylan. These cuts feature only McGuinn, Crosby, and Hillman, as do the final four selections, which are a part of a new Byrds album. The sound quality varies markedly from session to session and track to track, but overall, it is an improvement over other currently available CD versions, except for *Never Before,* which is generally sonically superior. It should also be noted that some songs are remixes, which are vastly different than previously released versions.

## David Byrne
b. May 14, 1952—Scotland
Founding force behind The Talking Heads and intellectual avatar of New York's post-punk scene. He began his involvement with world rhythms with

The Heads and has pursued it since that group's remission.

**Rei Momo (1989)**
Luaka Bop/Sire 25990-2 (63:43)  **[B]**
After presenting a couple of fascinating compilations of Caribbean, Latin, and South American pop music, the energetic, intellectual Mr. Byrne appropriates their compelling rhythms to support his vocals and lyrics. Backed by some of the finest players from New York's Latin musical community, he creates a sensuous, absorbing milieu for his ruminations. (Interestingly, shortly after its release, some of *Rei Momo*'s backing musicians made strong charges of cultural plundering). While Byrne is to be applauded for using his celebrity to bring a broader audience to the current, vital music of the Latin communities, there *is* something calculated about it. Perhaps it's the antiseptic precision of it all—even the extraordinary sound with its bell-like clarity—contributing to its bloodlessness. This is music to dance to, to sweat by, on a tropical night. *Rei Momo* is almost clinical.

# J.J. Cale
## (Jean Jacque Cale)
b. December 5, 1938—Oklahoma City, Oklahoma
**Special Edition (1984)**
Mercury 818 633-2 (39:22)  **[C+]**
The laconic, loping, blues-influenced Cale sound is fairly presented on this compilation disc. Since there is repetitive sameness to all of Cale's writing and performance, this probably represents as comprehensive an overview as any but the most ardent fan would desire. It does include his major claim to fame, the hit "Cocaine" (probably a triumph of timely subject matter over musical form) as well as some of his stronger, earlier compositions: "Magnolia," "After Midnight," "Lies," and "Crazy Momma." This is very listenable but also very limited music. Soundwise, there is some quality variation among the cuts, but overall the CD delivers more punch and detail than its LP counterparts.

**Travel Log (1990)**
Silvertone/RCA 1306-2J (42:50)  **[C+]**
With Cale's country-blues-based sound, generally less is best—he always seems to suggest more than he delivers, which, in itself, is an art. But he's done it better before. Maybe he's mined the same limited vein for too long and there just aren't any nuggets left. On some cuts, he does give way to larger production values, but they neither enhance nor fit the repetitive material. Cale used to do it a lot better. The sound quality is OK.

# Peter Case
Former member of The Nerves and lead singer for the talented, but ill-fated, L.A.-based Plimsouls.

**Peter Case (1986)**
Geffen/Warner Pioneer Corporation 32XD-812 (47:41)  **[B]**
"I said I didn't know any songs about America—these songs are about sin and salvation. Have fun." That's how Case describes this T-Bone Burnett–produced extraordinary debut, assisted by some of L.A.'s top players: Burnett, Mitchell Froom, Mike Campbell, Van Dyke Parks, Roger McGuinn, John Hiatt, and the ubiquitous Jim Keltner among them. This psychic troubadour wanders his strange terrain, visiting offbeat moments with affecting insights. Contemporary folk music, average voice, but there's something more at work here—or does there just seem to be? You really can't be sure, and therein lies the fascination. The sonics on this Japanese import are a disappointment—it sounds as though it was mastered from an equalized source, resulting in edgy, harsh vocals, and choppy instrumental production.

## The Man With the Blue Postmodern Fragmental Neo-Traditionalist Guitar (1989)
Geffen 24238-2 (40:27)   [A]
There's a terrible temptation to say "the title says it all," but other than being the bane of DJs and record retailers, it only suggests the wondrous elements that make Peter Case and his second solo release so special. Aided by some of the best side men around, Ry Cooder, Mitchell Froom, David Hidalgo, and David Lindley, this contemporary troubadour again provides a haunting, transient vision of the people and places of our times. Dubbed by some to be roots rock, the feel of *The Man With The Blue Postmodern Fragmental Neo-Traditionalist Guitar* is as much folk as it is rock. Regardless of the label, what counts are Case's insightful, evocative lyrics and intense vocals. It all comes together beautifully, making for one of the better recordings to come along in the late eighties. The CD's sound is bright but not edgy, with strong dynamics and well-rendered vocals.

## Rosanne Cash
b. May 24, 1955—Memphis, raised in southern California
Johnny's daughter, but very much her own woman.

### Right or Wrong (1979)
Columbia CK36155 (38:07)   [B–]
Released in late 1979, this recording was called by Dave Marsh "the first real country album for the eighties." Rosanne's fine vocal attributes and intelligent manner with a lyric are admirably showcased by her husband Rodney Crowell's production and compositional contributions. A striking marriage of Nashville and L.A. country, *Right Or Wrong* is a strong debut recording which holds up over time. The CD

sound, while a bit bright every now and again, is more dynamic and much cleaner that the LP.

### King's Record Shop (1987)
Columbia CK40777 (38:48)   [A–]
Rosanne's nimble, heartfelt country/pop succeeds because of her expressive talent as a singer—she has a good ear for a song. It's just that husband Rodney Crowell's production, while clean as a whistle, is merely serviceable, not enhancing. Nonetheless, the lady carries it off just fine, particularly on her John Hiatt cover and "The Real Me." The sound on this disc is simply superlative.

### Interiors (1990)
Columbia CK46079 (34:18)   [A + ]
Those who take the time to know *Interiors* will be rewarded with insights and enlightenments. Rosanne Cash is a warm and mature artist whose fine career reaches a lofty pinnacle with this self-produced album. Quiet and unassuming, this compelling litany of relationships, both private and politic, is nothing less than extraordinary. In lieu of easy hooks, her experiences are revealed through a candlelit glow and simple acoustic accompaniment. *Interiors* is both immediately familiar and newly revealing—an instant heirloom. On *Interiors,* Cash's expression has everything to do with integrity and nothing to do with current perceptions of musical product. The all-digital recording is state-of-the-art.

## Exene Cervenka (Christine)
### Old Wives' Tales (1989)
Rhino 122 70913 (34:32)   [B–]
With her first solo release since the demise of X, the great L.A. punk/folk/

rock band of the eighties, Cervenka settles somewhat comfortably into the folk/country vein that fueled X's heart even at its most agitated punk moments. Assisted by the bell-like clarity of Rhino's CD sound and ably abetted by Tony Gilkyson's instrumental and production skills, and his wife, Eliza's, vocal harmonies, this countrified outing is not without its charms, "Leave Heaven Alone," "She Wanted," and "Coyote On the Town" among them. Still, there is something almost cloying about it all—too cute, too offhand?

# Tracy Chapman
b. 1964—Cleveland
**Tracy Chapman (1988)**
Elektra 9 60774-2 (36:14)   **[A]**
This startling debut was probably the most potent new release of the decade, at least in terms of the rapidity with which it catapulted Chapman from obscurity to a stage with Bruce Springsteen, among others, in less than twelve months time. Musically and lyrically compelling, folk music for its urban times—prayers and screams—it achieved one of those rare moments when critic and customer shared a common passion. Often reminiscent of Joan Armatrading, Chapman stakes out her own territory and leaves it indelibly stamped. You can quarrel with her politics (I know I do), but you can't obliterate the passion. Time may tarnish this release a bit, but it was perfect for its moment, and honest feeling retains its power to touch, long after its evocation has passed from memory. "Fast Car," "Mountains O' Things," and "For My Lover" are extraordinary songs, and the others are not disappointments. Chapman's strengths are obvious: her well-written songs and her chilling, warm, haunting voice. One reason why this recording works so

effectively is David Kershenbaum's production: simple, basic accoustic instrumentation that never gets in the way, but illuminates, adding nuance. In addition, the all-digital sound is beautifully clear, spacious, and natural. All in all, one hell of a package.

**Crossroads (1989)**
Elektra 60888-2 (43:01)   **[B–]**
Second albums are often the litmus test for a debut artist labeled a "great new talent." Chapman's debut provided sufficient substance, both popularly and critically, to dispel any doubt of her talent. Thus, *Crossroads'* continuation of the feel and message of her debut was expected. The performance and production are more assured; the material is less defined and impactful. Partly the result of her catapult into stardom, her personal stance now reflects the self-questioning that often follows major life shifts. Her sociopolitical attitudes remain, but would be enhanced if they were less involved with inequities and more concerned with the lessons of self-reliance and assumption of personal responsibility, both skills this powerful talent possesses in abundance. The all-digital sound nicely showcases the understated, mostly acoustic, production, with openness and precision. If 1988's *Tracy Chapman* left you longing for more, *Crossroads* will fill that longing, but not in a totally satisfying way.

# Ray Charles (Ray Charles Robinson)
b. September 23, 1930—Albany, Georgia
Ray, who has been blind since the age of six and who suffered the often traditional impoverished youth of many southern blacks of his generation, has been accurately called the creator of soul music. His combination of gospel

forms with popular lyrics tinged with elements of jazz and blues was seminal in the formation of modern black popular music.

**Greatest Country & Western Hits (1962)**
Dunhill DS040 (61:39)   [A + ]
Talk about a blowaway—when Ray released *Modern Sounds in Country and Western Music* in 1962, the idea of the man who invented soul music, who gave us "What'd I Say" and "I Got a Woman," doing saccharine, sentimental, trite country music was incomprehensible. It hit the charts on April 21, 1962, held No. 1 for fourteen weeks, and spawned *Volume 2* in November of the same year. This twenty-track compilation includes seventeen songs from those recordings, plus three additions, "Crying Time," "Together Again," and "Don't Let Her Know." While six of the tracks are repeated on *His Greatest Hits Volumes 1 & 2* and "Careless Love" is included on *Greatest Country & Western Hits,* the other fourteen are more than worth the price of admission. A classic from one of the truly greats. The sound quality, again with Charles involved in the digital reworking, is superb.

**His Greatest Hits, Volume 1 (1960–1971)**
Dunhill DZS036 (63:24)   [A]
Pop music is showbiz, and that means wretched promotional excess and superlatives are the constant idiom, but Ray Charles is a musical genius by even the most conventional standards. Some have said he is the greatest pop singer we've heard, and they can make a credible case. Certainly there has never been anyone with his easy dexterity—R&B, soul, C&W, jazz, pop, ballads, and stomps—Charles's mastery has left an indelible stamp. In the fifties, while at Atlantic, he brought gospel forms to R&B sensibilities and virtually invented

soul music. In 1959 he left Atlantic for ABC/Paramount's greener pastures, where he remained until 1972. *His Greatest Hits, Volume 1* delivers twenty of his country/pop/R&B songs from that era, including "Georgia on My Mind," "Your Cheatin' Heart," "You Don't Know Me," "I Don't Need No Doctor," and "Let's Go Get Stoned"—it's a killer from beginning to end. One of the things that makes this disc special is its excellent sound quality, which is probably attributable to the fact that Ray was involved in the digital remastering. The word is that he has the truest ear in the business, and the sound of this disc (which is wonderfully consistent regardless of original source) will do nothing to diminish that reputation.

**His Greatest Hits, Volume 2 (1960–1972)**
Dunhill DZS037 (66:19)   [A + ]
If *Volume 1* doesn't scratch the itch in your soul for the sound of the Genius, here's twenty more in the best fidelity ever. This grouping includes "Hit the Road, Jack," "I Can't Stop Loving You," "You are My Sunshine," "Sticks and Stones," "Makin' Whooppee, Parts 1 & 2," "At the Club," and "Look What They Done to My Song, Ma." Hell, the man could sing the *phone book* (but maybe not the Beatles)!

**Anthology (1960–1968)**
Rhino R2 75759 (66:18)   [A + ]
This Rhino collection is drawn from the same ABC/Paramount masters used on Dunhill's *His Greatest Hits Volumes 1 & 2,* but these twenty tracks focus more on the upbeat soul/R&B material, and is a better compilation than either of those fine releases. It includes his three fifties groundbreaking classics: "What'd I Say," "I Got a Woman," and "Hallelujah I Love Her So" from his 1965 *Live in Concert* album, not quite as good as the Atlantic

originals, but not bad, either. Bill Inglot and Ken Perry's digital remastering, while excellent, is markedly different from Ray's Dunhill renderings. This disc has a harder live concert sound that more effectively captures the band's tightness and Charles's energy, but it lacks the expanse of the Dunhill releases. If you have the space, money, or taste for only one Ray Charles collection on CD, this is the one. And you gotta have one.

**Ray Charles Live (1973)**
Atlantic 781732-2 (72:02)   **[B–]**
A fascinating set of recordings, particularly considering their 1958 vintage—Ray is a musical sponge, equally at home with jazz, R&B, soul, and gospel sounds. These recordings cover some of those divergent elements and illustrate how "The Genius" bound them all together to create soul music, God bless him! Unfortunately, these were live recordings done thirty years ago, and while instrumentally the CD is an overall enhancement, on Ray's vocal mike distortion reigns sadly supreme; and, as we all know, that's where it's at. Nonetheless, the driving, pulsing rhythmic energy behind these cuts still comes through, loud and clear.

**The Legend Lives (1960–1968)**
Arcade ADEH/CD/780 (62:06)   **[B +]**
A rather strange German compilation that contains a few of the gospel-inflected "shouts" ("Hit The Road Jack" and "What'd I Say") which provide the basis for Ray's claim as the creator of soul music. However, a majority of the selections come from the *New Directions In Country Music* era, when the Genius exposed the kinship of country and his soulful blues-based sound. Called by some the finest vocalist in contemporary music, this CD enhances the exemplary subtlety of his singing. While the source material utilized is somewhat obscure (the liner notes are virtually non-existent), the sound, while dated, is generally of consistently high quality.

# Neneh Cherry
**Raw Like Sushi (1988)**
Virgin 7 91252-2 (46:13)   **[A]**
One hell of a debut. Blending rap, hip-hop, and contemporary soul with a tough female viewpoint, Cherry has delivered an underappreciated powerhouse recording. Complex and contemporary in its production, it's clear she knows where she's coming from and where she's going. The sound is fairly impressive, but has a nasty tendency toward shrillness at the very top end.

# Alex Chilton
b. December 28, 1950—Memphis
Both a founder and the lead voice of the legendary Box Tops, Chilton has scuffled in and out of the music scene since that band's demise in 1970 and the subsequent creation and termination of his follow-up group, Big Star.

**Stuff (1969–1977)**
New Rose Rose 68 CD (57:58)   **[D +]**
This compilation is made up of nine cuts recorded in 1986 in New Orleans and seven others recorded in the late sixties through the mid-seventies, most of which were written by Chilton. It's generally clean, straight-ahead rock (with the newer work reflecting a certain punk sensibility), but is more of minor historic interest than current musical validity. The sound on the more recent recordings is clean and dynamic, but with a marked tendency to overbrightness. The older selections are sonically pretty weak, muddy, and compressed.

# Eric Clapton
b. March 30, 1945—Ripley, England
During the late 1960s, as the featured guitarist with bands like the Blues-breakers, the Yardbirds, and Cream, Clapton became the first great English guitar hero. He has never really appeared totally comfortable in the role of individual star or group leader, but has sustained a career that has been negatively impacted by some of the more corrosive attributes of the rock & roll lifestyle.

### Timepieces (The Best of Eric Clapton) (1970–1978)
RSO 800 014-2 (44:58)   **[C + ]**
One of rock's great lead guitarists, his singing abilities are merely adequate, at best. Probably for this reason, the recordings which feature him as leader and vocalist have never attained the levels of intensity or importance accorded to his contributions as lead guitarist on other artists' albums. This collection of his seventies hits (originally released in 1982) certainly captures the highlights, "Layla," as well as essentially all of his most popular cuts from the decade. The sound is equivalent to that of a very clean LP, with occasional, not overwhelming, distortion.

### Crossroads (1963–1987)
Polygram 835261.2 (294:20—four discs)   **[B + ]**
One of the many benefits the CD has brought to music devotees has been the creation of multidisc anthologies that provide career overviews. When combined with effective packaging and liner information, plus the sound enhancement available in good digital conversions, these packages can be gems. Bob Dylan's *Biograph* (1985) set a high standard that *Crossroads* attempts to emulate.

Unfortunately, Clapton's stature doesn't approximate Dylan's, but he is the finest blues/rock guitarist we have known, and he has been a major player in the rock game for a quarter of a century. This four-disc compilation is a truly comprehensive overview of the varied career of a troubled, talented survivor who has had a discernable influence on rock since the explosive sixties. In the process, *Crossroads* provides a nice overview of the development of one of the music's major tributaries, the blues side of the British Invasion. While every fan will question some inclusions and regret a few omissions, there's probably as much of Clapton here as any devotee could possibly desire. All of Clapton's groundbreaking musical alliances are represented: the Yardbirds, John Mayall's Bluesbreakers, Cream, Blind Faith, Derek and the Dominoes—some with rare ("Ain't That Lovin' You" with Dave Mason) and others with previously unreleased (Cream's "Lawdy Mama") material. As expected with material spanning a quarter century, there is wide variation in the sound quality— some of the earlier material is a bit rough—but it's obvious that the care that went into the total package extended to the digital conversions, which are notable sonic improvements over earlier formats.

# The Clash
Formed 1977—London
Admittedly inspired by the Sex Pistols, who sounded punk's late seventies revolutionary cry, it was the Clash who ultimately brought intelligence, supplemented by powerfully compatible sounds to flesh out the British punk testament.

## The Clash (1977)

Epic EK36060 (43:55)   **[A]**

This was music to make your heart beat once again—it was an assault, a violation—it was rock & roll the way God meant it to sound. You loved it/you hated it; at least you felt something about it. The fifteen politically inspired cuts that make up this forty-four-minute attack on the "revised" edition of this, the band's debut recording, present as concise and complete a summary of the punk purview available. Not necessarily pleasant listening, but, in sad fact, one of the last real rock & roll albums to be issued. The CD sound has a bit more spaciousness than the LP, but this music wasn't made with great regard for its audio-technical aspects (the album was recorded over three weekends), so don't expect any miracles. Still superior to the LP.

## Sandinista! (1980)

Epic EZK37037 (144:33—two discs)   **[A–]**

Sprawling, formless, excessive, and frequently bursting with greatness ("The Magnificent Seven," "Charlie Don't Surf," "Junko Partner," "Hitsville U.K.," "Ivan Meets G.I. Joe," "Something About England," "Washington Bullets," and "Police on My Back"), *Sandinista!* is another (in this case punk) example of a great single album buried in the wretched excess of multiple sides. It's still memorable, but simply too diluted. The sound is clean enough, but subject to obvious compression.

## Combat Rock (1982)

Epic EK37689 (46:05)   **[A]**

The last (and most commercially successful) gasp of this mid-seventies British punk aggregation whose popular success doomed their aesthetic principles. This is punk polished with Glyn Johns's fine production hand and also with a bow to the New York rap scene. An arty and explosive mixture of their reggae-funk-based rock, *Combat Rock* produced the band's ultimate audience acceptance as evidenced by several genuine hits, "Rock the Casbah" and "Should I Stay or Should I Go?" In retrospect, this is probably a perfect eulogy for one of the most vital exponents of the English seventies punk explosion. The sound is clean and spatially well-defined, although it occasionally tends to overbrightness, but never excessively.

# Jimmy Cliff

b. 1949—Somenton, Jamaica

Reggae's first international star by virtue of his lead role in the cult film classic, *The Harder They Come* (1972). While he has retained star status, primarily in England, he ceased being a real creative force long ago.

## The Harder They Come (1973)

Mango CCD9201 (40:32)   **[A + ]**

One of America's introductions to the reggae music of Jamaica was an early seventies cult movie starring Jimmy Cliff, *The Harder They Come*. This rough film told the rags-to-riches story of a Jamaican youth who finds fame and success through the island's music. This soundtrack recording features the triumphant sounds that rose from that ghetto—music of joy, despair, hope, and anguish, both heartfelt and mesmerizing. Half the selections have become Cliff's classics: "You Can Get It if You Really Want It," "Many Rivers to Cross," and "Sitting in Limbo." The title track and the remainder by Desmond Dekker and the Maytals, among others, are equal to or better than the well-known Cliff compositions. While the sound is obviously compressed, it is such an improvement over the LP it borders on revelation. This CD delivers classic reggae, both historically and musically, and it sounds substantially better than ever.

### In Concert—The Best of Jimmy Cliff (1976)
Reprise 2256-2 (47:32)  [C+]
Reggae's first superstar revisits his strongest compositions, originally laid down earlier in the decade, with a competent instrumental backup and an enthusiastic audience. He brings energy and good voice to the effort, but the originals were better, and Cliff's reggae version of Cat Stevens's "Wild World" isn't reason enough to set this one apart. For a live recording, the sound quality is really pretty good—the vocal mix is occasionally too far behind the band, and there's too much audience noise. Still the sound, particularly that of the band, is just fine.

# The Coasters
Formed 1955—Los Angeles
### The Ultimate Coasters (1954–1961)
Warner Special Products 927604-2 (51:58)  [D–]
Working with Jerry Leiber and Mike Stoller, two of rock's most fascinating and talented "behind-the-scenes" pioneers, the Coasters created musical vignettes that were current, complete, often humorous, and consistently innovative in their production values. Unfortunately, Warner Bros.' digital conversion of this wonderful material is a crime—muddy, constrained, and distorted, so much so that some cuts ("Searchin'," "Youngblood," and "Along Came Jones") are painful to hear. The first time around much of this genuinely wonderful music never found the ear of the majority white audience; now that it's all here in a single package, it is the final injustice that slovenly engineering totally masks its true worth.

# Eddie Cochran
b. October 3, 1938—Albert Lea, Minnesota
d. April 17, 1960
### The Best Of . . . (1957–1959)
EMI America CDP7 46580 2 (31:53)  [B+]
Cochran possessed the true fever of rock & roll, but a blowout on a British road in 1960 brought an untimely end to a rockabilly career that had commenced three years earlier with "Sittin' in the Balcony." For those few years, Cochran's guitar burned and his raw voice howled. The sound on this musically comprehensive disc is bright and generally impressive, if a bit edgy in the upper midrange.

# Joe Cocker
# (John Robert Cocker)
b. May 20, 1944—Sheffield, England
This frenetic former steamfitter was one of the few genuine sixties rock "stars" who reached celebrity performing material principally written by others. Virtually untrained, but possessed of an emotionally charged roughhouse voice, a voice that launched a thousand parties, his expressive powers place him among rock's premier vocal interpreters.

### With a Little Help From My Friends (1969)
A&M CD3106 (40:43)  [B]
The first album release by the man who may be the music's least likely hero. Even working with some of England's better known rock artists (Jimmy Page, Chris Stainton, and Steve Winwood among them) the musicianship is a bit rough around the edges, but the intensity of Cocker's vocals perseveres. The ten selections, including compositions

by Bob Dylan and Lennon/McCartney as well as some penned by Cocker and Chris Stainton, have a certain rough, jam session feel which is very consistent with Cocker's general stage presence and vocal qualities. The sound is clean and precise, but lacks the general spatial ambiance which the best digital conversions can impart.

### Joe Cocker! (1969)
A&M CD4224 (35:24)　**[A]**
If he had made only this, his second album, Cocker's stature in the star-studded sixties would have been assured—his sensitive yet raucous readings of songs written by some of rock's best added new meaning and exposure to very valid material.

### Mad Dogs and Englishmen (Music From the Original Soundtrack) (1971)
A&M 396002-2 (76:19—two discs)　**[B]**
The 1970 Mad Dogs & Englishmen tour which featured a great, brass-enhanced driving band led by Leon Russell behind Cocker's frenzied vocal antics was one of the decade's more hysterical events—guaranteed excitement made pervasive by the successful motion picture diary of the tour, one of the first rock concert movies ever released. The sixteen selections are faultless picks (with the exception of Rita Coolidge's one contribution), but the fairly insistent high energy level, perhaps inevitable in this format, becomes somewhat wearing. The concert quality sound is also pretty consistent, and, while clean for its source, has a marked tendency to some overbrightness.

### The Very Best Of/Greatest Hits (1968–1972)
Fun FCD501 (58:02)　**[B+]**
The sixteen selections are all drawn from Cocker's first two albums. This is first-rate music by one of rock's best vocal interpreters, and affords a decent one-disc overview of the singer's early career. Its sound quality varies as expected, and, while a few cuts are burdened with minor distortion, overall the sound is essentially equivalent to that of a clean LP.

### Live (1990)
Capitol CDP793416 (73:53)　**[C–]**
This live retrospective delivers quantity in both total playing time and coverage of most of Joe's three decades of hits—and that's where it ends. The band plays like it's worked the same charts two hours too long, and Cocker resorts to mannerisms where his twitchy energy, inimitable style, and sense of phrasing once made him a rare interpretive rock vocalist. The quality of the live sound is adequate, but lacking in separation.

# Bootsy Collins
b. October 26, 1951—Cincinnati
At sixteen, he joined James Brown's band, the J.B.'s, established himself in P. Funk with fellow funkmeister George Clinton.

### What's Bootsy Doin'? (1988)
Columbia CK44107 (42:22)　**[B+]**
*What's Bootsy Doin'?* Laying out the funk, whatja' 'spect? More musical than his Parliament-Funkadelic collaborations, replete with samples from the Beatles to nursery rhymes, the recording is dedicated "to the greats no longer with us: Jackie Wilson, Jimi Hendrix, Otis Redding, Marvin Gaye, Count Basie, and Jackie Gleason"—within its musical melange there are echoes of them all. Its staccato sound for dancin' feet and inquiring minds works on both levels. The sound is bright and basically synthesized, but nicely punctuated with a

fine horn section that includes the re-doubtable Maceo Parken. It's a happenin' good time with enough humor and weirdness blended in to keep it more than interesting.

# Commander Cody and His Lost Planet Airmen
Formed 1967—Ann Arbor, Michigan
Rejuvenated in San Francisco in 1969.
The "Commander" is George Frayne IV,
b. July 19, 1944—Boise, Idaho.

**Lost in the Ozone (1971)**
MCA MCAD 31185 (38:23)  **[C + ]**
Sure it's hokey—hippie truck-drivin', booze-cryin' music made for Saturday night joints—liberal on the beer, 'cuz the more you drink, the better it sounds. The spirit moves the Commander and his Airmen—enough at times to surmount their technical limitations. But this one's got "Seeds and Stems" on it, and that seems like reason enough to me. The sound seems to have been taken from an equalized master; it's clean, but a bit too bright, a little weak at the bottom, and the vocals have a more recorded than a natural quality.

**Commander Cody and His Lost Planet Airmen (1973)**
MCA MCAD-661 (28:20)  **[D + ]**
This budget offering provides about one LP's worth of Cody's country/boogie sing-alongs. Fine for nostalgic hippies and retired truck drivers with the sound of the diesel echoing in their ears. There's always been more fervor than talent with this ersatz, but unpretentious, group, but enough is enough. Sound quality is pretty average, too.

# Ry Cooder
b. March 15, 1947—Los Angeles
Rock's preeminent musical archivist. Cooder's guitar prowess, among the best slide players ever, has been an important component of the recordings of countless major artists and his own recordings provide a breathtaking overview of the more esoteric, but nonetheless important, musical strains that have become a part of contemporary American pop music.

**Into the Purple Valley (1971)**
Reprise 2052-2 (37:48)  **[A–]**
On this, Cooder's second album, rock's resident archaeologist leads the listener on a simple stroll through some depression era thirties and forties musical Americana. Relying on his string virtuosity and deadpan vocal deliveries, he illuminates this country's richly diverse musical history, all the while reaffirming the material's lyrical currency. Cooder is backed by a few very talented musicians who deliver their message with the directness of a tintype. The emphasis here is musicianship, and while the CD adds little in the way of enhanced dynamics, it does provide a crystalline clarity befitting the subtle beauty of the strings as never before. Highlights of a fine collection include "Money Honey," "F.D.R. in Trinidad," "Teardrops Will Fall," and "Determination Blues."

**Paradise & Lunch (1974)**
Reprise 2179-2 (37:24)  **[A]**
Of all the musical potpourris Cooder has concocted over his almost twenty-year solo career, this melange of historic "Ditty Wah Ditty" to contemporary "Mexican Divorce;" gospel to Salvation Army Band, marvelously succeeds in blending the divergent musical elements that can be found in American

pop songs. This, of course, has been Ry's stated direction since he emerged as one of the sixties premier session players. For all its diverse components, this recording showcases American popular music and perhaps the American musical experience as well as anything to come out of the rock era. The sound, unfortunately, is not revelatory—it's equivalent to a good, clean LP.

### Chicken Skin Music (1976)
Reprise 2254-2 (40:01)   **[B + ]**
Our distinguished pickin' musicologist successfully blends some unlikely virtuosos from divergent musical strains, Flaco Jimenez, the Tex-Mex accordion legend, and Gabby Pahinui, acknowledged king of the Hawaiian steel guitar. Also joining in are Cooder stalwarts, vocalists Bobby King and Terry Evans, with added licks provided by Jim Keltner, Red Callender, and Milt Hollander, among others. The musicians vary from cut to cut, as does the material, which ranges from Leadbelly ("The Bourgeois Blues," "Goodnight Irene"), through Ben E. King ("Stand By Me"), to Gus Kahn ("Chloe"). While none of its is truly inspired, the musicianship is first-rate, and you have to admire Cooder's ability to maintain the integrity of such diverse material while contemporizing it. While the sound is occasionally a bit boxy, it has wonderful clarity and excellent separation, particularly among the strings.

### Jazz (1978)
Warner Bros. 3197-2 (38:31)   **[B–]**
The music played dates back to the turn of the century and before—the days of brass and string jazz bands (before Louis Armstrong modernized the form), where the bass line was often provided by a tuba. While the selections were composed by artists whose careers commenced in the last century; e.g.,

Jellyroll Morton, the New Orleans whorehouse pianist whose Creole-influenced sound still remains influential, and Bix Biederbecke, the first great white jazz trumpet virtuoso, it is the string playing conducted by famed Bahamian Joseph Spence, that adds a distinctive quality to these ragtime instrumentals. The sound is good, not great, like that of a clean LP.

### Bop Til You Drop (1979)
Warner Bros. 003358-2 (40:15)   **[B]**
A landmark: the first pop all digital recording released in 1979. While its musical sources touch on blues, jazz, and country sounds, the general orientation is toward fifties/sixties R&B. Featuring some of L.A.'s best session players and singers, among them Jim Keltner, David Lindley, and Bobby King, plus Chaka Khan vocals on a couple of tracks, this is classic material lovingly presented. It features the honest vision of Ry Cooder and his virtuoso string playing as central elements. The sound is detailed and dynamic with nice spatial attributes; although, a couple of cuts, "Little Sister" and "The Very Thing That Makes You Rich" are marred by muddy or extraneous sounds.

### Borderline (1980)
Warner Bros. 3489-2 (44:09)   **[B–]**
On this collection of early rock, R&B, and soul, Cooder is supported by his sometime touring band that includes John Hiatt (who contributes "The Way We Make a Broken Heart"), Jim Keltner, and fine soul singers Bobby King and Terry Evans. Cooder's level of *instrumental* competence is higher than most, it's just that it all seems extraneous, somehow. The CD delivers excellent sound—clean, airy, with excellent articulation among the voicings.

### Get Rhythm (1987)
Warner Bros. 9 25639-2 (40:55)   **[B+]**
A bit raw and raucous, and it works. Put together a first-rate group of players (Cooder, Van Dyke Parks, Flaco Jimenez, and Keltner among 'em), add the great blues voices of Bobby King, Terry Evans, Arnold McCuller, and Willie Green, Jr., mix some originals with some offbeat borrowings from Johnny Cash, Chuck Berry, and Otis Blackwell, spice with a twist of weird, and that pretty well sums it up. Oh yeah, Cooder still insists on "singing" most of the leads. A bit rough, but a good time, nonetheless. The sound on the mostly upbeat tracks is hard and sharp, with a tendency to overbrightness; on the few slower numbers, it has a nice open, spacious, clear quality.

## Sam Cooke
b. January 22, 1935—Chicago
d. December 11, 1964
Like many of the great black soul and R&B singers of the 1950s and 1960s, Cooke's career began singing gospel in the black church (in his case, his father's). This is a man who was born to sing. He always made it sound so easy, so smooth, and, oh, so very sweet. While his roots and appeal were clearly established in the world of gospel, with the Soul Stirrers, his ultimate message proved to be more glandular than godly. Like another fifties giant, Jerry Lee Lewis, Cooke clearly embodied the essential rock/life conflict of good versus evil, but Sam carried it off with more style, right to the very end.

### Gospel in My Soul (1950s)
Suite Beat Records SBCD2011 (31:22)   **[F]**
This is gospel conceived and produced as bleached fifties pop songs. If that's not bad enough, the cover portrait and title notwithstanding, Cooke sings only on four of the twelve cuts included. The sound quality is as bad as the rest of it. (It does have some fine R.H. Harris true gospel efforts, but they aren't that good.)

### The 2 Sides of Sam Cooke (mid-fifties)
Specialty, SPCD-2119-2 (31:15)   **[B+]**
Cooke, like so many other great soul singers, got his start in gospel. In his case, it was with the already established Soul Stirrers. This recording presents six gospel classics and six largely unknown pop songs, although "I'll Come Running Back to You" reached the R&B charts in 1957. Forget the pop side—both song and sound quality are sorely lacking. The gospel side is another matter—one listen and you'll easily understand how the man almost achieved rock-star status and female fanaticism while singing lead in an internationally renowned gospel quartet. The gospel performances are moving and Sam's vocals are a thing of wonder. The CD's sound is crisper, more intimate and dynamic than the LP, but the recording defects are also unfortunately heightened. Probably a must for die-hard Cooke or gospel fans.

### Live at the Harlem Square Club, 1963 One Night Stand (1963)
RCA PCD15181 (37:33)   **[B]**
The sound on this disc, particularly the first half, is pretty bad; but as bad as it is, the music comes through and just won't let go. A marvelous "window" into the real sounds of fifties American soul music on hot southern Saturday nights. This is Cooke at his roots raucous best.

### At the Copa (1964)
abko 29702 (40:45)   **[D+]**
Cooke moved from gospel to pop in an effort to cross over to a mass (white) audience. In 1964, the Copacabana was the establishment New York watering hole where the biggest pop stars worked

before the world's supposedly most sophisticated audiences. So Cooke played it with the most bleached material of his career. While he added his own rhythm section, including Bobby Womack on guitar, the musical accompaniment is provided by Joe Mele's Copacabana Band. It's obvious that Cooke never really connected with this audience, even if he does cover "Tennessee Waltz." Of interest only as a historical footnote (and a fascinating comparison to his other live CD, *Live at the Harlem Square Club*). Uninspired and uninspiring. The sound is terribly compressed and dated.

### Sam Cooke The Man and His Music (1953–1965)
RCA PCD1-7127 (70:06)   **[A + ]**
A comprehensive twenty-eight song collection, most of which are outstanding, that runs the gamut from commercial pop to gospel fervor, and through it all soars one of the greatest pop voices ever heard. The sound quality varies, as expected, but overall, a vast improvement over any other recordings of this classic work. (As is the case with much of the RCA material covering fifties artists released on compact discs, the name Gregg Geller is reflected as A&R director. Geller, who has unfortunately left RCA, has been a major contributor to the disc recompilations of RCA's classic rock material, making an invaluable contribution to the recorded library of this roots music. Generally speaking, Geller's name on a pop disc is a good indication of quality material.)

# Elvis Costello (Declan McManus)
b. 1955—Liverpool, England
The most important single artist to survive England's seventies punk explosion. Costello, the son of a big band singer, began his commercial life as a computer operator, but was soon working as a roadie for the Brinsley Schwarz Band. He first began releasing records in 1977, and has since proven amazingly prolific. A thorny, difficult personality (a natural adherent to the rude punk attitude) Costello has been quoted as saying that his artistic purpose was "revenge and guilt." This modern Elvis has never followed the traditional avenues to stardom, preferring his purposely obscure, often abrasive, public image. But Costello's massive talents, evidenced by his wit and mastery of wordplay as well as energetic commitment to musical intensity and inventiveness, rank him among the major artists in rock's thirty year pantheon.

### My Aim Is True (1977)
Columbia CK35037 (36:38)   **[B–]**
A truly stunning debut release. With it Costello announced his prickly presence to a musical world generally gone flat and fat. While it lacks the instrumental bite of later offerings, due, in part, to the fact that the backup musicians were the group Clover and not the later formed Attractions, who proved to be the glove to Elvis's hand. It does contain some of his most enduring music, "Less Than Zero," "Watching the Detectives," "The Angels Wanna Wear My Red Shoes," and the haunting "Alison." Sadly, this fine recording is very poorly served by the digital conversion which suffers from both too apparent hiss, distortion, and a severely compressed, dirty overall sound.

Columbia remastered and reissued this CD in 1989. The new version clocks in at 35:59 and the sonic improvement raises the rating to B+, but while the hiss is mostly eliminated, the sound still suffers from compression and muddiness.

## This Year's Model (1978)

Columbia CK35331 (33:24)  **[B+]**
With this release, Costello had found the backup band suited to his jagged vision and on this recording they underpin him with a dense, driving rock & roll sound that adds to the intensity of the statements, but doesn't necessarily clarify or enhance the fascinating lyrical excursions. With the exception of "Radio Radio," "Pump It Up," "Lip Service," and "No Action," none of the other individual tracks have achieved much recognition, but the overall lyrical involvement with sexual, personally oriented material is fascinating. The bite and acuteness of Costello's overview of male/female relations in the modern world remains compelling. The CD sound is not an appreciable improvement over the dense intensity of the original LP.

Remastered in 1989, new running time 33:14, with notable overall sonic improvement; rating now A.

## And the Attractions
## Armed Forces (1979)

Columbia CK35709 (36:50)  **[A−]**
Originally to be issued under the more descriptive title *Emotional Fascism, Armed Forces* is generally considered this artist's most successful recorded venture. The arrangements involve more variety and a far greater "pop" sensibility than were evident on earlier recordings, but, remain driving, intense statements. Costello's lyrical preoccupation with sexual politics remains the keystone to the wordplay; however, here he had enlarged his expressionistic canvas to reflect political concerns in a broader sense. As usual, his talents spill out all over the place, but the recording is highlighted by his classic "Oliver's Army" as well as "Accidents Will Happen" and "Green Shirt." The greater attention paid to production values is evident in the CD sound which has slightly enhanced dynamic and spatial qualities, but tends to excessive brightness.

Remastered in 1989, new running time 36:14, again resulting in sonic improvement, specifically by eliminating the edginess and notably tightening the bottom; still a bit compressed.

## Taking Liberties (1980)

Columbia CK36839 (51:37)  **[B+]**
A bit of a hodgepodge, twenty tracks culled from the B-sides of singles and songs included on English but not American versions of earlier album releases. Sprinkled with marvelous moments ("Girls Talk," "Radio Sweetheart," "Stranger in the Dark," "My Funny Valentine," [yes, *that* "My Funny Valentine"], "I Don't Want to Go to Chelsea," "Night Rally," and "Getting Mighty Crowded"); the recording is ultimately chaotic, but exhilarating. The sound varies, but is roughly equivalent to LP quality.

## And the Attractions
## Get Happy!! (1980)

Columbia CK36347 (48:20)  **[B+]**
This is Costello and the Attractions' New Wave reworking of the soul sounds of the sixties (including a frenetic cover of Sam and Dave's "I Can't Stand Up For Falling Down"). While it evidences a genuine feeling and affection for the roots reworked (particularly Steve "Nieve" Nason's always outstanding keyboards), it is a bit of a hodgepodge. Twenty cuts totaling forty-eight minutes—bits and snippets, interspersed with some true gems (among them "Motel Matches" and "High Fidelity"), yet, as Costello himself has said of it: "It wasn't in control, it was very maniacal and emotional." Not necessarily nega-

tive elements in the context of rock & roll, but here, they served to undermine the overall quality of the effort. Sound-wise, this is the class of the artist's seventies recordings, providing an openness and clarity missing from the earlier productions.

Remastered in 1989, again with an overall sonic enhancement; now clocks in at 48:27.

### Trust (1981)
Columbia CK37051 (41:45)  **[B + ]**
The complexities of modern romance shrouded in the tense mysteries of sex remain Costello's principal lyrical preoccupation, but this time around, they failed to produce any specifically memorable songs, though the quality of the material is pretty high. Somehow, one gets the feeling that at this point in his career, Costello, while still bitingly energetic, was somewhat stuck. The CD's sound is much punchier and better defined than on his prior disc releases, but it still suffers from compression and overbrightness.

Remastered in 1989, no change in playing time, but better dynamics and a generally smoother sound, resulting in rating upgrade to A–.

### Almost Blue (1981)
Imp Records Imp Fiend CD33 (32:34)  **[C–]**
Punk goes to Memphis for twelve country classics produced under the aegis of impresario Billy Sherrill, and the general critical consensus is that Elvis and the boys should have stayed on the other side of the pond. The pathos too often sounds like bathos, although, "Good Year for the Roses" works like a charm. The sound is clean, well separated, but clearly compressed.

### Imperial Bedroom (1982)
Columbia CK38157 (51:04)  **[A]**
The band plays better than ever before, and Geoff Emerick's deeply layered production has received frequent critical kudos, often invoking favorable comparisons to *Sgt. Pepper.* Costello's songs here move away from his often abrasive punk stance to pure Tin Pan Alley, making this perhaps his most listenable album. However, his lyrical preoccupations, paranoia and guilt, tend to lend an overall insularity to it all that retains the integrity of Costello's original stance. The sound is great: clean, defined, dynamic, and appreciably more open than on the LP.

### Punch the Clock (1983)
Columbia CK38897 (45:34)  **[A]**
For this guy, the word "prolific" is an understatement. The pop propensities evidenced on *Imperial Bedroom* continued unabated here. This time around, certain big band colorations and punctuation have been effectively added. Highlights include "Every Day I Write the Book," "Shipbuilding," "Pills and Soap," and "The World and His Wife." Surface and sound notwithstanding, Costello's acerbic, painful lyrical preoccupations remain at center stage. The sound, while not quite as remarkably transparent as that on *Imperial Bedroom,* is still a substantial improvement over the LP, adding a punch to the proceedings which are otherwise clean and fairly well defined.

Remastered in 1989, new time at 45:28, with improved definition and generally first-rate sound.

### The Best of Elvis Costello and the Attractions (1977–1984)
Columbia CK40101 (64:25)  **[A]**
The CD version adds three bonus tracks ("The Angels [Want To Wear My Red

Shoes]," "Man Out of Time," and "A Good Year for the Roses") to the sixteen originals included on the LP version of this fairly representative collection of the work of this most prolific of punk's pioneers. An effort has been made to clean up the mixes on the included tracks, and the result is a uniformity of sound usually not heard from such divergent sources. Overall, it's dynamic and fine, with some expected compression and a tendency to edgy brightness. As single disc collections go, this one is a winner, particularly considering the vast body of work from which it was drawn.

Also remastered in 1989 with notable, but varying, sonic improvements—most appreciated on the earliest material.

### The Costello Show
### (Featuring Elvis Costello)
### King of America (1986)
Columbia CK40173 (57:59)   [A–]
This time around, Elvis trots out a new/old (short-lived) persona; i.e., Declan McManus, but the music is clearly of a piece with that which preceded it. T-Bone Burnett's clean, open production highlights Costello's voice and the underlying material. On this outing, Elvis (oops, sorry, Declan) employs backup musicians who are principally drawn from the cream of contemporary American studio veterans (Jim Keltner, Mitchell Froom, James Burton, Ray Brown, and Earl Palmer among them) rather than the Attractions, a few of whom join on a couple of the selections. All said, it's a somewhat ambiguous effort which certainly has its moments, but one that doesn't rank with the best of Costello's work. (It probably sounded better initially than it really is because of the paucity of the competition at the time of its release.) The sound displays slight hiss and compression but retains

the punchy definition that is the ear-mark of a good digital recording.

### Blood & Chocolate (1986)
Columbia CK40518 (47:49)   [A]
Back with the Attractions (and his "old" name), Elvis is biting as ever. Dense, murky, and driving, this release hearkens back to the harrowing days of yore when Costello rode punk's screeching mayhem to personal stardom. Complex and ultimately aching music from a man whose misery is apparently constant, but whose talent is overwhelming ("I Want You"). The sound is clean, but its stage is a bit compressed.

### Spike (1989)
Warner Bros. 25848-2 (64:36)   [A+]
New persona, same enormous talent and witty, articulate irreverence. Spike covers it all with dazzling dexterity (including several Paul McCartney collaborations), breathtakingly naked vocals, and consistent relevance. Spike employs a multiplicity of name talents (Dirty Dozen Brass Band, Allen Toussaint, Chrissie Hynde, Paul McCartney, Roger McGuinn) and styles; but Costello's cohesive vision shapes this into one of the best releases in his prolific, extraordinarily creative career. Carlo Wolff probably said it best: "Costello has reclaimed his eminence as rock's best reporter, one of the premiere documentarians of a universe that goads, saddens, and amuses him." The sound on this disc is just about as good as it can get.

# Cowboy Junkies

Formed mid-eighties—Canada
Three Timmins' siblings, Margo (vocals),
Michael (guitar), and Peter (drums), abet-
ted by Alan Anton (bass).

### The Trinity Sessions (1988)
RCA 8568-2-R (52:57)  **[A–]**
Atmospheric in the extreme, Margo Timmins provides ethereal vocals that waft
through the dreamlike, druggy atmosphere created by this Canadian foursome in a Toronto church. It's haunting, evocative stuff, ranging from Hank
Williams's "I'm So Lonesome I Could
Cry," to the Velvet Underground's "Sweet
Jane," about which Lou Reed has supposedly said the Junkies' version is the
best he's ever heard. Along their som-
nambulistic way, the Junkies deliver
twelve selections, some written by
Margo and her lead-guitar-playing
brother, Michael, while throwing in
some Richard Rogers and Patsy Cline
covers. It all works. This is a deeply
affecting album that draws the listener
into a private dream that manages to
soothe and disquiet simultaneously. The
digital sound is in line with the performance, and with its muted echoes and
live sensibility, is a great addition.

### The Caution Horses (1990)
RCA 2058-2-R (44:37)  **[C +]**
The Timmins siblings' successor to their
haunting *Trinity Sessions* is a disappointment—the ethereal sound and subtle
hooks echo through *The Caution
Horses,* but this time around seem less
appropriate to the material. With the
exception of Neil Young's "Powder-
finger"—he hasn't called this the best
rendition of that song he's ever heard—
and Mary Margaret O'Hara's "You Will
Be Loved Again," all songs were written
by Michael Timmins, and therein lies

the problem. It's too much of the same,
and lacks the substance to sustain an
entire recording—sounds nice, fails to
linger. The disc's sound is distinguished
by its brooding clarity and intimacy.

# Creedence Clearwater Revival

Formed 1959—El Cerrito, California
Simply America's best singles rock & roll
band. While geographically aligned with
the psychedelic explosion that took
place across the bay in San Francisco,
Creedence never really was associated
with the posturings or prescriptions that
colored so much of the city's finery. In
fact, because of their rockabilly roots
and bayou sounding name, for years
many fans assumed that they were from
the South.

### The Best Of . . . (1968–1972)
Fantasy VDP1024 (43:55)  **[B +]**
Fourteen great singles which, while not
a comprehensive collection of CCR's
greatest hits, are fairly representative of
their work. The sound quality, with
slight deviation, is first-rate—clear,
bright (albeit a little edgy in a few
vocals), and dynamic.

### Chronicle (20 Greatest Hits) (1968–1976)
Fantasy FCD-623-CCR2 (68:13)  **[A +]**
This disc contains six more selections
and about fifteen more minutes of music
than the *Best of* collection reviewed
above; the additions ("Lodi," "Fortunate
Son," "Run Through The Jungle," "Com-
motion") make this a truly comprehensive overview of this wonderful band's
most popular work, as well as a showcase for one of the truest and most distinctive voices in the annals of rock &
roll, that of John Fogerty. The sound
does vary some ("Lodi" is unfortunately
afflicted with noticeable hiss), but overall a marked improvement over the LP.

### Chronicle Volume 2 (1968–1972)
Fantasy FCD-703-CCR3 (74:33)   [C+]
Because Fogerty's voice and talent are such a fundamental aspect of sixties American rock & roll, its hard to find fault with much of anything he does. But the twenty selections on this CD weren't hits, because they just didn't measure up to the twenty included on the first volume of *Chronicle*. There are some good numbers, but even the sound quality isn't up to that of Volume 1.

### Green River (1969)
Fantasy FCD-612-8393 (29:26)   [A]
Because Creedence was essentially a singles band (probably the best that rock & roll has yet produced), the compilation discs reviewed previously represent the best way to acquire their classic material. However, Fantasy has released most of the original albums on CD, which is not unexpected since this group has been that label's primary source of revenue for about two decades. This was the band's second recording, but the first that really defined its sound, and it's still a classic. The quality of the sound, while an improvement over the LP, is occasionally muffled, but it's generally clean and accurate, with some dynamic enhancement.

### Willie & the Poorboys (1970)
Fantasy FCD-613-8397 (35:02)   [A]
Creedence provided the music you wanted to hear on the car radio when the top was down and the highway smooth. This is their other really great original album release that was geared for going. On the whole, the CD sound provides a noticeable enhancement over the LP version except for "The Midnight Special" and "Side O' the Road" which suffer from muddy, boxy sound.

### Cosmo's Factory (1970)
Fantasy FCD 608 8402 (42:56)   [A–]
The last recording by the original band. Shortly after its release, older brother Tom Fogerty wearied of John's dominance and left the band, which marked the beginning of the end. Included are some of CCR's better known creations, "Travelin' Band," "Lookin' Out My Back Door," "Run Through the Jungle," "Up Around the Bend," "Who'll Stop the Rain," and "I Heard It Through the Grapevine." The CD sounds like a clean LP, similar to the sound on *Willie & The Poorboys*, but overall is less hampered by incidental distortion or hiss.

## Marshall Crenshaw
b. 1954—Detroit
Got his start playing John Lennon in the *Beatlemania* tour.

### Marshall Crenshaw (1982)
Warner Bros. 3673-2 (34:18)   [A]
This hot retro Buddy Holly–style debut evoked tremendous critical response. Ira Robbins, "Sparkling, tuneful gems that are instantly memorable and steadily enjoyable;" Robert Christgau, "Crenshaw captures a magic un-adolescent innocence without acting the wimp." Almost a decade after its release *Marshall Crenshaw* still holds up, another enduring statement of great pop/rock & roll, hook-based, basic, good songwriting, played without artifice. The fact that Crenshaw's debut release was the clear hightlight of his recording career doesn't make him unique; and it doesn't diminish the power of these twelve happy tracks. Soundwise, like the vinyl before it, the CD is remarkably close to demo quality.

**Maryjean & Nine Others (1987)**
Warner Bros. 9 25583-2 (42:22)　**[D]**
Promise, promise—all we get is promise.
The sound is muddy, too.

**Good Evening (1989)**
Warner Bros. 25908-2 (38:05)　**[B + ]**
*Good Evening* is the best thing Crenshaw
has done since he first displayed his
Buddy Holly-based good-time pop sensibility on his 1982 self-titled debut. He has
written or cowritten half of the ten bouncy
selections and displays his sure musical
sensibility on the other five: Richard
Thompson, John Hiatt, the Isley Brothers,
and Bobby Fuller covers. There's no
heavy message or earth-shaking music
here—just the happy sound of simple pop
played with infectious precision by the
likes of David Lindley and Kenny Aronoff,
and presented in a bright, crisp, dynamic
sonic package. A guaranteed good time.

# Jim Croce
b. January 10, 1943—Philadelphia
d. September 20, 1973
**Photographs & Memories His Greatest Hits
(1972–1974)**
21 Records 790467-2 (41:06)　**[B]**
The early seventies brought the singer/
songwriter to the fore in pop music, and
Croce, having begun his career in the
Greenwich Village sixties coffeehouse
scene, fit right in. While the pop productions afforded his folk-styled material
probably had much to do with his primarily posthumous success, his serviceable melodies, unpretentious singing,
and playing style—combined with an
eye for lyrical detail and laced with an
ironic sense of humor—all added up to a
consistently easy listenable experience.
The fourteen selections fairly represent
a comprehensive career overview. The
sound does vary among the selections,
but generally is acceptable, LP-like, but
clean with some spatial improvement.

# Crosby, Stills, Nash (and Young)
Formed 1968—Los Angeles
Superstar folk rock. Their celebrity
always outshone the limited quantity of
their recorded output. Hell, Crosby's
two-decade personal drug opera has
been accorded more ink than was ever
expended on critical reviews of their
artistic output. But every now and again
they had their musical moments, and
when they did, they generally managed
to resonate with some critical moments
in a momentous era.

**Crosby, Stills & Nash (1969)**
Atlantic 19119-2 (40:43)　**[C]**
They brought impeccable credentials to
the party, but somehow it never quite
managed to get off the ground. This,
their debut recording, was as good as it
ever got, and it wasn't that bad if you
don't mind what David Marsh adroitly
labeled "adult bubble gum." A slick-sur-
faced step to stardom. If you can bear
the hiss, which is no worse than on the
LP, the sound is significantly more open
and dynamic than on vinyl.

**So Far (1974)**
Atlantic SD 19119-2 (43:19)　**[C–]**
This was music made for the market, not
for the more personal expressive needs
of its creators, and it shows (occasional
quality additions from Neil Young notwithstanding). But popular older music
is often enduring for its nostalgic value,
if nothing else, and this collection provides a fair overview of some very popular late sixties and early seventies material. The sound is a mixed bag, sometimes compressed, sometimes harshly
bright, sometimes marred by loud hiss,
but it still surpasses the LP due to its
spatial and dynamic enhancement.

## Terence Trent D'Arby
b. March 15, 1962—New York
His immense musical ability is exceeded
only by his gross self-importance.

**Neither Fish Nor Flesh (1989)**
Columbia/CBS CK-45351 (51:30)   **[C + ]**
Too much production, too many stances,
and too self-indulgent—it all adds up to
a very disappointing second release
from a young artist of immense talent
and ego. He has the capacity to deliver
at the elite levels to which he aspires, as
is evident in some beautiful and driving
moments on this release, but the failure
of the highly touted whole obscures its
worthwhile parts. The sound, while not
perfect, is exemplary.

## Bobby Darin (Walden Robert Cassotto)
b. May 14, 1936—Bronx, New York
d. December 20, 1973
Darin, whose recording career commenced in 1958, represents a rather
unique hybrid of pop/rock artist. While
his major milieu really fell into the
realm of popular, Broadway/Las Vegas
music, his work was tinged with a fre-
neticism that related to the essence of
rock & roll.

**The Ultimate Bobby Darin (1958–1961)**
Warner Special Products 9-27606-2
(42:52)   **[C + ]**
The seventeen selections on this disc
contain all of Darin's classic material:
"Splish Splash," "Dream Lover," "Mack
the Knife," "Bill Bailey," and "Beyond
the Sea." It is a comprehensive package;
however, its quality is diminished by the
digital reproduction which, while generally clean, tends to be thin and often
harsh in the vocals.

## David & David
Formed 1985—Los Angeles
Sadly, appear to be one-shot wonders.

**Boomtown (1986)**
A&M cd5134 (41:04)   **[A]**
From L.A. (where else?)—modern fables
of sterile times in a world where reality
is often consumed with escape from the
real thing. Melodically compelling, lyrically intelligent, and supported by
sympathetic, effective production values, this is about as appealing as the
personal apocalypse is ever going to
sound. While some have said that the
vocal approach of the two Davids resem-
bles that of Hall and Oates, in fact, the
material is much more strongly reminiscent of that produced by Squeeze. The
sound is open, precisely detailed and
dynamic; perhaps a bit bright, really
only marred by pervasive hiss.

# Mink DeVille (Willy)

b. 1953—New York
Arose out of New York's mid-seventies
punk scene, DeVille's forte is R&B-based
rock & roll.

## Miracle (1987)

A&M CD5177/DX2162 (47:19)　**[C+]**
DeVille may be the perfect vocalist for
Dire Straits, and that's what this Mark
Knopfler–produced recording sounds
like. It's an appealing sound, like most of
Knopfler's work, but it lacks guts and
heart. DeVille is one of those fringe
figures who roared out of New York's
seventies new wave scene with a strong
retro rock sound and image. His *Le Chat
Belu,* released in 1980, remains his one
outstanding release. *Miracle* is slick, listenable, and forgettable. The all-digital
sound is demonstration quality, absolutely wonderful.

# Bo Diddley (Ellas McDaniel)

b. December 30, 1928—McComb, Mississippi
At an early age, Bo moved from Mississippi to Chicago's largely Mississippi-
based black community where he
picked up the nickname which he has
made famous, originally using it as an
amateur boxer. The proximity to the
urban blues-saturated sounds of Chicago
and an early discovered talent moved
Bo to music, and the result was a grafting of a very personal syncopated form
of rhythm on a basic blues form resulting in the "Bo Diddley beat" that echoes
through rock to this very day. Irreverent,
irrepressible, and underappreciated, Bo
Diddley continues to embody the spirit
of the music.

## Go Bo Diddley (Two On One) (1955–1958)

MCA CHD5904 (63:54)　**[B+]**
This disc covers Bo's '55 through '58
recordings and, for the most part,
crackles with the energy common to the
fundamental releases that rocked 1955
into musical history as the year that the
pop music world was turned upside
down by the first insolent roar of rock &
roll. His musical inventiveness (check
out "The Clock Struck 12" or "Bo's
Guitar") and eclecticism (marked by the
use of unique instrumentation in the
rock/blues form) is often overlooked, as
is the fact that he studied classical violin
for twelve years. The sound quality of
this recording, particularly on the first of
the two first records included, is pretty
awful, marred by distorted vocals and a
non-existent bottom. But the second
album on the disc is vastly superior and
the music's compelling rhythm retains
its potency after thirty years.

## The Chess Box (1955–1968)

Chess CHD2-19502 (128:34—two discs)　**[A]**
While the argument has raged for years
as to who was the creator of rock & roll,
one issue should not be subject to argument: Among the founding fathers, Bo
Diddley remains the most underappreciated. Fortunately, his original recordings
were done on the Chess label, which
was acquired by A&M Records with a
commitment to bring to market those
classics in a form appropriate to the
material. As A&M has done with Chuck
Berry, Willie Dixon, and Muddy Waters,
they have with Bo Diddley in this two-
disc compilation. This set includes forty-
five tracks, several of them instrumental, and thirteen rarities, including nine
tracks never before released. Also included is a book with Bo's brief autobiography, some fine notes by Robert Palmer
that place Bo Diddley not only in the
perspective of American rock & roll, but

show him to be a conduit for the black musical legacy. Too often thought of as the primal one-hit wonder, the fact is that Bo Diddley is a multifaceted talent who created a sound on his first historic release, "Bo Diddley," which has been borrowed for four decades. As an early member of the Chicago-based Chess recording family, it was inevitable that his work would reflect a strong urban blues influence. While he is a generally under-rated vocalist, it is in the "Bo Diddley beat" that his fame resides—a beat that draws on African tribal rhythms and American gospel permutations. As Palmer points out, it was an entire rhythmic atmosphere that created this infectious beat. While his lyrics are simplistic, they are also marvelously ritualistic. Drawn extensively from Chicago street jive and children's rhyming slang and games, they are simply another ingredient in the syncopated stew Bo brews with subtle but remarkable variety. This boxed collection provides all of the important material from his most productive decades, generally in first-rate mono sound. There are a few exceptions to this, notably "Diddley Daddy" and "Down Home Special," one of the previously released tracks. Unfortunately, several other selections are marred by slight edginess, one of which is "Cadillac" and the other, "You Know I Love You," is the undiscovered gem of the set, featuring Bo singing lead backed by the Flamingos. All in all, given the age of this material, A&M is to be complimented on the sound reproduction, which is of the same high quality as all elements in the package. It would have been nice if A&M identified the mono selections. Minor criticisms aside, this is a valuable addition to any basic rock library and, as noted by Palmer, it isn't overly difficult to trace antecedents of both funk and rap in the seminal work of Ellas McDaniel.

# Dion
# (Dion DiMucci)
b. July 18, 1939—Bronx, New York

As lead singer with the Belmonts (named after Belmont Avenue in the Bronx neighborhood where they were born), Dion created an interesting blend of pop standards combined with driving Italio-American doo-wop hits that endure to this day. His stay with the group was brief, but he has maintained an up and down solo career through the eighties.

### Dion and the Belmonts (1958–1963)
Ace CDCH176 (46:01)   **[B + ]**
From saccharin fifties Hit Parade to white-power doo-wop, this disc provides late fifties sounds in a digital mix that should knock your ears off. There's some pretty wretched stuff here, but there are also some pure gems: "A Teenager in Love," "Run Around Sue," "The Wanderer," and "Lovers Who Wander."

# Dire Straits
Formed 1977—London

The perfect rock band for the "new age era" of rock & roll. The band (really Mark Knopfler) isn't stretching the edges of the envelope, but within the territory they carved out for themselves, they make listenable, relatively sophisticated music.

### Dire Straits (1978)
Warner Bros. 3266 (41:28)   **[B + ]**
From the first note on this recording, it's apparent that Knopfler has assimilated the lessons laid down by the Beatles, Paul Simon, and Led Zeppelin, among others—the recording studio is every bit as much a component of a band's sound as its guitars or keyboards. Having come on the scene a few years before digital

reproduction became feasible, it appears that Knopfler maintained a keen ear for advances in studio technology. The lush, yet slightly removed, spatial quality of the group's attractive sound is the direct result of these concerns. Musically there is a strong kinship to J.J. Cale's vocal timbre and mannerisms, plus a reliance on his blues-oriented, loping rhythm. Because of Knopfler's limited performance prowess, the elements which lift this recording above the run of the mill are his acknowledged songwriting skills (as illustrated in the album's hit single "Sultans of Swing") and immaculate production values which produce a slightly compressed, but fine sounding CD.

**Making Movies (1980)**
Warner Bros. 3480-2 (37:41)   **[B–]**
Blues-based, guitar-centered pop sounds from Mark Knopfler, a man who has found his vein and mines it effectively. Knopfler's strengths are his compositional abilities and understanding of effective use of the modern recording studio. The former are best illustrated on "Tunnel of Love" and "Romeo And Juliette" (two of his better all-time songs), and the latter is evident throughout the recording. The CD's sound, while afflicted with some hiss, is beautifully open and dynamic with each voicing firmly centered in its own specific location.

**Love Over Gold (1982)**
Warner Bros. 9 23728-2 (41:24)   **[B–]**
More easy listening; romantic, elegantly produced sounds from Knopfler and his ever-changing band of backup players. This time out, there are only five selections, so each contains more space for instrumental meanderings. The sound effects are lovely; the substance is questionable. As always, the attention to detail in the recording studio pays off

with a fine sounding product, consistently among the best in the current pop scene.

**Brothers in Arms (1985)**
Warner Bros. 25264-2 (55:12)   **[B]**
The accurately aimed but ultimately blunted barb at MTV, "Money for Nothing" was the single that brought such great success for what is really a rather mediocre album. Knopfler does have the knack for writing engaging melodies and strong narrative lyrics, and he also has the ability to create a spacious, new-ish-wave soft-rock sound which has found a receptive audience. If the music is less than first-rate, the sound quality is another matter. This all-digital disc is simply one of the best sounding pop CDs around.

# Dr. John (Malcolm "Mac" Rebennack)
b. 1941—New Orleans
**The Ultimate Dr. John (1972–1987)**
Warner Special Products 9-27612-2 (54:43)   **[A]**
A fixture in the fertile New Orleans music scene from the mid-fifties forward, Dr. John has written, produced, played, and sung on countless records for almost thirty years. With his drawling "N'Orleans" rough, ragged-voiced vocals, respected musicianship, and voodoo preoccupations, he's an often overlooked musical natural. With production assistance from the likes of Allan Toussaint, Jerry Wexler, Tom Dowd, and Harold Battiste; and musical contributions from Plas Johnson, the Meters, David Spinoza, and Shirley Goodman, the good Doctor whips up a spicy brew of New Orleans R&B roots gumbo. This is year-round Mardi Gras from the soul of the city where the rhythm never stops. Sound quality varies from the thin

and slightly harsh to the fat and detailed, but it remains a marked improvement over vinyl versions, and the subtleties of the lead vocals are consistently
improved.

# Fats Domino
# (Antoine Domino)
b. February 26, 1928—New Orleans
The self-anointed "Fat Man" was the
artist who brought the New Orleans
barrelhouse (i.e., boogie whorehouse
piano) tradition into the pop mainstream, and became a one-man musical
industry in the process—with hits like
"Ain't That a Shame," "I'm Walkin'," and
"Blueberry Hill."

**The Best of Fats Domino (1949–1961)**
EMI America CDP7 465812 (32:39)   **[B+]**
The first of many New Orleans–based
rockers who drew upon a musical tradition uniquely rich among American
cities. The essential element of the New
Orleans sound, as it has evolved with
rock & roll for the past three decades,
has been its good time, party down
quality which the Fat Man pioneered
nationally. The sound quality here,
while generally good, is certainly flawed
on occasion, and varies appreciably
from cut to cut; but all the early hits are
included which means that the party
is still going strong.

**My Blue Heaven: The Best of Fats Domino
Volume One (1949–1961)**
Imperial EMI USA CDP7-92808-2 (44:18)   **[B–]**
Antoine "Fats" Domino's boogie-based
piano, smooth, yet rollicking vocals, and
ability to make each recording a party
proved irresistible, popularizing some of
rock & roll's original work. It was Fats
who identified New Orleans as one of
the cities that can lay claim to providing

the roots of rock & roll. All his seminal
work was on the Imperial label, and this
twenty-song collection covers a fair sampling, although the omissions of "Goin'
Home," "Goin' to the River," "All By
Myself," and "Poor Me" are mysterious.
Almost all of his chart hits are included:
"The Fat Man," "Ain't That a Shame,"
"I'm in Love Again," "Blueberry Hill,"
and "Walking to New Orleans." Some
critics have called this the best-sounding
Fats original hits package currently
available on disc, so the reason for my
less-than-stellar rating is based solely on
its sonic weakness: The sound quality
varies widely from track to track, and
too often the vocals sound as if they
were taken from a jukebox-worn 45.
Steve Kolanjian's liner notes are comprehensive and informative.

# The Doobie Brothers
Formed 1970—San Jose, California;
now, thankfully, disbanded
**Best of The Doobies (1976)**
Warner Bros. 3112 (45:11)   **[D–]**
To fault their musicianship would be
unfair, to fault their product is inevitable;
bleached soul/funk sounds geared to
meaningless hooks and corporate marketing all presided over by Michael
McDonald's adenoidal wail. A prime
example of the decline of quality in the
seventies version of rock music. The
sound is about equal to that of an LP, but
who cares?

# The Doors
Formed 1965—Los Angeles
Perhaps it is because Jim Morrison's
screams of rebellion were as loud as any
voiced in the sixties, or perhaps he was
more successful than we imagined in
conjuring up the darker spirits that he
sought to invoke, but for whatever rea-

son, the music of this highly influential group has managed to survive despite uneven, and frequently antagonistic, critical evaluation. Success and continuing popularity are clearly derived from Morrison's charismatic status, more icon than poet or musician.

### The Doors (1967)
Elektra 74007.2 (242 2012) (44:27)   **[A]**
Simply one of the strongest debut albums to come out in an era when giants came forth with unbelievable regularity. The sound is generally clean and dynamically enhanced, with some weakness in the lows. Some of the mixes tend to make Morrison's vocal secondary to the instrumentation, which is clearly an improper shift of the focus of the group. But this is all nitpicking. A part of Jim Morrison's message was to conjure up the darker powers that in earlier times were the province of sorcerers and wizards—this recording is as close as he ever got. Truly a breakthrough release in that it expanded both the vocabulary and scope of the subject matter covered by rock & roll.

Remastered in 1988–89 from the original master tapes, the sonically much-improved reissue clocks in at 44:31.

### Morrison Hotel/Hard Rock Cafe (1970)
Elektra EKS 75007-2 (37:27)   **[B]**
The band's apparent concept album that comes close and just doesn't quite make it—the Doors were primarily a singles band. That's not to say this is a failed effort, far from it, outside of their debut recording, it probably maintains the highest level of musicianship from cut to cut of any of the Doors' album releases. As always with this group, Jim Morrison is the center of it all, and as Robert Christgau said: "He's not the genius he makes himself out to be, so maybe his genius is that he doesn't let his preten-

sions cancel out his talent." The sound is a bit murky, close in quality to that of the LP.

### L.A. Woman (1971)
Elektra EKS-75011-2 (48:46)   **[B + ]**
Blues-based, often tongue-in-cheek, this was the group's last joint effort; prior to its release, Morrison, literate poet and pretender that he was, left for Paris. He never returned, dying of a heart attack there on July 3, 1971, at the age of twenty-seven. About half of this recording works; in part because the band seemed satisfied with simpler approaches, and Jim had apparently exhausted his overreaching stage persona (or maybe just his liver). Some cuts continue to hold up, "Love Her Madly," "L.A. Woman," "Hyacinth House," and "Riders on the Storm" among them. Sad to say, the sound is poor—muddy, with some apparent distortion.

Remastered in 1988–89 from the original master tapes, and the sonic improvement is striking—it now has strong dynamics and excellent clarity, resulting in a rating upgrade to A-.

### Alive She Cried (1968–1970)
Elektra 9 60269-2 (37:01)   **[C + ]**
Released in 1983, the performances that make up this recording took place in 1968, 1969, and 1970. One of the elements that made the Doors so exciting was Morrison's continuing tightrope walk over the abyss of self-parody and wretched excess, particularly in the free-form arena of live performance. On the seven cuts included on this relatively brief package, he teeters several times, but never hits bottom; or, for that matter, reaches the top. The sound expectedly varies, but a majority of the tracks are excellent: spacious and dynamic, while the others betray their live roots. This CD provides a live look at an important,

influential band (though not always a good one), including some of Morrison's brief readings of his strained verse.

### The Best of the Doors (1968–1971)
Elektra 2CD 960345 (89:31)   [A]
This two-disc compilation opens with "Break on Through" and closes with "The End," and the seventeen selections in between make up most (but not all) of the band's best music. What sets this two-disc set apart is its sound. The Doors' longtime producer, Paul Rothchild, who has become a part-time keeper of the legend, has stated that these are the only CD releases of the group's material remastered from the original master tapes; listeners won't question that statement. The sound is wonderful—perhaps a bit bright on occasion, but clean, clear, spacious, and dynamic. It clearly conveys the magic of digital reproduction.

# Nick Drake
b. June 19, 1948—Burma
d. November 25, 1974
Enigmatic, elegaic, and somewhat mysterious, Drake's very personal jazz-tinged folk/rock sound, while known primarily to a small, devoted cult, remains influential in the British folk/rock-based crowd.

### Five Leaves Left (1970)
Island CID 9105 (41:42)   [A]
The short-lived, hermetically disturbed Nick Drake fashioned a cult following on two albums released in 1969/1970, Five Leaves Left (which supposedly alludes to rolling papers) and Bryter Layter. Minimalist as it is, Five Leaves Left has the more textured musical arrangements, meshing beautifully with Drake's gentle, breathy tenor. This is hypnotic, elliptical music resonating with haunting echoes.

Interestingly, Richard Thompson plays electric guitar on the strong opening "Time Has Told Me," but it is Danny Thompson's fine bass that anchors these ethereal elegies. While there is a touch of chamber music, gentle jazz, and English folk, Drake's music is possessed of an undeniably affecting quality that makes it perfect for rainy nights, hazy autumn afternoons, or mountain mornings. Like the LP, the sound seems to emanate from behind a smoky screen, and there is a bit of tape hiss, but it retains nice dynamics and an enveloping warmth.

### Bryter Layter (1970)
Island CID 9134 (39:42)   [A + ]
Stephen Holden described Drake's songs as "narcotic," Sam Sutherland described his singing as "a murmur of smoke and velvet," Bruce Malamut described him as "the John Coltrane of folk singers," and John Cale (who plays viola, harpsichord, celeste organ, and piano on Bryter Layter) acknowledged Drake's inspiration in the creation of his own classic Paris 1919. Drake's fluid lyrical/musical images are reminiscent of a river-shaping rock. He carves shimmering moments in time. He leaves magical tracks on the soul. Yet it's all done with breathy simplicity and understated, elegant instrumentation. Like Five Leaves Left, Bryter Layter is a journey into a unique, enchanting space. While it's difficult to isolate a single selection from his mesmerizing few recordings, "Northern Sky," included on Bryter Layter, may well represent the fullest realization of his special talent. The sound quality of this disc, particularly considering its vintage, is first-rate.

# The Drifters

Formed 1953—New York City;
disbanded 1964/65
Original lead Clyde McPhatter. One of
the more sustaining, albeit transient,
innovative, and influential of the early
doo-wop, R&B-based pop groups of that
music's golden era. Their manager,
George Treadwell, disbanded the original group in 1958 and continued on
under the Drifters' name with a group
that had been known as the Five Crows.

### All Time Greatest Hits & More (1959–1965)

Atlantic 781931-2 (103:15—two discs)   **[A]**
In 1953 the Drifters' first hit, "Money
Honey," reached the top of the R&B
charts, with Clyde McPhatter providing
great lead tenor. Until 1954 this group
charted ten other Top Ten R&B hits,
including McPhatter's and Bill Pinkney's
classic duet on "White Christmas." In
1955 the original group departed the
name and a number of others took their
places through its last charted single in
1982. This comprehensive collection
features the Drifters' three different later
lead vocalists: Ben E. King, Rudy Lewis,
and Johnny Moore, and their greatest
hits: "There Goes My Baby," "This Magic
Moment," "Save the Last Dance for Me,"
"Up on the Roof," and "Under the Board-
walk," and fine unknowns, "Nobody But
Me," but a lot of it is pretty forgettable.
After McPhatter's departure the Drifters
became a producer's group, and Jerry
Leiber and Mike Stoller were among the
most innovative and influential. By
adding fuller instrumentation including
strings and Latin beats, they moved R&B
into mainstream pop. There's probably
more here than any but the most hardcore fans would care about, there's also a
hell of a lot that every true pop music
fan will find indispensable. In terms of
record sales, the Drifters, in all of their
incarnations, are the twenty-eighth best-
selling R&B artists in history. The sound
quality is nothing extraordinary, varying markedly from session to session,
although it gets better in the later
material.

# Bob Dylan (Robert Allen Zimmerman)

b. May 24, 1941—Duluth, Minnesota
Zimmerman begat Dylan and Dylan
(along with the Beatles) begat a form of
rock & roll that included an intellectual
element to complement the visceral. He
stands as the single individual whose
persona and legend loom largest from
the sixties, the decade of rock's richest
creativity. He gave the music relevance
to the moment—he literally exploded
the form—he created his own myth and
with the anonymity it afforded, he was
free to expose it all, the real and the
surreal. His work from the sixties defines an astonishing, electrifying creativity, which has not since been equaled.
Dylan's music, from folk to gospel, New
York to Nashville, Jew to Gentile, com-
prises a contribution that ranks with the
great cultural artifacts of this century.

### Bob Dylan (1961)

Columbia CK 08579 (36:52)   **[A]**
Folk/rock's Book of Genesis, Dylan's
first recording delivered eleven traditional folk/blues songs and two
incredible originals, "Talkin' New York"
and "Song to Woody," which, in a primitive way, anticipate the electrifying
output looming in his future. A clawing
testament to perhaps the single most
influential, impressive talent of the rock
era, the recording bristles with the
boundless, driven energy that would forever change the worlds of rock and folk

music. Three decades after its original release it remains an arresting, riveting performance—a twenty-year-old armed with a caustic, nasal voice, acoustic guitar, and yowling harmonica serving notice that his time, and that of his generation, were at hand. This budget-priced disc includes Stacey Williams's original liner notes as well as Robert Shelton's *New York Times* review of Dylan's 1961 performance at Greenwich Village's Gerdes Folk City, generally conceded to be Dylan's career catalyst. The disc's sound, while markedly more dynamic than its vinyl counterpart, is far from state-of-the-art due to the weird stereo mix that places the voice in the left channel, the harmonica in the middle, and the guitar on the right.

**The Freewheelin' Bob Dylan (1962)**
Columbia CK8786 (50:08)   **[A]**
The attack is less abrasive than that on Dylan's debut a year earlier, but this time out, with the exception of "Corrina, Corrina," traditional material has been set aside in favor of Dylan's own compositions, forever allaying any question about the depth and breadth of his genius. *Freewheelin'* opens with "Blowin' in the Wind," his first anthem, the song with which Peter, Paul & Mary catapulted him to celebrity. From the hilarious to the harrowing, the thirteen selections delivered political, social, and romantic commentary at a level rarely achieved in popular song. *Freewheelin'* also yields "Girl from the North Country" (still one of his most tender and most haunting ballads), the overly praised "Masters of War," plus "A Hard Rain's a-Gonna Fall," "Don't Think Twice, It's All Right," and "I Shall Be Free." With this record Dylan began to expand the political scope and intelligence of popular music through the magic of his words and the prescience of

his vision—it's truly one of those masterpieces that left an indelible imprint on the music and the audience that followed. Again, the music is as simple as the message is complex—harmonica, guitar, and the countrified nasal twang of his voice. But this time the sound has a more natural, though still dated, quality, which in clarity alone, is an improvement over the LP.

**The Times They Are A-Changin' (1964)**
Columbia CK8905 (45:37)   **[B]**
Two years after the seminal *Freewheelin',* Dylan returned with ten new songs preoccupied with the street politics that then swirled around him. Because of their greater topicality, many of the songs remain more icons of a turbulent era than abstract messages of universal truth. *The Times They Are A-Changin'* is an evolutionary, not a revolutionary, release—revolution was around the corner, two albums away. Yet this is anything but a weak album—it would be a decade before that description would be applied to any of Dylan's work. "One Too Many Mornings," "North Country Blues," "Restless Farewell," and the lingering love ballad "Boots of Spanish Leather" still sustain merit more than a quarter-century after their original release. Producer Tom Wilson brings a more natural coloration to the sound quality, expectedly emphasizing the vocals, but too often buries the acoustic guitar too low in the mix. It sounds a bit dated, but fine nonetheless.

**Another Side of Bob Dylan (1964)**
Columbia CK 8993 (50:44)   **[A–]**
Dylan's second Tom Wilson produced release of 1964 was a major improvement over its predecessor, and represents the culmination of the early pure-folk Dylan. The use of an acoustic piano actually represents the first major change

in his instrumental sound. It is on *Another Side* that we hear Dylan finding the lyrical context and form that suited his vision and message—verbose, oblique, but always evocative—the poet prophet finding his voice. His ambiguous stream-of-consciousness abstractions are at once immediate and profound, personal, and impenetrable. You may not know what it all means, but you know you've never heard anything quite like it before; you know it matters, even if you're not quite sure why. There is more balance in the mix between voice and guitar, but because of a less than clean background and a sense of distance between performer and microphone, the whole thing sounds a bit like it's coming through a scrim—roughly equivalent to how it sounds on vinyl.

### Bringing It All Back Home (1965)
Columbia CK9128 (47:29)   [A + ]
The year was 1965, and the savior of contemporary folk music was abandoning the purists by melding his lyrical topicality with the amplified beat at the heart of rock & roll. This obviously transitional recording (half recorded with rock instrumentation and half acoustic folk stylings) initiates yet another enlargement of the then burgeoning world of rock & roll. Dylan simply refused to be limited by prior conventions. His influence was pervasive, traceable in contemporary work of both the Stones and the Beatles as well as numerous other artists. The classics, "Subterranean Homesick Blues," "Maggie's Farm," "Mr. Tambourine Man," and "It's All Right Ma," as well as the clichés, began here. Soundwise, the low end lacks dynamics, but otherwise this is a very successful digital conversion.

### Highway 61 Revisited (1965)
Columbia CK9189 (51:40)   [A + ]
From the first resonant beat of "Like a Rolling Stone" (perhaps Dylan's finest song) to the piercing plaintive harmonica that closes "Desolation Row," this recording encompasses some of the best rock music ever made. The sound, while far from revelatory, is superior to the LP; it's clean and the detail enhancement is noticeable; this disc is essential.

### Blonde On Blonde (1966)
Columbia CGK841 (71:23)   [A + ]
A lot of critics have stated that this is Dylan's best—some even say that it is the best rock record of all time. It is the consummate work by a man who may be rock's single most important creator. When one stops to realize what Dylan had already released in 1965 and 1966, *Bringing It All Back Home* and *Highway 61 Revisited,* if he had done nothing else, his stature would have been assured. But, *Blonde On Blonde* may be the most fully realized album in the annals of rock & roll. It is the work of an obvious genius at the height of his creativity. Soundwise, the worst of it sounds like a cleaner, slightly enhanced version of the LP; at its best, the dynamic and special enhancements added by digital conversion are wonderful. Unfortunately, Columbia has also shaved a few seconds off the music to get the recording on a single disc—better it should have been released on two CDs; classics are classics.

In 1989, with technology adding greater playing time to the CD, Columbia reissued *Blonde on Blonde,* reinstating the several minutes (clocking in at 73:15) it had shaved off "Sad Eyed Lady of the Lowlands"—now, a classic *is* a classic.

**And The Band**
**The Basement Tapes (1967)**
Columbia C2K 33682 (77:29—two discs)  [A +]
These sessions which were done at the
Big Pink in upstate New York, away from
the glare of the spotlight and without
any public intent, are loose, funny,
touching, and moving. Dylan has never
sounded more relaxed on record, and
The Band, both as supporting group and
on their own, lays claim to the title of
America's greatest rock band (yeah, I
know, all but Levon are Canadian, but
this is essential American music). Of the
twenty-four included songs, eighteen are
by Dylan (many of which have surfaced
elsewhere), but this is the only recording
of The Band's six contributions. Greil
Marcus's always-insightful liner notes are
icing on the cake: "What was taking
shape, as Dylan and The Band fiddled
with the tunes, was less a style than a
spirit—a spirit that had to do with a
delight in friendship and invention."
The sound on these CDs is a revelation—not studio perfect, but production-
perfect for the material. *The Basement
Tapes* resonates with a truly enduring
power and sense of mystery.

**Greatest Hits (1967)**
Columbia CK9463 (40:20)  [A +]
With the exception of "Rainy Day
Women #12 and 35" the other nine clas-
sics included here are also available on
*Biograph.* That aside, this is essential
Dylan, with most of the early hits
included. The sound quality is analo-
gous to that on *Highway 61* reviewed
above.

**John Wesley Harding (1968)**
Columbia CK9604 (38:31)  [A +]
In July, 1966, Bob Dylan had a motorcycle accident that took him out of the
maelstrom of his own creativity and the
celebrity that attended it. During his

recuperation in upstate New York
(Woodstock), he privately explored his
roots with Canada's great American
roots group, The Band. This was summarized on *The Basement Tapes* not
released officially until 1975. But the
ambiance of this time was expressed in
1968 in *John Wesley Harding.* On it,
Dylan turned away from rock's frenet-
icism and returned to countrified folk
roots. It remains an enduring recording,
the first oblique expression of the
devoutness that would overtake his output a decade later, as well as a direct
precursor of the country sound that
would overwhelm *Nashville Skyline,*
which, like this album, was recorded in
Nashville. The sound is certainly adequate, much like the other Dylan CD
releases from this decade—clean, with
some enhancement of detail, but not
much dynamic or spatial improvement.

**Nashville Skyline (1969)**
Columbia CK9825 (27:08)  [C +]
Dylan's first really inferior release,
1969's *Nashville Skyline,* is not totally
without merit. The commercially successful "Lay Lady Lay" and the rerecording with Johnny Cash of the
lovely "Girl From the North Country"
are quality material even by Dylan's
high standards; but that's about it. The
sound is a little better than that of the
prior Dylan CD releases from this era,
but it doesn't matter a whole bunch.

**Self Portrait (1970)**
Columbia CGK 30050 (74:05)  [C–]
Of this unbelievable release, Greil Marcus wrote: "I once said I'd buy an album
of Bob Dylan breathing hard. But I never
said I'd buy an album of Bob Dylan
breathing softly;" David Marsh wrote:
"*Blonde on Blonde* is probably the best
two-record set in the history of rock &
roll. *Self Portrait* is almost certainly the

worst double set ever done by a major artist." And Robert Christgau added: "I don't know anyone, even vociferous supporters of this album, who plays more than one side at a time. I don't listen to it at all," while noting that Jon Landau wrote him requesting that Christgau assign it a "D" rating in his *Village Voice* review. Who am I to argue? I'll go with the flow. Oh, the sound quality of *Self Portrait* is also problematic—overly shrill and harsh in the upper midrange and weak in the lower midrange; generally constrained, but Columbia did manage to get the both LPs on a single CD, something they failed to accomplish with the original CD release of *Blonde on Blonde*—ain't that a gas?

### New Morning (1970)

Columbia CK 30290 (35:59)   **[B]**
Perhaps in response to the critical and market drubbing *Self Portrait* suffered, or perhaps just because he's Bob Dylan, three months after that disastrous double album Dylan was back with *New Morning,* a mixed bag of mostly minor pleasures. In the middle of it all are two songs, "Winterlude" and "If Dogs Run Free," stylistically very different, but both featuring a lighthearted, throwaway sensibility, giving them both a silly durability uncommon to the rest of the recording. The obvious exception is "Want to See the Gypsy," which stands among the best of his seventies songs. Overall, the very unpretentious (although chorale-inclusive) attitude toward this relatively simple, straightforward material wins out, resulting in endearingly pleasant, if not essential, Dylan. Many of his hard-core fans accord greater status than I've suggested. The CD's sound quality is adequate, although there is annoying low-level hiss throughout, and the bass has a muddy, boomy sound.

### Greatest Hits Volume II (1971)

Columbia C2K31120 (78:25—two discs)   **[A]**
Twenty-two examples of an artistic decade marked by Dylan's variety and virtuosity. Five selections were previously unreleased, and the remaining seventeen are all strong statements by a man who defined the term in sixties rock. Simply a first-rate collection. Expectedly, the sound is all over the place, rarely of surpassing quality and occasionally affected with rough distortion.

### Pat Garrett and Billy the Kid (1973)

Columbia CK32460 (35:25)   **[B + ]**
Almost three years passed (following *New Morning*) before Dylan returned to the studio, and instead of the hoped-for major statement, we got the soundtrack to the movie *Pat Garrett and Billy the Kid,* in which Dylan played a supporting role. It's effective as background for another dusty Sam Peckinpah Western yarn, but on its own there's not a whole lot to sink your teeth into. The music is fine (Dylan's music is too often wrongly written off as derivative) and the musicianship generally first-rate (Roger McGuinn, Booker T., Jim Keltner, among others), but it's Dylan's words that ultimately matter, and there aren't many this time out. Yet, when he does include a song, he does so with grace and power—"Knockin' on Heaven's Door" has justifiably become a favorite, and "Finale Theme," while lyrically identified with the movie, stands as one of his better narrative songs and gets a strong vocal reading. The sound quality of this budget-priced disc is generally impressive.

### And The Band
### Before the Flood (1974)

Columbia C2K 37661 (92:40—two discs)   **[A]**
A kick-ass live effort, on which Dylan applied his revisionist approach to his

old material, effectively trashing prior meanings and moments. The Band wails like banshees and Mr. Tambourine Man whips on a new mask for his seventies audience to contemplate. Released in 1974, these recordings were made during the last three performances of his 1974 twenty-one-city tour with The Band. Ever since the late sixties, when bootlegs of this musical combination's *Basement Tapes* were widely circulated among aficionados, the opportunity to see these two "naturals" perform together was compelling. Are the revised renditions of his classics successful? Not really, but obviously what matters was his willingness to do it in the first place, and, ultimately, that's what makes this first-rate rock & roll. The interspersed performances of The Band doing their own material are consistent with the whole and burn with raw energy. Given that these are dated live performance recordings the sound is surprisingly clear and punchy. There is some compression and some muddiness in the bottom end, but overall, not disappointing.

### Blood on the Tracks (1974)
Columbia 33235 (51:55)   [A + ]
The snarl was still there, but the shift in Dylan's attitude was marked and perceptible. The spotlight is completely on Dylan here, because the backup musicians added nothing but the briefest sort of filler sound. Dylan filled that spotlight with the best songwriting he'd done in years—honest, poetic, the voice of a survivor hopefully headed for less traumatic times, but carrying the scars and bitterness of savaged love. The music is lilting and haunting, making this Dylan's best release of the decade (acknowledging that the *Basement Tapes* were really sixties material, release date notwithstanding). His sing-

ing is stunningly honest, which adds dimension to his most mature musings about love lost and a time gone by—too quickly. It's folkish sound hearkens back to the sixties; its heart is the perspective it places on times recently past, irrevocably gone. The sound on this disc is wonderful, open, and full. It does have a few moments of overbrightness and slight compression is perceptible, but the vocal detail is greatly enhanced.

### Planet Waves (1974)
Columbia CK37637 (42:14)   [A–]
Even with a new record company (this release originally was Dylan's Geffen debut, commencing a brief absence from Columbia, which ultimately reacquired the rights to the master), and a reunion with The Band (clearly the finest backup group with which he has been associated), *Planet Waves* was greeted somewhat apathetically commercially and critically. Those that denigrated it were probably afflicted with unreal expectations because of the legendary Dylan/Band chemistry (*The Basement Tapes* being then the most notorious and coveted bootleg about). Time reveals a recording concerned with simple domestic involvements that yield enduring pleasures. It's no masterpiece, but it's far from the secondary product it is too often perceived to be. If anything, it has a somewhat unfinished quality about it, but that's not a foreign element in much of Dylan's work. While *Planet Waves* is best known for "Forever Young" (performed both up- and downtempo) and "You Angel You," it is not the individual tracks, but the sophisticated picture of loving and relationships that encourages repeated listenings. The sound quality is only fair; the whole seems unnaturally bunched together, and Dylan's vocals and harmonica flirt with edginess throughout.

## Desire (1975)

Columbia CK33893 (56:15)   **[B]**
A return to topicality and a movement
away from the more personal stance of
*Blood on the Tracks*. While it is a quality
work of ambitious scope, it somehow
has an unfinished quality about it;
probably attributable to the less than
polished instrumental "assistance" that
lends little of positive value to the proceedings. Still, one of his better offerings
of the seventies due to the inclusion of
some fine material, "Hurricane," "Isis,"
and "Sara" being the highlights. The
sound is overbright to the point of
harhness on some of the vocal and harmonica tracks, a distinct comedown
from the high quality of *Blood on the
Tracks*.

## Hard Rain (1976)

Columbia CK34349 (51:19)   **[C + ]**
When it comes to recording, Dylan dis-
dains anything other than a "live, one-
take" feel, which suggests that his live
recordings should exhibit him at his
best. Yet this has never really been the
case. This live postcard from the ragtag
Rolling Thunder tour is made up of a
first-rate group of Dylan songs performed by a second-rate group of
background musicians, who provide
anything but inspiration. Dylan's vocals,
and the inherent strength of the material, raise the level from time to time,
only to be quickly dissipated by lackluster instrumental backing and
breaks—maybe they were too busy con-
templating and conveying the gospel to
Bob to be overly concerned with the
business at hand. It's really too bad,
because Dylan's songs cry out for better,
but then if he really gave a damn. . . . To
bottom it all out, the sound quality is
atrocious—boxy, muddy, noisy, over-
audienced, and frequently distorted.

## Street Legal (1978)

CBS CDCBS 86067 (49:56)   **[D–]**
Dylan's released a lot of recordings over
a career now spanning more than two
decades, and it would be unfair to
expect them all to be good—this one's
not. The addition of a female chorus
detracts rather than adds to the proceedings, and the band plays like their last
gig was a Salvation Army affair. The
sound is appropriate to the contents:
compressed, muddy, distorted, and frequently harsh in the vocals.

## Slow Train Coming (1979)

Columbia CK36120 (46:47)   **[C]**
Dylan reborn, what else? This recording,
which heralded his conversion to Chris-
tianity (he was born a Jew), created a
huge stir in the late seventies, which
probably says more about the sterility of
the times than the importance of either
the event or the music. Actually, of all
his many poses, this one seemed most
suspect, but buoyed by the Jerry Wexler/
Berry Becket production and the fine
Muscle Shoals House Band, it had a professional sound to it that had never been
heard on Dylan's work before. It was
enough to earn him a Grammy (which
he personally accepted) and to lure Jann
Wenner out of his lofty publisher's office
of *Rolling Stone* to write an extended
review which concluded that this was
the artist's pinnacle accomplishment.
Time has not treated *Slow Train Coming*
quite so kindly. The sound is pretty
good—clean, detailed, and somewhat
open, though it still is noticeably compressed.

## Biograph (1961–1981)

Columbia DK38831/C3K38330 (216:57—three
discs)   **[A + ]**
Because of the permanence of CDs and
their introduction almost thirty years
after rock & roll commenced, they offer

a unique opportunity to package an artist's work in a permanent form valuable to the rock music collector. Columbia's pioneering efforts in this direction are evidenced in this three-disc release, meriting double commendation. The material, fifty-three songs spanning twenty years (1961–81), includes crucial prior releases plus a modicum of fresh, but obscure, previously unreleased material or unreleased versions of familiar cuts (e.g., the surpassing live version of "Visions of Johanna"), and makes this a remarkable collection. While Dylan is an artist famous for his casual, if not downright slovenly, attention to studio production values (and some of the masters utilized here were truly demo recordings), the sound quality evidences extreme care in the digital remastering. Obviously, the sound varies, given the vast diversity of sources, but only the most persnickety of listeners will be disappointed with either the sound or content of this release. In addition to the music itself, the packaging is enhanced by insightful printed material.

**Infidels (1983)**
Columbia CK38819 (46:15)  **[B–]**
Dylan's only all-digital recording, *Infidels* sounds great, particularly in the subtleties of the vocals, but the material is a different matter. This is gospel/pop/rock with a little politics thrown in for old time's sake. The motivation behind it feels more like a desire to continue a career than a need to express much deep conviction. *Melody Maker* was singularly unimpressed, calling it "as stimulating as an evening in a laundromat," but who knows what kind of laundromats they frequent. Because of its pop sensibility, fine production values, and polished musicianship, *Infidels* is appealing, albeit watered-down, Dylan, with a couple of stronger inclu-

sions: "Sweetheart Like You" and "Don't Fall Apart on Me Tonight."

**Real Live (1984)**
Columbia CK3944 (52:21)  **[D–]**
There's obviously some talent at work here, but it's pretty well hidden. It too often sounds more like a hootenanny than a rock concert. Dylan's recorded live efforts have rarely been successful, and this is no exception. The disc sound is simply terrible—constant hiss, murky, muffled vocals, heavy compression, and a band that sounds like it didn't make it to the stage from the bus. There may have been some quality moments on this tour, but you won't hear them here.

**Empire Burlesque (1985)**
Columbia CK40110 (46:56)  **[C–]**
The born-again phase had passed, but the female backup singers hadn't. Neither the material nor the performance provide much of lasting value. It's not that it's that bad (it really isn't), it's just that it's Bob Dylan, and, right or wrong, our expectations are pretty high. The sound, while slightly compressed, is pretty dynamic and clean; it's also subject to fairly continuous hiss.

**Knocked Out Loaded (1986)**
Columbia CK40439 (35:34)  **[B–]**
The mix came out of a dance club and the song selection is weird; much of it recorded with an echo chamber effect around the lead vocals which, with the female and children's choirs, gives many cuts an ordained quality. Forget the first five selections; the interest lies in the final three, each written by Dylan with a different cowriter. "Brownsville Girl," on which actor/playwright Sam Shepard is the collaborator, is an eleven-minute surreal cinematic montage that manages somehow to reflect a resonant American strain. Tom Petty provides that function

on "Got My Mind Made Up," an honest-to-God rocker on which Dylan sings with some real intensity. Finally, the fascinating collaboration with mainstream popster Carole Bayer Sager, "Under Your Spell," has the feel of pure pop product (with a slight gospel tinge), but in some subtle lyrical manner sustains the nervy quality that was the key to Dylan's classic work. The sound is punchy and dynamic, with nice instrumental separations, a strange vocal mix, and a lightly noisy background.

### Down in the Groove (1988)
Columbia CK40957 (32:09)   [C–]
For this eighties throwaway, Dylan has gathered a number of respectable talents—Danny Kortchmar, Steve Jordon, Steve Jones, Paul Simonon, Clydie King, Bobby King, Willie Green, Alan Clarke, Sly Dunbar, Robbie Shakespeare, Mitchell Froom, Ron Wood, Mark Knopfler, and Eric Clapton—and slapped them into homogenized submission. Maybe it's the material, sixty percent of which was neither written nor cowritten by Dylan; maybe it just was one of those days when Bob wasn't all that inspired. Whatever the reasons, Down in the Groove is far from memorable. The slight "Silvio" garnered some airplay, which gave the album a broader popular acceptance than the material merited, but the real highlight is "Ugliest Girl in the World" (cowritten with Dylan by longtime Grateful Dead writer Robert Hunter), which echoes the cracking wit and electricity of Dylan's great sixties work. The CD's sound has the same slapdash feel that affects the performances.

### Oh Mercy (1989)
Columbia CK 45281 (39:00)   [A + ]
There must have been something in the air in late 1989. Whatever it was, Oh Mercy is Dylan's best new release since 1974's Blood on the Tracks. With sympathetic, atmospheric production assistance from the incomparable Daniel Lanois, and instrumental assistance from a number of fine New Orleans players, including several members of the Neville Brothers Band, Dylan has brought forth a recording that resounds with his trademark topicality and Nashville twang. Of its ten cuts, only "Disease of Conceit" is really expendable (in fact it's much worse than that). The remainder reaffirm one of the great individual talents to have sprung from the rock & roll revolution. Lanois, of course, has provided magic for a number of artists since the mid-eighties, including U2 and Robbie Robertson, but this effort with Dylan is notable, especially in the haunting atmosphere he provides for "Man in the Long Black Coat," which is classic Dylan. This may sound like programmed radio hype, but on Oh Mercy Dylan has created some of the most meaningful and affecting music of the last thirty years. The other eight tracks are also vintage, yet current in their reflection of where a generation's tumultuous troubadour finds himself almost three decades after it all began. Lanois's production contribution extends to the clarity, spaciousness, and warmth of the sound.

### Under the Red Sky (1990)
Columbia CK 46794 (35:44)   [D]
Things didn't bode well when I saw Bruce Hornsby's name prominently displayed on the longbox. 1989's Oh Mercy was powerhouse, later-career Dylan, and Under the Red Sky was produced by preeminent pop producer Don Was, who previously had shown an almost unerring touch. Dylan has assembled his finest group of backup players: Kenny Aronoff, George Harrison, Stevie Ray Vaughan, Jimmie Vaughan, David Lindley, Waddy Wachtel, Slash, Elton

John, and Al (shades of *Blonde on Blonde*) Kooper. The puerile lyrics (e.g., "Wiggle, Wiggle") are either half-hearted attempts at parable or the most mundane trash Dylan has ever written. Lacking lyrical substance, his vocals ring hollow, and the merely adequate sound fails to provide the spatial separation that might have shifted the focus to the fine instrumentalists. Only the inclusion of "TV Talkin' Song" kept my rating from being lower. Maybe, out of respect, we could chalk this one up to the times, since he's often said to be a mirror of them, but the real Bob Dylan wouldn't buy that one, either.

# Eagles
Formed 1971—Los Angeles
Slick urbanizers of the L.A. country sound, the Eagles enjoyed great popularity throughout the decade. In retrospect, their sexist lyrics and commercial orientation lacks sustaining substance.

### Desperado (1973)
Asylum 5068-2 (36:02)  **[C–]**
The perfect band for the self-important seventies. On this, their second album, their adopted conceit was the creation of a Western outlaw concept which was designed to provide historical precedent for their sexist rock hero stance. But glossy production and country hooks aside, the general vapidness of the material undermines the myth. The sound on the CD is severely compressed and often muddy.

### Their Greatest Hits (1972–1974)
Asylum 105-2 (43:12)  **[B]**
These ten selections were integral to seventies rock radio. As an indictment of those times, it's nonpareil; yet, it remains slickly seductive. The sound is all over, mostly compressed, occasionally a bit harsh, though often equivalent to the LP version.

### Hotel California (1976)
Asylum 103-2 (43:33)  **[B+]**
The addition of Joe Walsh brought a harder, more rock edge to the band's material which made this their strongest album statement. Gone are the gunslingers of the past; it's tough enough to stay alive on the mean streets of Beverly Hills. In the end, it's a pretty hard look at the seamier side of success, still packaged for the adoring mass audience, and it works. They may not have been sincere, but they were pros; and Henley and Frey were among the era's better writers. The sound, while sometimes a bit bright in the vocals, is big, spacious, detailed, and a decided improvement over the LP.

# Steve Earle
b. January 17, 1955—Fort Monroe, Virginia
First made his name as a songwriter covered by Waylon Jennings and Carl Perkins, among others. Ultimately evolved a driving, clean country/rock sound that effectively showcases his fine writing.

### Guitar Town (1986)
MCA MCAD-5713 (34:33)  **[A]**
The seventies and early eighties brought commercialization to Nashville with the same vengeance that it attacked the rock community. The result was string-drenched music that was incredibly

vapid, even measured by the usual soap opera norms. The last half of the decade has brought the inevitable backlash—the return to scrawny, leather-lean, honest-to-God, roots country sound. The kind of music to drive your truck to (*big truck*). Earle is at the forefront of this hard-edged, hard-voiced resurrection. Earthy, well-honed lyrics two-steppin' across a lonesome twang—that's Steve Earle, and he's damn good. This is country music for a changed country—it sounds familiar, but it sounds fresh as well. The CD provides clean, crisp, well-defined, and nicely spaced sound qualities.

**Steve Earle and the Dukes**
**Exit 0 (1987)**
MCA MCAD5998 (38:42)    **[A]**
This one proves that *Guitar Town* weren't no fluke. The band plays simple, tight, kick-ass, pedal-steel country music, while Earle brings a hard-edged country drawl to his acutely observed, well-wrought lyrics that define a part of the contemporary American scene as well as any being written today. The sound is excellent, exhibiting all the positives of digital reproduction.

**Steve Earle and the Dukes**
**The Hard Way (1990)**
MCA MCAD-6430 (55:55)    **[B–]**
Is it country? Is it rock? Does it matter? Earle brings intensity to his hybrid musical form and writes lyrics with relevance, ideals, and meaning—something that is pretty rare in any pop form these days (other than rap). These qualities have marked Earle's work since his extraordinary debut, *Guitar Town*, but *The Hard Way* lacks the overall quality of the earlier releases. It does, however, contain some gems, from the moody "The Other Kind" through the powerful "Billy Austin" to the angry

"West Nashville Boogie." The sound quality overall tends a bit toward the ragged, but somehow with Earle, that's OK.

# Earth, Wind and Fire
Formed 1969—Chicago
**That's the Way of the World (1975)**
Columbia CK33280 (38:39)    **[B]**
Among the sleekest seventies funksters, Earth, Wind and Fire created some of the most uplifting and joyous pop music of the decade. Glorious arrangements, crescendos of sound anchored by a tight danceable beat produced truly irresistible musical moments: "That's the Way of the World" and "Shining Star" being the prime examples from this album. The words are empty, but the energy is contagious. The music is a compelling amalgam of jazz, gospel, R&B, and pure pop. The sound is clean, nicely detailed, and punchy, but still compressed.

# Joe Ely
b. 1947—Amarillo, Texas
The varied textures of the cultures which coexist in the Lone Star State have bred a kind of regional music rich in its sources; e.g., Tex-Mex, Western Swing, rockabilly, and honky tonk among them. The music that Ely plays reflects all those influences,with some R&B and rock & roll thrown in for good measure. He received his widest exposure when he opened for the Clash, both in England and the United States on their 1980 tour.

**Lord of the Highway (1987)**
Hightone Records HCD8008 (44:05)    **[B]**
This isn't Ely's best recording, but it is the first one available on disc. *Lord of the Highway* is a fair introduction to a fine artist about whom *Melody Maker*

said, "He has everything going for him except success." While the band touches upon the dark swamp power at the soul of rock & roll, Ely's vocal restraint keeps it all just this side of the edge. Still, there are some good moments, "Me and Billy the Kid" and "My Baby Thinks She's French" among them. The sound is first-rate: warm, open, and detailed with excellent separation.

## Dave Edmunds

b. April 15, 1947—Cardiff, Wales
Roots (retro) rock avatar who made mostly overlooked but genuinely joyous, pulsing rock & roll on his own and with Nick Lowe (Rockpile). Better known and ultimately more influential as a sought-after producer.

**Get It (1977)**
Swan Song 84482 (31:47)  **[A]**
Edmunds's energized, accelerated fifties rockabilly/Chuck Berry-influenced rock & roll reflects the simple directness of its roots. Exuberant and danceable, this is simply party music for the early punk era and it still rocks with authority. There's even some respectable country, "Worn Out Suits, Brand New Pockets," "Hey Good Lookin'," and ersatz doo-wop, "Where or When" and "Get It," but it's the burners, "Get Out of Denver," "JuJu Man," "I Knew the Bride," and Graham Parker's "Back to School Days" that lend *Get It* its good time/party down character. The purists will say that the originals did it better years before, but there's something about the garage nature of it all that allows the flame to be passed—diminished, perhaps. Edmunds's joy and sincerity shine through, as does his production sophistication, which has always served him well. The CD has nicely enhanced dynamics, which add a freshness to an enduring original.

## The English Beat

Formed 1978—Birmingham, England
A band of young and old, black and white, English and Jamaican players who rose out of the English late-seventies ska revival with a danceable beat, a proclivity for Motown covers, and a punk/political stance.

**What is Beat? (1983)**
IRS CD70040 (46:09)  **[B +]**
A compilation of some excellent late seventies/early eighties English ska-based pop music. A danceable, insistent beat propels bright melodies and lyrics that manifest the appropriate amount of political awareness. The Beat was one of the original, and most enduring, of the brief-lived two-tone movement that arose, in part, from England's substantial Jamaican population and the punk awareness of a socially stratified society. Good stuff. The sound varies with its divergent sources; overall, it's fairly clean, lightly dynamic, but primarily reflective of its mostly analog ancestry, hiss and all.

## Brian Eno
## (Brian Peter George St. John de Baptiste de la Salle Eno)

b. May 15, 1948—Woodbridge, England
**Thursday Afternoon (1985)**
EG EGCD64 (60:58)  **[B]**
Eno has employed his tape loops and other studio wizardry to create this composition specifically written for the uninterrupted one hour-plus playing time of the CD. Similar to his other "ambient" compositions; what at times feels like formless pleasantries of electro sound does exhibit a subtle, almost organic pattern as melodic repetitions ebb and flow through the contemplative

forms. The sound is all you can ask for from disc reproduction, even with its analog sources.

# Esquerita
# (Eskew Reeder, Jr.)
b. 1930?—Greenville, South Carolina
Little Richard on Esquerita: "He was one of the greatest pianists, and that's including Jerry Lee Lewis, Stevie Wonder, or anybody else I've heard. . . . He really taught me a lot."

### Esquerita (1958–1959)
Capitol Collectors Series CDP 7918712 (66:00)  [B]
Esquerita is an off-the-wall surprise for lovers of late-fifties rock/soul, particularly those with an ear for the esoteric. Little Richard, with whom he shares a wild falsetto (although Esquerita's lacks the total abandon that made Little Richard's unique), has written enthusiastically about Esquerita's piano technique, and validly so. Esquerita combines Jerry Lee Lewis's piano panic with Little Richard's vocal mayhem, lacking only their material and exposure; but for that, instead of being a footnote he might have made it to rock & roll fame and fortune. He certainly had the look down; the cover of this CD is worth the price of admission. This twenty-eight song collection is a comprehensive overview of some fine fifties party songs that still manage to raise the energy level. The sound is compressed, somewhat reedy and thin, but the enthusiasm and explosiveness of the material manage mostly to overcome the sonic shortcomings.

# Eurythmics
David Stewart, b. September 9, 1952—Scotland; Annie Lennox, b. December 25, 1954—Scotland
The high-style, gender-bender end of MTV rock & roll.

### Revenge (1986)
RCA PCD1-5847 (44:10)  [D]
More synthesized, programmed pop pap by a group whose appearance remains more interesting than its sounds. (Hooray for MTV!) England's *New Musical Express* said it all: ". . . the triumph of the mediocre art thief over the sources that arouse his envy more than they inspire him." Nonetheless, Dave Stewart's production is as predictably polished as ever, and Annie Lennox does her usual effective vocal job, but the material is far from exceptional, resulting in another bright, quickly forgettable pastiche. The CD sounds crisp, clean, and dynamic, although it's a bit overbright in the highs.

# The Everly Brothers
Don Everly, b. February 1, 1937—Brownie, Kentucky; Phil Everly, b. January 19, 1939, Chicago
The children of well-established country music artists Ike and Margaret Everly, Don and Phil brought country harmony, enhanced by their blood-relationship, to the formative years of rock & roll. It was their melodic contribution and truly gorgeous harmonies that distinguished and established this singing duo, who, after a long and sometimes troubled career, reformed in the 1980s with a renewed capacity to lend their special brand of singing to the world of rock & roll.

**Cadence Classics (Their 20 Greatest Hits) (1957–1960)**
Rhino RNCD5258 (45:57)   **[A]**
Aptly titled, this is classic fifties rock by the Brothers Everly, and that means that most of the selections included here will be familiar to any listener over the age of fifteen. Rhino, and its extraordinary digital producer, Bill Inglot, generally do a first-rate job with conversion from analog to digital material. This is no exception, providing bright, clean, and clear sound.

**(Highlights) The Reunion Concert (1983)**
Mercury 824 476-2 (68:36)   **[A]**
After growing up and performing together for over thirty years (their singing careers having begun when they were children), on July 14, 1973, in Hollywood, Phil literally smashed his guitar on stage in mid-show and walked out on what had been one of the most successful and enduring partnerships in rock music's history. On September 23, 1983, in London, Don and Phil Everly reunited on stage for the first time. This recording commemorates that occasion. As pure rock history, the event has sufficient stature to stand on its own, but, gloriously, it proved to be much more. The Everly's sound was undiminished; if anything, there was an added richness to their soaring harmonies, which may, in part, be the result of the digital sound used for this recording. Whatever the reasons, *The Reunion Concert* is a pure nostalgic delight. Given the fact that this was a live event, the sound is a blowaway. Clean, crisp, defined, and detailed, it's hard to fault. Sure the drums and bass are mixed too far forward and Don's guitar sound tends to overbrightness, but that's nitpicking. Two notes: (1) five songs included on the double LP album are deleted from the disc, leaving twenty; and (2) the accompanying liner text is very informative.

**The Everly Brothers (EB/84) (1984)**
Mercury 822 431-2 (33:22)   **[B]**
Not really a debut recording, but it is the Everlys' first studio release after a ten-year hiatus. It clearly establishes that the quality of their uniquely beautiful, influential harmonies remains undiminished. In addition to three fine new Don Everly compositions, the album, produced by Dave Edmunds, includes first-rate material from Paul McCartney ("On the Wings of a Nightingale"), Jeff Lynne ("The Story of Me"), and Bob Dylan ("Lay, Lady, Lay"). It also strongly reaffirms the duo's Kentucky country roots. Unfortunately, the weakest aspect of this fine album is the CD sound, which, while far from awful, isn't any addition to the proceedings. It suffers from a bad mix which overly emphasizes the bass/drum sound and too often drowns the vocals in the instrumentals (primarily on the up-tempo numbers) while displaying some muddiness, as well as an overall overbright sound.

**Born Yesterday (1985)**
Mercury 826 142-2 (45:03)   **[B + ]**
Another Dave Edmunds production, this 1985 release is studded with some beautiful country-tinged, current pop material impressively performed. Don Everly's title song again demonstrates his excellent composing abilities, but is, unfortuately, his only song included in this set. In addition to a soaring reading of the Sutherland Brothers, "Arms of Mary" (which sounds like it was written for the Everlys), they also cover Mark Knopfler's lovely "Why Worry" and Dylan's "Abandoned Love." But the real highlight is the bonus CD-only cut, the full-out Everly ballad magic applied to Sam Cooke's "You Send Me"—it does. The sound is a bit of a mixed bag: The ballad material is generally warm, nicely spacious and detailed, but the up-tempo numbers suffer from muddy mixes and too obvious compression.

# Donald Fagen
b. ca 1950—Passaic, New Jersey
**The Nightfly (1982)**
Warner Bros. 23696-2 (38:56)   **[D–]**
More pallid jazz rock sounds from half
of Steely Dan (the other being Walter
Becker). England's *Melody Maker*
summed it up, "Musically, lyrically,
spiritually, and conceptwise, this
album's a bummer." On the other
hand, the CD sound is first-rate.

# Marianne Faithfull
b. Circa 1947—London
**Broken English (1979)**
Island 90039-2 (37:44)   **[A]**
At age eighteen, in 1964, Marianne
Faithfull attained pop notoriety both for
her well-publicized liaisons with members of the Rolling Stones and for "As
Tears Go By," a Top Ten British hit that
year. After a decade and a half of living
in London's darker, more obscure fringes,
away from the music business, she
resurfaced with this recording. It is
almost the diametric opposite of the
stand she assumed in her first performances (sweet innocence)—her voice
had become a husky rasp; her message,
vitriolic, obscene, and ultimately cynical.
Yet, the overall effect is extremely strong
in its message and presentation. This is
a potent, though not necessarily pleasant musical statement, featuring a punk
attitude, a strong dance beat, and some

fine musical and production values. The
CD sound is very slightly compressed,
but clean and crisp with enough edge to
it to nicely accommodate the spirit of the
material.

**Strange Weather (1987)**
Island 7 90613-2 (38:15)   **[A–]**
A haunting excursion to the pre-World
War II sounds of Marlene Dietrich—it
conjures up a chanteuse, seamed-hosed
and high heeled amid a smoky blue
melancholy. Three of the cuts date back
more than half a century ("Penthouse
Serenade [When We're Alone]," 1932;
"Yesterdays," 1933; and "Boulevard of
Broken Dreams," 1934); while the
remainder include compositions by Tom
Waits, Bob Dylan, Leadbelly, and Doc
Pomus. The high (low) light has to be
Marianne's rerecording of her 1964 inge-
nue hit, "As Tears Go By;" if you don't
think that the times have changed, one
listen to this late eighties reading will
forever dispel that idea. The beautiful
Stones' playmate of twenty years ago
has grown into a tough, experienced
woman, now possessed of a deep burnished voice, which she employs to
effectively explore memories, times
past, and the general despair of life's and
love's losers. Impressive, but not for
sunny mornings or springtime afternoons. The sound is pretty decent, but is
plagued with hiss, as well as occasional
muddiness.

## Blazing Away (1990)
Island 842794-2 (72:41)  [A]
Rarely does a live recording equal studio product in sound or performance quality—many are released to satisfy record company contractual requirements. *Blazing Away* is an exception. The audience sounds are a distraction, but the intimacy of the interaction between Faithfull and that audience, combined with the wonderful acoustics of Brooklyn's St. Anne's Cathedral, add potency to the strong material. All her best-known songs, old and new, are covered in an extraordinary performance strongly enhanced by great backup musicians. For a live recording, the sound is damn near state-of-the-art.

# Bryan Ferry
b. September 26, 1945—Washington, England
The image may be rock's original lounge lizard, but, in reality, Ferry is one of the most intelligent, entertaining, and serious musicians the form produced in the seventies.

## These Foolish Things (1973)
E.G. 823 021-2 (43:58)  [A+]
One of the most fascinating records in the history of contemporary pop music. On it, Ferry re-invents a baker's dozen pop hits ranging from 1936 (the title selection) to a number of sixties goodies: "A Hard Rain's A-Gonna' Fall," "Piece Of My Heart," "It's My Party" (that's right, Leslie Gore's obnoxious 1963 No. 1 hit), "Sympathy for the Devil," "The Tracks of My Tears," and "You Won't See Me." At first contact it may sound like parody, but it's really a Master's thesis on the last fifty years of American pop music. It's wonderful! The CD's sound is a real enhancement; clear, clean, and well-defined; it occasionally sounds a bit

thin, but that's probably more intended than overlooked.

## Another Time Another Place (1974)
E.G. 813 654-2 (42:01)  [C–]
The cover shot is a killer. The contents are an extension of the concept behind *These Foolish Things* through another ten wide-ranging pop songs. It starts strong with a version of "The In Crowd" that justifies the cover, but it's pretty much downhill after that: repetitious in both concept and execution. This one didn't earn him his doctorate. The sound varies substantially from cut to cut, but is often harshly bright in the highs and muddy in the lows.

## The Bride Stripped Bare (1978)
E.G. 821 127-2 (42:02)  [B]
This is an admixture, four of the ten cuts are Ferry's compositions with the remainder ranging from R&B to traditional Irish music. The material is strong, and Bryan's singing is more honest and emotive than usual, but, the production misses more often than it succeeds, which is too bad because this one had the makings of something special. The sound has punch and dynamics that obviously are an improvement over the LP, but equally as obvious, it is still compressed throughout.

## Bryan Ferry/Roxy Music
## Street Life (20 Greatest Hits) (1972–1981)
Polystar/EG 829 362-2 (74:04)  [A–]
Perhaps Roxy Music's greatest virtue has been its accuracy as a mirror of its moment—unfortunately, the image reflected is not always real appealing, but, what the hell, that's life (at least life the way England's foremost seventies art rock band perceived it). What Bryan Ferry and Brian Eno created in the mid-to-late seventies was some of the sleekest, most fascinating music of a

fairly arid artistic period. Dave Marsh called their recording *Siren,* "A touchstone album of seventies art rock." Robert Christgau, on the other hand, observed of their debut release, *Roxy Music,* "This celebrates the kind of artifice that could come to seem as unhealthy as the sheen on a piece of rotten meat." (He liked the album.) This compilation covers both Ferry's and Roxy's recordings from the seventies through the early eighties, twenty selections all told. For the most part, the Ferry cuts are representative of his better solo work, but the seventies Roxy Music material, while good, omits some classics; e.g., "Serenade" and "The Thrill of It All," while leaning too heavily upon eighties material produced by the surviving three original members (Ferry, Phil Manzanera, and Andy Mackay). This most recent material has brought the band its greatest acceptance in both England and the U.S., but, while eminently listenable, it is romantic rock that lacks the inventiveness and stance that made earlier versions of this group so influential. The sound varies markedly, as must be expected; the eighties cuts, while exhibiting some compression, are still bright, dynamic, and clear with precise spatial separations. The early Roxy Music inclusions tend to be bright to the point of harshness.

**Boys & Girls (1985)**
Warner Bros./EG25082-2 (38:24)  **[B]**
Atmospheric, arty, and appealing, Ferry's very successful 1985 outing (which includes his hit, "Slave to Love") is an aural montage. His principle themes of self-involved melancholy and romance are expressed through multiple layers of synthesizers and multi-tracked vocals all in the service of mood rather than of message; and they work to perfection—ambient sounds for *distingué*

lovers. The sound quality is almost perfect, marred only by occasional hiss in some of the quieter sections; otherwise, it qualifies as one of the better sounding pop discs around.

**Bete Noire (1987)**
Reprise 25598-2 (43:46)  **[B–]**
Sophisticated eighties techno-soul for urban anguished souls in heat. Dance-driven, reggae-influenced with a dash of decadence. Slick, real slick music for high-tech elevators. Yet it is also very much the music of its cynical times. The sound is real slick too—dense, yet natural and open. Well recorded.

# Fine Young Cannibals
Formed 1985—England
**Fine Young Cannibals (1985)**
London 828004-2 (34:37)  **[F]**
Following the breakup of the English Beat, two of its original members (Andy Cox and David Steele) advertised for a vocalist and came up with a real winner in Roland Gift. Thus, Fine Young Cannibals and this, their 1985 debut, which is first-rate pop product that effectively displays Gift's prodigious singing style. The highlights are the tough "Johnny Come Home" and a rave-up version of the King's "Suspicious Minds." Sadly, the sound on this CD is awful: thin and distorted, with Gift's voice sounding like a trebly rasp. Stick with the LP.

# Roberta Flack
b. February 10, 1939—Asheville, North Carolina
**The Best Of (1972–1978)**
Atlantic 19317-2 (43:42)  **[B + ]**
Perhaps because she recorded for Atlantic in the late sixties to early seventies, or because she scored so strongly on her initial outing with "The First Time Ever I Saw Your Face," with resultant influence

on the black pop market, the expectations for Flack's career were extremely
high. They were never close to realized.
Trapped in the rut of her own success/
excess, she apparently lacked either the
insight or feeling necessary to capitalize
on her undeniable talents. Songs
included (some duets with Donny
Hathaway) are a fair snapshot of a sadly
lackluster career, but, the title notwithstanding, omitted are some of her better
efforts: "Hey That's No Way To Say Goodbye" and "Reverend Lee" among them.
The sound is all over the place, compressed, harshly bright, dynamic,
spacious, and frequently subject to audible hiss ("The First Time Ever I Saw Your
Face" being almost, if not completely,
ruined by it).

## The Flamin' Groovies
Formed 1965—San Francisco
Originally "The Chosen Few" and then
"Lost and Found," these Northern Cal-
ifornians have done nothing if not
persevere.

### Groovies' Greatest Grooves (1976–1979)
Sire 25948-2 (74:38)  [B–]
This compilation of the mid-to-late seventies purebred rock & roll by one of
San Francisco's better, but lesser-known,
bands, throbs with energy and rebellious excitement. Sure, the stance is
retro and the vocals are ragged, but if
you like it rough and simple, the
Groovies do their best to accommodate.
The sound varies, never reaching
decent levels—it's badly compressed
and there's plenty of tape hiss.

## Fleetwood Mac
Formed originally 1967—England; most recent
incarnation formed 1974—California
The remnants of a barely surviving sixties British blues band (Mick Fleetwood

and John McVie) find sunshine and success with the addition of California's
Lindsey Buckingham and Stevie Nicks,
along with Christine Perfect McVie, who
had joined the group in 1970. Buckingham is now gone and the women are
about to follow. In the past the redoubt-
able rhythm section has shown great
resiliency, but odds are their time is past.

### Bare Trees (1972)
Reprise 2278-2 (37:17)  [B–]
This band has gone through more cycles
than a modern microwave oven. Bare
Trees comes from what might loosely be
defined as their middle period (post-
Peter Green, pre-Lindsey Buckingham/
Stevie Nicks), when Christine Perfect
McVie's voice and keyboards brought a
more defined pop sensibility to their
work. It is also among the best releases
of this period, highlighted by the enduring "Sentimental Lady." The sound is
obviously compressed, somewhat
murky, and affected by hiss.

### Fleetwood Mac (1975)
Reprise 2281-2 (43:01)  [A–]
Timing is everything, and this may have
been one of the best timed releases in
the history of popular music—enor-
mously influential, if not overwhelmingly substantial. John Rockwell, writing
in Connoisseur Magazine, called it a
"rock landmark," one of "seven records
that define a musical age." Rockwell's
comments have the ring of truth; particularly when one considers how pervasive the Fleetwood Mac sound was in
the FM-oriented mid-seventies. And this
is material of enduring value—it exhibits
fine writing, singing, and guitar work, as
well as one of the best (and most experienced) bass/drum combos in the biz—
and don't let anybody kid you, the flash
may be out front, but the really great
rock bands are built from the bottom up.

The sound does justice to the material—spacious and beautifully detailed in the vocals and strings.

### Rumours (1977)
Warner Bros. 03010-2 (39:42)  **[A]**
*Fleetwood Mac* released in 1975, was a huge selling album for its time, with over four million copies sold. By the eighties, when Michael Jackson's *Thriller* sold over ten times that number, Fleetwood's earlier numbers seemed a bit diminished; but there's no accounting for taste or the power of the tube for that matter. *Rumours,* released in 1977, sold over two and a half times as many copies as *Fleetwood Mac* and while it may not have been two and a half times better, it was an improvement over its predecessor; all the virtues of which were preserved, but, this time out, enhanced by more inventive compositions. The sound is what keeps this recording from achieving a top rating. It provides some enhanced detailing, but is burdened with hiss and is generally compressed.

### Greatest Hits (1975–1978)
Warner Bros. 25801-2 (64:27)  **[B + ]**
For better or worse, the mid-seventies edition of Fleetwood Mac (with Lindsay Buckingham and Stevie Nicks) represents the purist distillation of the American pop/rock soundscape in the middle of a relatively boring decade. The band's driving, slick sound, cult of personality lyrics, sprinkled with Buckingham's ultrasophisticated pop licks, forged a hugely popular sound. The cool passion of Christine McVie combined with the ethereal quasimysticism of Nicks, in performance and writing, stamped an indelible image—a definite precursor to the cannibalism of rock & roll by mainstream markcting and MTV—their sophistication (as well as some claim to roots) meant their product

would be well-crafted. These sixteen selections cover most, but not all, of Fleetwood's favorites, as well as two newly recorded songs. Everyone is going to find something important missing, in my case it's the unforgivable absence of "Landslide" from *Fleetwood Mac,* the recording that established the band's mid-seventies primacy. I'm sure others will be equally distressed about the absence of "Second Hand News" from *Rumours,* or the general tilt away from Buckingham's creative contribution toward McVie and Nicks compositions. But the sound quality can't be faulted, so for the fan who doesn't want to acquire the individual albums, this greatest-hits collection should provide most of the desired nostalgia.

# The Flying Burrito Brothers
Formed 1968—Los Angeles
### The Gilded Palace of Sin (1969)
Edsel Records EDKC 191 (37:33)  **[B]**
After the Byrds released *Sweetheart of the Rodeo,* Gram Parsons and Chris Hillman joined Sneaky Pete Kleinow and Chris Ethridge and released *The Gilded Palace of Sin,* one of the classic country/rock recordings. After its release Parsons left the band, and with him went the magic that made this album special. But with Parsons's *pure* country lead vocals, this is a fine sampling of the brief period when country music was grafted to rock instrumentation to produce another facet in the gem that rock became in the experimental sixties. The sound is clear, with decent imaging, but it's also compressed and tends toward harshness.

# John Fogerty
b. May 28, 1945—Berkeley, California
The essence of Creedence Clearwater
Revival, which was America's greatest
rock singles band.

## Centerfield (1985)
Warner Bros. 25203-2 (35:37)   **[A–]**
In 1985, thirteen years after Creedence
disbanded, and ten years after Fogerty
released his last solo recording, John
came back with *Centerfield*, which
proved to be a breath of fresh air amid
the formula pop of the mid-eighties. This
album is a one-man studio effort—
Fogerty wrote, sang, and played it all,
which proved to be a somewhat insular
*tour de force*. Highlights are the title
track (which baseball should adopt
as its anthem), "The Old Man Down
the Road," "Rock & Roll Girls," and
his paean to the King, "Big Train From
Memphis." Perhaps there's too much bitterness between the lyrical lines, but the
sound is pure car radio rock & roll. The
CD sound is very good (particularly considering the overdubs that must have
been required), but reflects a certain
compressed sound stage.

## Eye of the Zombie (1986)
Warner Bros. 25449-2 (43:56)   **[A]**
From cover to contents, this is a scarify-
ing statement. *Eye of the Zombie* is the
second eighties release for Fogerty, who
had returned to the world of pop music
with full energy. This time out, he mastered the idiosyncrasies of the modern
recording studio and its stepchild, the
synthesizer. In addition, instead of doing
it all himself, he enlisted the aid of other
musicians, primarily on bass, drums,
and backup vocals. The whole outing
has a more open, current flavor than
*Centerfield*, and reflects a certain, almost
Old Testament vengeance in its seething

overview of a technological world frighteningly preoccupied with violence and
nihilism. It didn't enjoy the popular success of *Centerfield*, but may well prove
more enduring. The sound is great:
precise, detailed, and dynamic, with
wonderful openness and instrumental
separation.

# The Four Tops
Formed 1953—Detroit
**19 Greatest Hits (1964–1972)**
Motown MCD09042MD (58:46)   **[A–]**
The Temptations may have had more
flash, but the Four Tops had Levi Stubbs,
one of the great soul voices, and Holland-Dozier-Holland, the best of all the
fine Motown production teams. The
result was a justified string of hits, beginning with "Baby I Need Your Lovin'"
(8/15/64) and running through "I Can't
Help Myself" (5/15/65), to their all-time
classic, "Reach Out, I'll Be There"
(9/3/66). They're all included here—it's
sixties Motown soul-style music at its
best. You really don't need a whole lot
more. The sound is clearly superior to
the LPs', but that's easy given the quality
of Motown's LPs. There is some dynamic
enhancement and an increased instrumental clarity. Too often the lead vocals
are plagued by minor, but irritating, distortion.

# Frankie Goes to Hollywood
Formed 1984—England
**Welcome to the Pleasure Dome (1984)**
Island 7 90232-2 (70:11)   **[B]**
Frankie say: Trevor C. Horn (producer).
Of course, it's all hype. But Horn is nothing short of a production genius; a man
who really knows his way around a recording studio. Thus, hype or not, the
sound is spectacular. Substance, forget
it; this is disposable product for dispos-

able times. If you're looking for a demo disc to show off the wonders of CD sound, this all-digital recording would be a prime candidate: clean, tight, open, crystal clear, and occasionally sonically dazzling.

# Aretha Franklin
b. March 25, 1942—Memphis
The daughter of Detroit's well-known Baptist minister, Reverend C.L. Franklin, who was also known nationally as a gospel singer, Aretha defined female soul singing in the sixties; thus, her well-earned appellation, Lady Soul. Working with Jerry Wexler on the great R&B label of the era, Atlantic, Aretha has managed to score fifteen Top Ten hits since her recording career began in 1961. Her best work is infused with an energy and passion that sets it a cut above any of her peers.

### I Never Loved a Man the Way I Love You (1967)
Atlantic 8139-2 (32:33)   **[A + ]**
Aretha's Atlantic debut, with Jerry Wexler producing, is simply one of the great soul recordings of all time. In addition to the title cut, it includes "Respect," "Dr. Feelgood," "Do Right Woman—Do Right Man," a couple of Sam Cooke covers (the movin' "Good Times"), and a church-inspired reading of "A Change is Gonna Come." The other five tracks further define what soul is really all about. Her inspired vocals, fine piano, the Muscle Shoals rhythm section, and its struttin' horns all add up to a recording that is a classic by any standard. Unfortunately, as has too often been the case, Atlantic's digital remastering leaves a great deal to be desired—the tape hiss is constantly audible and annoying, and the compression inherent in the original analog recording plagues the CD. How-

ever, this is one of those cases where the message blows away the medium.

### Lady Soul (1968)
Atlantic 8176-2 (30:01)   **[A]**
Perhaps the most aptly named recording in R&B/soul history—she *is*! Aretha's recording career began on Columbia, but it was with her move to Atlantic in 1967, and her association with Jerry Wexler, that she not only found her format, soul music, she *defined* it. *Lady Soul* was her third album for Atlantic, and it contains a handful of classic Aretha: "Chain of Fools," "(You Make Me Feel Like) A Natural Woman," and "Since You've Been Gone (Sweet Baby);" it also has some weaker attempts at mainstream material ("People Get Ready" and "Groovin'"), but overall the ten cuts represent one of the greatest soul singers we have been privileged to hear, working at or near the peak of her considerable power. Soundwise, the recording's analog roots remain much too apparent, with very obvious hiss throughout, and noticeable compression.

### Aretha—Live at the Fillmore West (1971)
Mobile Fidelity Sound Lab MFCD 820 (48:12)   **[B]**
Aretha cooks, but something's wrong in the kitchen. In part, it's the backup band that never quite seems in sync, and that's a shame, because her vocals exude pure, soulful energy. The recording captures some strong performances: "Dr. Feelgood," "Bridge Over Troubled Water," "Eleanor Rigby," and a rare recorded duet with Ray Charles, an extended kickin' version of "Spirit in the Dark" (which, unfortunately, never meshes either), but, the remainder is just OK. The CD sound adds a bit to the punch of the material, but that sound is marred by hiss, mike hum, occasional dropout, and distortion. It's still the best

way to hear Lady Soul on one of her better nights; unless, of course, she happens to be in the neighborhood.

## Amazing Grace (1972)

Atlantic 2-906-2 (86:24—two discs)    **[A–]**
This is not a rock recording. It *is* a recording of a gospel church service featuring the glorious voice and spirit of Lady Soul returning to her home ground, with a little help from Rev. James Cleveland at the piano and conducting the Southern California Community Choir. It's a beautiful musical experience; Aretha was born to be Lady Soul. The sound is noticeably compressed, occasionally a bit edgy, distorted, and muddy, but the CD does add spatial clarity and some detail.

## 30 Greatest Hits (1967–1974)

Atlantic 81668-2 (99:31—two discs)    **[A +]**
The music on this double disc package defines female soul singing. The material spans the seven years between 1967 and 1974, Aretha's most productive years under the sympathetic aegis of producer Jerry Wexler. Soul music is the bastard child of the unholy union of gospel and the blues—Aretha *is* Lady Soul, and there ain't nobody near second place. The testament to all that is right here: "I Never Loved a Man," "Respect," "Baby I Love You," "Dr. Feelgood," "Chain of Fools," "Think," "Spirit in the Dark," "Don't Play That Song," "Bridge Over Troubled Water," "Spanish Harlem," and nineteen other gems make this an essential sacrament of sixties

sound. Obviously, the quality of that sound varies with the differing source material; the newer cuts sound generally better than the earlier ones. On the whole, compared to prior vinyl versions, the sound is a genuine, discernible improvement. The liner notes (reproduced from the album) are excellent and informative, unfortunately, a high-magnification microscope is required to read them.

## One Lord, One Faith, One Baptism (1987)

Arista AZCD-8497 (72:36)    **[B +]**
Home for Aretha is Detroit, and the heart of her home has always been the Baptist church, where her daddy, the Reverend C.L. Franklin, ministered to his huge flock. Over the years she has sung at the New Bethel Baptist Church on C.L. Franklin Blvd. in Detroit. *One Lord, One Faith, One Baptism* was conceived and produced by Aretha as a church service, with assistance from her sisters, Mavis Staples, Rev. Jasper Williams, and Joe Ligon of the Mighty Clouds of Joy. The inspired, inspiring gospel singing is interspersed with sermons and invocations by Aretha, Rev. Franklin, and Rev. Jesse Jackson. It's about the power and the glory as enunciated in word and song, and while it may not be everyone's cup of tea, her duet with Mavis Staples in "Oh Happy Day" is hair-raising. The acoustics of the church and the glory of the vocals are nicely captured in clear, resonant, dynamic sound.

# Peter Gabriel
b. May 13, 1950—England
**So (1986)**
Geffen 9 24088-2 (46:24)  **[A–]**
Eighties power pop by one of its most intelligent, creative, and sincere practitioners. Obviously the best thing to come out of Genesis, Gabriel is a man of great musical and production sophistication, who employs his architecturally structured sounds to exorcise personal demons. While there is an antiseptic, somewhat overworked coolness about it all, this is one of those rare recordings that has garnered both critical and popular acceptance. (The latter probably arising out of Gabriel's wondrous video dexterity as well as his musical creativity.) The sound is open, dynamic, detailed, clean, and well-separated, about all one could ask from a CD.

# Art Garfunkel
b. October 13, 1941—New York City
**Breakaway (1975)**
Columbia CK 33700 (37:06)  **[C + ]**
Garfunkel's voice is a beautiful instrument; a fact which has caused the singer to become so concerned with his sound that he ignores the meanings contained within the lyrics. Of course, this strips the recording of any real substance. The pure musicality of it is another matter. This is Richard Perry's glutinously rich production deployed with about as

much tastefulness as one is likely to hear—glistening mid-seventies pop product at its vacuous best. Overall the sound reflects the care employed in Perry's recording—it's beautifully spatial with lovely clarity and only minimal compression. On the negative side, there is occasional hiss audible in the quiet sections, and few overbright vocal moments, but these are minor complaints.

**Scissors Cut (1981)**
CBS/Sony 38 DP22 (31:46)  **[D]**
Lush early eighties pop/ballads which attempted to substitute production sheen for personal soul, resulting in aural cotton candy. The musicianship and studio perfectionism (thanks to Roy Hallee) are evident throughout, but neither the singer nor the songs justify the effort, Garfunkel's fifth solo release since the break-up of Simon and Garfunkel. The sound, given its analog origins, is very good: open and clean. However, some background noise is occasionally evident and the sound stage lacks depth and appropriate spaciousness.

**The Art Garfunkel Album (1973–1981)**
CBS CDCBC 10046 (50:06)  **[C–]**
If Garfunkel's post-Simon brand of pop pastry is your dish, this fourteen-selection compilation includes most of his better known material, e.g., "Breakaway," "A Heart in New York," "Wonder

ful World," "I Only Have Eyes for You," and "I Believe (When I Fall In Love It Will Be Forever)." As is always the case with Garfunkel, the sound production values are first-rate, resulting in a quality sounding CD, which does reflect the limitations of its analog origins.

# Marvin Gaye
b. April 2, 1939—Washington, D.C.
d. April 1, 1984

Gaye's history is almost archetypical black pop star—son of a preacher (in this case one of the most unusual to ever mount a pulpit), he began singing in church at three, then turned to doo-wop in the fifties; ultimately becoming a part of the Motown "family" in the fullest sense—he married Berry Gordy's sister, Anna. He also worked as a drummer and backup singer behind numerous Motown acts. Even though he enjoyed great success with the company during the sixties, it wasn't until he broke free from its production-line approach in 1971, with the classic "What's Going On," that his unique talents were given free rein. A deeply troubled, albeit fascinating man, he died from gunshot wounds administered by his father.

### What's Going On/Let's Get It On (1971/1973)
Tamla TCD 08013 TD (67:22)   [A + ]

You gotta buy this one, not only because it contains two of the seventies' best soul albums, but also to encourage Motown, and inform the rest of the industry that two-fer values in the disc market will be positively received. The two albums combined here are the highlights in the career of one of the seventies greatest soul singers. What's Going On, a singularly influential Motown recording, represents Gaye's autonomous recording ideas, executed with some distance from

the hit factory. It went a long way toward making black pop music meaningful to both its black and white audiences (but primarily the former). It helped bring a social consciousness to Motown, although the tenor of the times was also moving that way, and it delivers three great songs, "What's Going On," "Mercy, Mercy Me (The Ecology)," and "Inner City Blues (Make Me Wanna Holler)." In August, 1987, Rolling Stone ranked What's Going On tenth in its compilation of the "100 Best Albums of the Last 20 Years," saying of it: "Throw in hints of jazz . . . a pronounced gospel feeling, and you have a singular, exquisitely spiritual album." The "feel" of Let's Get It On, his next release, and the second album included on this disc, is not that far afield from What's Going On, but subjectwise, it's back to business, and, Gaye's end of the business was sex. This is music for two and whatever else feels good. The sound on both recordings is much brighter, cleaner, and more dynamic than on the LPs. What's Going On sounds better, if a bit compressed and occasionally overbright. Let's Get It On is generally overbright to the point of occasional edginess, but is more dynamic. Both suffer from too apparent hiss.

### Marvin Gaye and His Women—21 Classic Duets (1964–1974)
Tamla TCD 06153 TD (57:45)   [B]

The duet was a staple of Gaye's recorded repertoire, and over the years he recorded with four talented women, Diana Ross, Mary Wells, Kim Weston, and Tammi Terrell (actually five—see below). The highlights of those joint efforts are what make up this CD. Again, the disc, the sound of which varies from selection to selection, is a marked improvement over the inferior LP mixes and surfaces, yet, it is still far from what it might be. Specifically, the generally compressed sound stage on almost all selections and frequent harshness in the female vocals undermine what is conceptually a fine collection.

**15 Greatest Hits (1964–1977)**
Tamla TCD 06069 TD (58:51)  **[B +]**
Most of the major hits are included, providing a representative overview of this important artist's career. As expected, the sound quality varies markedly from cut to cut, and none of it is really outstanding. But considering the fact that Motown LPs often sounded as if they were pressed on used auto seat vinyl, just getting clean renditions is a major plus.

**Live at the London Palladium (1977)**
Tamla TCD 06191 TD (72:25)  **[C +]**
This is Motown showbiz captured in concert—long medleys featuring abbreviated glimpses of classic material and a lack of cohesiveness between the singer and the band. But Marvin was communicating that night, and the interaction between artist and audience creates genuine excitement every now and again, particularly on "Trouble Man." The sound is boxy and compressed. It's also overbright on some vocals, but never truly harsh. Still an improvement over the LP.

**Midnight Love (1982)**
Columbia CK38197 (39:40)  **[A]**
Like most pop stars (black, white, male, and female), sex appeal and love songs were Gaye's stock and trade, but Marvin got more explicit about it than most. This, the last release before Gaye's tragic death, marked a resurgence in a career that had been in disarray for a period of almost ten years, and brought Gaye back to the forefront with its smash hit, "Sexual Healing." While not the equal of his classic *What's Going On, Midnight Love*

has to rank with his best recorded work, and that automatically places it with the best soul releases of the era. The apparently contradictory themes of sexual and spiritual redemption are the cornerstones of this work and the artist blends them with seamless compatibility. It may not be a totally fitting epitaph, but it comes damn close. The sound is crisp, clean, detailed, and clear, with a slight tendency to excessive brightness in the highs.

**The Marvin Gaye Collection (1961–1982)**
Motown M0TD46311 (254:39—four discs)
**[A +]**
For too many years Motown treated their artists and releases simply as product designed and marketed to sell as many units as possible. On a purely commercial level, this approach worked so well that it turned the company into the most financially successful black-owned enterprise in American history. But the core of it all was a serendipitous roster of some of the greatest pop artists to assemble under one banner. A credible argument can be made that the greatest single talent to emerge from Berry Gordy's hit factory was Marvin Gaye. One thing is certain: Gaye was the most difficult among a stable of superstars who sang and danced their way to fame under the aegis of a dominant, determined impresario. This multidisc boxed set is a fitting tribute to the late, great Marvin Gaye. Except for the awful cover art, everything about this package is a collector's dream come true: a brief but informative booklet written by Gaye's friend, biographer, and sometime collaborator, David Ritz, with recording dates and chart information, but, no real information on backup singers and musicians. *The Marvin Gaye Collection* is divided into categories: "20 Top 20s," "The Duets," "Rare, Live, and Unre-

leased," and "The Balladeer," among which are thirty-four previously unreleased tracks. "20 Top 20s" is a best-of category beginning with 1962's "Stubborn Kind of Fellow" and closing with 1982's Grammy Award-winning "Sexual Healing." In most cases they've gone back to the original single mixes, and the sound is simply sensational. "The Duets" covers all the hits with Mary Wells, Kim Weston, Tammi Terrell, the weaker Diana Ross collaborations (since they didn't like each other, their parts were separately recorded), and, previously unreleased, four with a woman named Oma Page. Again, the sound quality is the best possible for this material. "Rare, Live, and Unreleased" is the weakest section, but only because at his best, Gaye was simply nonpareil. It closes with Marvin's chilling version of the national anthem performed with the Marine Corps band at the 1983 NBA All-Star game. The final section, "Balladeer," presents some early Gaye, emulating Nat "King" Cole and the work of other fifties crooners. It displays a lack of depth and lyrical understanding, but closes with seven selections from the unreleased 1978 LP *Vulnerable,* which contained some of Gaye's finest ballad singing, with multitracked Gaye harmonies—this work was hidden much too long. For the serious Gaye or Motown fan, much of this material may be redundant, but the production/sound values and previously unreleased material on this set make this somewhat expensive package a worthwhile listening/learning investment.

# Bob Geldof
b. October 5, 1954—Dublin
Founding member (1975) of Boomtown Rats, an early, influential Irish punk rock band. Achieved fame for his work (with

Midge Ure) on Band Aid, mid-eighties rock-led effort to deal with African famine.

### The Vegetarians of Love (1990)
Atlantic 7 82041-2 (57:24)   **[B+]**
Easily Geldof's finest solo recording, *Vegetarians* has an immediately appealing, loose, easy quality. Vocally, it echoes Bob Dylan and Van Morrison. Geldof employs accordions, violins, penny whistles, the ukelele, and assorted kitchen utensils—and his Irish roots. Lyrically, it is the best writing he's done, there's no stridency here—these are mature musings, phrased with wit and insight. Soundwise, it won't knock your socks off, but *Vegetarians of Love* has a warmth consistent with the performance.

# Georgia Satellites
Formed mid-eighties—Georgia
### Georgia Satellites (1986)
Elektra 9 60496-2 (38:53)   **[C+]**
Throwback southern rock & roll by a scruffy band from a state that has become a major source of eighties musical talent. The Satellites sound a bit like the London rock scene in the sixties, before psychedelia came along. They don't break any new ground, but there's always a place for good ol' Saturday night kick-ass rock & roll. These guys know that, and deliver ten strong doses on this, their debut release, including the hit, "Keep Your Hands to Yourself." The sound is just OK, pretty muddy in the mix and very compressed, given its current vintage.

# Grateful Dead
Formed 1965—San Francisco
Either you are or you're not—I'm not. So "Dead Heads" be warned; you won't be

real pleased with the following reviews, but you may find the comments about the sound quality helpful.

### Workingman's Dead (1970)
Warner Bros. 1869-2 (35:55) **[B]**
Probably the musical highlight of the band's career—but it won't blind you. Yet, this one comes closest to capturing the ambience that has made the Grateful Dead more an extended family than musical formulators. The sound quality varies from cut to cut, in some cases providing nice open clarity and in others detailing, but compressed. Still, overall, a noticeable improvement over the LP.

### American Beauty (1970)
Warner Bros. 1893-2 (42:28) **[C]**
It features a couple of slightly above average compositions (including their trademark "Truckin'") and the ambience is fairly rustic/hippie. But the ideas are far from original and the "sound" is purveyed far better by other nonlegendary bands. The singing and musicianship remain vaguely communal. The sound is a marked improvement over prior reproductions, providing a clear, more spacious feel, and some dynamic enhancement—some hiss too.

### Europe '72 (1972)
Warner Bros. 2668-2 (110:10—two discs) **[B–]**
"There simply isn't much about this group that's impressive, except the devotion of its fans to a mythology created in Haight-Ashbury, and now sustained in junior high schools across America"—so said Dave Marsh in *The Rolling Stone Record Guide*. He really tells it like it is, and pretty it ain't. Perhaps the most disturbing thing about this second-rate musical dinosaur is that many of their fans truly believe they make first-rate music—which is the saddest testimony I can think of for what passes as rock

music today. With that out of the way, the Grateful Dead, more than any other major attraction, has sustained, in fact, *prospered* on the concert circuit; of all their live recordings, this one stacks up as well as any (and it *was* Pigpen's last album). It has its highlights—"Sugar Magnolia," "China Cat Sunflower," and "Hurts Me Too" come immediately to mind—let's see, that's three out of seventeen, and it's really just the guitar that I like on "Hurts Me Too." Because the songs are taken from four different venues as well as some studio filler, there are very discernable differences in sound quality from track to track. Some of it is very acceptable for its vintage and recording conditions, but too much is thin and boxy, with noticeable tape hiss.

### From the Mars Hotel (1974)
Mobile Fidelity Sound Lab MFCD 830 (37:38) **[C]**
The songs are a little better than those on some of the other seventies recordings, and the playing is not as viscous as has been frequently exhibited. But it's still the Dead with all their limitations and all their meanings. The sound is like that of a very clean LP, hiss and all.

### Shakedown Street (1978)
Arista ARCD 8228 (39:28) **[D]**
From about 1970 on, everything the band produced was severely lacking in musical value—they don't sing real well, and while they are competent musicians, that about describes it. The sound is clean, occasionally a little thin, spacious, and well-detailed, but overall, a little bright.

### In the Dark (1987)
Arista ARCD8452 (40:52) **[C +]**
For twenty-two years, these aging hippies from the Haight have nurtured an extended family which now has

achieved mythical stature. More icons than musicians, the Dead and their enduring audience represent an almost perfect commercial/ideological symbiosis. *In the Dark* is their first studio effort in years, and while they still can't sing or play that well, it just doesn't matter anymore; hell, it never did (Kharma is Kharma). This *is* their best recorded outing in years and "Black Muddy Water" is a good song. The sound is first-rate: dynamic, open, tight, clean, and clear.

# Al Green
b. March 13, 1946—Forrest City, Arkansas
A great soul singer in an era when the competition was still pretty fierce. Probably underappreciated because he wasn't associated with a "major" label. He recorded for Memphis-based Hi Records where his fine producer, Willie Mitchell, still insisted on using tube amps and twenty-two mikes on the drum kit to get the sound just right.

### Let's Stay Together/I'm Still in Love With You (1972)
Motown MCD 08018MD (68:37)   **[A]**
Green's surface vocal sheen can seem like a be-all, end-all because it's so smooth and easy. But, beneath that surface is man who knows and respects his roots. This is best illustrated by the more emotive vocals and rougher instrumentation reflected on *Let's Stay Together.* *I'm Still In Love With You* has an overall sound not unlike it's companion on this two-fer, only this time, the writing and production failed to quite measure up, although it still has its moments. Sound-wise, *Let's Stay Together* generally evidences a detailed open clarity which is very appealing, but on a few cuts (e.g., "Judy") the sound is compressed, muddy, and noisy. *I'm Still In Love With*

*You* suffers from more hiss (particularly on the otherwise wonderful title selection) and is generally a bit overbright. Still, the overall sound of the CD is a major improvement over that previously available.

### Call Me/Living For You (1973/1974)
Motown MCD 08040MD (73:24)   **[A]**
Another dynamite two-fer from Motown. *Call Me* is easily this fine artist's best release and *Living For You* isn't that far behind. From the original music written by Green's producer, Willie Mitchell, with words penned by Green and arrangements sparked by Al Jackson's tailored drumming, to covers of country classics (á la Ray Charles), Green insinuates himself into a lyric like a serpent, with some truly breathtaking results. This is premier slick seventies soul with some overtly religious overtones that foreshadowed Green's 1977 change from secular to religious material, corresponding with his ordination as a minister. Whatever his guise, the man can sing. The sound on both recordings is fine—clear, defined, and subtly dynamic, all with an easy flowing naturalness that nicely compliments the material. There is some slight hiss, but it's negligible.

### Greatest Hits (1975)
Motown MCD 0611MD (55:32)   **[B + ]**
Admittedly, Al worked in a narrow spectrum of material, but with his wondrous, elastic voice, he worked every nook and cranny of it. The fourteen cuts cover all of Green's seventies hits, and while their sonic sameness discourages repetition, they all contain a sinuous sensuality that is compelling and makes them ripe material for certain of life's moments. Willie Mitchell's production precision pays dividends on the CD reproduction—the drums, always a sound marvel

on his recordings, have a lifelike presence, and there is an open, smooth quality to the sound that is noticeably superior to the LP. Several tracks are marred by hiss, however.

**Love Ritual—Rare and Previously Unreleased (1968–1979)**
MCA MCAD42038 (50:20)   **[B + ]**
Before Green fled the travails of pop stardom and disco boredom, he was the quintessential black balladeer of the early seventies: heir apparent to Sam Cooke, but with a hit formula that was wearing thin. But that voice, with its silken gyrations, was without peer. MCA has unearthed some rare material for

this disc, so rare that its primary appeal will be to die-hard fans for whom Al's vocal acrobatics are a never-ending source of joy—or at least the best make-out sound around. Some of the tracks, "Love Ritual," "Strong As Death (Sweet As Love)," "Ride Sally Ride," and an extended mix of his classic "Beware" stand with his well-known album material; the remainder are sometimes interesting, but admittedly unfinished in concept and production. Green's production foil, bandleader/producer Willie Mitchell, always took great pains to achieve that rhythm section-oriented "Hi Records" sound, and MCA's digital remix adds enhanced clarity.

# Bill Haley and the Comets

This group formed about 1950, ultimately attained a stature in the pantheon of rock & roll not so much predicated on talent or musical contribution, but rather on the fortuitous fact that their work was chosen as the first rock movie soundtrack in a non-musical.

**Bill Haley and His Comets—From the Original Master Tapes**
MCA MCAD5539 Dida 202 (52:33)  **[B–]**
It may be cocktail rock, but since it was the soundtrack to *Blackboard Jungle* (one of the first "serious" movies about and aimed at fifties youth audiences), that's about all it took when the alternative was Mitch Miller. The CD is a sonic marvel—the stuff simply never sounded better.

# Jerry Harrison

b. February 21, 1949—Milwaukee
Originally the keyboard player with Jonathan Richman's Modern Lovers.

**Casual Gods (1988)**
Sire 25663-2 (55:37)  **[B]**
Harvard graduate, former Modern Lover and full-time keyboard and guitar player for the highly influential Talking Heads, this is Jerry Harrison's second solo album (his first being 1981's less successful *The Red and the Black*). The dense, swirling rhythmic underpinnings that keynote the Heads' sound are very much a part of the sound of *Casual Gods,* but somehow they sound darker and more ominous here. Harrison lacks David Byrne's prickly but compelling vocal affectations, but his efforts are more than serviceable. Given the generally lackluster state of late-eighties American popular music, *Casual Gods* stands above the majority of releases with its multilayered musical textures and Harrison's often troubled lyrical inventions. It's a quality effort from beginning to end, with the highlights being "Rev it Up" and "Man With a Gun." The CD's sound is a dramatic improvement over the LP—bright, punchy, and dynamic, with clarity and reasonable spaciousness. If you're a Talking Heads fan, *Casual Gods* will be a welcome addition to your collection; if you're not, it's a reasonable introduction to the current synthetic-based, dance-paced state of pop music, but it suffers from a lack of variety in the sound and feel of the material.

# The Havalinas

L.A.-based acoustic trio. Tim McConnell, the songwriting, singing, harmonica-playing guitarist, and Dennis "Smutty" Smith, bassist, both played with the Rockhats, a New Jersey punkabilly group from the late seventies and early eighties and Chalo Quintana who also played drums for the Cruzados. The name, "havalinas," means wild pigs.

## The Havalinas (1990)
Elektra 60938-2 (39:39)   [B]
Eleven well-written, passionately played songs dealing with a variety of topics, most of which are current—false prophets, both political and evangelical, ecology, greed, and feminism. John Mellencamp's fine producer, Don Gehman, handles their acoustic sound with his usual skill, which means this disc is a sonic treat. The music sounds real, as do the sentiments, and that's about all anyone can ask for.

# Jimi Hendrix
b. November 27, 1942—Seattle
d. September 18, 1970—London
The self-appointed voodoo child of rock & roll, his voice was nothing to write home about (he was once quoted as saying that it was only after hearing Dylan that he had the courage to sing), but his playing was something completely different. The amplified guitar is the instrumental trademark of the rock sound and Hendrix was its greatest master; possessed of incredible dexterity with the instrument, he was simply nonpareil. It has been twenty-some years since Jimi first laid down his fantastic left-handed licks on a right-handed guitar, and nobody has come close to approximating the magic that he could force out of those six metal strings. In his hands, the instrument contained all the sounds of the modern technological world, and Hendrix was able to call upon them at will. Blues-based, psychedelically colored, and jazz-tinged, Jimi's classic material is indigenous to the music's greatest era.

## Are You Experienced? (1967)
Reprise 6261-2 (41:07)   [A + ]
Dave Marsh called it "probably the most stunning debut album of all time." Peppered with honest-to-God classics like "Purple Haze," "I Don't Live Today," "Hey Joe," "Fire," and "Manic Depression," it exploded on the scene in what may have been music's greatest year, 1967, and was the equal of the best that came out. While Jimi's Telecaster was always the star of the show. The Experience, Noel Redding and Mitch Mitchell, were a cohesive unit whose strength was underpinning as well as magnifying the greatest rock guitar player that we've known. While Jimi "grew" in subsequent releases, this is probably his most accessible work and contains all the elements that remained central to his unique musical vision. The sound is a significant improvement over its vinyl counterpart.
  Remastered in 1988–89, *Are You Experienced?* now times in at 41:01, and while there is still some minor tape hiss and a slight tendency toward overbrightness in the vocals, it is a major sonic improvement.

## Radio One (1967)
Rykodisc RCD 20078 (59:37)   [B–]
Amidst the slew of posthumous reissues of Hendrix's recordings, *Radio One* is among the better efforts. This is due to strong performances and relatively clean mono sound. It's not an essential release, however, unless you're a Hendrix completist. His covers of "Day Tripper" (rumored to include John Lennon on backing vocals) and the King's "Hound Dog" make interesting additions to Hendrix's brief but prodigious legacy. While there are moments of stunning power among the seventeen selections, many of which are Hendrix standards, the overall effort lacks the

cohesiveness or sustaining power that established his unique niche. Taken from five different BBC radio broadcasts, the sound is a bit rough and sometimes edgy, as are many of the performances.

## Jimi Plays Monterey (1967)
Polydor 827990-2 (41:17)   [A+]
Woodstock and Altamont became sixties bywords, but the Monterey Pop Festival held in June of 1967 was clearly the musical event of the decade. In no small part this was because of Hendrix and the Experience, whose appearance marked a triumphant return from England. With this performance, Jimi introduced the American audience to another vocabulary for the rock guitar. On Sunday, June 18, in the clear coastal California night, Jimi's guitar burned—figuratively and literally. This historic moment has been captured with wonderful fidelity on the CD, particularly given its vintage and the fact that it is an outdoor concert recording.

## Axis: Bold as Love (1968)
Reprise 6281-2 (39:30)   [A–]
Clearly a transition between *Are You Experienced?* and *Electric Ladyland,* *Axis* contains some of Jimi's prime ballad material, "Little Wing" and "Castles Made of Sand." Given the fact that so many of Hendrix's sounds were built on feedback and distortion (all precisely planned and executed), the sound on this CD is excellent, close to crystal clear with more dynamics than are realistically expected from recordings of this era.
    Remastered in 1988–89, with a playing time of 39:33, resulting in an improvement over the sound of the original CD release.

## Electric Ladyland (1968)
Reprise 6307-2 (75:36—two discs)   [A+]
Jim was a space pilot, whose frontiers were sound. He bared his blues' soul from beneath psychedelic finery, but he was always true to that soul, cognizant of the dues paid and still due. Called genius, called wizard, he was a black light that burned like the sun at night. He was magic, mythic, and momentary. But the moment is partially captured here. Experience it. The sound easily surpasses the LP, but live cuts have noticeable mike hum; other minor glitches are apparent, although not extensive or intensive enough to affect a unique sonic statement.

## The Singles Album (1967–1971)
Polydor 827 369-2 (90:00—two discs)   [A]
The twenty-three selections represent the A and B sides of all this important artist's important singles. The fact that Jimi's musical canvas covered a wide variety of styles, each somehow expressing his otherworldly persona, is amply illustrated on this fine compilation. The sound, while sometimes muddy in the bass and drums, still crackles with the electricity of Hendrix's genius. Distortion is supposed to sound distorted, but some cuts (e.g., "Gloria") sound very muffled. The liner notes, while brief, are factual and informative.

## Kiss the Sky (1966–1969)
Polydor 823 704-2 (46:36)   [B+]
This eleven-selection compilation includes work from various sources (albums, singles, and concerts) which is representative of the best of his groundbreaking contribution to the music in the 1960s. The sound quality varies all over the place, but compared to the LP counterparts of this material, it's a substantial improvement.

### The Jimi Hendrix Experience Live at Winterland (1968)
Rykodisc RCD 200338 (71:45)   [B + ]
This CD-only concert release recorded October 10–12, 1968, contains the only live versions of some of Hendrix's stronger material: "Manic Depression," "Sunshine Of Your Love," "Spanish Castle Magic," and "Tax Free," probably making this a "must" recording for hardcore Hendrix fans. While Ryko has done an admirable job with the cleanness of the sound, it's still a concert recording (with mike hum, etc.) of a band for whom distortion was stock and trade. Given these limitations, it's a quality production right down to the packaging, which includes a reprint of the wonderful sixties psychedelic poster used by Bill Graham to promote the performances at which these recordings were made. This is a very good Hendrix concert release, but it lacks the fire that made *Live at Monterey* such an incendiary experience.

# Don Henley
b. July 22, 1947—Gilmer, Texas
Drummer, writer, and vocalist with the Eagles.

### The End of the Innocence (1989)
Geffen M2G 24217 (53:24)   [C–]
Like that of his former star vehicle, the Eagles, Henley's music elicits a certain love/hate response. It's so easy to be seduced by his smooth hooks, production, and evocative lyrics, that the cynicism and ultimate banality of his work only sneaks up after repeated listenings. The title track is an immensely appealing pop song; the rest of the recording has little to distinguish it. If it matters, the sound quality meets current standards.

# John Hiatt
b. 1952—Indianapolis
### Slug Line (1979)
MCA MCAD-31358 (39:01)   [B + ]
Hiatt's first two recordings, 1974's *Hangin' Around the Observatory* and 1975's *Overcoats*, both on Epic, were promising singer/songwriter efforts lacking focus and intensity. In 1979 he came back to MCA with *Slugline*, which has both. Fueled by R&B and reggae rhythms, sharp lyrics, and punk sensibility, Hiatt served notice that his was a talent to be reckoned with. While the mass audience has yet to really acknowledge this, his critics and his peers certainly have. He may be bitter, but he's bright, and the high-energy *Slug Line* captures his significant talent and his intentions. "You're My Love Interest" is the most interesting track, and "Washable Ink" has garnered some cover attention. The sound is merely adequate, being consistently compressed.

### Two Bit Monsters (1980)
MCA MCAD-31359 (35:45)   [B–]
Primitive, stripped-down production values and consistently urgent high-tempo rhythms earmark Hiatt's first release of the decade. His promise was becoming more widely recognized—*Time* covered him. While not without its moments ("Back to the War," the Costelloesque "Back to Normal," and "New Numbers" come immediately to mind), *Two Bit Monsters* doesn't measure up to 1979's *Slug Line*. And he really should have hired a better photographer (or improved his self-image). The hard-edged, punk, dirty sound quality was desired—and attained.

### Riding With the King (1983)

Geffen 4017-2 (42:21)   **[B]**

For a long time Hiatt's reputation was based on his tough rock/country/pop songwriting, replete with requisite hard edges and witty wordplay. It is the quality of that writing, plus some sympathetic production by Ron Nagel, Scott Mathews, and Nick Lowe that makes this one of his better early outings. Hiatt's rough and ready vocal style may be offputting, but he understands that its the words that count, and he gets those across. In addition to the title cut, "Death by Misadventure," "Don't Even Try," and "Lover's Will" are all strong examples of Hiatt's craft. The sound on the Nagel/Mathews productions is a bit more open and natural than that on the slightly compressed Lowe contributions, but all in all it's pretty good quality.

### Warming Up to the Ice Age (1985)

Geffen 24055 (38:58)   **[A–]**

Sure, it's a little slick and a little cynical, but the hooks and smart lines just keep flowing. My personal favorite: "Besides the buttons on our shirts, girl, what else did we leave undone?" Hiatt picks up some strong vocal support from guests Elvis Costello, Bobby King, Willie Greene, Jr., and Tracy Nelson. So while the stance may be problematic, the music is anything but. The sound is bright, clean, and appropriately punchy.

### Y'all Caught the Ones that Got Away (1979–1985)

Geffen 24247-2 (48:15)   **[A–]**

It wasn't until 1987's *Bring the Family* that Hiatt's artistry was fully commercially exposed. While his recording career dates from 1974's *Hangin' Around the Observatory* (which he now disowns, along with 1975's *Overcoats*), it really wasn't until *Bring The Family* that a broader listening public was exposed

to this artist, whose creativity had long been lauded in the critical press. His songs have been covered in both country (by Conway Twitty) and rock and pop (by Rick Nelson and Bonnie Raitt, among others). This compilation captures the best of Hiatt's cult career from 1979's *Slugline* through 1985's fine *Warming Up to the Ice Age*. While the writing on *Bring the Family* was extraordinary, it didn't eclipse the best of what Hiatt had proffered on the recordings that preceded it. What set *Bring the Family* apart was its production—a number of sympathetic, top-flight professionals (Jim Keltner, Nick Lowe, and Ry Cooder) providing uncluttered backing that showcased Hiatt's songs and performances in a direct and natural manner. It is the lack of similar production values that is the major detraction from this otherwise totally recommended disc. While seven different producers are represented in these thirteen selections, none really provides a sound that effectively showcases the material—at their best they're unobtrusive; at their worst, downright distracting. The intensity of Hiatt's country/punk renditions of "She Loves the Jerk," "When We Ran," "My Edge of the Razor," "Riding With the King," "She Said the Same Things to Me," and "The Crush," make this release a good way to get into the work of a man who knows how music can sound when intelligence, wit, and commitment come together. The CD's sound varies with the source recordings, in some cases a bit overbright, but overall, it isn't a problem.

### Bring the Family (1987)

A&M CD5158 (45:33)   **[A + ]**

Hiatt is one of the undiscovered gems of the current rock world. He writes some of the very best lyrics you're likely to hear ("Besides the buttons on our shirts, girl—what else did we leave undone?").

And if the buying public has missed that fact (and to date they have), his fellow musicians haven't. Hiatt songs have been covered by a number of rock artists. In addition to his compositional skills, he is a first-rate interpreter, with an elastic voice and an honest way with a lyric. Principally known for his work with Ry Cooder's touring band, he has now released eight albums, generally to critical acclaim and little else. On *Bring the Family* he is joined by Ry Cooder on guitar, Nick Lowe on bass, and Jim Keltner on drums for what is clearly his strongest album statement—and it's an absolute killer. From the clever lyrics and good-time upbeat sound of "Memphis in the Meantime" to the aching beauty of "Lipstick Sunset," the ten selections reflect the scope of an artist whose concerns and musical abilities encompass a large spectrum of rock & roll music. To top it all off, the fine musicianship displayed here is beautifully showcased in some of the best CD sound you are likely to hear.

### Slow Turning (1988)
A&M CD5206 (49:06)   **[B + ]**
*Bring the Family* was a hard act to follow. Originally the word was that Hiatt would reunite the heavies for the follow-up. It didn't happen, so Hiatt turned to the guys in his road band, and the results are comfortable. Hiatt writes some of the best rock/country lyrics around, which gives him a running start, and his expressive, blue-collar voice gets better each time out. There's bite and insight, as well as telling detail (even if the wordplay is, at times, a bit forced). No truly great songs, but there aren't any dogs, either. The sound is just OK; it has a slightly confined quality.

### Stolen Moments (1990)
A&M 75021-5310-2 (52:59)   **[B]**
After too many years, too much booze, and too little attention, Hiatt has found personal redemption and audience acceptance to go along with the critical acclaim and peer respect he earned years ago. A lyricist capable of some of the best turns of phrase in pop music, his previous release (*Slow Turning*) too often seemed more concerned with word play than with real feelings. *Stolen Moments*' heavily autobiographical content avoids the sharp verbal moments that spiced his earlier work, replacing them with fewer cutting images and more heartfelt sentiment: "With no education higher/Than the streets of my hometown/I went lookin' for a fire/Just to burn it all down." The result is a very good, but not great, recording, probably because it lacks any songs where the words, music, and performance are truly memorable. Glyn Johns's production nicely frames Hiatt's gruff vocals, but maintains a sameness that ultimately blurs the separation between the twelve selections. The analog recording is clear and warm, although a little more spaciousness would have helped.

# Hindu Love Gods
### Hindu Love Gods (1990)
Giant 24406-2 (37:09)   **[C]**
This is one of those off-the-wall entries that pops up out of nowhere that will either turn you completely on or off. *Hindu Love Gods* combines three-fourths of R.E.M. (Bill Berry, Peter Buck, and Mike Mills) backing Warren Zevon on an impromptu live studio session that took place in 1987. The material leans toward bashing blues, and includes songs from Robert Johnson, Woody Guthrie, Prince ("Raspberry Beret"), and the Georgia Satellites ("Bat-

tleship Chains"). Instrumentally, the Love Gods manage to generate a fair amount of heat. It's Zevon's vocals that are problematic—he lacks the looseness of a true blues singer, so instead of igniting the fire, he too often seems to be confining it. It does sound like these guys had a rough good time paying homage to the blues foundations of much of rock & roll, but there isn't much here to encourage repeated listenings. The sound quality reflects the hasty nature of the enterprise, lacking spacial definition and clarity among the individual players.

# The Hollies
Formed 1962—Manchester, England
This sweet singing quintet represented England's most successful sixties singles band, after, of course, the Beatles.

### The Hollies Greatest Hits (1964–1972)
Epic CK 32061 (37:03)   **[B]**
Pop pastry elegantly served, but pastry nonetheless. This accurately titled twelve-selection disc should induce a little honest nostalgia for those who experienced these well-crafted confections firsthand in the mid- to late-1960s, and, whether one was there or not, "Long Cool Woman (in a Black Dress)" still sounds great. The sound quality varies among the cuts; overall it is more clear and spacious than expected, but the upper mid-range on the vocals tends toward an edgy harshness too often.

### Anthology: From the Original Master Tapes (1967–1975)
Epic EGK 46161 (68:48)   **[B]**
If you're a fan, this compilation is a must—the clever, bright pop production and slick harmonies never *sounded* better. The remastering from the original tapes gives the music depth, detail, and

clarity not heard before. Because this collection is limited to their Epic recordings, some of the sixties Imperial singles, "Bus Stop" and "Stop Stop Stop" are missing, but "Carrie Anne," "Long Cool Woman (in a Black Dress)" and "He Ain't Heavy, He's My Brother" are among the twenty included. The fact is there ain't much of real substance here, except, of course, some glorious pop memories.

# Buddy Holly (Charles Hardin Holley)
b. September 7, 1936—Lubbock, Texas
d. February 3, 1959—Clear Lake, Iowa
("the day the music died")
A major, often underrated influence, whose music and visions (pioneering use of the Stratocaster guitar and importance of record production) have sustained with massive influence far beyond their limited original exposure and his sadly brief recording/performing career.

### For the Last Time Anywhere (1956–1958)
MCA MCAD-3D48 (21:22)   **[D + ]**
The material was originally released on LP in 1983 as "Lost Masters." There really aren't any true revelations on this brief package, and the sound, while generally clear, is largely harsh and edgy. "Bo Diddley" sounds like it came from a used edition of a bad 78. This is an interesting, bargain price CD for the compulsive fan only, although "That's My Desire" is a lot of fun.

### From the Original Master Tapes (1957–1959)
MCA MCAD5540 DIDX-203 (44:00)   **[A + ]**
The musical reasons for Holly's somewhat subtle but pervasive influence are all here, with the original energy main-

tained intact. Due to the brevity of his career, this single disc can truly provide a comprehensive overview of his major contributions to rock's formative years. Sound-wise, this may represent the zenith of digital enhancement of older recordings. Clear, spacious, complete sound that is nothing short of phenomenal.

# The Holmes Brothers
## In the Spirit (1990)
Rounder CD2056 (47:08)  **[B +]**
There is a resonant strain in American black music bounded on one side by the gospel sounds of the black church and on the other by the blues sounds of black experience. Imbued with pure, intense expressions of the extremes of human emotion, it has been the wellspring that has nourished much of the great pop/rock music that revolutionized world listening since it was popularized by Chuck Berry, Elvis Presley, and Little Richard in the mid-fifties. The Holmes Brothers (Wendall, Sherman, and Popsy Dixon) evoke that strain with sweat-drenched, soaring soul on each of the eleven selections on *In the Spirit*. Eschewing the drivel masquerading as today's pop, these veterans combine Saturday night and Sunday morning realities in joyous moments of pure feeling. As Peter Guralnick writes in his informative liner notes, "These are songs—standards and originals alike—that are being reinvented each time they are played and sung." There's not a bad track here, and among the highlights are "When Something is Wrong With My Baby," "Going Down Slow," "Baby, What You Want Me to Do," and the soaring spiritual, "None But the Righteous." The CD's sound is clear and

defined, with a natural warmth and grit befitting the material, however, it sometimes reveals a certain cramped, thin quality.

# The Honeydrippers
## The Honeydrippers Vol. 1
Esperanza 7 90220-2 (18:20)  **[C–]**
A negligible but nice idea that was probably more fun for the participants than for their audience, although, "Young Boy Blues" has a certain perverse appeal. The sound is clean and pretty open, but clearly evidences its analog roots.

# John Lee Hooker
b. August 22, 1917—Clarksdale, Mississippi
One of the truly seminal delta cum urban blues musicians, his alienated, laconic sensibility has proved a strong influence on the English/American blues-based facets of rock & roll.

### The Hook (1949–1962)
Chameleon Records D2-74794 (47:06)  **[A–]**
Hooker's urban blues and delta roots have influenced many who have followed—in both the contemporary blues scene and seminal rock & rollers. Within the limited range of his smoky, almost monotone but resonant voice, he conveys a weary but naked classic blues message of too much booze, many women, and not enough bread. This excellent compilation (sixteen cuts, five of which were previously unreleased) provides a first-rate overview of his early classic work—"Boogie Chillun," "Boom Boom," "Big Hips, Tight Skirt," and "Crawlin' Kingsnake" among them (sorry, no "Tupelo"), material originally released on the Vee Jay label dating back to the late forties. Given its age, the sound quality is impressive, audible hiss notwithstanding. The real thing gets

harder and harder to find; this *is* the real thing.

### The Healer (1989)
Chameleon Records D2 74808 (41:44)   **[A]**
Blues incantations from the mojo man whose power seems to grow with the passage of time—he's been mumbling his magic for sixty years. For *The Healer,* some of the many artists the Hook has influenced were invited by producer Roy Rogers to join—a sound idea in concept and execution. Bonnie Raitt's Grammy Award–winning duet on "I'm in the Mood" surpasses anything on her own Grammy Award–winning *Nick of Time,* and the collaborations with Los Lobos, Robert Cray, Santana, George Thorogood, and the remnants of Canned Heat are consistently first-rate. Yet it is his solo work, "Sally Mae," "Rockin' Chair," and "My Dream," that capture Hooker's special dreamy intensity. The sound quality is fine, a bit affected by Hooker's trademark reverb, but it's too late to stop now.

## Hothouse Flowers
Late-eighties Irish band
**Home, London (1990)**
London 828197-2 (56:03)   **[B + ]**
Rooted in their native Ireland, Hothouse Flowers makes moody, melodic music that swirls with energy and lingers like mist. Their often overly simple lyrics are preoccupied with time, the environment, lost love, and a belief in positive thought and action—fully mainstream, and packaged in an appealing acoustic/electric blend. What sets them apart are Fiachna O'Braanain's throbbing bass and Liam O'Maonlai's expressive lead vocals. Hothouse Flowers is a group with a rich instrumental texture and core energy that portend better things for the future, although *Home* is a very reputable outing. Soundwise, it's fine, with full, rich, warm dynamics and a big sound stage.

## Howlin' Wolf (Chester Arthur Burnett)
b. June 10, 1910—West Point, Mississippi
d. January 10, 1976—Hines, Illinois
Delta/urban blues singer/guitar/harmonica player whose voice had the power of an elemental force of nature—too raw and potent for comfort.

### The London Howlin' Wolf Sessions (1970)
Chess/MCA CHD 9297 (41:30)   **[B]**
It was a hell of a concept. Combine the living legend—one of the inspirations for the British blues renaissance—with some of the superstars whose careers he inspired, and the end result should be spectacular. On these sessions, Wolf works with Eric Clapton, Steve Winwood, Bill Wyman, Charlie Watts, Ringo Starr, and Klaus Voorman. The youngsters hold up their end just fine, particularly Clapton. Unfortunately, when these sessions went down, Wolf was sixty years old; the thing that keeps this from being extraordinary is the weakness of Wolf's vocal performance. The voice still has its ringing power, but the menacing, primal nature that reverberated through his earlier, sometimes scary work is gone. Yet, this remains the last of Wolf's recordings, and for that reason, this disc remains a priority for blues or British Invasion blues fans. The sound is adequate, but exhibits certain harshness, and too often sounds more boxy than open.

## Chris Isaak
b. Stockton, California
**Silvertone (1985)**
Warner Bros. 925 156-2 (36:42)   **[B]**
The retro-Presley label is truth in marketing, the guy also happens to play and sing real well. So *Silvertone's* atmospheric, dreamlike rockabilly has real appeal. There have been all kinds of big expectations for Isaak, but they have yet to become reality, probably because his musical vein is too narrow—what he does, he does well, it just slightly misses the mark, although its pleasures are palpable, notably "Dancin'." The sound on this CD is generally adequate, except for some troublesome vocal miking.

### Chris Isaak (1987)
Warner Bros. 25536-2 (36:19)   **[B + ]**
Swamp rock from Stockton, California. Isaak is one of the few genuinely exciting artists to emerge in the mostly arid eighties. He's a throwback to the sound and image that arose out of Memphis over thirty years ago. His smoky voice is sometimes reminiscent of Roy Orbison, his band is tight and true, and his songs echo with the history of the best of rock & roll. The sound is first-rate: warm, open, detailed, and dynamic, with heavy, though intended, echo.

### Heart Shaped World (1989)
Reprise 25837-2 (46:12)   **[B–]**
Isaak possesses the looks, the tools, and the attitude to hit it big—in live performance, he's a rockin' good time. His first release, *Silvertone*, had some fine, promising moments, but the much-awaited *Heart Shaped World* is a case of genuine talent stuck in an artistic dead end. With his voice and his sound he might do well recording covers—clearly the strongest track on *Heart Shaped World*, "Diddley Daddy," is the only cut among the eleven he didn't write. In lieu of stroger material, producer Eric Jacobsen has settled for augmented instrumentation—Hawaiian slack-string guitars, horns, and vocal overdubs—all of which are tasteful enough; perhaps that's the problem. Next time out, someone ought to strip away all of the deft packaging and let the man burn. Now *that* would be something to look forward to. The sound is warm, clear, and natural.

# The Jacksons

Formed 1967—Gary, Indiana

**Michael Jackson and the Jackson Five**
**18 Greatest Hits (1969–1981)**
Motown MCD06070MD (59:43)   **[B]**

The Jacksons have sold well over 100 million records as a group and Michael alone has sold about that many again. They've done it with well-produced, seamless, eminently forgettable pop music. This disc brings a complete overview of the group's most memorable moments, and while their roots may be funk, the results ain't. The sound quality of the disc is a real plus: clean, spacious, and clear.

# Joe Jackson

b. August 11, 1955—Burton-On-Trent, England

Another intellectual new waver who brings taste, chops, and respect for popular music to all that he does.

**Look Sharp! (1979)**
A&M CD-3187 (36:40)   **[B]**

New wave was punk for the masses and it never really caught on, but Jackson's brand, particularly as exemplified on *Look Sharp!* was about as popular as it got, with "Is She Really Going Out With Him?" included here, being a major hit for him. Joe Jackson is a calculated musician of talent but little exposed soul. Still, this recording is filled with bright, catchy music and is a prime example of the seventies new wave movement. The sound on the disc is very bright, at times to the point of harshness at high volume, and the sound stage is somewhat confined. Other than that, it is clear and clean.

**Joe Jackson's Jumpin' Jive (1981)**
A&M CD3271 (42:17)   **[C + ]**

If not in musical form, the jitter-bugging era that was the forties bears a certain kinship to the rock & roll spirit. Certainly Louis Jordan has been referenced by a few rock critics as a prehistoric progenitor of what has come to be known as rock & roll. On *Jumpin' Jive*, Joe Jackson has gathered together a big band that accurately mirrors the sound of the great swing jump bands of that bygone era. In the process, they cover several of Louis Jordan's classics. Like most of Jackson's work, *Jumpin' Jive* is a technical *tour de force*, the only missing ingredient is that spark that gave rise to the adage "it don't mean a thing if it ain't got that swing." The sound is clean and nicely separated, but it's thin and obviously compressed, resulting in a small stage—music confined by the speakers.

# Mick Jagger
# (Michael Philip Jagger)
b. July 26, 1943—Dantford, Kent, England
**Primitive Cool (1987)**
Columbia CK 40919 (49:24)  **[D–]**
Jagger's sometimes contrived but artful vocal mannerisms grow out of and play best against the live nastiness of his band. Lacking the Stones' magic, and particularly the catalytic impact of his Glimmer Twin, Keith Richards, he simply doesn't have it solo, and what's left ain't worth either the money or the time. The sound is adequate for its vintage—so what?

# Etta James
# (Jamesetta Hawkins)
b. January 25, 1938
Truly great R&B singer with hits in four decades, a victory over a long-term heroin habit, and the nickname "Miss Peaches." The real thing.

**Seven Year Itch (1988)**
Island 7 91018-2 (38:46)  **[A]**
Take an established, reinvigorated R&B veteran, turn the production over to another veteran, Barry Beckett, whose history dates back to the sixties, add a group of great backup players (including Steve Cropper and Jim Horn), and turn them loose on some lesser-known Stax/Volt burners, and you come up with one of the most satisfying soul sessions in years. James, whose career spans three decades, has been a favorite with black audiences for years but was not well-known among white listeners. Her inability to crossover prior to this release is attributed to her addictive life-style. Lord knows it hasn't been from lack of talent—Etta has one of the rough, dirty, sly, sexy voices that leaves no doubt about whats going on: a little lovin' and a lot of losin.' The production, song selection, and vocals all fit like the proverbial hand in glove, but when the smoke clears, it's Etta's party and knowing soul that makes this recording something to return to. Like everything else about *Seven Year Itch*, the sound quality is fine—real fine.

# Rick James
# (James Johnson)
b. February 1, 1952—Buffalo, New York
**Reflections (All the Greatest Hits)**
**(1978–1984)**
Gordy GCD06095 CD (57:22)  **[C]**
Producer, writer, and performer, James began his musical career in Canada fronting the Mynah Birds which included Neil Young and Bruce Palmer who both went on to Buffalo Springfield and beyond. But by the seventies, Rick was fronting his Stone City Band, extolling the virtues of partying in all respects, and laying down what he dubbed punk/funk—really just more slick, techno-black seventies sounds which did enjoy strong support from the black audience plus some crossover success. The eleven selections cover almost all of the group's seventies to early eighties successes. The sound varies some from cut to cut, generally in degree of clarity and dynamic enhancement, but overall, it's pretty clean and detailed, if not very spacious.

# Tommy James and the Shondells

Formed 1960—Niles, Michigan
**The Best of Tommy James and the Shondells (1966–1969)**
Roulette RCD42040 (33:10)   **[C]**
In case you thought the sixties were a garden of Beatles and Stones, consider this: in a recording career of less than four years (the band broke up in 1970), Tommy James and the Shondells produced seven million-seller singles, including "Crimson & Clover" which alone sold five-and-a-half-million copies. But two decades after the fact, there isn't much to recommend here. It's not that it's bad, it just isn't that good.

# Jan and Dean
# (Jan Berry)
b. April 3, 1941—Los Angeles
# (Dean Torrance)
b. March 10, 1940—Los Angeles
The Beach Boys had the biggest waves, but these guys were there when it all began.

**Greatest Hits (1959–1964)**
Hollywood Nites HNC0014 (37:00)   **[B–]**
Surf music was a narrow form that gave rock a fresh, scrubbed image in the late fifties/early sixties, which went a long way toward spreading the music to a mass audience. While Dick Dale is generally credited with being the founder of the instrumental surf sound, it was the Beach Boys and Jan and Dean who created the vocal overlay that moved it into the mainstream. Jan and Dean were neither great singers nor writers—many of their best singles were written by Brian Wilson—but they personified Southern California's surf/hot-rod culture. This sixteen-track compilation includes their first non-surf hit, "Baby Talk"; a cover of the Crows' doo-wop classic, "Gee"; and their four early sixties Top Ten hits "Surf City," "Drag City," "Dead Man's Curve," and "The Little Old Lady (From Pasadena)"—pretty light stuff. The Beach Boys did it so much better, but for the rock historian or surf nut, this is about the only CD collection of their work, which is acknowledged to be a minor classic of the form. As expected, sound quality varies markedly from track to track; some of it isn't bad, but generally, the vocal mix and reproduction are weak, buried, or overly manipulated, but they didn't have a lot to work with, either.

# The Jefferson Airplane

Formed 1965—San Francisco
This group took folk rock to the land of chemistry (San Francisco was Owsley Stanley's home territory) and then were the first (by virtue of a national recording contract with RCA) to export the message around the world. While their earliest efforts were a bit rustic, the original lineup was made up of quality musicians whose work between 1967 and 1969 attained a richness and complexity sometimes overlooked. After that they caved in to the weirdness. The Airplane became a Starship, unfortunately, in name only.

**Surrealistic Pillow (1967)**
RCA PCD13766 (34:55)   **[C–]**
What sounds so innocent today was revolutionary two decades ago. "White Rabbit," introduced here, became the first national anthem to the common drug experience. Musically, this is a fine release that is poorly served by the digital conversion. It sounds as if it was recorded at the end of a bowling alley. It

is recommended that you either save your LP or check out the Jefferson Airplane compilation recording, *2400 Fulton Street* (reviewed below) which covers the key selections on this otherwise fine release.

### Crown of Creation (1968)
Mobile Fidelity UDCD 523 (38:18)  **[C +]**
Psychedelics gone soft, *Crown of Creation* too vividly illustrates reputation outstripping creativity. Mobile Fidelity has developed a better sounding CD product with their gold ultradiscs and cultivated an audiophile audience for their product, but you have to wonder about the recordings upon which they choose to lavish this expertise, particularly this third rate echo of the dimming of the fabled San Francisco scene. Grace Slick provides an affecting reading of David Crosby's ode to multiparty intimacy, "Triad," Paul Kantner stakes his claim as drum major of the science fiction chemical marching band, and Marty Balin's "House at Pooneil's Corner" was probably his last meaningful contribution to the fragmenting band. The splendid ultradisc sound nicely showcases Jack Casady's creative bass as well as the general sonic weirdness that was expected of the territory.

### Volunteers (1969)
Mobile Fidelity UDCD540 (44:40)  **[B +]**
Political chemistry as exploding light and sound, *Volunteers* was the apex of this turbulent, transient, archetypical San Francisco band's career. A flowering of sixties visionary utopia from folk roots, the ten songs on *Volunteers* run the gamut from street revolution to moments of true mystery to the arcanely incomprehensible—all the attributes that elevated Grace Slick, Marty Balin, Paul Kantner, and company to legendary status. Several decades' lapse reveals the album's relevance more as an icon of the sixties rather than for any enduring qualities of the music itself. But for many it was the best of times in the most magical of places. Mobile Fidelity's gold ultradisc opens up the sound when compared with the vinyl, but still suffers from tape hiss and a general murkiness in the mix that dates it. The package includes a reproduction of the peanut butter and jelly liner graphics that were a part of the original album presentation.

### 2400 Fulton Street (The CD Collection) (1967–1971)
RCA 5724-2-RP1&P2 (133:13—two discs)  **[B +]**
For all intents and purposes it's all here (maybe even a little more than you really want)—the major components of the psychedelic sound of San Francisco in the sixties. The sound quality obviously varies, but overall it's a bit muffled and boxy, though still better and much cleaner than the LP versions. During the Airplane's period of strongest creativity (1966–70), they moved from folk rock through psychedelic acid weirdness to political activism and science fiction babble. Their dense, often demented sound still conjures up the Summer of Love more potently than any other band for most Americans. This is what the "heads" in the beads, sandals, and tie-dyes grooved on two decades past, and while it sounds a bit dated, it still sounds good.

# Elton John (Reginald Kenneth Dwight)
b. March 25, 1947—Pinner, England
Heralded at the beginning of the seventies as the next wave of the British Rock invasion, John, while wildly successful, proved to be a bit of a Trojan Horse

spearheading the pop ethic takeover of seventies rock. With his excessively camp stage extravaganzas, gospel-based piano, and Bernie Taupin's sophomoric, but sometimes effective lyrics over his hook-filled melodies, John scored fifteen Top Ten hits (five went to No. 1) during the decade of the seventies.

### Elton John (1970)
DJM CD8 (39:31)   [B–]
The first of Elton's 1970 releases (the other being *Tumbleweed Connection*), it introduced American audiences to his chunky piano, enthusiastic vocals, and the juxtaposition of yearning ballads with all-out production rockers. It was obviously a formula whose time had come. The musicianship is polished and tight; the Gus Dudgeon production precise and complementary, all of which resulted in a massively appealing pop product. John's recorded work has always been notable for its sound quality, and given the vintage of this material, it doesn't sound that bad on disc. That doesn't mean that compression and occasional harshness aren't evident; they are, but detailing and dynamics are also improved.

### Tumbleweed Connection (1970)
MCA MCAD37199 (46:57)   [B]
The songs have more structure and the production, again by Gus Dudgeon, shows a lighter more varied touch. The fictional Western slant to the lyrics and packaging (not uncommon to rock at the time, but from England with specs?) is not an enhancement. That conceit appeared to have come primarily from lyricist Bernie Taupin, but Elton was also obviously a willing participant. Weak as the early selections of the recording may be, the final two bring the proceedings to a strong conclusion. A ballad ("Talking Old Soldiers") and a rocker ("Burn

Down The Mission") rank among the duo's best efforts. The sound isn't that clean or dynamically enhanced, and it does suffer from some hiss, but, it has nice spatial attributes and greatly enhanced vocal clarity.

### Madman Across the Water (1971)
DJN CD5 (45:19)   [C+]
The opening cut, "Tiny Dancer," for all its lyrical foolishness, is still one of the most compelling cuts John has ever recorded. Unfortunately, it's pretty much downhill from there, although "Levon" isn't that bad. While there still is some evident compression (the recording was released in 1971), the overall sound quality of the disc is impressive.

### Madman Across the Water (1971)
Mobile Fidelity Sound Lab UCD 516 (45:21)   [A–]
This, one of the pop maestro's early efforts, has a darker feel than most of his work and is susceptible to the claim that the cobbled lyrics keep it from achieving real stature. Yet it still sounds good, particularly "Tiny Dancer" and "Levon." This gold CD captures every nuance of the album's original fine production values.

### Honky Chateau (1972)
MCA MCAD 16111 (45:04)   [B+]
More slickly produced music for the masses, but this time out the whole affair is more crisp and up-tempo; less impeded with obvious filler. In addition, the piano playing and overall tone of the work take on the old English music hall sound (á la *Sgt. Pepper*) and because it's all so obviously showbiz, it works. There is nothing momentous or even very meaningful here—but when some good time, silly pop music will fill the bill, look no further (and it does have the absurdly wonderful "Rocket Man"). The

production is impressive in its crisp, spatial definition, but suffers from a slight overbrightness.

### Don't Shoot Me, I'm Only the Piano Player (1973)
DJM CD10 (42:54)   [C−]
The songs; e.g., "Daniel" and "Crocodile Rock" are every bit as good as those on *Honky Chateau* as far as the writing goes. The performance, unfortunately, is a different matter. For some reason, on this album, Elton is just going through the motions (a fact which is highlighted by the clarity the CD imposes on the vocals). Now, some would say that is all he ever does, but sometimes, he did it with more feeling than others, and this ain't one of those times. The production often sounds forced. The sound is nothing to write home about, its sharp clarity being more than offset by brightness which is often excessive to the point of harshness. They ought to try this one all over again, from scratch. The material deserves it.

### Goodbye Yellow Brick Road (1973)
MCA MCAD6894-2 (76:21—two discs)   [A−]
Edited down to one disc, this would easily be John's recorded pinnacle. *Goodbye Yellow Brick Road* somehow managed to blend Taupin's lyrical fantasy and Elton's grandiose musical melanges into something greater than the sum of their parts—the romantic spirit of seventies pop captured in all its excessive, multicolored glory. The title song, the opening instrumental, "Funeral for a Friend," followed by the vocal "Love Lies Bleeding," and "Candle in the Wind" are the highlights, with the remainder made up of some strong material, as well as some pretty forgettable exercises. The sound is a great enhancement over the LP, clear, detailed and dynamic with nice spatial quality,

albeit with a slight tendency to overbrightness.

### Goodbye Yellow Brick Road (1973)
Mobile Fidelity Sound Labs UDCD 526
[76:21]   [A]
This expensive (about $40) single CD gets the whole double LP (MCA double CD reviewed above) on one gold disc, and it is. The notably improved sound and convenience justify the heady price for one of Elton's true pop classics.

### to be continued (1965–1990)
MCA MCAD4-10110 (301:58—four discs)   [A]
The much-hyped seventies savior of rock & roll (at least that's the way the rock press described him in 1970) has been recording for a quarter of a century. His up-and-down career may have failed to provide the resurrection, but he returned music to juke box-oriented pop that shared a common sensibilty with fifties and early-sixties Top Forty, ultimately qualifying him as the popmeister of the rock generation. And Elton John has been responsible for some glorious pop music which has become an integral part of the soundtrack of a lot of lives—he's had more than twenty Top Ten hits and numerous other charted successes. That he's done this while relying principally on the adrift, insipid lyrics of Bernie Taupin may be the truest testimony to the magnitude of his talent. His infectious energy, consummate showmanship, and hook-laden music have legitimately elevated him to pop superstar. Among the revelations of this excellent set is the extraordinary quality of his craftmanship—Gus Dudgeon's production has long been acknowledged as a pop benchmark and Paul Buckmaster's string arrangements set a standard by which all others should be measured. The sixty-seven included songs fairly cover John's highlights, although hard-

core fans will miss "Talking Old Soldiers," "Burn Down The Mission," and "Blues For Baby and Me," to name just a few. But then you get some rarities, including a better version of "Your Song," and a drivin' duet with John Lennon on "I Saw Her Standing There," recorded live at Madison Square Garden in 1974, plus four new tracks recorded in 1990, produced by Don Was specifically for this boxed set. All of this is presented in a package that includes a thirty-seven-page booklet with an informative Elton John/Bernie Taupin interview, detailed personnel and recording information, and hot graphics. As is the case with most multidisc releases, *to be continued* has more than its share of dross, but the overall quality here is higher than most, even acknowledging its sometimes overblown, formulaic qualities. Soundwise, it's a pure joy.

# Robert Johnson
b. May 8, 1911—Hazelhurst, Mississippi
d. August 16, 1938—Three Forks, Mississippi
Part shaman, part totem—Johnson was the spiritual inspiration to many whose road to rock & roll began with the blues.

### The Complete Recordings (1936–1937)
Columbia C2K 46222 (106:54—two discs)
[A + ]
Robert Palmer summarized Johnson's recording history with the following: "Robert Johnson recorded twenty-nine songs in 1936 and 1937. . .and then vanished into the murky Mississippi Delta world of juke joints, voodoo lore, violence, and perpetually indentured black sharecroppers who worked in the cotton fields all week and were serious about Saturday nights." Those twenty-nine songs, along with a dozen alternate takes, make up this historic blues package. Those songs are the basis for a leg-

end (and a myth) that ignited much of the blues-based rock & roll that fueled the sixties British Invasion. The extraordinary booklet accompanying this boxed set includes comments from two rock giants whose inspiration can be traced to these recordings, Keith Richards ("I've never heard anybody before or since use the form and bend it quite so much to make it work for himself . . . he was like a comet or a meteor that comes along and, *boom,* suddenly he raised the ante, suddenly you had to aim just that much higher") and Eric Clapton ("I have never found anything more deeply soulful than Robert Johnson. His music remains the most powerful cry that I think you can find in the human voice, really"). Stephen C. LaVere provides a biography that puts the man and his music in its context. Yet all of this fine packaging is merely a wrapper for the music itself—honest, almost unbearably intense, and compelling—music that probes the basic impulses of the human soul, expressed with anguish, joy, carnal power, and an aloneness that echoes in the darkest recesses of the spirit. Johnson was not the first great American blues artist, nor, obviously, the last, though an argument can be made that his mastery of the guitar has never been equaled. But he was the most primal, and perhaps the most influential. Ultimately his music eludes description—it must be experienced. This compilation provides the best means available for that experience. Its often strangled, tinny sound is markedly better than any previous Johnson releases. For all of that, it is a treasure.

# Rickie Lee Jones

b. November 8, 1954—Chicago
**Rickie Lee Jones (1979)**
Warner Bros. 3296-2 (42:16)   **[A]**
One of the seventies' better debut
releases, featuring the hit "Chuck E.'s in
Love" and including a number of
Rickie's quirky, jazz-tinged sagas of
losers on the loose: "Easy Money," "Last
Chance Texaco," and "Coolsville"
among them. It all sounds a bit like John
Steinbeck writing for a hip Broadway
fifties musical. The arrangements are
spare and tasty, focusing on Ms. Jones's
throaty, expressive interpretations of her
offbeat but compelling material. The
sound has an intensely intimate quality
about it, with effective enhancement of
the subtle vocal shadings augmented by
nice instrumental spacing and clarity. It's
not quite as sonically clean as it might
be and at times feels a little compressed,
while at others a little vocally harsh, but,
these are minor complaints.

**Flying Cowboys (1989)**
Geffen 24246-2 (55:58)   **[A]**
1989 was the decade's best year for new
music and one of the reasons why was
this fine release from Rickie Lee Jones.
Coming ten years after her classic debut,
it is clearly her best work since that auspicious introduction. While I am not a
great fan of the producer, Walter Becker,
it is clear that his production is a significant element in *Flying Cowboys'* overall
high quality. Jones's urban/jazz sensibility is nicely reflected in his
production work, and its cool overall
quality emphasizes the warmth of her
expressive vocals. The somewhat
morose denseness of her mid-eighties,
infrequent releases is supplanted in
*Flying Cowboys* with a more upbeat
attitude and greater diversity of emotional content. There's not a weak cut

among the eleven, all of which are
Jones's originals, except for "Don't Let
the Sun Catch You Crying," a hit in 1964
for Gerry and the Pacemakers. There's a
radiance and openness to this material,
and Jones's voicings are extremely compelling. Pop/rock music for thinking
adults, Rickie Lee Jones reaffirms the
fact that she is one of the most interesting talents to have come into the mainstream. The sound on this all-digital disc
is exemplary, with an airy spaciousness
and vocal warmth.

# Janis Joplin

b. January 19, 1943—Port Arthur, Texas
d. October 4, 1970—Hollywood
During the halcyon days of the mid/late
sixties in San Francisco, Janis stood as
the queen of that area's acknowledged
and thriving rock community. A truly
talented blues shouter, she came to per-
sonify the female rock star of the era,
but her life was probably best summed
up by her own quote: "On stage I make
love to 25,000 people, then go home
alone."

**Pearl (1971)**
Columbia CK 30322 (34:20)   **[B + ]**
Clearly Janis's best recorded effort after
her original Columbia release, *Cheap
Thrills,* done with Big Brother and the
Holding Company. Sadly, the stature of
Joplin's myth is not matched by either
the quality or the quantity of her recorded output. Not even this relatively
brief outing captures the legend at her
best. But on "Me And Bobby McGee,"
"Mercedes Benz," and "A Woman Left
Lonely" she manages to convey the
nakedly honest intensity that, at its best,
made her work incendiary. Even though
the Full Tilt Boogie Band provides first-
rate instrumental assistance, too often,
the other cuts seem either slightly out

of sync or overly marred by excessive vocal hystrionics. The sound isn't great, marred by a general muddiness, consistent hiss, and occasional excessively bright upper mid-range.

**Janis Joplin's Greatest Hits (1968–1972)**
Columbia CK 32168 (41:52)   **[A]**
It's a good career overview, including both live and studio work with all three of her major backup aggregations, Big Brother and the Holding Company, Kozmic Blues Band, and the Full Tilt Boogie Band, represented. Unfortu-

nately, nothing on record really captured this blues urchin's awesome musical moments. For that you might want to check the Monterey Pop Video to see and hear Janis give one of the most electrifying performances in the recorded history of rock & roll, as witnessed and attested to by Mama Cass Elliot, (the rest of the film is prime as well). The disc's sound is, as expected, all over the place; much of it sounding pretty dated. But sonic imperfections duly noted, it is still superior to its vinyl counterparts.

# B.B. King
# (Riley B. King)
b. September 16, 1925—Indianola, Mississippi
**Live at the Regal (1971)**
MCA MCAD 31106 (34:57)  **[A]**
By now B.B. King is ubiquitous to the blues, a form that holds a devoted audience, many of whom get their musical sustenance in noisy, smoky dives where the dance floor's too small and the music's too much. The interplay between artist and audience is almost as integral to urban blues as the congregation is to gospel. King knows this, and has recorded a number of live outings that tap into the electricity of that interplay. A natural, intelligent showman, he has the capacity to electrify with both his heartfelt vocals and his stinging guitar. While the man's recording career spans six decades, his live releases reflect his best work, and on *Live at the Regal,* with its great horn riffs, King is at the top of his form. The CD's sound is a marked improvement over its vinyl predecessor, but still betrays substantial compression and the acoustic problems common to live performance.

**The Best Of (1953–1986)**
MCA MCAD 31040 (40:33)  **[A–]**
The Blues Boy whose guitar (Lucille) only plays leads, usually searing, soaring ones at that; B.B. King is the standard by which urban blues guitar players have been measured for literally decades. His influence on both the white rock and black blues communities is obvious and extensive. B.B. is also a great blues singer and innovator. This collection of late sixties/early seventies songs is a fair sampling from a long and prolific career. It includes some fine workouts: "How Blue Can You Get," "The Thrill Is Gone," and "Nobody Loves Me but My Mother," and there are no dogs included (B.B. may never have recorded one). Frankly, his best recordings are the concert releases with *Live at the Regal* leading the list. The sound quality is a bit dynamically enhanced over the LP, but hiss and compression are still evident, and the quality does vary substantially from track to track.

# Ben E. King
# (Benjamin Earl Nelson)
b. September 28, 1938—Henderson, North Carolina
Whether working with vocal groups (Moonglows/Drifters) or solo, King has epitomized smooth soul singing.

**The Ultimate Collection (Stand By Me) (1959–1975)**
Atlantic 7 80213-2 (56:33)  **[B+]**
Working with the Drifters' producers Leiber and Stoller (two of rock's least acknowledged, but most influential early architects) and Phil Spector, King

was part of some of the most influential soul music cut in the early sixties. Perhaps because he was the lead voice on the reputed first soul hit to employ strings, "There Goes My Baby" (with the Drifters 6/1/59), his work has been too often smothered with overly sweet instrumental settings. In addition to being one of the premier male soul singers of the early sixties, King was a fine composer who had a hand in the writing of many of his hit recordings. As with all collections assembled from recordings made at different times and places, it is difficult to generalize about the sound. Also, as is almost always the case with Atlantic, it is best described as sounding like a good LP; the CD does suffer from some vocal distortion and an overbright edge to some of the vocal tracks.

# Carole King
# (Carole Klein)
b. February 9, 1942—Brooklyn, New York
From Brill Building tunesmith to back country recluse, King has to be recognized as one of the great pop songwriters of her era.

### Tapestry (1971)
Ode EK 34946 (44:49)   [A]
In the sixties, she was an integral part of the Brill Building's brand of hot pop product, participating in writing over 100 hits, including "Loco-Motion," "Up On the Roof," and "Will You Love Me Tomorrow." In the seventies, she moved into the spotlight with this recording which was on the charts for almost six years, in the process selling over thirteen million copies, making it one of the most commercially successful pop albums ever released. It isn't a fluke. King has written or cowritten these twelve sensitive, yet streetwise, pop vignettes, representative of the best of

the form. She sings them straight at you, without artifice or affectation, all backed by simple but very effective instrumental settings. In the seventies, rock branched into a number of subforms and this recording was instrumental in establishing (both artistically and commercially) what has come to be known as the singer/songwriter form of pop rock music. The sound is not real clean, and is marred by insistent hiss, but it's superior to the LP, both in its dynamics and spatial attributes.

# The Kinks
Formed 1963—London
During the halcyon days of the mid-sixties British Invasion, the Beatles and the Stones vied for the championship, with third place a distance back. But the Kinks and the Who stand as the bands most deserving of the bronze. Ray Davies's quirky, absolutely English lyrical perspective, plus performance problems, kept them from achieving major stardom in the United States, but their sophisticated, often cinematic music has maintained a substantial world following for over two decades.

### Backtrackin Vol. I (1960s–1970s)
Starblend CD Track 1/1 (40:48)   [F]
You can't fault the fourteen selections covering this eccentric, creative group's best known singles from the mid-sixties to the early seventies. But you can fault the production—it's godawful. The masters must have been third generation cassettes originally recorded off AM radio. It's a shame; the material merits much better.

### Greatest Hits (1964–1966)
Rhino R2 70086 (45:20)   [A]
These eighteen selections cover the most creative—certainly the most high-

energy—period in this great rock band's history, including all the requisite goodies, in strong mono reproductions. If you're a fan, this is *the* essential Kinks disc; if you're not, but are interested in experiencing the diversity and creativity of one of the genuine leaders of the British Invasion, this package should prove a delight.

**Lola Versus Powerman and the Moneygoround (1970)**
PRT CDMP8836 (40:17)  [B−]
The band's 1970 concept release. The concept involved was the story of a group trying to get a No. 1 hit record. The best thing about the whole affair is the "record" they're promoting: "Lola," one of the decade's best rock songs. The rest of it is OK, but a bit heavy in the tone of the singing and the lyrics sung. To appreciate the Kinks, one has to have a certain intimacy with their large body of recorded work. Unfortunately, because the band has not garnered a world of commercial success, their better early LPs are frequently deleted, and very little of that material has reached CD yet. It's anyone's guess if it ever will. This album is a fair sampling of one facet. The sound is about equivalent to that of a clean LP.

**Muswell Hillbillies (1971)**
Rhino R2 70936 (44:39)  [A−]
One of Ray Davies's greatest assets is the Achilles' heel of American acceptance of his work. As much narrator as lyricist, his sensitivity to and handling of the details of time, place, and class have set his often satirical work apart. But because the world he chronicles is that of working-class London in the sixties and seventies, it has never been totally transportable to America where his (and the Kinks') audience seems more at home with the crude neo-punk rock &

roll that kept the band from playing in the U.S. for a time. That's truly a shame, and *Muswell Hillbillies* is a prime example. While excluding any of the Kinks' historic singles, it does include a dozen first-rate, mostly acoustic examples of a truly gifted songwriter's work. Augmented at times by New Orleans old-time brass (which somehow suggests the English music hall tradition), this heavily blues/country influenced set also incorporates accordion and clarinet, creating an old-time flavor over which Davies deadpans his remarkable verbal vignettes. Given its vintage, Bill Inglot and Ken Perry of Rhino have, once again, provided substantial sonic improvement over the original vinyl.

**Come Dancing With the Kinks (The Best of the Kinks 1977–86) (1986)**
Arista AZCD 8428 (69:51)  [B−]
The band's output of the last ten years or so has retained their appealing quirkiness, both musically and lyrically, but, their classic work was done in their first decade. This is emphasized by the less than wondrous live versions of earlier classics "Lola" and "You Really Got Me" included here. Ray Davies still tracks the same themes with his unique musical approach, but they fail to resonate any longer, valid though they still may be. The sound is all over the place with newer items having a fine aural sheen ("Don't Forget to Dance" and "Livin' on a Thin Line"); but earlier material obviously suffers from analogic shortcomings and muddy digital conversions.

# Gladys Knight and the Pips
Formed 1952—Atlanta
This family group began as children in church and reached soul stardom through amateur competitions.

**Greatest Hits (1961–1974)**
Curb D2-77321 (35:29)   **[B]**
Each of the ten selections on this budget collection reached one of the top three spots on the R&B charts. The warm, full, gospel-influenced voice of Gladys Knight has found a home on those charts for the better part of thirty years. Gladys and the Pips' best work occurred in the early seventies with "Midnight Train to Georgia," "Neither One of Us," and "I've Got To Use My Imagination," and they're all here. In retrospect, the formulaic production values reveal a dated quality, but the nostalgic appeal is undeniable and the smoothness of their singing is notable. Some of the early sixties tracks ("I Heard It Through the Grapevine," "Every Beat of My Heart") suffer from a severely compressed bottom, but the sound quality of the seventies releases is the best currently on disc from the group.

**The Best of Gladys Knight and the Pips (1970–1974)**
Buddah BCD 68001 (67:50)   **[C +]**
Gladys Knight can sing, and when she gets a good song and a solid arrangement, she and the Pips make some sweet seventies' pop/soul sounds ("Midnight Train to Georgia" and "I've Got To Use My Imagination"). Unfortunately, during the seventies Buddah phase of their career, the group consistently settled for production over purpose. However, even in the lesser material, there are times when Knight's warmly sensual voice raises things to a level to be reckoned with. The CD does add a half-dozen "bonus" cuts to this compilation, which was originally released on LP. The sound is relatively clean and spacious but not particularly dynamic or detailed. ("Midnight Train to Georgia" remains one of the great pop/soul songs of the era.)

# Kool Moe Dee (Mohandas Dewese)
b. circa 1970—New York
**Knowledge is King (1989)**
Jive/RCA 1182-2 (44:51)   **[B]**
Propelled by a thunderous bass line, Kool Moe Dee fashions his impassioned raps around themes that are contemporary and socially redemptive—assailing the evils of materialism and the drug culture while endorsing determined ambition, learning, and spirituality. This is music that needs to be heard, music that proves its own importance—a true continuation of the positive power of pop, of which real rock is a legacy. The title selection is one of the best rap songs to come along in the rapidly evolving form—as the man says, "Knowledge is infinite/Suckers ain't into it/Ignorance is bliss/And they're kin to it." The sound's OK, with a heavy bottom and good vocal clarity.

## Ladysmith Black Mambaza
Formed 1965—Ladysmith, South Africa
(originally from Swaziland)
**Shaka Zulu (1987)**
Warner Bros. 9 25582-2 (36:48)   **[A]**
This ten-voice male church choir
under the leadership of Joseph
Shabalala has had import recordings
available in the United States for a
number of years. But it wasn't until 1986
when they joined Paul Simon on his
classic *Graceland* that their wondrous
vocal prowess received anything like
mass exposure. This 1987 release was
produced by Simon and engineered by
the extraordinary Roy Halee with results
that are among the best pure vocal
music on record. Eight of the ten songs
are sung in English (the other two in
their native Zulu), but, Black Mambaza's
voice is universal—music from the heart
to the heart—that celebrates life as majestically as you are ever likely to hear.
An amazing record by an amazing group.
The sound is perfect—crystal clear and
as open as the spirit of the music.

## Daniel Lanois
**Acadie (1989)**
Opal/Warner Bros. 25969-2 (41:21)   **[B + ]**
This debut release from one of the
eighties' most successful producers captures the essence of his Cajun roots
intermingled with the mists from bayou
swamp waters. Ably assisted by Brian

Eno, the Neville Brothers, U2's fine
rhythm section, and legendary New
Orleans guitarist Mason Ruffner, Lanois
reflects regional feelings through modern sensibilities with generally first-rate
results. There are moments of excessive
self-indulgence, but the simple charm of
most of the selections succeeds admirably. Lanois's notes on the varied sources
for each selection, and the production
processes employed to realize them, are
interesting and insightful. The sound
won't blow you away, but it won't get in
your way, either.

## k.d. lang
b. Canada
**And the Reclines**
**Angel with a Lariat (1987)**
Sire 25441-2 (31:07)   **[B + ]**
Two-steppin' rockified traditional country by k.d. lang and her crack cohorts,
this is a prime example of the good-time,
off-the-wall new C&W sound that has
defied both traditionalists and music
marketers. Its energy is undeniable—
k.d. is one of the best singers to come
along in years, but those who flocked to
her Patsy Cline-evocative *Shadowland*
for its sheer vocal virtuosity will find this
(except for the closing ballad, "Three
Cigarettes in an Ashtray") a bit of a rinky
dink party. Dave Edmunds's tasty production lends authenticity, however.
This album is an impressive debut that

didn't fully portend what was to follow. Soundwise, it's better than OK, but it's no audiophile's dream.

**Shadowland (1988)**
Sire 9 25724-2 (35:56)   **[A]**
lang has learned the lesson of the successful pop artist: how to play the media like a twelve-string, and it was this recording that gave her public stature. While her early supporters saw *Shadowland* as a retreat from her attempts to broaden and revitalize current country music, one thing she has never kept secret is her abiding feeling for Patsy Cline—how could she keep working in front of the Reclines? A gifted artist with one of the best pop/country voices to come along, k.d. enlisted the production talents of Cline's legendary producer, Owen Bradley, to recreate that country/ pop ballad sound, with strings, crying pedal steel, and backup voices. The sound is sumptuous, the mood, heartbreaking, and the voice, astonishing. There are a few two-steps, but it's the weepers, "Lock, Stock and Teardrops," "I Wish I Didn't Love You So," "Black Coffee," "Shadowland," "Busy Being Blue," and the blue-ribbon country quartet's (lang, Brenda Lee, Loretta Lynn, and Kitty Wells) "Honky Tonk Angels' Melody" that make this a genuine keeper. The echo-laden sound is perfect for the mood, and all the soaring textures of lang's voice are warmly and intimately revealed.

**And the Reclines**
**Absolute Torch and Twang (1989)**
Sire 25877 2 (41:45)   **[A]**
k.d. and crew capture the controlled energy that make for memorable live performances, and in the process define the direction for vitalization and updating the classic, traditional country sound. Nine of the selections were written or cowritten by lang, and there's not a weak track in the bunch, with "Big Boned Girl" the upbeat standout, the oblique, searing "Pullin' Back the Reins," and perhaps the best song ever written about child abuse, "Nowhere to Stand," being the most notable. Best of all is lang's agile, expressive voice, one of the most affecting and potent currently recorded. Those looking for another nostalgic echo of Patsy Cline may be disappointed; for those looking for an intelligent, moving talent whose roots are country but whose vision is unconfined, this is simply a first-rate offering. The disc has a bright, dynamic, yet natural sound, with an excellent balance of voice to instruments. Damn the politics—this woman can sing!

## Cyndi Lauper
b. June 20, 1954—New York City
**She's So Unusual (1983)**
Portrait/CBS RK38930 (38:37)   **[A]**
It may have sold as much on visual image as musical content, but those who bought the package got a bonus—Cyndi Lauper is a natural; one of the most engaging pop talents to emerge in the eighties. *She's So Unusual* is a class debut release—good songs (some written by Lauper, with inclusions from Prince and Jules Shear among others), great singing, and bright supportive production. "Time After Time" is among the best ballads to come out in the decade; "She Bop" and "Girls Just Want to Have Fun" brought feminist values (both personal and social) to a teen audience in positively compelling form—a delight that sustains. The sound is dynamic and fairly clean, but a bit overbright and somewhat compressed, very analagous to the sound of a good quality LP.

**True Colors (1986)**
Portrait/CBS RK40313 (38:08)  **[A]**
Cyndi's second, released in 1986, reaffirms her status as one of the major female pop talents of the decade. She sings her heart out, whether it be ballad or up-tempo number, and she communicates both her unique personality and emotions through every lyric. Ably assisted by such diverse talents as the Bangles, Adrian Belew, Nile Rodgers, Billy Joel, Aimee Mann, and Pee-Wee Herman, Lauper has produced an album that covers a wide range of pop territory, and all of it well. The centerpiece is her cover of Marvin Gaye's "What's Going On" segueing into the New Orleans classic, "Iko Iko," which is inspired in both concept and execution. The sound is a revelation; spacious, clean, open, and dynamic with precise separation. The vocal mix is set back a bit, but Cyndi's penetrating voice still gets through.

# Led Zeppelin
Formed 1968—England
Originally formed under the name the New Yardbirds, Led Zeppelin was the first exponent of the bombast that has mutated into the young white male phenomenon now known as "heavy metal," a subgenre which often seems like the indestructible cockroach of rock & roll. To ignore their instrumental talents and preconceived intent would be uninformed; to ascribe much meaning or importance to their extraordinarily popular output would be misguided.

**Led Zeppelin (1969)**
Atlantic SD19126-2 (44:58)  **[B]**
The first explosion. To their blues-based madness, which Jimmy Page, their lead guitarist (and the producer of this self-titled debut effort) had developed during his stint with John Mayall's Bluesbreakers,

they added a theatrical sense of dynamics which both heightened the bombast and sustained interest. Their form of rock was defined by *The Rolling Stone Encyclopedia of Rock & Roll,* "as sculptured noise." They were one of the earliest bands to understand and use the recording studio as another distinct element of their sound, and, with the excellent Glyn Johns providing engineering, the sound of their recordings is big and "bad." The CD sound, while free of hiss and powerful, remains compressed and muffled around the edges.

**Led Zeppelin II (1969)**
Atlantic 19127-2 (41:40)  **[B–]**
Chosen by a panel of critics in *Rolling Stone* (August 27, 1987) as one of the hundred best rock albums released between 1967 and 1987, it was described by the publication as "The Book of Revelation scored for an electric boogie quartet." It did codify the monster sound that rapidly became a sound heard around the world. This was rock's primal message of rebellion expressed in elementary form—almost pure deafening noise. Young male teen rockers understood it loud and clear, as have legions of heavy metal successors who have recombined Zeppelin's explosive sonic blast and occult preoccupations into a consistently successful commercial form. While not a concert recording, the album was cut in various locations during the band's initial touring phase, with resultant variation in its sound, which sometimes includes mike hum and tape hiss and often sounds dampened as if it were recorded in a padded cell; which, come to think of it. . . .

**Untitled (IV) (1971)**
Atlantic 19129-2 (42:40)  **[A]**
It all culminates here. Ponderous as it may sometimes be, Led Zep's powerful,

mythic thunder is rock & roll (unfortunately, the same can rarely, if ever, be said about their legions of heavy metal successors). This time out they were in full control of their dynamic vision and the end result is an early seventies classic highlighted by "Black Dog," "Rock And Roll," "When The Levee Breaks," and what became the anthem of the decade, "Stairway to Heaven." Of course, Zeppelin's music was about much more than bombast; it was music of shading and contrast, of instrumental and production precision, all of which are generally well-displayed on the CD. Its dynamics and clarity will make you a believer. It does have slight flaws, some hiss and some vocal compression, particularly on the Joni Mitchell tribute "Goin' To California," but these are ultimately inconsequential.

### Led Zeppelin (1969–1979)
Atlantic 7 82144-2 (290:23—four discs)   [A]
This 1990 boxed set covers material recorded between 1968 and 1978, compiled and remastered under the personal supervision of Zeppelin founder and former Yardbird, Jimmy Page, whose searing, soaring guitar provided the framework around which the houses of the holy were built. So in its way, this is heavy metal's revised book of Genesis— the digital restatement of one of rock's best-selling and most influential bands. The fifty-four tracks included are drawn from nine of their ten albums, excluding only the soundtrack to *The Song Remains the Same,* but including a few B-sides and previously unreleased takes: "Travelling Riverside Blues" and "White Summer/Black Mountain Side," both from 1969 radio broadcasts, thrown in for good measure. It's all here: the ponderous pontification, the crashing power, the wretched excess, the subtle genius, the boorish noise, the soaring

spirit, John Bonham's unholy drumming, Page's probing, throbbing blues-based guitar, John Paul Jones's underappreciated musicality, and Robert Plant's erotic banshee wails. That Zeppelin, more than a decade after its demise, continues to totally eclipse its host of imitators, is probably the ultimate testimony to their reverberating energy. For their legions of followers, this boxed set is a must, simply because Page has realized their studio perfectionism in the digital transfer, opening up the recordings without sacrificing the intensity of the originals—it's a sonic masterpiece. This digital remix uncovers the care and subtlety at the heart of their mega bombast and the wonder of Page's guitar. There's a well-designed thirty-six-page booklet with informative essays by Cameron Crowe, Kurt Loder, and Robert Palmer, as well as requisite photos and detailed information on the recording sources and dates, plus Led Zeppelin's complete discography. A class package from a group that always knew their emotional, incendiary music was important.

# John Lennon
b. October 9, 1940—Liverpool, England
d. December 8, 1980—New York City
The rock & roll soul of the Beatles who tried to fulfill that role for all mankind. One of the truly great artists to have expressed his very personal vision through the medium of popular music.

### Plastic Ono Band (1970)
Parlophone CDP7 46770-2 (39:18)   [A + ]
Rock & roll as public confession/personal catharsis/primal scream. It's powerful but questionable stuff. The group celebrity of the Beatles and a difficult personal history combined to unleash Lennon's furies and wracking

self-doubts. On this harsh, stark, stinging recording, Lennon lets it all hang
out, without instrumental coloration
or personal reservation. Working with
Phil Spector, their brutally raw production values illuminate Lennon's masterful singing and bruised psyche with an
intense, pitiless spotlight; their artistry
is manifest in the way John's voice,
through subtle manipulation, becomes
the perfect rock & roll vehicle. The outstanding track is "Working Class Hero,"
but *Plastic Ono Band* isn't about singles
(that was the Beatles' ultimate bag)—it
stands as a powerful, flawed expression
of the artist as canvas. While the sound
stage is a bit constrained and has a
"recorded" feel to it, the sound is perfect, integral, and substantially better
than the LP.

### Imagine (1971)
Parlophone CDP7 46641 2 (39:26)   **[A]**
Arriving hard on the heels of the icy
blast that was *Plastic Ono Band, Imagine*—particularly given the title cut—
almost seemed like a warm, fuzzy
blanket. Certainly the Beatlesque pop
sensibility had returned, and John
always *was* the barbed Beatle. Obviously "Imagine" has now ascended to such
anthemic status that criticism of its
underlying naivete is a waste of effort,
and it *is* a beautiful song of love, both
personal and political. The remaining
nine tracks wander over rock's musical
terrain while yielding listenable, oft-
times fascinating material, from his
infamous attack on Paul ("How Do You
Sleep?") to almost giddy, girl-group pop
("Oh Yoko!") coproduced by Phil Spector. With a myth of this magnitude, it is
difficult to separate the artist from the
legend, or, for that matter, to accept
Lennon on his non-Beatle terms. But
*Imagine* ultimately reestablishes the fact
that, politics and persona notwithstand-

ing, John Lennon was a consummate
rock/pop artist, and songs like "Jealous
Guy," "I Don't Want to Be a Soldier," and
"Oh Yoko!" are worthy additions to
contemporary music's all-time great
songbook. The sound quality varies
markedly from track to track: "Crippled
Inside" and "Jealous Guy" are both
open, clear, and dynamic; "Imagine" suffers from excessive compression, and
the rest have a strong "recorded" feel,
sometimes distorted, probably reflecting
Lennon's and Spector's use of the studio
as a sound palette. "Whip and Mirror by
Yoko"—now what exactly did he mean
by *that?*

### John Lennon & Yoko Ono/
### Plastic Ono Band
### Sometime in New York City/Live Jam
### (1972)
EMI CDS7 467282 (91:08—two discs)   **[D]**
God knows the man had his demons (he
lived with one), as well as his political
preoccupations, and general topical pur-
suits. This time out he also had Yoko,
the awful Elephant's Memory Band,
some misguided Phil Spector production, and a little Frank Zappa thrown in
for good measure. It's a mess—a sad
mess. If it matters, the sound on both
studio and concert discs sucks—distorted, muddy, and compressed.

### Live in New York City (1972)
Parlophone CDP 7 461962 (42:20)   **[B]**
Recorded on August 30, 1972, at a
Madison Square Garden benefit concert,
but not released until 1986, this is music
that's as rough as a cob. As Lennon says
between the cuts, "Welcome to the
rehearsal." Perhaps it was the vibe that
night, perhaps it was just because it was
John Lennon in America, New York in
1972; whatever the reason, the performance often rises above its often too

apparent limitations. The very "live" sound on the disc captures it all, warts and everything—mike hum and occasional distortion included. But through the entire proceedings shines John's sincere desire to touch all who heard his song. The medium may have been flawed that August night, but the message sounded loud and clear.

### Shaved Fish (1975—compilation release date)
Capitol CDP 7 46642 2 (41:42)   **[A–]**
A collection of post-Beatles sloganeering—but the message is so important and the artist was so sincere that it rises to pure rock & roll. While not everything included is of lasting quality, each cut does evidence the rock production sensitivities of one of the best to ever record within the form. The sound varies appreciably from cut to cut; i.e., at times it is a bit bright, at others it's afflicted with hiss and some compression, but, on average the dynamic punch and enhanced clarity make it a clear choice over the LP.

### The John Lennon Collection (1969–1981)
Capitol CDP7 91516 2 (71:31)   **[A–]**
This nineteen-track compilation runs from the sublime to the ill-conceived. It includes the only complete CD version of the single "Give Peace a Chance" (an abbreviated version is on *Shaved Fish*), "Instant Karma!," "Happy Xmas (War is Over)," "Cold Turkey," "Power to the People" (ugh), (originally released on singles, then collected on *Shaved Fish*), and the relatively obscene B side "Move Over Ms. L." The balance comes from *Walls and Bridges, Plastic Ono Band* ("Love"), *Mind Games, Imagine, Rock'n'Roll* ("Stand By Me"), with the majority drawn from *Double Fantasy.* Most of the tracks will be familiar to

Lennon fans; on the whole, *The John Lennon Collection* provides a fair overview of the pop side of his post-Beatles career. Yet without the hard-edged, more personal songs, it cannot be considered balanced. As expected, the sound quality varies markedly from track to track, but there aren't any real clunkers—generally good analog-source reproduction.

# Jerry Lee Lewis
b. September 29, 1935—Ferriday, Louisiana
If one were to seek the story of thirty years of rock & roll as personified in the life and style of one human being, Jerry Lee Lewis probably stands as the single primal incarnation of the form (Nick Toshes has captured this fact beautifully in his marvelous biography of the artist, *Hellfire*). In his prime, Lewis and a piano were the only ingredients really necessary to ignite the inferno of rock & roll any time, anywhere. Trapped in the conflict between the good as exemplified by his church history and the bad, as exemplified by the Devil's music he played so urgently, Jerry Lee continues to act out this conflict with a power and a passion that is elemental to the best of the form.

### Classic Jerry Lee Lewis (1956–1963)
Bear Family Records BCD 15240 (600:32—eight discs)   **[A +]**
Subtitled "The Definitive Edition of his Sun Recordings," this monster, mastered from digital transfers of the original tapes, includes 246 tracks, the original versions of each of his Sun singles, the fabled "religious discussion" between Lewis and Sam Phillips preceding the recording of "Great Balls of Fire," thirty previously unreleased performances, and "fifty-six performances in stereo—most for the first time!" Of course that's

more than any sane listener would ever want—hell, its playing time runs over ten hours! (Talk about a day in the life.) Then there's the thirty-six-page booklet, filled with great photos and detailed recording information on each and every track—an archivist's dream. The fact is that the great roar that changed the world of popular music, maybe the world, was the creation of a handful of rockin' rebels who had the talent, drive, and guts to make their joyful noise while the staid establishment invoked its mighty powers to smite them down. Of all of them, Jerry Lee may have been the wildest. Little Richard, another piano player, may have exceeded him on record, but Lewis's private brand of madness wasn't just for showtime—this dude lived it out to the fullest, each and every brash day. They humbled him, but he ain't down yet, and the testimony contained in these eight discs is pounding proof that the undaunted spirit of rock & roll will live on. It's all here—the country, the boogie, and the sexual simmer that shook preachers in pulpits across America. It's interesting to note that during the eight years he recorded for Sun (the period covered by this boxed set), he only had ten singles that reached the Top 100; "Whole Lotta Shakin' Goin' On" reached number 3; "Great Balls of Fire," No. 2; "Breathless," No. 7—none reached No. 1 and no others made the Top Ten. Yet he remains for many the leering incarnation of the lecherous rebellion at the heart of rock & roll. His talent has never been questioned—his *lifestyle* has. At Sun he recorded rock, country, blues, folk, and spirituals, all of it represented here, complete with alternate takes, X-rated studio banter, and cover versions of many of the hits made famous by his illustrious contemporaries—Elvis, Little Richard, Carl Perkins, and Chuck Berry. Soundwise,

these are the best digital transfers of this material available from any source, generally very clean and nicely detailed, mostly mono, but limited by the dynamic capacities of the recording equipment available at the time.

**18 Sun Greatest Hits (1957–1973)**
Rhino 5255 (39:54)   **[C–]**
Definitely not up to Rhino's usual high standards for compilation discs of early rockers. Its eighteen selections include all the essentials covered in the disc *Ferriday Fireball* as well as some offbeat others, but the sound quality is nothing special, and the Ferriday compilation is clearly the better value.

**Ferriday Fireball (1957–1973)**
Sun CD Charlie 1 (60:03)   **[A]**
Twenty-five of the historic original Sun recordings which comprehensively cover Lewis's initial rock & roll days, before bad PR drove him to country audiences. In other words, it's all here. The sound is good, given the age of the masters, but the dynamic range of the work is not greatly enhanced by the digital transfer.

**The Greatest Hits Volume II (1958–1968)**
IMP (Pickwick) PCD 840 (45:56)   **[D]**
Mostly second-rate renditions of second-rate material afforded third-rate production.

# Little Feat
Formed 1969—Los Angeles
Zapped Southern–fried travelin' blues.

**Little Feat (1971)**
Warner Bros. 1890-2 (33:29)   **[B]**
It was inevitable that a bunch of escapees from Frank Zappa's Mothers of Invention wouldn't be just another Southern rock/boogie band, roots not-

withstanding. Musically, there's a bit of everything: blues, R&B, rockabilly, nascent funk, and pure country, and these guys can play it. What sets it apart from the mainstream are the gear-grindin', smoke-filled, whisky-swillin' lyrics that belie just a touch of crazed weirdness. An interesting debut from a band that would become one of America's seventies favorites—they got better, but this ain't a bad beginning. Soundwise the disc is obviously compressed, but generally clean.

### Sailin' Shoes (1972)
Warner Bros. 2600-2 (38:22)   **[A]**
Where the weirdness meets the road there's "A sign that turns from red to green/It says chop suey and join the U.S. Marines/From Tuscon to Tucumcari/Tripe my guacamole baby." It's all here—somewhere, their second album, the last one with the original lineup; after this release bassist Roy Estrada left to rejoin the Mothers, and Kenny Gradney, with his funkier inflections, along with percussionist Sam Clayton, joined up. If you think there's a foot fetishist on the loose here, you may not be far off the mark—this is the band's loosest, hottest studio effort, laying claim to being their best all-around work. Blues drenched, funk syncopated, and a bit off-the-wall, *Sailin' Shoes* is one of the better second albums to come along in the seventies. The recording has an appropriately bright, nicely dynamic, rollicking sound.

### Dixie Chicken (1973)
Warner Bros. 2686-2 (36:48)   **[A–]**
The third recording from a hardworking band that occasionally reveals the strain. But their brand of blues, boogie, and echoes of The Band still provides some of the most listenable music of the somewhat arid seventies, and *Dixie*

*Chicken* is clearly among their strongest outings. From the greasy title track to the almost haunting "Roll Um Easy," Allen Toussaint's "On Your Way Down," the nicely syncopated "Fat Man in a Bathtub," and the snaking instrumental "Lafayette Railroad," this is their Crescent City album, and they almost manage to sound like natives of America's city with the richest musical heritage. Paul Barrere and George contribute some nice guitar licks; as always, Bill Payne's keyboards are superlative. The sound quality of this CD, while betraying its analog roots, is really pretty strong.

### Feats Don't Fail Me Now (1974)
Warner Bros. 2784-2 (34:31)   **[B]**
With founder Lowell George's writing contributions giving way to the efforts of other band members, there is a noticeable decline in the quality of the material. But the group's strong chops and George's funky vocals still result in a superior effort, capped by the ten-minute closer, "Cold Cold Cold/Tripe Face Boogie"—Southern boogie gothic weirdness still simmering. The sound quality of this disc is best described as good analog.

### Waiting for Columbus (1978)
Warner Bros. 3140-2 (74:17)   **[B +]**
Somehow it all sounds a little pat, which, for a live album from a boogie band known for its looseness and live performances, makes no sense at all. Maybe the fact that it was their *first* live recording had something to do with it. As the packaging clearly notes, "Don't Bogart that Joint" and "Apolitical Blues," included on the original double LP, are deleted from the CD "to facilitate a single specially priced compact disc." *Uh huh.* This was their last recording in which Lowell George fully participated,

and it isn't bad, particularly for a concert recording. It's just not what those who'd experienced their live performances had hoped for. The recording was taken from several concerts, and some of the tracks boast exceptional live sound, while others suffer from poor vocal mix and a somewhat boxy, thin quality. The fifteen tracks provide a representative overview of the band's career, and there are moments when everything comes together and it really begins to cook.

# Little Richard (Richard Wayne Penniman)

b. December 5, 1932—Macon, Georgia
While Little Richard stands alone in the annals of rock & roll, his history is not uncommon to that of many blacks who came to the music in the early to mid-1950s. As the third of fourteen children, he found himself dancing in the streets of Macon for nickels and dimes at the age of seven and was the lead singer in his church choir before he was fourteen years of age. Before his career as a pop performer got under way, he was working at the Greyhound bus station in Macon washing dishes. While Richard's recorded output is not extensive, the sheer intensity, exuberance, and irreverence (not to mention perceived lack of taste) embodied in those few releases added a coloration to the music which continues to this day.

### 18 Greatest Hits (1955–1964)
Rhino RNCD 75899 (42:21)  [A + ]
This was music guaranteed to piss off Mom and Dad as maniacally performed by the self-claimed bronze Liberace—it still sounds great. Nasty songs sung in a wildly, primally orgasmic voice pulsating to the rhythms of New Orleans voodoo music. (And all this at a time when Cole Porter's lyrics to "Love For Sale" were essentially banned from radio air play in America, for God's sake!) The sound is clean and outstanding given the age of the masters. This is rock & roll, the real thing! This disc contains music that seethes with energy and screams with rebellion. The sounds have truly left an indelible mark on all rock music that has followed.

### The Specialty Sessions (1955–1964)
Ace ABOXBK1 (277:36—six discs)  [A + ]
This is it—the whole outrageous, screamin' enchilada—the taproot of rock & roll—the testimony in support of the Great One's claim as the founding father (and son and holy ghost) of the music that changed the world. And nothing rings hollow. This English import collection begins with Richard and his hot touring band, the Upsetters,' 1955 demo ("Baby" and "All Night Long") as recorded at WMBL's Macon studio. Most of the eighty-two tracks are famous Bumps Blackwell/Art Rap sessions cut at New Orleans' J&M Studios with the hot studio band of Lee Allen, Alvin "Red" Tyler, Frank Fields, and Earl Palmer, creating the spark that ignited rock & roll. In other words, it's all here, the famous, alternate takes, studio dialog, unreleased material, and a thirty-page booklet that includes a thorough, detailed history, plus precise session information, and rare photos. There is an abbreviated American release of this set that eliminates a number of the alternate takes, the audience for which is probably limited to the most ardent fans or nascent historians. What comes through, of course, is unparalleled energy and abandon, but the breadth of this package reveals more—a clarity of vision, the perfection of a great sound, and often overlooked musicianship and vocal prowess. While the sound quality re-

veals somewhat primitive elements, this lovingly produced effort delivers surprisingly high-quality sonics. These reproductions preserve that physical sound of a great rock & roll studio with enhanced clarity. "A wop bob a loo bop a lop bam boom!!"

# Lone Justice
Formed 1984—Los Angeles
**Lone Justice (1985)**
Geffen 24060-2 (36:09)   **[B–]**
This pop countryish album is principally notable for one thing: Maria McKee, who happens to be one of the hottest female voices to hit rock in recent memory. She's not a bad writer either, having had a hand in the writing of half of the disc's ten selections, the most notable being "After the Flood." This is the recording that produced the driving hit, "Ways to Be Wicked" written by Tom Petty and Benmont Tench, the Heartbreakers' talented keyboard player who contributed substantially to these proceedings. The sound has its moments, but generally is analagous to that of a clean LP.

# Los Lobos
Formed 1974—East Los Angeles
Performing proof that rock & roll is the voice of every strain in the great melting pot.

**And a Time to Dance (1984)**
Slash/London 828-026-2 (18:34)   **[B + ]**
The musical texture may be *nortenas,* but the spirit is rock & roll. The debut EP from the hardest-working band in L.A.'s barrio crackles with tight musicianship and impassioned vocals. Among its seven tracks are a couple of classic Mexican folk songs performed with infectious spirit, a buoyant cover of Ritchie Valens's "Come On, Let's Go" and

four rockin' originals by Hildalgo, Perez, and Rosas. The only complaint about this disc is that it is so brief—a spicy appetizer for great things yet to come. Soundwise, there's really nothing to complain about.

**How Will the Wolf Survive? (1984)**
Slash/Warner Bros. 9 25177-2 (33:29)   **[A]**
This is pretty impressive stuff. Its roots are real, and so are the dues it took get this L.A.-based Chicano band acceptance within the mostly white mainstream of pop success. From straight ahead Saturday night rockers through traditional Mexican folk material, to contemporary compositions that express the valid and growing point of view of one of America's largest minorities (and one that has not as yet made that much impact on its adopted culture), Los Lobos brings absolutely first-rate musicianship, real sensitivity, and obviously heartfelt meaning to whatever they perform. They are one of the most valid of the decade's new rock bands, and the title selection on this collection is their greatest recorded work yet. The sound quality reflects excellent instrumental separation; T-Bone Burnett's straightforward, clean production values; relatively clean sound; and some evidence of analog compression.

**By the Light of the Moon (1987)**
Slash/Warner Bros. 9 25523-2 (40:37)   **[A–]**
The worthy follow-up by David Hidalgo, Cesar Rosas, and company suffers from dichotomy of intent; i.e., it's partially made up of Rosas's energetic rock numbers and partially of Hidalgo's lyrical expressions of the difficult aspects of life for many Spanish-speaking immigrants in America in the 1980s. But these concerns are every American's because the problems addressed involve universal disillusionment, heightened by prox-

imity to the world's most affluent culture ("The Hardest Time"). That aside, on a track-by-track basis, each selection reflects this fine band's strengths, which are numerous. It is arguable that the future hope for real creativity in rock (and maybe for the nation) may depend upon the continued diversity of a society that draws fresh inspiration and attitudes from a multiplicity of cultures—Los Lobos certainly supports that premise. There is a realness to their music which transcends language or cultural boundaries and assures its continuing currency. There is no single cut on *By the Light of the Moon* to rival "Will The Wolf Survive?," but the overall quality of the release is almost the equal of its fine predecessor. Again, T-Bone Burnett's direct, open production pays dividends in the sound, which is clear and separate, and this recording reflects dynamics and openness that are markedly superior to that of their first full album release.

### La Pistola Y El Corazon (1988)
Slash/Warner Bros. 9 25790-2 (25:11)  **[B +]**
Building on the independence spawned by the wide commercial success of their contribution to the popular *La Bamba* soundtrack, Los Lobos chose not to capitalize upon, but to return to, their roots—the *nortenas* music of northern Mexico—with this brief, all-Spanish release. This potent band derives much of its easy compatability from its musical and cultural heritage. *La Pistola Y El Corazon* is a vital testimony to both. The result is impressive, but those not conversant with Spanish or the cultural tradition out of which it arises must feel somewhat distanced. Fortunately, the feeling and vitality often transcend the language barrier. Soundwise, the vocals tend to the overbright side; the instrumental mix is a bit jumbled on occasion; however, it does not ultimately distract.

### The Neighborhood (1990)
Slash/Warner Bros. 26131 (45:23)  **[A–]**
Some music is made as a cry of outrage, some music is made to make a buck, and some music is made because it is a celebration of life. Los Lobos makes music that celebrates. Whether it is acoustic or electric recreations of traditional Mexican folk songs, or simple, current anthems to the joys and sorrows of everyday life, this fine band plays it as naturally as they breathe. *The Neighborhood* is a recording of simple pleasures, a window to dreams and desperation, the parties and the pains that enhance and afflict commonplace souls. It's not about big themes or issues, but emotions that make up everyone's daily experiences. Sounds simple, but it's not. The thirteen selections run the gamut from the mythic "Down on the Riverbed" to the sublime "Little John of God," but the overall emphasis is on the upbeat, danceable, Saturday night goodtime escapism that makes the rest of the week endurable. It's all done with instrumental virtuosity and the magic of David Hidalgo's earnest, aching voice. Add to it some vocal assistance from John Hiatt and Levon Helm and you end up with an album that sounds great the first time you play it and better the tenth or hundredth. The sound is driving, dynamic, and generally clean and crisp, although the bottom muddies up a little every now and again.

# Darlene Love (Darlene Wright)
b. 1938—Los Angeles
### Paint Another Picture (1988)
Columbia CK40602 (33:53)  **[D]**
You've heard of one-hit wonders—this recording is a one-track wonder. "He's Sure the Man I Love" resounds with

Spectorian drive and production, raising the blood pressure a couple of notches and generating a smile worthy of remembered girl-group glories. But that's all there is. The other eight overblown tracks are underwritten and overproduced. It's really too bad, because Love's voice is warm, rich, and powerful, and the one good track is so damn much fun. The sound varies, with tape hiss on "You'll Never Walk Alone" (yeah, that one), and vocal disintegration on "We Stand a Chance," but it really doesn't matter.

## Love & Rockets
**Love & Rockets (1989)**
RCA/Beggars Banquet 97152-2-R
(41:54)   **[D + ]**
These three former members of Bauhaus have come some distance from that group's gloom rock. Talk about a seductive surface—there's enough fuzz, feedback, and echo to hide a roaring Harley, but in this case, there's nothing to hide. Soundwise, particularly for those drawn to distortion, there's little to complain about.

## Lyle Lovett
b. November 1, 1957—Houston
Described by the *Washington Post* as "a Lone Star Tom Waits."

**Lyle Lovett (1986)**
MCA MCAD-31307 (33:42)   **[B + ]**
From western swing to jumpin' jazz (which isn't the leap it may seem) through classic country, Lyle Lovett debuted with this flawed, but arresting release. Like k.d. lang, this wry, wavy Texan has no interest in joining the Ricky Skaggs aesthetic—no, this guy wants to bust down the fences and head off in a whole new direction or two.

When he doesn't get hung up in contrived down-home wordplay, he writes a strong country lyric and delivers it with a nuanced ease that makes the goin' real easy. Maybe *too* easy—with his obvious smarts and sensitivity, it feels like he's got the stuff to really rattle the Nashville establishment—after all there are a lot of folks with a lot less going for them who are giving it a try. If you like your country with a twist, Lovett's worth your attention. The sound quality fits the acoustic instrumentation and laid-back feel to near perfection.

**Pontiac (1987)**
MCA MCAD-42028 (35:41)   **[A–]**
Lovett continues down the multipathed trail he staked out on his auspicious debut. This time out the telling detail, wicked wit, and casually arched vocal delivery feels more comfortable, as do the fine backup musicians. Through it all is a touch of the bizarre (Tonto in a boat) thereby establishing a real marketing challenge in this era of demographied playlist programming. A diverse talent of undeniable appeal, Lovett works a variety of musical forms—pure ballads, country ballads (which have an uncanny resemblance to Jesse Winchester, particularly on "Walk Through The Bottomland" with Emmylou Harris), jumpin' jazz, and some upbeat, pedal-steel-fueled country romps. With his easy yet sophisticated vocals, he manages to blend the styles comfortably. A greater synthesis of styles could prove fascinating, but then so would a mastery of any of them. The recording quality on this all-digital release is wonderful.

**Lyle Lovett and His Large Band (1989)**
MCA Curb MCAD-42263 (41:14)   **[B–]**
His Large Band may get top billing, but it's the aching country ballad that takes

center stage on Lovett's third release, along with a little jazz and pop. But whether it's a crying tenor sax, fiddle, or pedal steel in the background, the prevailing mood is down and blue. The writing this time out isn't quite as sharp, leaving an impression of stylistic tour de force as opposed to the form serving the message. Still, it's done with a lot of polish, and Lovett's fine singing becomes stronger and more assured with each album. Again, the all-digital sound is first-rate, warm, clean, and natural. "Stand By Your Man," indeed!

# The Lovin' Spoonful
Formed 1965—New York City
**Greatest Hits (1965–1968)**
Deluxe CD1022 (23:20)   **[D–]**
This is a disc to avoid; abbreviated playing time with sound values roughly equivalent to a clean LP.

**The Very Best of the Lovin' Spoonful (1965–1968)**
Buddah BCD68002 (41:33)   **[C]**
This was East Coast folk rock at its friendliest. "Do You Believe in Magic," "Daydream," "Younger Girl," and "Summer in the City," you gotta love it. Not a lot of substance, but sure a lot of appeal. The sound wanders all over the place ranging from the merely pedestrian to a substantial improvement over prior LPs.

**Anthology (1965–1968)**
Rhino R2 70944 (70:09)   **[A]**
This compilation is exactly what Rhino does best—assembling a comprehensive "best of" CD of a second-tier rock group, packaged with illuminating liner notes, and mastered with revelatory sound quality. Stated another way, if you are a fan of Greenwich Village mid-sixties folk/rock sounds pioneered by John Sebastian and his cohorts, this *is* the collection.

# Nick Lowe
b. March 25, 1949—Woodbridge, Suffolk, England
He got his start in Brinsley Schwarz, the seventies British pub-rock band whose alums have proved extremely influential in the rejuvenation of the seventies and eighties English pop scene. He has also been a mainstay (on bass) of Rockpile, as well as handling production chores for both Elvis Costello and Graham Parker.

**16 All-Time Lowes (1976–1980)**
Demon Fiend CD20 (47:43)   **[B]**
This compilation provides a fair overview of the witty, facile pop playfulness of one of the most ubiquitous members of the late seventies and eighties English music scene. His talent is undeniable, but his stance is sometimes questionable. It would have been nice to have "Rollers Show" among the disc's included selections, but otherwise it does cover most of his highlights; including the hit "Cruel to Be Kind," and the bizarrely funny "Marie Provost." The sound varies, but is, overall, equivalent to that of a clean LP, hiss and all.

**Party of One (1990)**
Reprise 26132-2 (36:02)   **[B + ]**
For a good time call on Nick Lowe's *Party of One.* The sophistication of Lowe's music is disguised in the straightforward Saturday night rock & roll format in which he revels. On *Party of One* his hook-laden singles sensibility and bright, witty lyrics are given a first-rate workout by Ry Cooder, Paul Carrack, Jim Keltner, and producer/ participant Dave Edmunds, who again proves that he's *this* producer's producer. Though not the equal of *Pure Pop for Now People* (U.K.'s *Jesus of Cool*) or

*Labour of Lust, Party of One* holds its own just fine, thank you. Music that moves both the mind and the feet has been a fairly rare commodity of late, and Lowe nicely fills the void. There are a couple of ballads, but it's the rockers like "Refrigerator White" that elevate *Party of One* over his last few releases. The sound is open, airy, and accurate, with nice dynamics. Lowe ain't heavy, but he's honest ("All Men are Liars") and a consistent good time.

## The Lucy Show
### Mania (1987)
Bigtime 6012-2-B (39:52)   **[B–]**
The Lucy Show sounds a bit like R.E.M. on speed, but it's a good sound from a tight, energetic band working the punk New Wave side of the eighties American musical street. The twelve brief selections reflect a promising young band on the verge of establishing an individual identity—here's hoping they make it. The sound is clean, but compressed, rarely escaping the speakers. It is also afflicted with constant, if not overwhelming hiss.

## Lynyrd Skynyrd
Formed 1966—Jacksonville, Florida
**Pronounced Leh-Nerd Skin-Nerd (1973)**
MCA MCAD-1685 (43:05)   **[A–]**
The debut from this Southern road/roots stomping aggregation served notice that worthy successors to the groundbreaking Allman Brothers had arrived, with one foot in rock and the other in southern sociomythology. They lived and played as if the music and the party were the only things that mattered. Strong song writing, sympathetic production provided by Al Kooper, and Ronnie Van Zant's redneck holler vocals add up to a Dixie-fried good time, mak-

ing the intelligence of the lyrics an added bonus. This release includes "Gimme Three Steps," "Poison Whiskey," and the ubiquitous, progressive "Free Bird." The sound is bright and tight, occasionally a bit edgy in the highs and mushy in the lows, but generally clean and dynamic.

### Second Helping (1974)
MCA MCAD 1686 (37:17)   **[A]**
Their second album leads off which "Sweet Home Alabama," the band's only Top Ten hit (that's right, "Free Bird" never reached the Top Ten). Alternating between hard driving, beer swilling anthems and longing regional ballads, the energy level, production values, and hard-assed swagger surpass their fine debut. "Workin' for MCA" is one of the more insightful biz songs around, and "The Needle and the Spoon" is an excellent example of the band's continuing concern for violent social issues. As is the case with their debut, the highs, particularly on the vocals, tend to be a bit overbright, but the bottom is much tighter; aside from slight overall compression, the sound is appropriately driving.

### One More For the Road (1976)
MCA MCAD6897 (71:17)   **[B + ]**
The height of mid-seventies Southern rock, served up live and kickin' by the band that earned its reputation doin' it live on the road. Covered among its twelve strong selections (almost totally drawn from their hot first and second album releases, *Pronounced Leh-Nerd Skin-Nerd* and *Second Helping*) are "Saturday Night Special," "Sweet Home Alabama," "The Needle and the Spoon," and "Free Bird," each an enduring testament to the power of Ronnie Van Zant's writing and performance. This is definitely a live outing, albeit a well-

recorded one. The band and the crowd cook—this was stirring Southern rock with a gritty edge, but, on record, the studio cuts of these songs remain definitive. The sound is clean, live, obviously lacking in studio sheen and definition, but, nonetheless, a plus.

**Street Survivors (1977)**
MCA MCAD-1687 (35:51)   **[A]**
As others have noted, *Street Survivors* makes an eerily perfect epitaph for what may have been the last of the truly great Southern road bands. It was the last recording (other than *Skynyrd's First . . .*

*and Last* issued posthumously the following year) as far as Ronnie Van Zandt, Steve Gaines, and Cassie Gaines, were concerned—they were victims of a fatal plane crash shortly after *Street Survivors'* release. Easily the best of the albums produced by Tom Dowd, it was their best new work in several years. The first two tracks are the strongest, "What's Your Name," and the strangely prophetic "That Smell," which ranks with the band's very best work. Though a bit overbright, the recording has a tight, bright, dynamic sound.

# Madonna
## (Madonna Louise Ciccone)
b. August 16, 1958—Rochester, Michigan
One of the best bits of barroom advice I
ever heard was: "For a good time, find a
Catholic girl gone bad."

**The Immaculate Collection (1983–1990)**
Sire/Warner Bros. 9 26440-2 (73:32)   **[B + ]**
"The coolest queen of white heat." "Nar-
cissistic, brazen, comic . . . the goddess
of the nineties." So trumpet the liner
notes to this MTV Video Vanguard's first
greatest-hits collection. You have to
hand it to her—building on techno-
spruced disco dreck, Madonna used a
licentious image and a little-girl voice to
keep at the pinnacle of pop for the better
part of the eighties. This disc assembles
most of her milestones.

Many of today's music critics have
conceded the existence of talent within
the hype, even though there probably
isn't an original idea or sound in her
considerable repetoire. Madonna's real
achievement is in her marketing prescience, her ability to understand the
currency of combining the visual, the
audio, and the slightly outrageous to rise
to the top of the mediocre contemporary
pop music scene. Yet it must be acknowledged that she is a real pro, and
polish and professionalism are the
benchmarks of all of her products.
Madonna's music is designed to make
you shake your booty, and shake it you
will. To those who would insist that
there is much of real significance here, I
would suggest that *The Immaculate Collection* has all the impact of the 23rd
Psalm flashed on the Times Square moving message sign—there may be something there, but the distractions, flatness, and mechanization drain it of any
real impact. Yet the era she exemplifies
was itself fairly bereft of honest emotion,
so this seventeen-track compilation
(which includes the new "Justify My
Love" and "Rescue Me") provides an
accurate souvenir of a predominate
musical form best forgotten. What is
truly outstanding about this CD is its
sound quality. Mixed with a new process
dubbed Q Sound, which produces enhanced depth and more specific sound
placement in the reproduced stereo
stage, and it works—the recording
sounds sumptuous and sensational.

# The Mamas and the Papas
Formed 1965—New York City
The members of this fine singing group
paid their dues in the Greenwich Village
folk scene of the early to mid-sixties, but
came together as a group in California.
They employed their fine harmonies to
extol the virtues of life in the golden
state.

**16 of Their Greatest Hits (1966–1968)**
MCA MCAD5701 (49:23)  **[B + ]**
In the early sixties the Beach Boys established Southern California as the home
of harmonious rock singles and this late
sixties quartet, augmented by slick (but
generally tasteful) Hollywood production, continued those traditions
beautifully. The Mamas and The Papas
were the perfect southern California
sound during the Summer of Love;
happy faces and peace signs. They were
also instrumental in the creation of the
1967 Monterey Pop Festival. As usual,
MCA has done a more than credible job
of digital transfer—the sound is clean,
clear, and appreciably more spacious
than the LP. The beauty of the interplay
of the individual voicings within these
familiar harmonies is markedly
enhanced.

# Bob Marley
b. April 6, 1945—Rhoden Hall, Jamaica
d. May 11, 1981
Though his musical career began in the
early sixties, it was during the seventies
that Bob Marley, and with him, reggae,
began to permeate the world of popular
music. In its native form, reggae has
achieved great popularity, not only in
Jamaica (its home ground), but also in
England, Europe, South America, and
Africa. During the seventies, its influence was felt throughout the pop music
of the Western world, either through
straight cover versions of the material by
white stars (e.g., Eric Clapton's rendition
of Marley's "I Shot the Sheriff") or more
pervasively, through incorporation of its
distinctive rhythm/instrumentation into
the framework of white/black artists'
musical canvases; e.g., Paul Simon, the
Clash, the Rolling Stones, and the Police
among many others. Musically, reggae is
marked by an inversion of the standard

rock instrumental format; i.e., the guitar
is used as a rhythmic rather than melodic
voice and the bass becomes a melodic as
opposed to rhythmic instrument, both
playing over a complex/hesitation percussive beat. Lyrically the music combines the concepts and vernacular of the
Rastafarian faith, as well as the politics
of oppressed, deprived minorities, specifically in cultures still suffering from
the financial dislocations of colonialism.
Marley, by virtue of his charisma, intensity, and total commitment to both the
music and its meanings became the
form's one true superstar with a worldwide following. Because of its protest-
message lyrics and R&B roots (derived
from U.S. records and radio received in
Jamaica since the forties) reggae represents a valid permutation of the rock
sound and spirit, and reflects rock's
absorption as a part of the popular
culture of the Third World. Marley's
death from cancer at age thirty-six was
a tragedy perhaps not fully appreciated
by the American audience, only a small
portion of whom had truly identified
with the pure expressions of the form.

**The Birth of a Legend (1963–1966)**
Epic Associated ZGK 46769 (56:46)  **[B + ]**
Before there was reggae, there was
ska—the musical mixture of traditional
folk, R&B, and jazz, which drove the
dance floors of Jamaica during the fifties
and sixties—pure party music to which
Marley brought socially relevant messages, driven by an irresistible beat, and
tight, joyous musicianship. The original
Wailers—Marley, Peter Tosh, Bunny
Livingston, and Beverly Kelso—were
each naturally talented musicians, capable of developing into effective solo
performers. According to Timothy
White's excellent liner notes, from the
outset it was Marley's intense drive and
vision that set them apart. This good-

time compilation delivers twenty tracks, ranging from Marley's stony, early compositions ("Simmer Down") to classic doo-wop/soul/R&B covers ("The Ten Commandments of Love")—all performed with rough abandon. The sound quality is a deterrent—very compressed, thin, and often raggedly edgy.

## And the Wailers
### Catch a Fire (1973)
Tuff Gong 422-846 201-2 (36:12)   [B+]
The Wailers—Bob Marley, Peter Tosh and Bunny Livingston—began their reggae career in the mid-to-late sixties. *Catch a Fire* was their first American album release. When it arrived, the critics raved, but the American public had not yet developed a taste for Jamaica's music of hypnotic beats and politico-religious messages. While the polish that came with popular ascendancy is missing, the nascent power, R&B/soul roots, and messages are evident on "400 Years," "Stir it Up," and "Concrete Jungle." The Tuff Gong remix from the master tapes in revelatory, with resonant bass supporting haunting harmonies that remain a bit set back in the mix.

## The Wailers
### Burnin' (1973)
Tuff Gong 422-846 200-2 (38:33)   [A]
Exactly who made up the Wailers on this recording remains a question. Some say it was the last American release on which Marley, Tosh, and Livingston all appeared; others suggest that Livingston had abandoned the group, in part because of Chris Blackwell's decision to give Marley name billing, and in part because of his own solo ambitions. The cover, on the other hand, would suggest that all three were involved; neither the album nor the CD list personnel. The growth on this recording is obvious compared with *Catch a Fire*. Their politi-

cal agenda moves to the fore, with classics like "I Shot the Sheriff," "Get Up, Stand Up," and "Burnin' and Lootin'." In addition, Marley establishes clearly his individuality and power as the lead voice in the group—previously, it was his guitar that was featured. The strongest of their early U.S. albums, the digital remix of the Tuff Gong CD is a sonic revelation.

### Natty Dread (1974)
Island 7 90037-2 (38:56)   [B+]
Recorded after Peter Tosh and Bunny Livingston (nee Wailer) left the group and were replaced with the effective support of the female I-Threes, which placed Marley's vocals at center stage, illuminating raw passion bubbling over the music's laconic beat. This is one of the first American Marley releases, if not *the* very first to begin to attract more than a hardcore audience; it contains his classic, "No Woman, No Cry." Soundwise, there is obvious compression throughout, but the vocals suffer most; the disc's overall sound is clean and while the rhythm tracks remain a bit murky, they do receive a dynamic lift.

### Natty Dread (1974)
Tuff Gong 422-846 204-2 (38:53)   [A]
The Marley catalog originally issued on the Island label was reissued in late 1989 on the Tuff Gong label using all-new digital mixes. The sound quality of the Tuff Gong recordings is consistently markedly superior to the earlier Island discs. In a sense this is the first real Bob Marley & the Wailers album. With the departure of Peter Tosh and Bunny Livingston, center stage, writing responsibilities, and direction of the group came together in Marley. *Natty Dread* is proof that he was not only up to the challenge, but that it was inevitable. A majority of the tracks, "Lively Up Yourself," "Them

Belly Full (But We Hungry)," "Rebel Music (3 O'Clock Road Block)," "Natty Dread," and especially "No Woman, No Cry," are extraordinary. The sound of the Wailers is markedly different, with the female trio the I-Threes providing very effective vocal backup, and the rock guitar of Al Anderson added to the mix. Soundwise, *Natty Dread* is more in-your-face than the echo-laden, laid-back feel of their previous releases. The Tuff Gong remix captures the enhanced dynamics and is marred only by occasional thinness in the I-Threes' vocals.

**Live! (1975)**
Island 7 90032-2 (40:34)  **[B + ]**
Recorded in London in July, 1975, this concert release features seven classic Wailers' songs, some of which go back to the original group that featured Tosh and Livingston. Marley was a hypnotically enthralling performer whose status went beyond the music to that of accepted spokesman for Third World political positions (he was wounded when he became the object of an assassination attempt in Jamaica). That intensity shows on this release, perhaps better than anywhere else on record. Both the sound (very "live" but muffled, dirty, and severely compressed) and the performance are on the ragged side. However, Marley's intensity more than carries the day, particularly his very moving reading of "No Woman, No Cry."

**Live! (1975)**
Tuff Gong 422-846 203-2 (37:27)  **[A + ]**
In addition to all the qualities that set Marley apart as an artist of the highest magnitude, he was a mesmerizing performer—a man able to elevate a concert to a spiritual level, lovingly shared, making the moment something beyond entertainment. *Live!*, his best concert recording, is ample proof. From pacing

to performance, it's about as good as a live recording can get. It builds like a Baptist sermon—rock-steady, anchored with voodoo bass, at times literally exploding with passion. The seven tracks are all first-rate Wailers chestnuts. While the opening "Trenchtown Rock" lacks focus, it's full speed ahead after that, and the version of "No Woman, No Cry" is definitive. The Tuff Gong remix is an improvement over the earlier Island disc, but there is a muddiness in the middle that keeps the overall sound quality at a level below that of the performance, and with a performance like this, that's a disappointment.

**Rastaman Vibration (1976)**
Island 7-90033-2 (35:10)  **[C + ]**
From political passion to more laid-back social commentary, *Rastaman Vibration* provides a continuation of the smooth groove that Marley and the Wailers had defined and occupied since earlier in the decade. While it lacks a single "classic" track, the recording is of consistent high quality. The sound is obviously compressed with some added detail in the upper midrange, but, it's really not much different from the LP—probably a little cleaner.

**Rastaman Vibration (1976)**
Tuff Gong 422-846 205-2 (35:23)  **[B–]**
This is a transitional recording, with the elimination of Island founder Chris Blackwell as a coproducer, as well as a change in instrumental lineup. In a political/lyrical sense, *Rastaman Vibration* is a continuation of Marley's revolutionary Rasta vision. Marley's vocal stance seems a bit askew, lacking the passion and intensity that would sustain the lyrical messages; overall, the quality of the songs, while listenable, is not up to the group's usual standards.

The sound quality is superior, but not as strong as most of the Tuff Gong remixes.

### Exodus (1977)

Tuff Gong 422-846 208-2 (37:21)  **[B + ]**
Less politically strident than its predecessors, *Exodus* features the affecting harmonies of the I-Threes and generally sweeter Marley vocals. Not all the cuts are strong, but the title track, "So Much to Say," "Jamming," and "Waiting in Vain" are all strong entries. Rasta roots (and buds) are integral to the reggae aesthetic and permeate the lyrics of this disc, not always an enhancement for the non-Jamaican listener. Still, *Exodus* remains a meaningful addition to the Marley catalog. Barry Diament's digital remastering tightens the bottom while opening and adding clarity to the total sound.

### Kaya (1978)

Tuff Gong 422-846-209-2 (37:16)  **[A + ]**
Clearly Marley's most accessible recording. This time out the Rasta and revolution have been set aside for more personal matters: love, joyous island moments, the glory of the sacred herb. An album infused with warmth and subtle, evocative vocals, *Kaya* may be Marley for the masses—it's ebullient, easy music, performed by a master at the top of his form. While strong from beginning to end, the very popular "Is This Love," "Easy Skanking," and "Time Will Tell" are particular highlights. The sound of *Kaya* has always been the best of any in the Marley catalog, and this remix enhances an already good thing to near perfection—a sonic delight.

### Babylon by Bus (1978)

Tuff Gong 422-846 297-2 (73:44)  **[B]**
Bob Marley was a riveting, mesmerizing performer who could turn a concert into a quasi-mystical experience. *Live* captures that magic more effectively than this double-LP concert recording taken from performances in Paris, Copenhagen, London, and Amsterdam. With the exception of the wondrous "Lively Up Yourself," all the selections on *Babylon* are different from those on *Live,* and Marley seems inspired by the audience response. The problem is in the instrumental portions, which tend to meander and drain the impact from Marley's songs. Yet the ardent fan will still derive satisfaction from live versions of "Punky Reggae Party," "Stir it Up," "Is This Love," and "Jamming," performed by a great reggae band backing a legend. The sound quality on this live release is excellent, and consistent from venue to venue.

### Survival (1979)

Tuff Gong 422-846 202-2 (38:09)  **[B–]**
By the end of the seventies Marley's music had become an anthem for the emerging Third World—in 1980 Bob Marley and the Wailers performed in the new government's independence ceremony in the African nation of Zimbabwe. The music on *Survival* reflects their political importance to the Third World, dealing with Marley's involvements with faith and oppression. Because of the generalized/politicized bent of the lyrics it often veers close to sloganizing, and because of many topical references, it has become dated, so *Survival* lacks the immediacy and durability of Marley's better work. Again, the digital remastering is a major sonic improvement.

### Uprising (1980)

Tuff Gong 422-846 211-2 (36:09)  **[A + ]**
Marley's final recording may be his finest—clearly one of the best from an awesomely influential career. All of his personal and lyrical concerns are

covered in these ten cuts—hope for personal and world redemption ("Coming in From the Cold"), political revolution ("Real Situation"), personal, pop-oriented music ("Could You Be Loved"). While it was "Could You Be Loved" that captured Western dance clubs, it is the album's final track, "Redemption Song," that comes closest to capturing the transcendent spirit that elevated Marley to a stature which, like only John Lennon and Bob Dylan before him, goes vastly beyond performance/entertainment. Too often during the seventies Marley seemed willing to accept a level of creative expression that only vaguely approached the sheer mastery within his grasp. On *Uprising* that mastery has been achieved, his singing, song writing, and sound coalesce into an enduring testament. He is sorely missed. This has always been one of the better sounding Marley recordings, and the Tuff Gong CD makes the good sound great.

### Confrontation (1983)
Tuff Gong 422-846 207-2 (37:52)   **[B]**
Posthumous releases are generally problematic at best (check out what's been done to Janis and Jimi), but as these things go, *Confrontation* is a respectable addition to the Marley catalog. This is attributable to the fact that the project was supervised by his widow, Rita Marley, a member of the I-Threes (the backup vocalists who joined the Wailers following the departures of Tosh and Livingston). The problem with *Confrontation* is in the songs: There were valid reasons why they never made it onto prior releases. But it's not without its moments: "Buffalo Soldier," which ended up in the excellent *Legend* compilation, and "Mix Up, Mix Up," a happy dance track. Even though these cuts were taken from different recording ses-

sions, there is consistency in the sound quality, which, as is the case with all the Tuff Gong reissues, is first-rate.

### Legend (The Best of Bob Marley and the Wailers) (1984)
Island 7 90169-2 (50:26)   **[A + ]**
The fourteen selections, released originally between 1972 and 1982, provide a fair overview of the career of one of the decade's most influential musical figures. From "Get Up, Stand Up," "Stir It Up," and "I Shot the Sheriff" through the live version of "No Woman, No Cry" to "Buffalo Soldier" and "Jamming," the collection captures the highlights by a man who understood the politics of his music and performed for much more than monetary sustenance. The sound is erratic, exhibiting both the positives and negatives of digital conversion in abundance. However, if you're looking for a one-disc sampler of the work of a reggae artist of first-rank importance, this would be the one.

### Rebel Music (1986)
Tuff Gong 422-846 206 2 (42:58)   **[A]**
This posthumous compilation focuses on the revolutionary, inspirational core of Marley's music—the part of the man that more than any other locked him in a special place in the hearts of dispossessed people the world over—the insinuating sounds of rebellion, the speaking of eternal truth. It is a powerful collection. It's also an excellent companion to *Legend,* the other compilation recording, which effectively captures Marley's more pop/personal/lyrical side. Though I'm sure that every fan will feel something is missing—in my case, I want to know what the hell happened to "Burnin' and Lootin'"—it's difficult to fault any of the ten included tracks. The CD includes excellent liner notes by Neil Spencer, which nicely capture the scope

of Marley's legend, primarily in the Third World. While there is some variation in the sound from track to track, the overall quality is excellent.

# Martha (Reeves) and the Vandellas

Formed 1962—Detroit

This group represented the "blackest" of the Motown girl group sound, in that Reeves's impassioned vocals were closer to her R&B roots than the pure pop product which Motown marketed so expertly.

### Dance Party (1964–1965)

Motown MOTO-5433 (30:22)   **[B–]**

Originally released in 1965, this Motown album includes two of their all-time classics, "Dancin' in the Streets" and "Nowhere to Run," but it's not a greatest-hits compilation. The remaining ten tunes are mostly filler, although their cover of "Mickey's Monkey" is notable. Reeves was probably the gutsiest female singer in the Motown stable, and with the Vandellas made some of the label's best party-down, shake-your-booty sides, but their *Compact Classics* or *Greatest Hits* CDs are a better way to go. The sound on this CD is clean, thin, and almost painfully shrill in the vocals.

### 24 Greatest Hits (1963–1971)

Gordy GCD06170 GD (65:08)   **[B+]**

Bright, brassy, and blues-based, Martha and the Vandellas showed more roots than any other female group to come off of Gordy's wondrous assembly line. This is get down party music, Motown style, and a quarter of a century after it first fueled a Friday groove, it still performs. The sound is thin and overbright, but as is usually the case with old Motown vinyl, this disc is still an improvement over the LP.

# John Martyn

b. 1948—Glasgow, Scotland

**Piece by Piece (1986)**

Island 7 90507-2 (58:44)   **[B+]**

Martyn weaves highly individualistic tapestries of sound, which include folk, jazz, blues, and light rock elements. There is a kinship between these sounds and the haunting works of Nick Drake. Since the late sixties, this artist has created a series of atmospheric recordings reflecting diverse influences, but resolving them in cohesive, appealing works which have enjoyed critical accolades and created a cult following, but they still remain outside of the ever-changing mainstream. While marred with continuous hiss, the CD's sound is very open, clean, and dynamic; a notable enhancement over the LP.

# Dave Mason

b. May 10, 1946—Worcester, England

**Alone Together 1970)**

MCA MCAD-31170 (35:06)   **[B–]**

Mason's first solo effort after leaving the legendary Traffic, *Alone Together* is a good, but not great record—too well-crafted, too safe. Nonetheless, his reputation as a composer, guitarist, and singer of the first rank is both merited and in evidence here. In addition, Mason is supported by first-rate musicians who work effectively together. The highlights include: "Only You Know and I Know," "World In Changes," and "Look at You Look at Me." The sound is essentially equivalent to that of the LP.

## John Mayall's Bluesbreakers
Formed 1963—England
**Mayall's Bluesbreakers with Eric Clapton (1966)**
London 800-086-2 (37:43)   **[B +]**
Before rock & roll was commandeered by the British in the early 1960s, there was an active audience in that country for local interpreters of American blues. This English musical tradition formed the launching pad for a number of major rock figures. While Mayall is a respectable blues musician (particularly on harmonica), his name is remembered more for the musicians who played in the Bluesbreakers from time to time than for the music actually made by that group. This disc features Eric Clapton—and arguably includes his finest recorded guitar work. The sound has a slight "distance" to it (because of the subtle reverberations that make it sound like it was recorded in a small dive), but it's much cleaner than any prior form of release, with a slight, unobtrusive, brightness or edge to it.

## Curtis Mayfield
b. June 3, 1942—Chicago
**Soundtrack: Superfly (1972)**
Custom CUR2002-CD (36:51)   **[B +]**
What could have been a slick soundtrack for another black exploitation film is elevated to another level by the Impression's former lead singer. "Freddie's Dead" and the title track charted, but there's an insinuating quality through all nine, and lyrics that speak truth. With disco beginning to drain the black music scene of its vitality, *Superfly* stands out for both its craft and creativity, benefitting from one of the sweetest soul voices of the era, coupled with some well-produced, light funk sounds. The sonics of this recording are impressive on CD, a minor problem being an occasional tendency to let the vocals slide a bit far into the mix.

## Paul McCartney
b. June 18, 1942—Liverpool, England
The son of a twenties jazz band leader, McCartney is a nonpareil writer of polished pop material. While his association with John Lennon in the Beatles provided a musical balance that turned the world of pop music on its ear, on his own (and with his traveling band, Wings), his lack of incisive lyrical intelligence and passionate commitment to more than commercial success has left a residue of emminently listenable but forgettable material.

**Band on the Run (1973)**
Parlophone CDP 7 46055-2 (41:13)   **[B]**
Easily, McCartney's most successful and listenable outing, *Band on the Run* was recorded in Nigeria and reflects both his fine pop sensibility and production acumen (most of the sounds that make up the recording were, in fact, done by McCartney alone in the studio). It does contain some strong seventies pop product, "Band on the Run," "Jet," and "Let Me Roll It" being the highlights. While it goes beyond mere aural wallpaper, it isn't any masterpiece either. The sound, marred by some hiss as well as harshness and distortion, is more open, dynamic, and warm than that of the LP.

**Venus and Mars (1973)**
Columbia CK36801 (43:30)   **[B–]**
Released in 1973, *Venus and Mars* was the follow-up to *Band on the Run* (which was basically all McCartney in the studio). With this recording, Wings again became a real rock band, notably through the addition of guitarist Jimmy McCulloch and drummer Joe English. For this

outing, the group went to New Orleans and availed themselves of the local musical riches, notably Allen Toussaint. The result is probably the best rock & roll that McCartney has made since departing his original group, particularly in the selections, "Rock Show" and "Listen to What the Man Said;" in no small part because Paul's songs here also have more spine than most of the post-Beatles saccharin pop with which he has been associated. The sound of the disc generally leaves a bit to be desired—heavy hiss, buried vocals, and occasional distortion are too much in evidence.

# Maria McKee
b. August 17, 1964—Los Angeles
**Maria McKee (1989)**
Geffen 24229-2 (45:06)   **[B]**
Ms. McKee, the former core of the short-lived Lone Justice, is one of the very best country/pop singers to appear in the eighties. Blessed with great pipes, the openness to convey her heart's message, and a riveting presence, her promise is yet to be fully realized. This may be because while she writes fine material, including all of these eleven selections, her songs never quite fully focus her major strengths. This, her first solo effort, sounds great, as is usually the result of Mitchell Froom's sympathetic production. The material is more confessional than country, and it's sung with open commitment.

# John Cougar Mellencamp
b. October 7, 1951—Seymour, Indiana
Originally, little more than another Midwestern Bruce clone. By the mid-eighties, he had turned his composing skills to his Midwestern, small-town roots, becoming a part of what has been dubbed "Heartland Rock."

**Uh-huh (1983)**
Polygram 814 450-2M-1 (32:59)   **[B–]**
*American Fool,* this album's predecessor, provided the first inkling that Mellencamp might have an independent point of view to express along with his acknowledged ability to create catchy musical hooks. The return to his surname was meant to mean something, but the retention of the bogus "Cougar" as a middle name sadly means more. This is the release that produced "Crumblin' Down," "Pink Houses," and "Authority Song," all of which are improvements over his previous output, but his simplicity, cynicism, and sameness overwhelm the remaining six tracks, Kenny Aronoff's drumming notwithstanding. Fortunately, the return to his Midwestern home and its values establishes *Uh-huh* as a base upon which Mellencamp eventually built a more respectable body of work. Don Gehman's fine engineering and production touches provide a clean, somewhat overbright sound with nice detail, a slightly soft bottom, and appropriate emphasis on drums.

**Scarecrow (1985)**
Mercury 824 865-2 M-1 (41:10)   **[B + ]**
*Scarecrow* is music concerned with the economic hard times and loss of traditional rural values that has affected much of America's midsection. The subject matter is valid, obviously heartfelt from Mellencamp's perspective (he still resides in his home state), and is presented on this album with power and precision. Musically, this artist doesn't break any new ground; Springsteen's powerful romantic rock echoes from every note, but Mellencamp writes some decent lyrics and his spirit appears to be more consistent with his roots. The title cut is the best item on the record, and it's a winner. The sound is dynamic, crisp,

and relatively open, with an unfortunate tendency toward overbrightness.

**The Lonesome Jubilee (1987)**
Polygram 832 465-2 Q-1 (39:47)   **[A]**
If rock & roll is any kind of political harbinger, then this fine recording may presage a populist revival to be reckoned with. With *Scarecrow*, John Mellencamp turned his lyrical focus to the life and concerns of America's rural heartland. Since the artist's feelings seem heartfelt, this redirection has increased the stature of his work significantly. Yet, populist ideals are only one facet of this complex effort. Mellencamp is dealing here with questions pertaining to the essence of the life experience itself, its joys, despairs, and ultimate inevitability. This context is presented within simple, yet sophisticated musical settings that employ a number of classic American folk instruments; e.g., Dobro, accordion, and violin, in addition to the standard rock band lineup, all of which connect the songs and themes to their somewhat obvious, but nonetheless enduring antecedents. Don Gehman's production has an energetic immediacy that the excellent digital sound fully communicates.

**Big Daddy (1989)**
Mercury/Polygram 838 220-2 (42:08)   **[A]**
There is a stark beauty to the level flatness of America's gutland illuminated by its seasonality. John Mellencamp and his crack band and production team come closer to capturing its myriad faces than probably anyone else. Kenny Aronoff's rifle-shot-in-the-wind drumming, Larry Crane's stark, driven guitar, and Mellencamp's coarse, country-tinged vocals stand together like stoic silos on a county highway. Mellencamp writes and sings of tradition and change, toughness and tenderness, memories and dreams,

with the conviction of a man who knows his heart's song. *Big Daddy* is further retrenchment from Mellencamp's early career built on hook-filled singles and snappy lyrics. At the time of its release, he announced he wouldn't tour in support of *Big Daddy*—but the videos diminished the import of that stance. Mellencamp is clearly an artist for whom maturity has meant introspection, committed concern, and a sense of self and place rare in modern pop. Less focused than *Scarecrow* and more insular than *The Lonesome Jubilee*, *Big Daddy* seems somehow sturdier. As is the case with earlier releases, his fine band is augmented with occasional fiddles and accordions that lend authenticity to Mellencamp's everyday observations on the details that define a moment or a lifetime. The disc has a stark purity of sound, with enough warmth to perfectly fit the mood and the message.

# Harold Melvin and the Blue Notes
Formed 1954—Philadelphia
Originally a doo-wop group, in 1970, Teddy Pendergrass moved from drums to lead vocal and the group signed with Gamble-Huff's Philadelphia International label.

**Collectors Item (All Their Greatest Hits) (1972–1975)**
Philadelphia International Label CK 34232 (46:51)   **[C + ]**
For the four years (1972–76) that Teddy Pendergrass's voice burned through the lovely Melvin vocal arrangements and Gamble and Huffs overburdened strings, Harold Melvin and the Blue Notes created some of the better disco/soul sounds to be heard. But Harold kept trying to hide Teddy until he finally lost

him. While Pendergrass was not featured on every cut on this collection, he is what elevates it above the run-of-the-mill. The man can emote with one of the biggest voices in the biz. The sound is generally clean (there is some very audible hiss in the quiet sections), but clear and dynamic; although some compression also remains evident, it is still a marked improvement over the LP.

## The Meters
Formed 1966—New Orleans
**Struttin' (1970)**
CD Charly 63 (53:27)   **[B +]**
As Roger St. Pierre's informative notes indicate, in the sixties many recording studios were used for their "house" bands as much as for their sound and advanced technology. The house band at Sea Saint Studios, co-owned by New Orleans's resident musical savant Allen Toussaint, was the Meters, probably best known for their crackling, propulsive drive behind Lee Dorsey's hits. Anchored by keyboardest Art Neville, this tight-knit house band could simply play. *Struttin'* is a compilation of their three prior albums, and its primarily instrumental content moves with rhythm and sass. The groove is pretty constant, which ultimately detracts from an otherwise first-rate compilation. The disc's sound is about as tight and dynamic as the playing, if occasionally a bit overbright in the upper midrange.

## George Michael
## (Georgios Panayiotou)
b. June 25, 1963—Finchley, Middlesex, England
**Faith (1987)**
Columbia CK40867 (58:04)   **[B +]**
Sure, he's the archetypical MTV mannequin. Sure, he began it all in a duo sadly

called Wham!. Forget it! The kid's a natural—he wrote, produced, arranged, and, of course, sings and plays his way through eleven selections, the best of which, "Faith" and "I Want Your Sex" are the apex of eighties techno-soul sounds. *Faith* is far from perfect, but at its best it shimmers, radiating considerable heat, and portends what may be quite a career. The sound is full, dynamic, and impressive overall.

**Listen Without Prejudice Vol. I (1990)**
Columbia CK 46898   **[F]**
Ptooey!

## Joni Mitchell
## (Roberta Joan Anderson)
b. November 7, 1943—Alberta, Canada
One of the most respected, covered, and influential of the singer/songwriters; her intelligently personal lyrical statements and sophisticated folk/jazz voicings have created a readily identifiable, honest body of lasting work.

**Ladies of the Canyon (1970)**
Reprise 6376-2 (45:00)   **[B]**
The folk song as art song, successfully transmitted by an honest enlightenment as youthful illusions acknowledge harder edged reality. Here Mitchell focuses on the piano rather than the guitar for accompaniment, adding to the more melodic flow of the material and the singing. While the compositions are uneven, "Big Yellow Taxi," "Circle Game," "Woodstock," and "For Free" have all become Mitchell favorites. The recording has a pleasant, clean analog feel.

**Blue (1971)**
Reprise 2038-2 (36:16)   **[A–]**
Poetic, confessional pop/folk/jazz by the one female singer-songwriter with

the guts and intellect to stand equally in the male-dominated world of early seventies pop/rock. Her painfully exposed experience and L.A. musical and production sensibility reached their zenith on *Blue*, which includes some of her strongest compositions: "All I Want," "Blue," and "The Last Time I Saw Richard." The minimal instrumental settings provided by Stephen Stills, James Taylor, Sneaky Pete, and Russ Kunkel add subtle nuance to a primarily vocal/acoustic guitar effort. The intimacy of the original recording is nicely preserved on the CD.

**For the Roses (1972)**
Asylum 5057-2 (40:36)   **[A–]**
Often complex, introverted, and confessional, this is arty (as opposed to emotional) folk music for moderns. Joni's work exhibits a certain pristine, strongly feminine quality. On *For the Roses*, her vocals are set amidst beautifully conceived, almost classical instrumental accompaniments. This is music which, for the most part, demands more attention than what usually is marketed under the "pop" label. It is also music that rewards the attentive listener. The sound, while sometimes disclosing slight hiss, is, overall, clear, and the disc accords the acoustic instrumentals full and detailed clarity, with Joni's unique voice preserved with all its idiosyncrasies.

**Miles of Aisles (1974)**
Asylum 202-2 (74:07)   **[B–]**
The eighteen selections, providing almost an hour and a quarter of early seventies concert performances, primarily cover Joni's most popular material: "You Turn Me On I'm a Radio," "Big Yellow Taxi," "Woodstock," "Blue," "Circle Game," "Real Good For Free," and "Both Sides Now" among them. Also included are lesser known, but

high-quality compositions such as, "Cold Blue Steel and Sweet Fire," "The Last Time I Saw Richard," and the fascinating "Jericho." Her performance, supported by Tom Scott's jazz-oriented L.A. Express and by her own solo accompaniment on piano, guitar, or dulcimer, has a very "live" feel in its straightforward unpretentiousness. The sound is definitely concert quality, not bad, but very compressed; somewhat noisy and occasionally strident. The CD sound emphasizes both the strengths and the weaknesses, and there is a fair share of both here.

**Court and Spark (1974)**
Asylum 1001-2 (37:00)   **[A + ]**
Because of the more melodic nature of the material and its less intricate lyrical convolutions, this is the highlight of Joni's major musical career. It is also as fine an example of the singer/songwriter genre as you will ever hear. Fortunately, the sound of the CD is clean, clear, and warm; of the same consistent high level as the rest of the package, making this a must disc.

**Wild Things Run Fast (1982)**
Geffen 2019-2 (36:45)   **[B]**
Joni's first record of the eighties and her first album of new material since 1974's *Court and Spark*, made with a nod to mainstream acceptance, is really a pretty good outing. The opening track "Chinese Cafe/Unchained Melody" creates effective, haunting resonance, and the cover of Elvis Presley's "(You're So Square) Baby, I Don't Care" has enough sass and pop to stand on its own. The other nine tracks, which are mostly wordy and upbeat, lack any obvious standouts, though all are more than acceptable. The music is synth-dominated, light jazz, provided by a diverse group of extras including Wayne Shorter,

Lionel Ritchie, and James Taylor. Sound-wise, *Wild Things* has a natural, clean, intimate quality that nicely enhances the material.

### Dog Eat Dog (1985)
Geffen 9 24074-2 (43:34)   **[A]**
A dense, multilayered, complex, and ultimately satisfying recording. This is the seventies singer/songwriter embracing the synthesized techno-rock of the eighties, which she employs with great dexterity and assuredness. Her lyrical preoccupations have moved from the self-confessional to the political. The melodies here aren't exactly hummable, but her vision is acute and her presentation ultimately sophisticated. The sound of the disc cuts the LP all to hell—its dynamic, precise openness adds an entire additional dimension, allowing the CD listener to hear the material the way it was intended.

### Chalk Mark in a Rain Storm (1988)
Geffen 24172-2 (46:27)   **[C]**
Not a real memorable outing. Let's leave it at that. Oh, yes, the sound quality is pretty good.

# The Modern Lovers
Formed 1972—Boston
Hans Christian Andersen discovers the Velvet Underground. Leader Jonathan Richman is an unselfconscious, natural contrarian who has joyously preserved the wondrous eye of a child for us all to see through. This is fragile rock & roll. Jonathan Richman loves Jonathan Richman and through his music, he communicates that love on a truly universal level that transcends explanation. Warning: This may be an acquired taste.

**The Beserkley Years**
**(The Best of Jonathan Richman and the Modern Lovers) (1971–1974)**
Rhino RNC 75889 (59:45)   **[A]**
This collection covers multiple versions of the Modern Lovers. The first incarnation (which included Jerry Harrison, later of Talking Heads, and Dave Robinson, later of the Cars) featured the production of John Cale (the original Velvet Underground cellist) resulting in the classics: "Roadrunner" and "Pablo Picasso" (included), as well as first-rate live and studio takes of material performed by Jonathan with subsequent versions of the band. The sound had to be tough to work with. Some cuts were literally recorded in a bathroom (Richman liked the echo), and Harrison has stated that the original band's recording philosophy was that "anything that was worked over lost its energy." Rhino's usual first-rate production efforts result in a detailed, spacious, nicely dynamic sound that is seriously marred with hiss and a generally noisy background.

# The Moonglows
Formed 1951—Louisville, Kentucky
**Look! It's the Moonglows (1956–1958)**
MCA CHD31267 (33:56)   **[B–]**
Among the mid-fifties doo-wop groups, the Moonglows were standouts for their smooth, mellow ballads, notably their 1954 No. 1 R&B hit, "Sincerely," which isn't included in this Chess album, originally released in 1977. While Bobby Lester provided most of the leads, Harvey Fuqua ultimately had the most impact, particularly through his later affiliation with Motown. *Look! It's The Moonglows* includes "Ten Commandments of Love" in all its hokey glory, and a smooth cover of the Clovers' 1955 moody hit, "Blue Velvet." Overall the

performance is better than the material, but there are some warm memories here for those who remember the pre-Elvis world. The sound is nothing special, particularly because of excessive tape hiss, but it is also noticeably compressed, suffering from dropout. This budget disc does include nice liner information.

# Van Morrison (George Ivan Morrison)

b. August 31, 1945—Belfast, Northern Ireland
The mystic Irish minstrel of rock & roll who, after leaving Them (the band that first brought him international acclaim) in 1966, has pursued his private vision, on his own terms. In the process he has created a legacy of unique music rooted in the blues, jazz, and Celtic mysticism that maintains an enduring potency, perhaps unique in the annals of rock & roll.

### Astral Weeks (1968)
Warner Bros. 1768-2 (47:16)   [A+]
Perhaps the single most enduring recording in the history of rock & roll, and it probably really isn't rock & roll at all, with his jazz musicians and mystical vocal flights into another "land on high." A recording for those tranquil yet vibrant moments when another reality seems to hover over the day to day like the mists over Van's native Ireland. The CD is very clean and clear, but adds little dynamic or spatial enhancement to its analog predecessor. The most apparent difference is an overall "brightening" of the sound, especially in the vocals, which, while short of the edginess often criticized in digital sound, is not necessarily an improvement.

### Moondance (1970)
Warner Bros. 3103-2 (39:17)   [A+]
Robert Christgau said it best: "Morrison's soul, like that of the black music he loves, is mortal and immortal simultaneously; this is a man who gets stoned on a drink of water and urges us to turn up our radios all the way into . . . the mystic." This is as good as it ever gets. The CD suffers from consistent hiss and a slight tendency to overbrightness in Van's vocals, but, on the positive side, it's detailed and dynamic with a warm, spacious sound.

### His Band and the Street Choir (1970)
Warner Bros. 1884-2 (42:22)   [A−]
The mystical Irish minstrel of rock & roll mixes some contemporary soul with some Crescent City rhythms as a follow-up to his formidable *Moondance*. It's a comedown; it almost had to be, but it's still a damn fine outing. The tone is less visionary and more soul party, which yields some rousing up-tempo numbers, notably the hits, "Domino" and "Blue Money." Sound quality varies (actually it's easy to distinguish between the various recording sessions); most cuts are compressed with little, if any, enhancement over the LP, whereas others are marred by very audible hiss and edgy overbright sound, but exhibit more dynamics and detail.

### Tupelo Honey (1971)
Warner Bros. 1950-2 (40:50)   [B]
The happily, hippily Marin County domesticated version of Van Morrison. It fit its era, and reflects some of the better qualities of the Summer of Love. Yet in retrospect (and, in fact, at the time of its release) the lack of apparent struggle seems to sap some of the mystery and intensity simmering at the core of Morrison's more enduring work. There are moments when the sheer joy illuminating his vocals ("Wild Night," "Moonshine Whiskey" and "Tupelo Honey" come immediately to mind) seems contagious—but then how many Irish

minstrels get to marry Janet Planet? The sound is clearer and brighter than the original vinyl, with enhanced vocal subtlety, but the bottom is a bit weak and muddy.

### St. Dominic's Preview (1972)
Warner Bros. 2633-2 (41:34)  **[A]**
*St. Dominic's Preview* is where Van Morrison unleashes his soul's soaring voice and claims that special place where magic resides. The sounds are jazz and R&B, the voice and vision are uniquely Morrison's—music of images and visions. Not everything included is far reaching—"Gypsy" never overcomes its trite concept, "I Will Be There" is a proficient light-jazz throwaway, and "Redwood Tree," despite its minor chart success and ecological bent, is too bucolic and naive. But "Jackie Wilson Said (I'm in Heaven When You Smile)," "Listen to the Lion," "St. Dominic's Preview," and "Almost Independence Day" are among the man's best recordings, and that's really all that needs to be said. The sound quality is crisp and clean, but a bit thin and boxy.

### Hard Nose the Highway (1973)
Warner Bros. 2712-2 (43:12)  **[B−]**
Certainly a comedown from its predecessor, *St. Dominic's Preview*, *Hard Nose the Highway*'s sound is more jazz than R&B, the lyrics too often a disparate patchwork, and the musicianship tends toward the lackadaisical and overblown (check out the Oakland Symphony Chamber Chorus on "Snow in San Angelino"). Still, it is not without its rewards: "Warm Love" is an enduring uptempo ballad, and "Wild Children" is an obliquely offbeat ballad that is one of the most haunting songs in Morrison's extensive repertoire—and one to which he has returned in concert. Unfortunately, the rest is hardly memorable,

although his very personal reworking of "Purple Heather" is not without its charm. Other than occasional slight edginess to the vocals, the sound has a nice spaciousness, decent separation, and dynamic range. One of Morrison's most perplexing and poorly received recordings.

### T.B. Sheets (1974)
Bellaphone 288-07-001 (42:52)  **[B]**
Contains the fascinating transitional recordings done around 1967, between the end of Them and the beginning of the Warner Bros. solo career in 1968, which commenced with the breathtaking *Astral Weeks*. From "Madam George," which is included on both recordings in markedly different readings, to elements of other selections, this is the obvious precursor to Van's better-known work. It also contains the truly frighteningly title cut, and one of the two best rock singles of his long recording career, "Brown-Eyed Girl" (the other being "Gloria" from his Them period). The disc has a clean but dated, hard-edged, overbright sound, which suffers occasionally from some nasty distortion.

### It's Too Late to Stop Now (1974)
Warner Bros. 2760-2 (92:32—two discs)  **[A + ]**
Hearing this live Morrison recording, it's difficult to accept the common perception that he is an erratic, generally uncomfortable, live performer. When he's right, as he was on the three shows from which this live set is drawn, it's damn near sanctified. The eighteen included tracks are mostly gems from Morrison's songbook—"Into the Mystic," "Listen to the Lion," "Cyprus Avenue," "Gloria," "St. Dominic's Preview," "Wild Children," "Caravan" and "Domino"; he also uses the occasion to revisit the blues, soul, and R&B roots that originally shaped his music. Backed by the

Caledonia Soul Orchestra, which could hold its own on a Saturday night in a South Chicago blues joint, Morrison cooks with conviction throughout. In this heady environment, the originals take on new, immediate textures, and the covers confirm Morrison's stature as one of the greatest blues/soul/R&B singers of his era. To top it all off, someone spent a fair amount of time with digital conversion from the master tapes, resulting in an excellent improvement over the vinyl—it is one of the best-sounding concert recordings around, obviously live, but with a full, nicely balanced sound.

### Veedon Fleece (1974)
Warner Bros. 2805-2 (47:48)   **[B]**
Melancholy, contemplative, and pastoral, *Veedon Fleece* proved to be Van's last release before a three-year hiatus from recording and performing. Its first five tracks create a lyrically abstract, lilting musical web, swirling with mystery but calming in effect. Then comes "Bulbs," an ebullient rocker squarely in the tradition of Morrison's buoyant upbeat best. Unfortunately, the remaining four selections meander meaninglessly nowhere—an extended fade. For the hardcore Morrison fan, sixty percent is good enough, particularly if it includes "Linden Arden Stole the Highlights," "Sheets of Arklow," and "Bulbs." For the less ardent, there are any number of other Morrison recordings that are better overall. The sound quality is just OK, suffering from an overall thinness and some vocal harshness.

### A Period of Transition (1977)
Warner Bros. 2987-2 (34:12)   **[C]**
After Van's three-year retreat from recording, *Period of Transition* was greeted with much expectation; in retrospect, it is one of his weaker efforts. Hell,

I'm *from* Kansas City, and I find "The Eternal Kansas City" an embarrassment. Produced by Morrison and Dr. John, *Period of Transition* is generally New Orleans upbeat, but the repetitive nature of the simplistic lyrics and a less than stellar vocal outing by Morrison take their toll. The occasional use of choirs adds nothing but heavy-handed production. The mediocre-to-poor sound quality—harsh, thin, edgy, bereft of bottom—detract further. Sadly, it all adds down to a major disappointment.

### Into the Music (1979)
Mercury 800 057-2 (49:50)   **[A + ]**
After 1972's *St. Dominic's Preview,* Morrison released four albums (one of which, *It's Too Late To Stop Now,* was a live double-record set) over the next six years which declined in both content and popular acceptance. 1979's *Into the Music* celebrated a resurgence of the creative powers that he had exhibited at the end of the prior decade. On this recording, he sounds more in command of his prodigious talents than, perhaps, anywhere else on record. His singing is a testament to the expressive powers of the human voice; the instrumental combination of strings (Toni Marcus on violin, etc.) and R&B horns (beautifully arranged by Pee Wee Ellis and Mark Isham) has proved to be a resonant background for Van's religious and fleshly visions since the time of this release. The whole thing is great, but the last four selections, concluding with the almost eleven minute "It's All In the Game/You Know What They're Writing About" may be his recorded tour de force. The sound is clean and nicely detailed, though the "stage" is not overly spacious and there is an overall tendency toward too much brightness, particularly on the uptempo numbers, but, these aren't major complaints.

## Wavelength (1978)

Warner Bros. 3212-2 (50:08)  **[B +]**

*Wavelength* confirmed that our darkest fears were unfounded—*Period of Transition* notwithstanding, Morrison was returning to form. Very pop-oriented, particularly the first six tracks, this is a good, not great, Van Morrison recording, which means it still stands head-and-shoulders above most of the music released in 1978. From the late sixties to the early eighties, Morrison lived in Marin County, California, and his fascination with the U.S. provided much of the lyrical basis for *Wavelength,* particularly the final track, "Take it Where You Find it," which, along with "Santa Fe/Beautiful Obsession," are the highlights of one of his most listenable efforts. Notable for Morrison's soaring voice throughout, the CD's sound is first-rate—resonant, detailed, and spacious.

## Common One (1980)

Mercury 830043-2 (55:06)  **[A–]**

*Common One* is, in many ways, a seminal recording in this fascinating artist's career. After a dozen generally successful years with Warner Bros., he was dropped from its roster as "part of an overall artistic realignment"—probably due to his reputation as a difficult artist who refused to participate in the market-driven eighties hype. Morrison moved back to Europe—the result was unpretentious jazz/classic R&B augmented by judicious use of strings and organ. Morrison sails on a stream of literary and R&B allusions guided by his growing spirituality. *Common One* is a noble, often moving experiment that may not be totally realized, but it is a serious work by an artist who has followed his muse more consistently than any of his peers. Made up of only six selections, two of which, "Summertime in England" and "When Heart is Open," take up over

thirty minutes, this is a recording that has been embraced by his fans and pilloried by critics. It's clearly not your everyday pop product, and it only infrequently attains the heights of Van's most incandescent work, but the first three tracks make it a worthwhile addition to the collection of any serious Morrison fan. The sound on the disc is full and rich, with dynamic subtleties that give digital sound an edge over its analog predecessor.

## Beautiful Vision (1982)

Mercury 800036-2 (45:08)  **[A]**

Van's first great album of the eighties—it works as a whole, revealing lovely, lyrical moments, and includes one of the best rockers from his prolific career, "Cleaning Windows," a killer track that speaks of musical and personal history, social strata, and telling influences with natural ease. The central element remains Morrison's growing preoccupation with more orthodox spirituality, but on *Beautiful Vision* it is imbued with a buoyant beat that emphasizes and effectively communicates its pure sense of joy. The album closes with a gorgeous instrumental, "Scandinavia," that presages and surpasses the increased use of instrumentals on its successor, *Inarticulate Speech of the Heart.* The sound of this release is a disappointment—too often thin and reedy in its upper ranges, tending toward harsh and edgy vocals.

## Inarticulate Speech of the Heart (1983)

Mercury 811 140-2 (47:01)  **[A]**

Van as ecstatic Irish spiritual visionary. *Inarticulate Speech of the Heart* is a beautifully conceived and executed homage to the "auld sod." Notable for its orchestral textures (a number of the cuts are instrumentals), it has a conceptual completeness which is rare in pop music. Van's return to his ancestral homeland seems to have had a salutory effect on both the man and his music. Thus, while the mood is often almost elegaic (there is not a cut on the album that even approximates a "rocker"), *Inarticulate Speech of the Heart* proves to be an uplifting, even joyous listening experience. The highlights are "River of Time," the instrumental "Celtic Swing," "The Street Only Knew Your Name," and "Cry For Home." The CD's sound is open, expansive, clear, and defined—it completes an almost perfect recorded presentation.

**Live at the Opera House Belfast (1985)**
Mercury 818 336-2 (52:05)  **[B + ]**
Morrison's discomfort in live performance is legendary. This is only the second release of concert material in a recording career that spans more than twenty years (the first being *It's Too Late to Stop Now*). With the exception of the briefest instrumental reference to "Into the Mystic" in the intro, the eleven selections are drawn from Van's post-1978 recordings. While nothing included is an enhancement over the studio originals, it is a polished, well-received performance on which Morrison sounds confident, if not exactly comfortable. The CD sound is excellent for a live recorded effort, with clear separation, impressive dynamics, and a tendency to overbrightness in the vocals and brass.

**A Sense of Wonder (1985)**
Mercury 822 896-2 (43:39)  **[B + ]**
Morrison's most specific, spiritually directed recording—the sounds of a sensitive, caring man dealing with the cosmic wonders of pure spirituality. As such, it is generally about as far from rock & roll as anything this fascinating artist has recorded. The usual diversity of influences (blues, rock, jazz, and tra-

ditional) is clearly reflected here, and Van is singing at the height of his powers, which is about as good as it gets. The sound is a revelation: open, spacious, defined, warm, and clean.

**No Guru, No Method, No Teacher (1986)**
Mercury 830 077-2 (51:14)  **[A + ]**
Rich instrumental textures, some great songs ("Got To Go Back," "A Town Called Paradise," and the best upbeat song he has done in years, "Ivory Tower"), plus some of the most impressive singing by anyone in pop music, make this Morrison's strongest album in years. His influence within the world of pop music has been incredibly direct and broad, but it is only a hardcore cult within the mass market that appreciates and supports this man who is a treasure in our contemporary musical culture. The sound is crystal clear, defined, open, and warm.

**Poetic Champions Compose (1987)**
Polygram 832 585-2 (48:13)  **[A]**
Stilted title notwithstanding, this is one of Morrison's most lyrical outings—more song cycle than collection of disparate elements. *Poetic Champions Compose* opens ("Spanish Steps") and closes ("Allow Me") with lovely instrumentals featuring Van's alto saxophone and is intersected by a third ("Celtic Excavation"). While there are no individual selections that stand out (with a possible exception of his evocative reading of the traditional "Motherless Child"), it is precisely the flowing continuity of the work that ultimately provides its special appeal. The instrumentation employed is very consistent with all of this artist's post-eighties recordings, featuring both strings and horns to create almost orchestral textures. Morrison's singing is direct and natural. All of this adds up to lovely music for a Sunday morning or an

autumn evening. The sound is well-defined, smooth, and generally clean. The only real criticism is a certain lack of spaciousness which an all-digital recording might well have added.

## And the Chieftains
## Irish Heartbeat (1988)
Mercury 834496-2 (39:01)   **[C]**
While Morrison gets top billing, this is really another Chieftains flute-and-fiddle-flogging Irish folk fest—the kind that has kept these graying traditionalists at the forefront of Erin's worldwide nostalgia merchants for too many years. Eight of the ten included selections are traditionals arranged by Morrison, the other two are his originals, "Celtic Ray," given a stronger reading on *Beautiful Vision,* and the mournful, traditional "Raglan Road," the clear standout. Soundwise, there is nothing extraordinary about *Irish Heartbeat,* it feels compressed and somehow shallow.

## Avalon Sunset (1989)
Mercury 839 262-2 (42:38)   **[A–]**
Rock's great Irish minstrel has followed his personal musical vision since "Gloria" burst upon the world in 1962. It has been an arduous and varied journey that at the end of the eighties found him more overtly religious, but enduringly compelling. *Avalon Sunset* is infused with his faith, love, and mystery, carried by some of his most soulful singing in years—it has moments of beauty ("Have I Told You Lately"), pure pop pleasure ("Whenever God Shines His Light"), as well as evocative reflection ("Coney Island"). Morrison's fine musicianship is evident in the musical atmospheres underpinning his romantically inclined, worshipful lyrics. The sound is close to flawless. A worthy addition to a career of artistry and integrity that now spans three decades.

## Enlightenment (1990)
Mercury 847 100-2 (51:07)   **[A]**
Morrison continues to track his private muse as he has done since his 1968 stylistic breakthrough, *Astral Weeks.* Since 1980's *Common One,* he has chosen to further isolate himself from the commercial American music scene, living in his native Ireland and working in England. There have been occasional limited U.S. tours, just enough to reward a few of the longstanding faithful while frustrating others. His abbreviated American tour in support of 1989's *Avalon Sunset* featured English pop legend George Farme on keyboards and vocals, and even included some rare club appearances. Farme joins him on *Enlightenment,* which continues the textures, pacing, and lyrical concerns that have shaped Morrison's creative output for more than a decade—his spiritual and secular hymns to God and sensual love. Despite its title, *Enlightenment* feels more secular than its immediate predecessor and is, perhaps, a bit more joyous for it. While strings and choirs are used to orchestrate his musical visions, they always swing. What he has abandoned in vocal mannerisms results in his most effective singing in years. The days have apparently passed when Van Morrison will reveal substantial shifts from one recording to the next. He has passed the years of evolution and has justly won a loyal following. While *Enlightenment* may not bring him many new converts, it will more than satisfy those for whom his roots-based music occupies a unique place. This is nourishment for the spirit. This is an expression of the gentler joys of the middle years. This is just another great Van Morrison recording. Its sound quality meets the same high standards—first-rate.

**The Best of (1965–1989)**
Mercury 841 970-2 (76:24)   **[B + ]**
Twenty selections from a recording
career that embodies more than twenty
years and twenty albums. The word is
that Van had a hand in selecting the
tracks that comprise his first and only
"best-of" collection, which only confirms
his reputation as a difficult artist. It's not
that there are any truly weak inclusions,
this overview runs from classic work
with Them ("Gloria," "Here Comes the
Night," and "Baby Please Don't Go"),
through a sample from his brief, frustrating Bang collaborations ("Brown Eyed
Girl"), to 1989's fine *Avalon Sunset*
("Wherever God Shines His Light,"
"Have I Told You Lately")—most coming
from his eighties releases. Devoid of previously unreleased material, it does
include the only CD version of the good,
not great, "Wonderful Remark," Van's
contribution to the *King of Comedy*
soundtrack. Obviously a decision was
made to stay away from his longer
songs, thus, the painful omission of "Listen to the Lion" in an effort to make
room for twenty songs, but there's no
logical reason to omit "Slim Slow Slider"
and "Into the Mystic." Morrison is a very
personal voice for most of his devoted
fans, all of whom probably feel their
own sense of outrage at the absence of
one or more meaningful songs. Since his
material has never produced much chart
success, a "greatest hits" approach
would not have provided a meaningful
criteria. In addition to the aforementioned, *Best of* does include a fair
sampling of his more upbeat classics,
"Moondance," "Jackie Wilson Said,"
"Domino," and "Cleaning Windows." So,
overall, it's a fair, not great, sampling,
and the song sequencing is about as
arbitrary as the songs themselves.
Soundwise, there is noticeable variation
in quality among the tracks, ranging
from first-rate to fairly average. Sonic
quality is not a major distraction on any
track, and the reproduction of the Them
selections is the best available.

## Mott the Hoople
Formed 1968—Hereford, England
**Greatest Hits (1972–1974)**
Columbia CK 34368 (38:40)   **[B]**
Mott is a bit of an anomaly. They began
their existence as a hard rock band, but
with the addition of Ian Hunter as lead
singer and principal writer, they took on
a Dylanesque coloration. However, it
was their affiliation with David Bowie
during his early-seventies glitter period
that provided them with "All the Young
Dudes," a song that catapulted them to
brief fame. Consummate borrowers
from their better- and lesser-known rock
brethren, Mott melded disparate elements into a dynamic, often humorous,
sound that combined the bombast of
early heavy metal with seventies glitter,
and just about everything else you or
they could think of. In retrospect, Mott
was a more potent band than originally
perceived. *Greatest Hits* is a reasonable
sampler, but is inferior to both *All the
Young Dudes* and *Mott*. As an overview,
thirty-eight minutes isn't long enough;
too much quality material is omitted,
such as "Ready For Love," "Sea Diver,"
and "Sweet Jane." What remains is generally first-rate, it's just too bad that
Columbia didn't take advantage of the
other half of the CD's capacity and provide a disc that is a fairer sample of this
fun band's erratic but rocking career.
Given the diversity of original material,
the disc's sound is remarkably consistent
and generally acceptable. However, it
does suffer from compression, some
muddiness, and rather closed imaging.

# Bob Mould
Former lead guitarist, creative fount of
Hüsker Dü.

**Workbook (1989)**
Virgin 91240-2 (52:47)   **[A]**
Sometimes the best of contemporary
music is the toughest to grasp. Certainly
with his prior band, Hüsker Dü, Mould's
complexity and personal intensity were
often obliterated by the slashing energy
of the band's attack. All of that and much
more are brought to the fore in this
haunting, searing solo work that chronicles pain, disenchantment, hope, and
perhaps catharsis. The musical palette
provided by Mould, Tony Maimone (Pere
Ubu), Anton Fier (Golden Palominos),
and Jane Scarpantoni (Tiny Lights) is
impressive in its scope. While Mould is
clearly an original of great talent, *Workbook* echoes the instrumentals and
vocals of Richard Thompson. This one
probably won't grab you at first or even
second listening, but Bob Mould is an
artist of complexity and honesty, in
whom an investment of time will yield
meaningful rewards. The sound on the
disc is sensational.

# Elliott Murphy
b. March 16, 1949—Garden City, New York
**Aquashow (1973)**
Polydor 835 587-2 (37:19)   **[A–]**
This little-known early-seventies gem is
a delightful CD discovery. The lyrical
form and instrumental configurations
are strongly reminiscent of classic Dylan
and, yeah, Murphy also plays harp.
What sets it apart is his ability to write
a decent tune and an insightful, knowing lyric. In his liner notes to this CD
reissue, Murphy rightfully acknowledges
Pete Seigel's production, which goes a
long way toward explaining the quality
sound on this release—it isn't perfect,
but it's bright and accurate. Pretty damn
good singer/songwriter stuff. Murphy
released three follow-up albums, but
*Aquashow* was his watermark.

## Loey Nelson
### Venus Kissed the Moon (1990)
Warner Bros. 26089-2 (50:44)  **[B]**
A solid sleeper from a promising new-comer. Loey writes much of her own material, but her covers range from Ste-phen Sondheim to Dr. John and Doc Pomus. Upbeat and melodic, if not inspired, this is music that brings a smile. The big-rep L.A. studio musicians are competent, but it's Loey's freshness that carries the day, and she does just fine. The sound won't set you on your ear, but it isn't a distraction, either. Her next outing could be very interesting. Here's hoping she gets a shot at it.

## Rick Nelson
## (Eric Hilliard Nelson)
b. May 8, 1940—New Jersey (raised Los Angeles)
d. December 31, 1985
Riding the exposure of the famous "Ozzie & Harriet Show" radio and TV series, Rick brought his brand of Holly-wood rockabilly into many American homes in the fifties, where otherwise rock & roll would have been totally unwelcome. Working with premier musicians, particularly James Burton on lead guitar, Rick Nelson ultimately proved to be sincerely committed to the simple, basic form of rockabilly which he presented with integrity and appeal.

### In Concert—the Troubadour 1969 (1970)
MCA MCAD 25983 (40:03)  **[B]**
Nelson's easygoing brand of country/rockabilly/folk/rock grew up in L.A., so it's only natural that he and his band, which included Randy Meisner on bass, would sound completely comfortable at that city's folk/rock mecca. You certainly can't fault his choice of cover material: Bob Dylan, Tim Hardin, Eric Anderson, to name a few. The fact that this album never really went anywhere probably has more to do with the era of its origi-nal release than with the fact that his performances often sacrifice potency for stylistic consistency. All in all, it's a fairly laid-back good time, of particular inter-est to hard-core fans. The live sound is nothing great, but its OK for what it is.

### The Best of Rick Nelson (1957–1962)
EMI America CDP-7 46558 2 (34:30)  **[B + ]**
Most, but not all, of Nelson's hits are included among the fifteen selections comprising this brief disc. The sound quality, while generally clear and spa-cious, is weak and often muddy in the low end, and on certain cuts reproduc-tion is far from ideal. But considering the technology available when these recordings were made, the digital enhancement is still apparent. James Burton's guitar work alone is worth the price of admission.

# Aaron Neville
b. January 24, 1941—New Orleans
**Orchid in the Storm (1985)**
Rhino R270956 (21:00)   [C+]
The choice of material is fine, doo-wop
classics like "Pledging My Love," "The
Ten Commandments of Love," and
"Earth Angel," and Aaron is in fine
voice (which is always saying a lot), with
brother Art joining him on three selections. It just doesn't make it somehow;
the ethereal instrumental backing blurs
rather than frames the unique, almost
otherworldly, sound that is Aaron
Neville's. Still, when the hour's late. . . .
Soundwise, Rhino's mix emphasizes the
overall smooth quality of the production.

# The Neville Brothers
Formed 1977—New Orleans
As much a part of the Crescent City's
R&B scene as the gumbo or crawfish
pies for which this most fertile of Ameri-
can musical cities is justifiably famous.

### Fiyo on the Bayou (1981)
Demon Fiend CD65 (35:44)   [A−]
Dave Marsh said it as well as it could be
said: ". . . as fine a set of New Orleans
rhythm and blues workouts as anyone's
put together in the past decade." The CD
sound is clean and generally clear, but
reflects some slight muddiness in the
mix and an overall compressed LP-like
quality.

### Neville-Ization (1984)
Demon Fiend CD31 (43:01)   [A−]
It's live gigs, not record sales, that have
kept these guys earning a living since
the fifties, and this recording from a
night at the famed Tipitina's in New
Orleans paints a pretty clear picture of
the reason why. Great vocal harmonies,

insinuating rhythms, and Aaron's aching, amazing voice all combine to create
bar-band music New Orleans style—like
it's supposed to be. They immerse a
number of sources into their spicy musical gumbo: Peggy Lee's hit "Fever,"
Bobby Womack's "Woman's Got to Have
It," a classic reworking of Aaron's "Tell it
Like it Is" (which can turn the rowdiest
Saturday night crowd into a church-like
atmosphere), and Duke Ellington's "Caravan." For a live recording, the sound
quality of this disc is pretty impressive.

### Treacherous: A History of the Neville
Brothers (1955–1985)
Rhino R2 71494 (102:51—two discs)   [A]
The Nevilles are one of the great enig-
mas of American popular music—the
No. 1 band in New Orleans, with strong
work covering four decades; their failure
to achieve major national stature has
been a concern of rock reviewers for
almost as long as the Nevilles have been
around. Some argue that their music is
too regional. Some complain that no
record producer has managed to capture
the riveting rhythms and voodoo energy
that make their live sets breathtaking.
Probably they're too black and too
regional for a white audience, and too
regional for a black audience. Thankfully they have maintained a cult following of sufficient size to keep them recording since the mid-fifties. *Treacherous*
is an effective overview of an illustrious
career, presented in an excellent Rhino
package, which means comprehensive
liner notes and the best possible sound—
although it varies substantially depending on the age and source of the original
material. While the Nevilles, jointly and
individually, have appeared in many
permutations (the Neville Brothers Band
itself was formed in 1977), consistent
strains flow through it all—marvelous
polyrhythms, R&B roots, and an endur-

ing belief in the redemptive power of faith. To top it off there is the soaring, almost angelic voice of Aaron, whose hair-raising classic, "Tell It Like It Is," is one of four live cuts included among the twenty-eight.

**Live at Tipitina's Volume II (1987)**
Spindletop Records (62:14)   **[B + ]**
The follow-up to 1986's *Neville-Ization*, which was also recorded live at Tipitina's. For current New Orleans sounds, Tipitina's is considered the place to be; one of the reasons for its rep is its close affiliation with the first family of New Orleans music. Since the 1982 incarnation of the band included Ivan Neville, this family included two generations. *Live* is a good, but not great, New Orleans party disc, with a little reggae ("Wake Up"), Motown ("My Girl"), some gospel ("Riverside"), a children's song ("Little Liza Jane"), and fine leads from Aaron on "Wildflower" and "Doo-Wop Melody." It could have been enhanced by tighter arrangements, but it's clear that the band and the house were gettin' in to a good time. The sound reflects its live source, too often muddy, and occasionally a bit edgy.

**Yellow Moon (1989)**
A&M CD5240 (53:03)   **[A]**
One of the great production challenges for more than three decades has been how to capture the fire and excitement of New Orleans' first family of contemporary music. Daniel Lanois brings his atmospheric approach to the party, coming closer than most, but still the live Nevilles and the recorded Nevilles remain distinctly different experiences. But this time out it doesn't matter—this is the band's best studio statement to date—and it's one hell of a statement. Combining religious/political themes into the seven originals, and five covers

from such worthy sources as Link Wray, A.P. Carter, Sam Cooke, and Bob Dylan, they turn the obvious into a true testament, all the while immersing us into the voodoo gumbo of the Big Easy's real roots. The Nevilles get sympathetic support from Lanois, Brian Eno, and the Dirty Dozen Brass Band, but it is the soulful singing of Aaron, Art, and Cyril, and Charles's saxophones, that create the reverent spirit illuminating this fine release. The sound quality is of the same high caliber as the performance.

**Brother's Keeper (1990)**
A&M 75021-5312-2 (55:58)   **[B + ]**
Combine the love of God, religion, politics, and social concern with a heady dose of New Orleans' rhythmic gumbo, add the voices of one of pop's premiere musical families, and the results are engaging—at times splendid. This is another damn good release by a group that has waited for literally generations to be discovered by the mass market. The overall feel of *Brother's Keeper* is more laid back than prior recordings, yet it does have moments of moving intensity and the usual strong rhythmic underpinnings. Old fans won't be disappointed, but I'm not sure how many new ones this will attract. The sound has a warm clarity that feels appropriate to the overall mood. ("Mystery Train" still belongs to the King.)

# Randy Newman
b. November 28, 1944—Los Angeles
Misanthropic, mischievous and hideously insecure, Newman remains one of the few genuinely intelligent, humorous, and truly musically creative artists still at work in the pop arena.

## 12 Songs (1970)
Reprise 6373-2 (29:54)  [A + ]
This release by L.A.'s resident rock
weirdo was described by the often
astringent Robert Christgau of the *Village Voice* as "a perfect album." From
menace to metaphor, Newman reveals
his truths with a simplistic brevity that
often belies its universality. In less than
thirty minutes he explores a world of
offbeat American experience with a sly
delivery and marvelously jaundiced eye.
Newman's original version of "Mama
Told Me Not to Come" is a totally different version than Three Dog Night's No. 1
cover, and the other eleven are every bit
its equal or better. Using a limited instrumental backup featuring Ry Cooder
on bottleneck, Newman and his piano
conjure up a variety of musical styles
that provide perfect settings for his off-
center lyrics. Sadly, the sound quality
reveals its analog origins, from tape hiss
to limited dynamic range, boxy sound-
stage, and noticeable variation from
track to track—yet it remains an improvement over its vinyl counterpart.

## Sail Away (1972)
Reprise 2064-2 (30:38)  [A]
Generally thought to be Newman's best
recording, *Sail Away* offers fascinating
textures and some of Newman's most
effective songwriting, notably the title
track, "Lonely at the Top," and the wick-
edly weird "You Can Leave Your Hat
On." It doesn't all succeed, but then he
grapples with some basic concepts—
"God's Song (That's Why I Love Mankind)," and some cheap-shot humor,
"Political Science"—all in the name of
irony, of course. One of the more
encouraging things about the world of
commercial pop music is that whenever
the reticent Newman garners enough
inspiration to fashion an album, not
only does it get released, but enough

people buy it to repeat the cycle—it's
enough to make you wonder (I'm sure
Newman does). But releases like *Sail
Away* give validity to the pop song as a
vehicle for meaningful expression. The
sound is a shade compressed, but still
strong.

## Good Old Boys (1974)
Reprise 2193-2 (33:56)  [A]
A portion of Newman's youth was spent
in the South, and this biting musical
evocation of America's most creative and
problematic region may be more caricature than insight. It also provides the
most conceptually complete work of
Newman's career. While "Rednecks,"
with its racially abusive lyrics, may have
garnered the most attention (certainly
controversy), it is "Marie," "Louisiana
1927," and "A Wedding in Cherokee
Country" that are the album's highlights.
They are all top-flight Newman, particularly the latter, which captures his
tortured humor and twisted vision as
well as anything in his repertoire. As
always, his musical settings are imagi-
natively perfect, with able assistance
provided by Ry Cooder, Bernie Leadon,
Glenn Frey, and Don Henley, among
others. The sound quality varies a bit
from track to track and is, overall, a bit
flat, but is superior to the LP. It all adds
up to one of Newman's better recordings.

## Little Criminals (1977)
Warner Bros. 3079-2 (38:41)  [B–]
Because it included "Short People,"
Newman's only hit single (it charted for
twenty weeks, holding down the No. 2
position for three weeks), this was easily
Newman's most popular album, reaching No. 9. Unfortunately, it is far from
his best—his lyrical muse seems to have
deserted him. He goes through the usual
motions all right, but too often the results are cruel, rather than creative, let

alone insightful. It does have its moments: "Sigmund Freud's Impersonation of Albert Einstein in America" and the L.A. country send-up, "Rider in the Rain," performed with the Eagles. But two out of twelve is a lousy batting average, even for a lesser artist. What it does have are creative, lush musical arrangements, which are fairly effectively reproduced on the CD, albeit with slight compression and a tendency toward harshness in the heavier vocal passages.

### Born Again (1979)
Warner Bros. 3346-2 (35:20)   **[B–]**
With *Born Again*, Newman moves from character to caricature. It's not that his obvious targets (hideously pretentious rock bands, money-warped TV evangelists, plus various other unpalatable denizens of the misplaced eighties) don't merit the slings and arrows—it's just that somehow it used to matter more. At least it exposes the razor's edge on which Newman so deftly trod for so long. This is one of his best-sounding recordings, with strong, occasionally overbright dynamics and presence.

### Lonely at the Top—The Best of Randy Newman (1968–1983)
Warner Bros. 241 126-2 (69:44)   **[A–]**
As compilations go, this import has a lot to recommend it—twenty-seven samplings from fifteen years of regional, erudite, wry, sometimes weird, but generally wonderful, music. Newman is a unique case, as talented as he is uncomfortable. Obviously with an artist this perverse you'll never get agreement on his best recordings, but with the general high quality of all his work there really aren't that many dogs in the bunch—just some interesting inclusions and omissions. Since his albums generally are somewhat conceptual, any extractions have to be viewed as just that. But

beginning with "Love Story," his brilliant three-minute encapsulation of a lifetime, to a 1971 live version of his "Lonely at the Top" (which Sinatra would have recorded, if he had a sense of humor), this CD covers seven albums, the most recent being 1983's *Trouble in Paradise*, with more than a casual visit to each. So if you're looking for a career overview with a fair sampling of the familiar, you can turn this one up. As expected, the sound is all over the map, but nothing's awful and nothing's extraordinary.

### Land of Dreams (1988)
Reprise 25773-2 (40:18)   **[A–]**
Middle age hasn't mellowed Newman, nor has it dimmed his brilliance. Brooding and bruised, *Land of Dreams* is a keyboard-flavored, lushly produced peaen to the insecurity and ruthlessness of his L.A. environment, and his geographically and socially transient history. Randy Newman may not be a happy man, but he is an honest one, and music is his genius. The recording opens with two storytelling autobiographies: "Dixie Flyer" and "New Orleans Wins the War," both of which evoke innocence and uncertainty. It flirts with rap, "Masterman and Baby J," and closes with one of the toughest songs of recent memory, "I Want You to Hurt Like I Do." There are some up moments, "Falling in Love," as well as some social consciousness, "Roll with the Punches" and "It's Money That Matters," but the overall tone is personal and painful. What makes it matter is a unique talent at the top of his often sardonic form. The sound is natural, full, and nicely detailed.

# New Riders of the Purple Sage
Formed 1969—Marin County, California
The country offshoot of the Grateful
Dead.

### The Best Of (1976—compilation release date)
Columbia CK34367 (30:50)  **[D–]**
Second-rate country by ersatz second-
rate country players. Suffice it to say,
their timing was about the only thing
right about this group. The sound varies,
from roughly LP equivalence to some
cuts with slight detail and dynamic
enhancement.

# Harry Nilsson
# (Harry Nelson)
b. June 15, 1941—New York City
**Nilsson Sings Newman (1970)**
RCA 4289-2-R (25:49)  **[B + ]**
The Newman is, of course, Randy, who
provides the ten songs, piano accompaniment, some vocals, and occasional
audible cues. It's a tribute to both the
material and the performance that such
low-key, simple production values and
minimal musical elements can evoke so
much, so easily. Newman is one of pop
music's honest-to-God composers whose
jaundiced lyrics can evoke nostalgia and
insight simultaneously—no mean feat.
This deceptively simple excursion into
the art of the pop song has remained a
cult classic for twenty years now, and it
retains an ageless grace and charm.
Given the apparently low-tech nature of
the master tape, the sound nicely com-
plements the warmth and intimacy of
the performance, but lacks breathing
room.

# The Nitty Gritty Dirt Band
Formed 1966—Long Beach, California
More country than rock, in 1977 became
first American band to tour U.S.S.R.

### Will the Circle Be Unbroken (1972)
EMI American CDPB7 46589 1/2
(119:34—two discs)  **[A]**
After Gram Parsons and the Byrds made
their way to Nashville and created coun-
try/rock with *Sweetheart of the Rodeo,* a
veritable subculture of country/rock
sprung up in Southern California—given
the Dust Bowl roots of many of the earlier immigrants to that area, this really
isn't as far-fetched as it might have first
appeared. Until 1972, the Nitty Gritty
Dirt Band was among the moderately
successful practitioners of this pop-based
hybrid. Then they had a bright idea:
Bring the prior generation's stars of the
Grand Ole Opry to the rock audience and
join in the fun. Assembling a half-dozen
of country's living legends—Mother
Maybelle Carter, Earl Scruggs, Doc Watson, Roy Acuff, Merle Travis, and
others—they gathered at Woodland
Sound Studios in Nashville and recorded
some hallowed classics of American
bluegrass in an atmosphere that readily
conveys the easy respect and informal
joy of making music that is an integral
part of their lives and the lives of their
forebears. Interspersed with occasional
conversation, there is a laid-back naturalness to the enterprise, elevating it to
near-classic status. It went a long way
toward realizing the Dirt Band's objec-
tive of bringing indigenous white
American music to a generation that
was revolutionizing the world's popular
music by building on indigenous black
American music. These thirty-eight
songs—a few of them instrumental—
pretty much cover the acknowledged
classics of the form. If you even *think*

you like country music, this set is a must, and if you're not sure, it may convert you. Great care was obviously taken in the original recording process, because the sound on this release is uniformly excellent—clean, crystal-clear, with a natural warmth.

**Will the Circle Be Unbroken Vol. 2 (1989)**
Universal OVLD-12600 (72:27)   **[A]**
Back in 1971, when the Nitty Gritty Dirt Band went to Nashville and enlisted legends to bring classic country sounds to the generations, they created an influential, classic recording, *Will the Circle Be Unbroken.* Their vision on this 1989 all-digital sequel may have been less grandiose, but the end result is equally listenable. Joined by Johnny Cash, John Hiatt, Johnny Rivers, John Denver, Levon Helm, Emmylou Harris, Roseanne Cash, Bruce Hornsby, Ricky Skaggs, and Roger McGuinn on individual tracks, the feeling is one of musicians playing for the joy and the interplay. There's not a weak track among the twenty included, and the highlights—the John Hiatt/Roseanne Cash erotic celebration of "One Step Over the Line," Highway 101's Paulette Carlson's heartbreaking "Lovin' on the Side," the Byrds-like reprise with Roger McGuinn and Chris Hillman of Bob Dylan's "You Ain't Goin' Nowhere," or the Dirt Band's original "When it's Gone" are what make down-home country playing an enduring delight—after all, this is the music that weaned Elvis, Carl Perkins, Buddy Holly, and the Everly Brothers. The sound is a pure delight—clear, distinct, intimate, and warm; it just doesn't get much better than this.

# The Notting Hillbillies
**Missing . . . Presumed Having a Good Time (1990)**
Warner Bros. 26147-2 (40:45)   **[B]**
The clarity, ambience, and spaciousness of this all-digital recording is seductive as hell. Mark Knopfler and some lesser-known English pickin' and singin' buddies revisit traditional American folk/country material with generally satisfying results. Also included are old Delmore Brothers and Louvin Brothers standards, along with Charlie Rich's "Feel Like Going Home," plus some similar new material from members of the group, including Knopfler. Though somewhat out of step in concept, the easy interplay of these talented players provides a surprisingly enjoyable outing.

# The Nylons
Formed 1979—Toronto, Canada
An a cappella quartet whose repertoire runs from doo-wop to gospel and pop.

**One Size Fits All (1982)**
Open Air OD0301 (30:24)   **[C + ]**
Slick, proficient, eminently listenable vocal music by four guys who are at least keeping the idea (if not the spirit) of the fifties great street corner harmonies alive and well. The standouts on this, their debut release, are, "Silhouettes" and "Bop! Til You Drop." The sound is simply faultless—this is a demonstration-quality disc.

**Seamless (1984)**
Open Air OD-0304 (33:48)   **[B−]**
Aptly titled, although soulless is equally applicable. They sing four-voiced harmony with dynamic precision, but there is little beneath the shimmering surface. *Seamless* is their best recorded effort as a result of the superior song selections.

"The Lion Sleeps Tonight" ("Wimoweh") even garnered commercial airplay, no mean feat for an almost a cappella group. Again, the sound quality is extraordinary.

### Happy Together (1986)
Open Air OD 0306 (33:51)   [C–]
At least they didn't call this one *Support*. More of the same, with a few more sound effects added to the mix. The title cut is as good as anything they've recorded, the rest of it is more shiny surface without substance; pop music for the new-age, no-soul crowd. If it's possible, the sound is even better (more definition) then on their two earlier disc releases.

# Laura Nyro
b. October 18, 1947—Bronx, New York
### Eli and the Thirteenth Confession (1968)
Columbia CK9626 (47:04)   [C–]
Let's just get it up front on this one: I'm not a fan. I respect her ability as a songwriter, but as a performer, I find her voice artificial and grating. However, during the late sixties and early seventies, Nyro had a devoted following for her confessional, soulful material, and this album is considered to be among her strongest recordings. Sadly, the CD's sound is abysmal, replete with obvious tape hiss with a thin, harsh quality overall. Purchase only if it's a personal favorite and your LP is missing.

# Sinead O'Connor

b. 1966—Ireland

Intense, outspoken, excruciatingly honest, stunningly talented, and bald. One of the most potent artists to arrive in the last decade.

## The Lion and the Cobra (1987)
Chrysalis VK41612 (42:23)  **[B]**

The highly acclaimed debut by the young woman whose princely inspiration three years later would turn her into a household word. *The Lion and the Cobra* is a bit too pretentious, and the heavy Kate Bush and Peter Gabriel influences tend to constrict its visions, but the youthful ambitions of O'Connor more than redeem the effort. It's not that the material, mostly written and produced by O'Connor, is that weak, it's just that it's not that distinguished—too often the production techniques overwhelm the message rather than amplify it. It's the way she sings—naked, without artifice, and with total intensity and commitment—"Drink Before the War" and "I Want Your (Hands On Me)" are the most fully realized and successful of the nine tracks. The disc's sound is somewhat problematic, often sacrificing clarity for opacity, which was probably intended, but wholly unnecessary. An uncommonly powerful pop voice.

## I Do Not Want What I Haven't Got (1990)
Chrysalis F2 21759 (51:10)  **[A]**

According to the rock press, O'Connor's record company resisted releasing this potent and immensely popular recording "because it was too personal." What further proof is needed that the industry and its audience are functioning in totally different spheres? Blessed with scorching intensity and one of the most expressive, impressive voices in recent memory, the visually riveting O'Connor delivers ten strong songs expressing a brief (she's twenty-five), turbulent life already exposed to personal and political perfidy. But in her performance, she overcomes and transcends it all to deliver what may be the first great album of the nineties—a statement of harmony, honesty, and musical diversity. Great pop music often extends personal exorcism to common experience, and this is great pop music. The excellent sound manages to balance crystal clarity with human warmth; you simply can't ask for much more.

# Roy Orbison

b. April 23, 1936—Vernon, Texas
d. December 7, 1988—Hendersonville, Tennessee

One of the second tier of rock's founders, Orbison pursued his pop/rock "outsider" vision through a life filled with tragedy and a voice of near operatic dimension, leaving a unique and enduring musical legacy.

**For the Lonely: 18 Greatest Hits (1956–1964)**
Rhino R2 74193 (46:31)   [A + ]
This balladeer of broken hearts and hidden dreams added a dimension to the early rock era by drawing inspiration from pre-rock pop music rather than from the gospel/R&B/country/blues sounds that fueled most of the revolution. Yet in a very intimate and personal way Orbison's operatic classics partake more of the spirit of Elvis than of Tin Pan Alley. This compilation is one of Rhino's historic best, and given the overall quality of the label's CD catalog, that is high praise. *For the Lonely* covers 1956 ("Ooby Dooby," Sam Phillips's attempt to convert Roy's Texas roots to rockabilly fame) through 1964's No. 1 "Oh, Pretty Woman," all of his Top Ten hits ("Only the Lonely," "Blue Angel," "Running Scared," "Crying," "Dream Baby," "In Dreams," "It's Over," and "Mean Woman Blues"), plus "Blue Bayou," and more. The excellent sound quality of this disc not only captures Orbison's classic songs, it vividly demonstrates his remarkable range, expressive voice, and the creativity of his productions. A fitting tribute to one of pop's often overlooked major contributors.

**Mystery Girl (1988)**
Virgin 91058-2 (38:17)   [B]
Imbued with the sadness at the heart of all of Orbison's best work, and the knowledge that its release followed his untimely death just as his star was deservedly rising again, *Mystery Girl* is a double disappointment. The problem is not the performance—Roy's operatic voice soars with richness and clarity in first-rate sonic reproduction. The problem is weak material, especially the ridiculously insulting "Windsurfer." Producer Jeff Lynne's pop/schlock tendencies sabotage more than a few otherwise quality performances, and on *Mystery Girl* his insipid vision almost overwhelms a truly great and original talent. Thankfully, a slew of other first-rate performers were involved—T-Bone Burnett, Elvis Costello, Tom Petty, George Harrison, and Bono—adding a few classics to the Orbison legacy: "In The Real World," "She's a Mystery to Me," and "The Comedians." The recording fully captures the sound and unbelievable richness of Orbison's voice, as well as the fully orchestrated but sometimes bombastic instrumentation.

# Graham Parker
b. 1950—East London
The largely undiscovered major talent to arise out of the later seventies British musical rennaisance.

### Howlin' Wind (1976)
Mercury Polygram 826273-2 (42:15) **[A]**
It took forever for Parker's label to get this classic on CD, but then Parker's career has been one long wrestle with popular acceptance. Too honest, sensitive, and smart to sell out to the hype, Parker has worked within the industry since 1976 to produce over a dozen albums, most of which garnered critical raves and consumer yawns. The lack of popular response is a mystery, particularly when it comes to this, his debut with his driving band, the Rumour (descended from Brinsley Schwarz). From the midst of mid-seventies pop lethargy and self-indulgence roars *Howlin' Wind,* driven by a vocal passion rooted in R&B and quickly emulated by the punks that soon followed. This is rock & roll smoldering with edgy honesty—music as emotional catharsis. The set includes "White Honey," "Back to Schooldays," the title track, and "Don't Ask Me Questions," perhaps Parker's best song, all of which belong in any comprehensive collection of meaningful seventies rock & roll. The sound, while far from state-of-the-art, is a notable enhancement over the original vinyl.

### Heat Treatment (1976)
Mercury/Polygram 826274-2 (35:59) **[A]**
It's rare that the promise of a debut album is realized in the follow-up, particularly when that follow-up is released within the same year as the debut. Sure, in the sixties, Dylan, the Beatles, and the Stones did that, but in the mid-to-late seventies when disco ruled? Yet that's precisely what Parker did with *Heat Treatment,* the charging, rage-driven successor to *Howlin' Wind.* Again backed by one of the era's few great bands, the Rumour, Parker sneers, rages, and sings the hell out of ten tough songs written from the gut of an artist for whom rock & roll means redemption (or, at least when he cut this one, it did). The title cut, "That's What They All Say," "Hotel Chambermaid," and especially, "Fool's Gold" are standouts, but there's not a weak sister in the bunch. The music is driven R&B, complete with snappy horns this time around, and the vocals are pre-punk paeans to disillusionment, both romantic and political. The sound on the CD is bright, clean, and generally wonderful.

### And the Rumour
### Stick to Me (1977)
Mercury 624808-2 (37:10) **[B–]**
This Nick Lowe–roughly produced effort doesn't succeed, but there are still some strong statements by Parker amidst the overblown and the pretentious. The title

track more than musters the requisite rebellious raunch, and his cover of "I'm Gonna Tear Your Playhouse Down" captures his trademark snarl effectively. Too much of the rest is merely good, not great; some of it ("The Heat in Harlem") just ain't worth a shit. The sound is dirty, raw, and edgy—it fits.

**Squeezing Out Sparks (1979)**
Arista ARCD 8075 (34:59)  **[A]**
This is hard-assed, hard-edged, hard-workin' rock & roll in the fullest classic, yet current, sense. The Rumour, one of the era's best pub-rock bands, drives with near manic intensity while Parker spews out his truthful, honest anger above it all. R&B-based, rock-rooted, these are the outpourings of a man who believes in the power of rock & roll with all the fervor he possesses. Sheer excitement enhanced by bright, hard, crisp dynamic sound. There wasn't a lot of great rock & roll made in the latter half of rock's transitional decade, but this was some of it, and it's tough stuff.

**And the Shot**
**Steady Nerves (1985)**
Elektra 9 60388-2 (43:21)  **[B]**
A bit of return to form for the struggling Mr. Parker. The addition of old cohorts from Brinsley Schwarz and Parker's slash-and-burn intensity turn the whole thing up a needed notch. Yet the lack of commercial acceptance plagues him and his effort misses the intensity required to cut through the pop/slick overlays; although "Wake Up (Next to You)" is a strong rock/pop ballad he handles effectively. Even with the radio airplay that song engendered, this wasn't the one to put Parker on top, either. This CD has a big, bright, clean, dynamic sound.

**The Mona Lisa's Sister (1988)**
RCA 8316-2-R (39:09)  **[C + ]**
Parker's honesty, anger, and bitter lyrics made him the darling of rock critics in the last half of the seventies. It was also perceived to be the reason for his failure to build a major audience—money and fame notwithstanding, this guy wanted his message to reach the masses. Since his original classics, he has moved from record company to record company, constantly fiddling with his production approach, trying to find the common code. This time out, he has recalled Brinsley Schwarz, which would suggest new sparks for the old fire. Forget it—this is laid-back pop that is dilution, not rejuvenation. Oh, it's listenable enough, and there are some nice lyrical moments, but what the hell happened to the snarling bastard punk pioneer whose music so obviously mattered? The sound is first-rate—open, clean, and as dynamic as the material will allow.

**Human Soul (1989)**
RCA 9876-2-R (43:49)  **[B + ]**
Graham Parker remains one of the unwashed legion of second-tier rock stars whose candle is carried by rock critics, yet who never manages to ignite a mass-audience spark. Over the years this progenitor of the English punk sound has approached various record companies to break through to popular success. For a brief period, he even took some of the bite out of his acerbic lyrics in the hope of finding more popular acceptance. Happily, *Human Soul*—his third release on RCA in two years—evidences a strong return to his root energy, wit, and bite. Assisted by some fine British musicians schooled in the pub and punk scenes (including members of Elvis Costello's Attractions and Brinsley Schwarz), Parker delivers an album that

contains moments of the same energy and cantankerousness that marked his best work. *Human Soul* is not equal to *Howlin' Wind* or *Heat Treatment,* but it is still one of the better things he's done in the eighties. The instrumentation, which is bright, brassy, and appropriately brittle, draws heavily on Parker's interest in American R&B. This high-energy release is notable for Graham's impressive and impassioned vocals, as well as the expected sprinkling of corrosive lyrics evidencing his continually jaundiced view. The CD sound quality is a little boxy, but overall does not detract from the end result

### Live! Alone in America (1989)
RCA 9673-2R (52:31)   [C]
The title tells it all. The critics know Parker is great; the listening public isn't buying. Of the fourteen tracks, ten are covers of his classic mid-seventies material ("White Honey," "Hotel Chambermaid"); one is a Sam Cooke cover ("A Change is Gonna Come"); and the remaining three are new. Parker is in great voice, and the CD's sound is warm, but obviously live. The sad fact is that there's really not much happening here.

# Gram Parsons (Cecil Connor)
b. November 5, 1946—Winter Haven, Florida (raised Georgia)
d. September 19, 1973—Joshua Tree National Monument, California
The son of country singer/songwriter Coon Dog Connor, Parsons came by his roots legitimately. During his sadly brief career, he proved to be one of the least recognized but most influential figures of the late sixties and early seventies musical scene. Parsons's brief association with the Byrds resulted in 1968's *Sweetheart of the Rodeo,* the seminal country rock album that gave rise to an L.A.-based genre that became a dominant strain in early seventies rock music.

### And the Fallen Angels Featuring Emmylou Harris Live 1973
Magnum CDSD 003 (47:23)   [B + ]
Parsons's heartfelt, haunting music is a true expression of an American cultural heritage which he made compatible with rock. These sounds have bound people and regions together for generations; Parsons, Harris, and crew perform them with a commitment and respect that establish both their history and immediacy. This album contains many of his and other writers' contemporary country classics performed live, and with the exception of his wondrous "Hickory Wind" is essentially comprehensive. One listen to this fine recording should explain Dave Marsh's observation that, "Parsons's influence is wide, deep, and likely to last." Of the eleven selections on this club-recorded disc, seven are included on the *GP/Grievous Angel* two-fer. "California Cottonfields," "Country Baptizing," "Drug Store Truck Driving Men," and "Six Days on the Road" are all pleasant enough, but not exceptional, although "Six Days" does have a certain buoyant urgency about it. The production values are pretty archaic; Emmylou's vocal mike is out of balance and given to distortion, and there is occasional feedback. While it appears the digital remastering did as much as possible with the source material, the sound is rough, thin, and boxy. Still the whole affair has a pleasant informality, interspersed with ad lib, but basically inane, spoken intros and asides.

### GP/Grievous Angel (1973/1974)
Reprise 9 26108-2 (75:11)   [A]
The disparity between Parsons's influence and his public awareness may be

greater than that of any contemporary musician. His brief, highly individualistic, intense life probably accounts for much of it. Yet, he's the guy who turned the Byrds from a folk/rock band to the founders of country/rock with *Sweetheart of the Rodeo*. Out of that, for better and worse, a whole L.A.-based school of contemporary music has evolved. Parsons's cult following is principally built on these, his only two major studio releases, which make for a perfect pairing on CD. His voice isn't the equal of his aesthetic, but most of the time his heartfelt commitment to the material more than gets him through. He also judiciously teamed up with newcomer Emmylou Harris, who provides her crystalline country support. The choice of musicians is also hard to fault: James Burton's guitar, Al Perkins, Buddy Emmons, and Byron Berline. There are twenty tracks on this disc, twelve of which were written or cowritten by Parsons. The remaining are drawn from an interesting cross-section of country writers: Tompall Glaser, Tom T. Hall, Peter Wolff, Seth Justman, the Louvin Brothers, and Boudleaux Bryant. There are some magic moments and some near misses, but overall, it's a wondrous compilation of country rock. Given the vintage of these recordings, their sound is impressive. Sonically *Grievous Angel*, because it's not quite as bright as *GP*, gets the nod, and the material on that album is a bit stronger than that on *GP*.

## Paul Revere and the Raiders
Formed 1959—Boise, Idaho
**The Legend of Paul Revere (1961–1971)**
Columbia C2K45311 (151:43—two discs)   [C + ]
With Dylan's *Biograph*, Columbia pioneered the concept of the boxed career overview aimed at the CD market, and established a high standard for

the format. While Columbia withdrew from that market until late 1990, other manufacturers have advanced the form to curatorial levels. Columbia is now returning to the fray—and well it should, given the vast array of meaningful material in its vaults. Why they have chosen to turn their efforts to a popular, but not really significant, American band for purposes of a premium package remains a bit of a mystery. The only apparent reason is that Paul Revere and the Raiders is one of the better-known acts that escaped CD conversion until fairly late in the game. With over two hours of music, this is an exhaustive set. This means fifty-five separate tracks from a group that charted only twenty-four songs, five Top Tens and one No. 1, "Indian Reservation." This overkill does deliver extensive and apparently complete factual information, and the theme song to Dick Clark's mid-sixties TV show, "Where the Action Is." It's all here, perhaps proving that the whole is substantially lesser than the sum of its parts. My biggest criticism of this overblown endeavor is the brutalization of the original mixes—the producers of this set chose to replace the original, lost stereo mixes with newly created ones, managing to bury or obscure the drum and guitar that originally gave these songs their exuberance. The resulting sound, if you care, is merely adequate.

## Ann Peebles
b. April 27, 1947—East St. Louis, Illinois
**Greatest Hits (1969–1988)**
MCA MCAD-25225 (33:44)   [C + ]
Like Al Green, Ann Peebles's recordings were shaped by the meticulous production of Memphis-based Willie Mitchell and the wondrous rhythm in Al Jackson's drums, which Mitchell would record with up to twenty-two separate

mikes. Peebles is a capable soul singer whose minor R&B hits have been covered by the likes of Tina Turner ("I Can't Stand the Rain"). On CD, the clarity and snap of Mitchell's production moves up front and the slight thinness in Peebles's voice is unfortunately betrayed. This slick package with informative notes features excellent sound and tight arrangements. Unfortunately, just like Peebles's career, it just never really takes off, but if you're already a fan, you won't be disappointed.

# Michael Penn
**March (1989)**
RCA 9692-2-R (42:32)   **[C+]**
Penn wears his influences, principally the Beatles, on his sleeve, but rock's other sixties and seventies elite make their presence felt in this debut. The basically simple production celebrates the tunes themselves, which are all first-rate, if somewhat derivative; Penn writes lyrics with more intelligence and maturity than are usually found on debut albums. This may be because he is not a youngster. The only thing missing from the Penn package is a singing voice; sadly, his is mundane at best. In the hands of an artist with greater vocal ability, the strength of the material would have resulted in a stronger release. *March*'s sound has a mechanical, hard edge that adversely affects its appeal, and the vocal mix is often muddy.

# The Pentangle
Formed 1967—England
**Basket of Light (1969)**
Transatlantic TRACD 205 (41:04)   **[B–]**
This band attempted to preserve the English folk music tradition and instrumentation by enhancing it with modern recording technology tinged with some

jazz overtones and rhythms. The result is apparently soulless, beautiful music that sounds like fine crystal. The disc does nothing to diminish the extraordinary sound quality that made the LP an audiophile favorite for years. It's clean, amazingly detailed, and spacious, with marginal hiss.

# Carl Perkins
b. April 9, 1932—Jackson, Tennessee
Another of the originators whose sounds first emanated from the Sun Studios in Memphis, Tennessee, Perkins's role would have been assured by virtue of the fact that he wrote the rock anthem of the 1950s, "Blue Suede Shoes." In addition to that achievement, Perkins remains an extraordinary guitarist and exponent of pure rockabilly sounds, with the emphasis on the country aspect of that form.

**Dixie Fried (1956–1959)**
Sun CD Charly 2 (59:56)   **[B+]**
All of the key original Sun recordings are included. The sound quality varies from cut to cut, and the overall dynamic range is expectedly limited; however, the general clarity and mix are good. The musical content of this disc is great, including the obvious popular hits as well as some lesser known true gems like the title cut.

# The Persuasions
Formed 1962—Brooklyn, New York
The only known surviving U.S. sixties doo-wop group, the Persuasions (with help from Frank Zappa, who gave them their first recorded exposure) have maintained a career doing pure a cappella music for more than a quarter of a century.

## Chirpin' (1977)

Elektra 1099-2 (34:42)   **[A]**

When it comes to a cappella/doo-wop music, no group has left a more indelible imprint than the Persuasions. For almost thirty years these four extraordinary singers raised Brooklyn street-corner harmonies to wondrous, soaring levels, anchored by the orchestral bass voice of the late Herbert "Tubo" Rhoad. *Chirpin'* is generally considered their strongest recording; if it's not, I want to hear what *is*. Each of the ten selections presents the art of a cappella/doo-wop/soul/gospel singing as well as you're ever likely to hear it, and "Pappa Oom Mow Mow," Tony Joe White's wonderful "Willie and Laura Mae Jones," and "Moonlight and Music" are special. The clean surface afforded by good digital reproduction frames and adds depth to this musical marvel, and the warmth and clarity of the voices never sounded better. As they say: "If you only own one a cappella CD. . . ."

## No Frills (1986)

Rounder 3083 (35:52)   **[B + ]**

This 1986 release isn't the equal of the 1977 classic, *Chirpin'*, but it provides the CD buyer a historic footnote—the unaccompanied street-corner (so-called "doo-wop") harmonies that fueled much of the fifties nascent rock sounds. Built on one of the most resonant bass voices you'll ever hear ("Tubo" Rhoad), their repertoire runs from gospel, to pop and doo-wop (all of which are fairly represented here). The pure expressive joy of the human voice raised in song is their stock in trade. The sound is clean, but it exhibits the limitations of its analog roots in its compression and somewhat closed space.

# Tom Petty (and the Heartbreakers)

b. 1952—Gainesville, Florida
Formed 1975—Los Angeles

One of the forms of rock to take shape in the seventies has been dubbed "arena rock"—potent, anthemic statements delivered with sufficient impact and sonic drive to be heard in the huge venues to which the rock promoters moved the audience during the decade. Petty, along with Springsteen and Seger, represented the best examples of the genre.

## Damn the Torpedos (1979)

MCA MCAD5105 (36:54)   **[B + ]**

Classic late seventies American rock & roll—bright, tight, forceful, well-written, and produced music played by a first-rate group of musicians whose joy comes through. Quality rock anthems for the assembled masses. The sound is clean, punchy, and well-defined, with a slightly edgy overall brightness that sometimes teeters on the edge of discomfort.

## Hard Promises (1981)

MCA MCAD37239 (40:09)   **[B + ]**

This is top-quality American mainstream rock & roll performed with a hard edge and honest intent. Perhaps not the equal of *Damn the Torpedos* (its immediate predecessor), but it's close enough. Highlighted by "The Waiting," "The Insider," "King's Road," and "A Thing About You," this recording, along with *Damn the Torpedos*, constitutes the best work by one of the most powerful late seventies/early eighties rock bands working. Jimmy Iovine's deft production captures every nuance. *Hard Promises* on disc reveals a clean open sound, precise separation, and sparkling dynamics that bring new life to a fine outing by a first-rate band working at the top of its not inconsiderable powers.

**Full Moon Fever (1989)**
MCA MCAD 6253 (40:00)   **[B]**
Southern roots and British Invasion
memories continue to define Petty's
musical domain. His unique, affecting
voice is in strong mettle on this Jeff
Lynne–produced solo release. The
whole thing has a loose, easy ambience
that adds to its accessible charm. If you
believe that each new release from a
major artist must represent some notable growth from its predecessor (a
common misconception), then *Full
Moon Fever* may prove a disappointment. Working with Lynne, George
Harrison, Roy Orbison, Benmont Tench,
Mike Campbell, and Jim Keltner, Petty
fashions a listenable, sometimes affecting outing that includes "Free Fallin',"
another hot, great love song by a man
who's written more than a few memorable ones. Yeah, I could do without the
Byrds cover, but big deal! The sound
quality is first-rate—clear, chiming,
warm, and propulsive.

# Wilson Pickett

b. March 18, 1941—Prattville, Alabama
The "Midnight Mover," "Wicked Mr.
Pickett's" raw, sexy sounds remain as
primal and effective as any in R&B.

**Greatest Hits (1963–1971)**
Atlantic 7813737-2 (71:18)   **[A]**
The wicked Mr. Pickett was one of the
most macho of the soul giants who recorded for Atlantic Records during the
sixties, the label's golden era. Beginning
in gospel music, Pickett moved to R&B
with the Falcons, and in 1962 scored his
first hit with that group, "I Found A
Love" (which is one of this collection's
twenty-four selections, but one which is
terribly reproduced). Essentially all of
his raw, high-energy hits are included on
this CD, the only exceptions being "Call

My Name, I'll Be There" (5/18/71) and
"Fire And Water" (12/25/67). "In The
Midnight Hour," "Land Of A Thousand
Dances," "Mustang Sally," and "Funky
Broadway" plus numerous other gems
that never really moved out of the black
market make this an essential collection. Sound quality, not a forte of Atlantic, is a little above their average, but
it is very uneven. Some cuts are plagued
with hiss, others have vocal distortions,
yet, the question is: against what sonic
standard are these twenty-year-old recordings to be measured? Compared to
digitally recorded, mixed, and reproduced quality eighties music, they obviously fail to measure up. But compared
to their vinyl counterparts, they are substantial audio improvements.

# Pink Floyd
Formed 1965—London
One of England's first psychedelic-rock
bands, their sixties output was a little
more than imitative of the San Francisco
acid-rock scene. However, with the seventies, and particularly the release of
their enduring *Dark Side of the Moon,*
Pink Floyd catapulted itself into a special
role in the hearts of rock listeners.

**The Piper at the Gates of Dawn (1967)**
EMI CDP7 463842 (41:58)   **[C+]**
England's answer to the Jefferson Airplane, Pink Floyd persevered and
prospered long after the Airplane
crashed and burned. This, their original
statement (recorded at London's Abbey
Road Studio at the same time the Beatles
were recording *Sgt. Pepper* there) is revered by hardcore Floyd fans because
it represents the vision of the band's
founder and original prime mover, Syd
Barrett, who shortly thereafter suc-
cumbed to a permanent drug-assisted
psychedelia known more commonly as

mental illness. As musical history, it's an interesting, but not really innovative, recording. However, the seeds of Pink Floyd's later success clearly germinated in this wacky soil. The CD's sound is impressive.

### Meddle (1971)
Mobile Fidelity UDCD 518 (46:50)   **[B–]**
The cult of Pink Floyd is bifurcated between those who still hold that Syd Barrett was English pop music's great post-Beatles genius and those who never heard of the mad Mr. Barrett but find his band's techno-spacey studio wizardry the realization of some cosmic window. In retrospect, the best of the group's music provides an ersatz soundtrack for sound nuts or space toddlers. *Meddle* preceded their classic *Dark Side of the Moon* by a couple of years, and its title track suggests the atmospherics that were finally fully realized on *Dark Side*, but it lacks the cohesiveness and structure that established the 1973 release as a multiyear best seller. The rest of the recording, with the possible exception of "One of These Days," is less than memorable, even when presented in Mobile Fidelity's enhanced gold disc sound, which is generally first-rate.

### Dark Side of the Moon (1973)
Harvest CDP746001-2 (42:58)   **[A +]**

### Dark Side of the Moon (1973)
Capitol CDP746001-2 (42:54)   **[A–]**
Released in 1973, this album was still on the *Billboard* pop charts in 1986 after selling more than ten million copies in the United States alone. The original, and obviously most enduring, of the seventies English concept-art rock albums. The eclectic techno-sound was very much attributable to the contribution of Alan Parsons, the project's Abbey Road engineer, the saxophone of Dick Perry,

and Clair Torry's expressive, wordless vocals. *Dark Side of the Moon* has become, perhaps, the essential icon of seventies rock. The sound quality depends on which of the two versions (Capitol or Harvest) is heard. The import Harvest release is now almost impossible to find (unless one is willing to pay a hefty price) but it affords much the superior sound—fuller, more rounded with significantly reduced tape hiss. The Capitol version is still a spatial and dynamic enhancement over the LP, but suffers from some muddiness and much more annoying hiss than the Harvest recording which, interestingly enough, runs four seconds longer.

### Dark Side of the Moon (1973)
Mobile Fidelity UDCD 517 (42:58)   **[A +]**
A natural section for Mobile Fidelity's gold ultradisc state-of-the-art sound, this is probably the cleanest, most resonant recording of this war horse, but it still has minor tape hiss. It's really not that much better sounding than the Harvest release, but is more accessible.

### The Wall (1979)
Columbia C2K36183 (81:23—two discs)   **[B]**
It's overlong, and won't bear close scrutiny, either musically or (especially) lyrically, but, it is listenable. *The Wall* is the pinnacle of English art rock at the end of the decade. Yet, this is a band that understands the art of the recording studio with more acumen than most; thus, if only on a sonic level, it succeeds. The CD adds marvelous dynamics, clarity of detail, and stage/depth to all the ingenious sound effects.

### The Final Cut (1983)
CBS CK38243 (43:28)   **[C–]**
Subtitled "A Requiem For the Post-War Dream" this is Roger Waters's musical eulogy to his father. It is also Waters's last

effort with Pink Floyd. *The Final Cut* is a somber, heavy record with a few memorable moments, but overall, it sinks under Waters's gloomy, vaguely cosmic visions. The sound is clean and open, but its compression impedes the dynamics upon which much of its production punch is predicated.

**A Momentary Lapse of Reason (1987)**
Columbia CK40599 (51:16)  [C + ]
The rock album as an aural movie. This is Pink Floyd devoid of Roger Waters, which means that it is principally a David Gilmour recording. Once again, it isn't *Dark Side of the Moon,* although it's an obvious descendant of that landmark recording. Sonically, this is an extraordinary outing. Recorded digitally (except for the bass and drums which were done on analog), the sound is the best part of it all. (It should be noted that there is a slight tendency to occasional overbrightness even on this all-digital effort.) The lyrics have all the stilted banality we have come to expect from England's pioneer art rockers, and its musical attributes are, for the most part, clearly secondary to the sonic effects upon which this band has built its not inconsiderable reputation.

# Gene Pitney
b. February 17, 1941—Hartford, Connecticut
**Anthology (1961–1968)**
Rhino RNCD75896 (44:34)  [C + ]
If you happen to be one of the rare, surviving Pitney fans, you're gonna love this. Pitney, who at times sounded like a poor man's Roy Orbison, is a hard artist to pigeonhole. As a rock composer, he wrote or cowrote "Hello, Marylou" and "He's a Rebel," both clearly rock numbers. His own repertoire ran the gamut from rock to pop to country. All the essentials, plus some true rarities, are

included among the disc's sixteen selections, all rendered in marvelous digital sound, thanks, once again, to Rhino's Bill Inglot.

# The Platters
Formed 1953—Los Angeles
Perhaps the premier doo-wop group of the fifties. During their heyday, the Platters provided some of the smoothest, most listenable hits available on fifties radio.

**Greatest Hits (1955–1959)**
Atoll Music ATO 8604 (32:26)  [C + ]
The contents live up to the title, although the group certainly provided much more in the way of fine doo-wop listening than is included on this relatively brief offering. The sound quality is generally clean, but does not really provide a great deal of dynamic enhancement.

# The Pogues
Formed 1982—Ireland
**Rum, Sodomy and the Lash (1985)**
Stiff 2223270 1 (43:07)  [A]
Traditional Irish folk music dragged screaming through the punk dump. If *Rum, Sodomy and the Lash* proves anything, it is that the spirit of rock & roll lives in many guises. By infusing the old songs with that irreverent spirit, those songs regain the currency that gave them original meaning. Lead singer Shane MacGowan is the living incarnation of the Irish hooligan as the devil; and he sings just like you hope he will. The Pogues are six Irish lads and one woman, Cait O'Riordan, who is Elvis Costello's wife. Produced by Costello, this sometimes crass album is infused with his sense of edgy anger, but what lingers is the passion and the caring.

Also what lingers is one of the strongest anti-war songs ever recorded, "And the Band Played Waltzing Matilda." The sound is clean, clear, and "live."

### If I Should Fall From Grace With God (1988)
Island 790872-7 (51:53)  **[A–]**
Shane MacGowan and six other punk hooligans who are the Pogues make some of the most vital and interesting music to be heard during these generally arid musical times. You play the Pogues when you want to dance with the devil—and dance you will. Image notwithstanding, these minstrels can play; MacGowan's bloodcurdling, dark, primal vocals pierce like lightning in a stormy sky. In sound and sensibility, the Pogues' music is very much a piece of Ireland's rich traditional musical heritage. That's not to suggest that their sound is limited to a narrow traditional spectrum. Far from it: The Pogues' musical milieu encompasses punk, rock, ersatz midstream, cocktail jazz, and Spike Jones, and somehow it all works, particularly the uniquely moving "Fairytale of New York," the madcap "Fiesta," and the impassioned "Streets of Sorrow/Birmingham Six." Produced by Steve Lillywhite, the CD's sound is clear and relatively dynamic, but not as open or precise as might be hoped. Proud, profane, and potent, the Pogues are the wind in the hills and the tears in a mourner's eye.

### Peace and Love (1989)
Island 92225-2 (45:06)  **[A–]**
The Irish have been punk since before Jimmy Cagney, and the Pogues are living proof of the vitality of the stance. Probably not for everyone because of their strong Irish folk roots, but their slashing individuality reverberates in a time sadly dominated by packaged pro-

ductions. This is so even when they overlay their bile with effective, heavy production and instrumentation, as *Peace and Love* amply illustrates. Some of their scruffy charm has been lost in the sometimes dense mix, but their musicianship and versatility fill most of the void and, thank God, Shane MacGowan's lead vocals remain unrepentant. The overall sound quality, while a bit dense (a frequent by-product of Steve Lillywhite's production sensibilities), is generally pretty good. A damn fine recording from a damn fine band.

### Hell's Ditch (1990)
Island 422-46-99 2 (41:46)  **[A]**
For all his Irish rage and gallows visions, Shane MacGowan can't overcome the joyous music in his soul. As a result, *Hell's Ditch* is another venom-dipped rollick through the pub into Siam, Spain, and Katmandu. Brimming with poetic imagery and musical mayhem, revealed with directness through Joe Strummer's no-bullshit production, *Hell's Ditch* is this potent band's best work since 1985's *Rum, Sodomy and the Lash.* The thirteen selections run the gamut from the unabated joy of "Summer in Siam" to the title track (not for the faint of heart), with stops along the way for Spanish poets and Greek goddesses. A heady, happy brew that should remind a few folks what the spirit of rock & roll is all about, while confirming the fact that today it is truly the world's music. Its sound is direct and clear, enough to make MacGowan's mewlings comprehensible.

# Poi Dog Pondering
**Wishing Like a Mountain and Thinking Like the Sea (1989)**
Columbia CK 45335 (57:28)   **[B]**
In an age where big production and big promotion are the bywords of the music industry, finding a band whose principal tenets seem to be fun and joy is about as rare as finding a thinking member of the Parents Music Resource Center. For this outing, Poi Dog is made up of sixteen musicians working out on accordion, cello, Latvian kokle, virginal tin whistle, frying pan, steel guitar, and horns to name a few. Out of all this come sounds of rock, Hawaii, Ireland, country, and Latin music, with equally diverse elements bubbling under it all. The guiding spirit behind this is Frank Orrall, who espouses his positive view through weird, wacky, and sometimes wonderful lyrics ("If I should die in a car wreck/ May I have Van Morrison on my tape deck"). While an acoustic sound overall, its joyous intensity is excellently captured with clear spaciousness.

# Buster Poindexter
**Buster Goes Berserk (1989)**
RCA 9665-2-R (37:12)   **[C + ]**
David Johansen's throwback party persona, Buster Poindexter, romps through ten uptempo jump tunes that span many musical eras and styles. A high-energy, good-time, party-down attitude is the byword. Buster's Banshees of Blue are joined by the Uptown Horns and a host of additional vocalists who build the beat, adding fine musicianship and an almost "live" ambience—there are even a couple of ballads amid the calypso rhythms and funk flourishes. It's polished, just not inspired. The sound quality is fine; nothing extraordinary.

# The Pointer Sisters
Formed Oakland, California
**Breakout (1984)**
RCA PCD1-4705A (43:45)   **[D]**
Packaged pop for a packaged age. Mostly studio technique and production in which the three female voices are one more element. Slick and senseless. The CD sound is extremely overbright, subject to hiss, distortion, and compression in both dynamics and space.

# The Police
Formed 1977—England
**Synchronicity (1983)**
A&M CD-3735 (44:30)   **[C]**
Pseudo-music by intellectual and emotional poseurs who enjoyed a brief vogue, but have thankfully managed to cash in their numerous chips and go their separate ways. (That said, "Every Breath You Take" is a stunning pop song.) The sound is an almost state-of-the-art analog to digital conversion with barely noticeable compression.

**Synchronicity (1983)**
Mobile Fidelity Sound Lab UDCD 511 (44:27)
**[B]**
Perhaps I am seduced by the breathtaking realism and crystalline openness of this gold CD's sound, or maybe the years have mellowed me since I first reviewed the A&M release (see above), but the pure pop sensibility of "Wrapped Around Your Finger," "King of Pain," and the still stunning "Every Breath You Take," have caused me to revise my opinion—this is one hell of a demo record. If you, like many, are a Police fan, the sound will simply knock your ears off.

# Elvis Presley

b. January 8, 1935—Tupelo, Mississippi
d. August 16, 1977—Memphis, Tennessee

In terms of record sales, and more importantly, influence, Elvis Presley is simply the greatest pop artist of all time. Elvis was the incarnation of America itself, from its crass commercialism to its brash vitality, as well as its gross self-indulgence—beautifully obscene, irresistibly potent, he articulated our roots, perhaps more honestly than we ever imagined. He was and is the king simply because he was the first to claim the kingdom. The true American original, the total realization of the American dream, he ascended to the throne because he wanted it badly enough—but at a hideous price. By the time he had attained legal majority, his celebrity had reached a level which set him totally outside everyone else's "real world."

**The Sun Sessions CD (1954–1956)**
RCA 6414 2 R (72:33)   **[A + ]**

**Elvis Presley (1956)**
RCA PCD 1-5199 (28:40)   **[A + ]**

**Elvis (1956)**
RCA PCD 1-5198 (30:23)   **[A + ]**
Dave Marsh stated it as well as it can be stated: "Suffice it to say that these records, more than any others, contain the seeds of everything rock & roll was, has been, and most likely what it may forseeably become." The chemistry and exuberance on the Sun Sessions are uniquely compelling—if you listen closely, you can almost feel the energy that infused these historic recordings. Soundwise, while the string reproductions are stunning, the vocals are sometimes a shade harsh (and occasionally badly distorted) but, this stuff *was* recorded over thirty years ago.

Bottom line: all the primal elements of rock & roll are here, generally reproduced with a sonic clarity heretofore unknown, 'nuff said?

On the two orignal RCA compilation discs (*Elvis* and *Elvis Presley*), Elvis conveys the amazing breadth of his musical vision, which was pervasive; he could sing it all and make it all uniquely his own in the process. By making the digital remixes from the original mono tapes and retaining that format, RCA has done a marvelous job of sound reproduction (particularly vocal nuances). The fact that the clarity reveals all the blemishes is hardly a problem!

**The Million Dollar Quartet (1956)**
RCA 2023-2R (66:58)   **[B + ]**
The title is, of course, a misnomer—the quartet is really a trio (Presley, Jerry Lee Lewis, and Carl Perkins), and the fourth, Johnny Cash, makes his most significant appearance on the cover. Given the phenomenal numbers of records Sun Records' founding fathers of rockabilly/rock & roll have sold, the "Million Dollars" was pocket change. Enough about what it isn't, because it is one of the more fascinating historic recordings available on CD. It seems that one afternoon, December 4, 1956, to be exact, Elvis returned to Sam Phillips's Memphis Sun Studios, having been "sold" to RCA and major stardom a year before. His old friend and sometimes touring companion, Carl Perkins, was just finishing a session in which a then virtually unknown Jerry Lee Lewis had played piano. There were some relatives, friends, and backup musicians around, and a few guitars. The ever-prescient Phillips placed some mikes and rolled some tape. The result provides a little over an hour of song snippets and conversation from that session. There are bits and pieces of over forty songs,

including multiple attempts at "Brown Eyed Handsome Man," "Crazy Arms," and "Don't Be Cruel," some of which last a mere five seconds. But as Colin Escots's informative liner notes emphasize, this is a keyhole insight to the common background roots of rock & roll, country/gospel, country/western, and bluegrass. That, and this rare insight into Presley (who Colonel Tom almost completely shielded from the press thereafter), make this a worthy addition to the collecton of any true Presley fan or student of rock history. The mono sound on this disc nicely captures the spontaneity and intimacy of the event and its era, but this isn't an audiophile experience.

### Elvis' Golden Records (1958—compilation release date)
RCA PCD1-5196 (33:40)   [A]
They're all here, the early monster RCA hits (fourteen of them, including "Hound Dog," "Heartbreak Hotel," "Love Me Tender," and "Don't Be Cruel") "restored" to their original mono formats before digital conversion. Thus, the sound, while sometimes uneven, is generally first-rate for material of this vintage.

### The Memphis Record (1969)
RCA 6221-2-R (72:07)   [A + ]
In 1969, Elvis released one of his stronger recordings entitled *From Elvis in Memphis*. This disc contains that album in full, reproduced with marvelous digital enhancement which would make the CD, if nothing else were added, an outstanding addition to any rock library. However, fourteen uneven tracks have been added to the CD including some gems ("Rubberneckin'" and "I'm Movin' On"). All twenty-three tracks were cut in Memphis over roughly a two-week period when approximately

thirty-five selections were produced. The ones that did not appear on the *From Elvis in Memphis* LP turned up later as singles or B sides on other recordings. In addition, some of this work appeared in the double album *Vegas to Memphis and Memphis to Vegas* which was abbreviated into a single album and sold for a period of time under the name *Back in Memphis*.

But this was the last time in the King's career that he appeared to really care about putting all that fierce talent on the line—it was early 1969, hard on the heels of the historic 1968 TV special that showed the sixties' upstarts once and for all why the King held the throne. This was, sadly, the final display of the essence of it all. Perhaps it was the return to home turf (it had been fourteen years since Elvis started it all at the old Sun Studios in Memphis), but as Peter Guralnick accurately observes in his liner notes to this release, on these sessions, Presley was infused with the gospel spirit that is at the heart of much of the music and clearly was a part of the heart of the man.

### Reconsider Baby (1954/55–1971)
RCA PCD15418 (38:11)   [A]
This is music made for the sake of music, not material tailored and produced to capitalize on the myth. The musicianship, production, and sound quality are sometimes rough, but this is the rock & roll blues performed by the man who began it all in the first place with a blues song, "That's All Right, Mama." The material ranges from the earliest Sun sessions to 1971 (his killer version of Charlie Brown's "Merry Christmas, Baby"). If you like roots—this is roots, muddy, raw, and wonderful.

# The Pretenders
Formed 1978—London, England
**The Pretenders (1980)**
Sire 6083-2 (47:15)   **[A+]**
Chrissie Hynde, whose vocals, rhythm guitar, and songwriting define the Pretenders, is one of the most honestly real artists to come along in the last decade. She makes rock & roll; no apologies, no regrets. This debut recording is stunning in its power, intimacy, directness, and variety. There's not a weak cut, but the standouts, "Precious," "Stop Your Sobbing," and "Brass In Pocket" were the reason this release established the Pretenders as one of the most successful of the new wave bands to come out of England in the late seventies. Hynde is a major contributor and this is a major work. The sound is pretty much the equivalent to that of the LP.

**Get Close (1986)**
Sire 25488-2 (45:22)   **[A]**
Working with three premier producers, Jimmy Iovine, Bob Clearmountain, and Steve Lillywhite, and a variety of musicians, including the only other surviving member of the original group, Martin Chambers (on drums), on one number, Chrissie Hynde has again fashioned a first-rate release. All the attributes which the original band exhibited six years previously remain, albeit softened with a more pop-oriented sensibility. Yet, there is no sense of compromise—Chrissie's too blunt and basic for artifice; that's why she consistently makes great rock & roll. This time around, the sound, too, is great—clean, defined, open, and dynamic.

**The Singles (1979–1986)**
Sire 25664-2 (57:39)   **[A]**
While the backup players have changed, the core element has been Chrissie Hynde. This compilation covers the Pretenders' seven years. Hers is a pure, perhaps unique rock vision among women artists, as honest, naked, and genuine as any. Though she comes from a woman's perspective into a male-dominated arena, Chrissie's "who-gives-a-shit?" attitude is totally consistent with rock's fundamentals. She makes her *own* music, possessed of power and commercial appeal, and that's what it's all about. Tough, uncompromising, and clear-eyed, *The Singles* is a satisfying dose of some of the best rock & roll of the last ten years. The sound quality varies a bit—overall hard and edgy, a bit overbright—but appropriate to the message.

**Packed! (1990)**
Sire/Warner Bros. 26219-2 (38:49)   **[B+]**
Expatriate Chrissie Hynde may just be the one great woman rock artist the form has produced to date. With her acerbic "in-your-face" style and instantly recognizable voice, her work has been consistently compelling and frequently truly great. Her band, the Pretenders, released their great debut in January, 1980, to both critical and popular acclaim, suggesting unlimited future delights. The ravages of drugs, success, and time have decimated the original band, so that while their (her) subsequent work has consistently reflected her remarkable talent, nothing has equalled that first brilliant burst. *Packed!,* their first new release in years, rightfully keeps the focus on Chrissie, but with those wonderful hard edges somewhat blunted, a few more mannerisms, and a more confessional bent to the lyrics, this is a mellower Chrissie. The result is a gentler, more melodic sound, wonderfully listenable, but the ballsy bitch of a decade past is sorely missed—subtlety is generally not a

prime ingredient in successful pop product. The all-digital recording occasionally edges toward harshness and is a bit thin in the midrange, but that's really nitpicking.

# Prince
# (Prince Rogers Nelson)
b. June 7, 1960—Minneapolis
The brief history of rock music has included a handful of black artists (Ray Charles, James Brown, Sly Stone, and Stevie Wonder) who, while enjoying various degrees of crossover recognition have, in fact, had immense impact on all the pop music that came after them. Prince clearly is the latest to enter this august group. The son of musical parents, he signed with Warner Bros. at age eighteen, releasing his first one-man album (he plays all the keyboards, guitars, and other instruments as well as multi-tracking his vocals) the same year. Before he was twenty-one, he had been credited with creating the widely influential "Minneapolis Sound" with his inventive pop/funk/rock blend.

### Dirty Mind (1980)
Warner Bros. 3478-2 (30:18)   [A]
Talk about truth in labeling, this one lays it right out up front and then delivers. Prince's sexual preoccupations, ranging from oral sex to incest, make up the lyrical subject matter here. Make no mistake, he doesn't pull any punches. This recording had been called "positively filthy" even before the PMRC had been heard from. However, by flaunting his explicit lyrics over a synth-based, propulsively insinuating pop/funk sound, with hooks aplenty and a danceable beat, the Minnesota *wunderkind* established his own very influential niche in the eighties pop market ("When

You Were Mine" from this release was covered by a number of other artists, and over the ensuing years, he's given songs to numerous artists in both the pop and funk markets). Subject matter aside, these are simply some of the freshest, brightest, most engaging sounds to have entered the pop mainstream in years. The CD sound is clean and clear, but also reflects some compression in both dynamics and audio stage size.

### 1999 (1982)
Warner Bros. 23720-2 (62:19)   [A + ]
If there was any question about Prince's musical stature and true genius, it was this recording which resolved the matter in his favor, once and for all. Masterfully building upon funk, soul, disco, rock, and pop sounds and influences, Prince has constructed an album of dance music that manages to sound totally fresh and is consistently inventive. "Little Red Corvette" and "1999" are the popular highlights. But his unstoppable groove runs through the ten irresistible selections (one less than the original double LP collection, "D.M.S.R." having been omitted by Prince to get the double LP package on a single CD), resulting in a landmark eighties effort. The sound is more open and dynamic on CD, but is impaired by continuous hiss and background noise, overbrightness, and noticeable weakness in the drum sounds.

### And the Revolution
### Purple Rain (1984)
Warner Bros./Paisley Park 9 25110-2 (43:55)   [A + ]
In 1984, his purple majesty brought out the soundtrack to what may well be the definitive rock movie, and delivered one of the best pop records of the year. A major aspect of this highly visible genius's music is his ability to create

songs which sound totally new, yet manage to be accepted and retained on first hearing. This is well illustrated here with "When Doves Cry." As usual, Prince's music runs the gamut among multiple, currently popular forms (soul, funk, psychedelia, etc.) and he handles each with freshness and individuality. The addition of the Revolution on this disc, while mostly functioning as a backdrop for the master's performance, does open up the feel and texture of the sound. It is here, also, that Prince demonstrates his guitar prowess, which alone would grant him major status in the current music scene. The CD sound is clear, open, dynamic, and well-separated, but does have a tendency toward excessive brightness and retains some noticeable hiss.

### And the Revolution
### Parade (1986)
Warner Bros. 25395-2 (41:0)   **[A]**
The follow-up soundtrack to the follow-up film *Under the Cherry Moon,* the soundtrack fares much better than its celluloid counterpart, but that's not saying much because the movie was a bona fide bomb. Actually, it's a shame the movie came out, because the record, clearly does stand alone. The music on *Parade* reflects an even broader musical palette than Prince had demonstrated on prior recordings, with a somewhat sweeter sound overall. Upon its release, it met with mixed critical and public response, but after the passage of time, it seems clear that this represents another massively creative musical step for a young man who continues to dazzle with his unceasing innovation. True, one of the cuts is so tied to the film that it doesn't really work on the recording ("Sometimes It Snows in April"), but the rest stand up in any context, particularly "Girls & Boys," "Kiss," and "Anotherloverholenyohead."

The sound is an unreserved success— open, crystal clear, and beautifully spaced and defined.

### Sign O The Times (1987)
Paisley Park/Warner Bros. 25577-2 (80:03—two discs)   **[A + ]**
The prolific one returns this time with a double disc outing that once again explores the multiple sounds and nuances of current (rap) and past (funk, soul, you name it) popular music. This time around, it's mostly Prince working solo (but who can tell?), although some additional musicians do make an occasional appearance. It's simply another brilliant *tour de force,* although, in all honesty, it would probably have been the ultimate pop statement that the critics have been awaiting from him if it had been edited into a single disc recording. As it is, it's a little bit of a lot of things with some dross, but more than its share of brilliant gems. The sound is first-rate—clean, very open, crisply dynamic, and nicely detailed.

### Soundtrack: Batman (1989)
Warner Bros. 9 25936-2 (43:34)   **[B–]**
As a souvenir of one of the most commercially successful films of the eighties, this soundtrack may be valid. As a Prince album, it is a disappointing commercial sellout. Maybe the movie was just too big for even his purple majesty. The danceable surface explodes with energy, but there's not much else to recommend it—the Sheena Easton duet is too lame for words, and too much of the rest of it is too hopelessly referential to the movie. It's not without its fair share of shakin' funk, its just that one expects more from Prince. The mostly synthesized sound is devastatingly potent—it'll blow you out of the room.

**Graffiti Bridge (1990)**
Paisley Park/Warner Bros. 9 27493-2 (68:34)
**[A + ]**
The most innovative, creative, and influential artist to appear since the late
seventies proves why he is so on this
soundtrack to his third film. Melding
funk, rock, R&B, rap, and soul with a
passion for the pious and profane,
Prince displays unrivaled genius where
the unexpected is the rule and almost
always inevitably right. Those who are
put off by the persona or the sometimes
explicit lyrics are ignoring a talent of
gargantuan proportions. *Graffiti Bridge*
displays both his own solo/production
wizardry ("Can't Stop This Feeling I
Got," "New Power Generation," "The
Question of U," and "Thieves in the
Temple") and the work of other contributors, The Time ("Release It," "Shake!"),
Mavis Staples ("Melody Cool"), and
funkster extraordinaire George Clinton
("We Can Funk"), with his standard
audacity. It may not be another *Purple
Rain*, but there are only a handful of
recordings comparable to that epic.
Soundwise, the disc is also impressive—
open, intimate, and dynamic, even on
his multitrack personal constructions.

# Public Enemy
Formed late 1980's—Los Angeles
**Fear of a Black Planet (1990)**
Def Jam/Columbia CK45413 (63:21)   **[B + ]**
Rock & roll, the musical revolution of
the fifties, traces its ancestry—gospel,
the blues, and country/western—from
the rural South. Rap, the musical revolution sweeping the nineties, traces its
roots to the the seething, angry, per-
secuted ghettos of big-city America.
Public Enemy, generally acknowledged
to represent the leading edge musically
and politically, is a group for its time and
of its roots. Their sound and message
are an assault borne of too much frustration and too little concern for the
fundamental causes of that frustration.
Maybe the first wave can only attack,
but when they choose the weapons of
their oppressors, bigotry and hatred,
attack is all they may ever accomplish.
Their anti-Semitism, anti-gay, and somewhat anti-feminist leanings bespeak
more ignorance than causal justice.
Sure, you have to know the problem to
solve it, but they shed heat, not light;
violence, not constructive solutions.
They do this with a sonic barrage and
vocal intensity that make their work
undeniably potent. Using modern
instrumentation and studio wizardry
with the deftness of masters, they combine the sounds of the most current
events with snippets of black aural history as the crashing, dense backdrop for
their urgent, timely messages. Are they
important? In the valid political context
of popular music, you're damn right
they are. Will they endure and be valid
in the greater scheme of the music's history? That is a somewhat more doubtful
premise. But if you want to know what's
happening in the urban cauldron of current American life, this, for better or
worse, is where it's at. The disc's sound
quality is an integral, effective part of the
message.

# The Radiators

**Zigzagging Through Ghostland (1989)**
Epic EK44343 (51:53)  **[D]**
Critically touted as another of the great
New Orleans bands, the Rads do little to
distinguish themselves on this very
repetitive outing. Either the studio or
their producer has managed to straight-
jacket their highly touted live wildness—
maybe it's just something about the Big
Easy; it just doesn't travel all that well.
The sound is about as adequate as the
playing, maybe a little muddier.

# Bonnie Raitt

b. November 8, 1949—Burbank, California
Blues/rock singer, slide guitarist who
has followed her private muse for several decades, building a devoted cult
and a memorable career.

**Bonnie Raitt (1971)**
Warner Bros. 1953-2 (37:50)  **[B + ]**
Her spirit and artistic bent may be based
in the folk/blues world where her performing career got its start, but her
sensitivities are as contemporary as any
other female recording. Thus, the material on her debut runs from Stephen
Stills's "Bluebird" to Robert Johnson's
"Walking Blues," with a couple of originals tossed in for good measure. With
Junior Wells's harp and A.C. Reed's tenor
sax adding coloration, the mood is
infused with the blues, and Raitt's

expressive vocals and slide guitar are
first-rate. The recording was captured
live in a remote Minnesota studio;
according to Bonnie, "We wanted a more
spontaneous and natural feeling in the
music . . . it also reflects the difference
between music made among friends living together in the country, and the kind
squeezed out trying to beat city traffic
and studio clocks." The sound quality
reflects the live feel, but is hampered by
slight compression.

**Give it Up (1972)**
Warner Bros. 2643-2 (36:57)  **[A–]**
Raitt has now released ten albums,
including 1989's *Nick of Time,* which
won her the audience and awards she
richly deserves, but this one's the best of
the bunch. Her second release, it retains
the root blues textures and attitudes of
her fine debut, tempered with a more
pop approach. It works. This time
around she recorded at Bearsville, near
Woodstock, N.Y., with locally based
musicians plus some assistance from
Paul Butterfield and Merl Saunders. She
also has chosen some fine, diverse material, "Love Me Like a Man," "Too Long at
the Fair," and the definitive version of
"Love Has No Pride." The whole undertaking has an easy rocking energy,
devoid of pretentious production. Sadly,
the sound is another matter—thin, compressed, edgy, and with apparent tape
hiss—it mars an otherwise excellent
recording.

**Sweet Forgiveness (1977)**
Warner Bros. 2990-2 (38:13)   **[B]**
This album almost put Bonnie into the big time because of the success of her cover of Del Shannon's "Runaway." Since it is arguably the weakest cut on the album, its success must have been the result of her gender reversal on the acknowledged classic. As usual, Bonnie brings great talent, intelligence, vocals, and instrumental chops to the party; as usual, her producer and record company (presumably with her consent) dilute it in the quest for pop success. Since Raitt isn't a writer, her choice of songs is crucial, and on *Sweet Forgiveness* she again displays her somewhat eclectic good taste, covering work by Paul Siebel, Eric Kaz, and Bill Payne; she still leans too heavily on the L.A. pop/country ethic. Personal history notwithstanding, Raitt's empathy, voice, and slide bottleneck guitar skills are clearly aligned with the blues—she ought to stick with personal predilections. The sound of this CD is disappointing—compressed and often muddy.

**Nick of Time (1989)**
Capitol CDP7 91268 2 (42:58)   **[B + ]**
This is the one that won Bonnie something closer to a mass audience and helped propel Don Was's production charisma to greater heights. It also won four Grammys (in a fairly competitive year), but then so did Milli Vanilli. That's an unfair comparison, because if Raitt is anything, she is a genuine, honest, albeit somewhat limited talent—a more than competent vocalist, a damn fine slide guitar player, and one bitchin' woman. It's just that Was's production is too derivative and slick, draining feeling from the above-average material instead of adding shadings and meanings to the words and intent. Raitt's real triumph is that she still comes so close to making

the material personal in the face of such production. Was does earn his overblown credentials with the sound quality of the recording—intimate, open, and warm—it's difficult to fault. The whole thing just needs a little more smoke, beer, and sweat.

## The Rascals
Formed 1965—New York City
**The Ultimate Rascals (1965–1970)**
Warner Bros. 9-27605-2 (60:33)   **[D]**
The sixties white soul band that launched the career of Felix Cavaliere also scored some major chart success with "Good Lovin'," "Groovin'," and "People Got to Be Free," all included here. Unfortunately, the digital remastering of this material is pathetic; in short, the sound stinks.

## The Raspberries
Formed 1970—Cleveland, Ohio
**Overnight Sensation—The Very Best of the Raspberries (1972–1974)**
Zap CD1 (60:53)   **[B + ]**
From 1972 to 1974 the Raspberries was where Eric Carmen learned his craft, particularly as a writer. Clearly a "second generation" rock band, their admiration for the Beatles, Beach Boys, and the Who, among others, reverberates through their repertoire. This and the excess and mawkishness they often exhibited would seem a basis for oblivion, but the Raspberries had an energy and sense of pop appeal that surmounted their limitations. This pure seventies pop extravaganza contains sixteen examples, including "Overnight Sensation," "Go All the Way," "I Wanna Be With You," and "All Through the Night." On the other hand, missing are, "I'm a Rocker," "Don't Want to Say Goodbye," and "Hands on You." Not a frontline

band, but a first-rate example of the joyous side of the early-to-mid-seventies pop music scene. The sound on this English import CD is generally a major improvement over the vinyl in dynamics, clarity, and spatial detail.

# The Rave Ups
## Chance (1990)
Epic/CBS EK 45255 (39:23)   **[B + ]**
The Rave Ups have heart and energy. Led by writer/vocalist Jimmer Podrasky (whose name alone should make him a star), this foursome employs some offbeat instrumentation, such as the Sri Lankan cobra flute, to distinguish their basic guitar-driven, country-tinged sound. Podrasky's affection for his musical forebears and strong, hoarse, expressive voice, combined with the band's tight musicianship honed though life on the road, result in one damn fine but generally overlooked release. Joyous and wise, *Chance* has an enduring feel. The sound is bright, clean, and dynamic.

# Otis Redding
b. September 9, 1941—Dawson, Georgia
d. December 10, 1967—Madison, Wisconsin
One of the truly great male soul singers of the sixties, Redding's principal audience (at least prior to 1967 when he appeared at Monterey Pop) was the black community that supported soul music generally; however, his influence on numerous sixties rock stars is undeniable.

## The Ultimate Otis Redding (1962–1967)
Warner Special Products 9-27608-2 (54:53)   **[C]**
In the golden age of great soul singers, Redding's raw, honest readings of classic material easily placed him near the top of the hierarchy. His influence on both white performers of the day, and on the

young audience that was just discovering the diversity of material upon which rock was formulated, was immense. His performance was one of the highlights of the legendary Monterey Pop affair. The compilation covers essentially all of his important studio sides, but suffers from uneven, often weak, sound. The recording has an arid, almost sterile quality about it which is diametrically opposed to the gut-wrenching passion that fueled this major artist's best work. It's suggested that the buyer wait for disc versions of Redding's live material (*Live in Europe* or *At Monterey*), since this collection just doesn't make it.

## The Otis Redding Story (1962–1967)
Atlantic 781762-2 (170:39—three discs)   **[A + ]**
Between 1962 and 1967, Otis Redding produced thirty-one Top 100 R&B hits. All of them, except "I Love You More Than Words Can Say," "Glory of Love," and "A Lover's Question" are included among the sixty tracks in this compilation. That, of course, means it includes "These Arms of Mine," "I've Been Loving You Too Long (To Stop Now)," "Respect," "Satisfaction," "Try a Little Tenderness," "Tramp" (with Carla Thomas), "The Happy Song," his sole No. 1 hit "(Sittin' On) The Dock of the Bay," and, as they say, many, many more. In this case that's true. This Canadian package is one of the best multidisc retrospectives to have come along so far—its one fault being the miniature ten-page booklet of recording and release dates, with no backing musician information, and a comprehensive career essay by Rob Bowman in type so small you need a power magnifier to read it—relatively minor quibbles compared to the driving, moving, sweet soul music on these discs. Redding began as a raw, rough R&B singer, and died as he was moving his music toward the masses. Using

chitlin circuit performance energy and his signature vocal gravel, "Mr. Pitiful," as he was sometimes known, infused each performance with emotional power and personal feeling. Influenced by Sam Cooke and Little Richard (both of whose songs he effectively covered), Redding was one of the truly great and influential soul singers of the sixties—the golden age for black pop. While many of the sixties' greatest artists have long since passed, and a good number departed with their best work behind them, in Otis's case you get the feeling that what might have followed could have been phenomenal. Certainly, what he left behind, at least as far as his studio work is concerned, is effectively explored by this set. The sound quality is all over the place, and generally leaves a lot to be desired, with too much compression, poor vocal mixes, and tape hiss adversely affecting the final product, but it is still better than its vinyl predecessors. Now, if only *Live in Europe* makes it to CD. . . .

# Lou Reed

b. March 2, 1943—Brooklyn, New York
Reed, principal writer and lead singer of the massively influential Velvet Underground, is that rare animal possessed of a rock & roll heart and a poetic mind. Not everything he had done since leaving the Underground in 1972 has worked; in fact, most hasn't.

### Transformer (1972)
RCA PCD14807 (37:03)   **[C–]**
While the Summer of Love and Me Decades passed merrily by, Lou Reed continued to sing about the seamier side of things. In the case of *Transformer,* the premise is "affected trendiness." Aided and abetted by David Bowie and Mick Ronson, this results in some engaging

moments, "Walk on the Wild Side" being the obvious one. The rest of the recording delivers more of the same, but it's not nearly as well realized. The sound varies, with some muddiness and compression evident, but a number of the cuts, (notably "Walk on the Wild Side") are beautifully rendered on disc; clear, detailed, and open.

### Rock'n'Roll Animal (1974)
RCA 3664-2F (40:00)   **[B +]**
Considered by many to be Reed's best live recording of classic Velvet Underground material, this five-song disc benefits from the strong backup efforts of a band that includes the guitars of Steve Hunter and Dick Wagner. "Sweet Jane," "Heroin," "White Light/White Heat," and "Rock'n'Roll" are all here. Robert Christgau said it most succinctly: "This is a live album with a reason for living." The sound quality on the CD is really very good for a concert recording. The unforgivable absence of any real information in the almost nonexistent liner notes is an all-too-common omission from so-called budget releases.

### New Sensations (1984)
RCA PCD1-4998 (43:02)   **[B]**
Reed has adopted a lot of personas in the recording career that he fashioned for himself since departing the Velvet Underground in the early 1970s. This, the eighties model, may well be the most accessible yet. It's true that the brutally edgy guitar sound is buried in the mix, along with female backup singers; and the lyrical preoccupations are now concerned more with the elements of middle-class pleasures than underclass horrors, but there is still some bite left. His eye for lyrical detail may also be a little diminished, but he's far from blind. Yeah, it could be a bit nastier and angrier, but everybody grows up sometime, for

better or for worse. The sound isn't bad, except for too noticeable, too frequent hiss.

## New York (1989)
Sire 25829-2 (56:55)   **[A +]**
Reed remains one of the most charismatic and influential artists of the rock era, and *New York* proves why. Working with the most sympathetic band (second guitar, bass, and drums) he's had since the glorious days of the Velvet Underground, he has created a series of searing home-turf vignettes at the end of the greed decade via his deadpan (but always pop sensitive) delivery and street poetry. On *New York* Reed touches on the evils and sins of urban America at a time when the gulf between the haves and the have-nots widened to expose a hideously gaping maw. This ain't the pretty side of life, and at times it rings closer to cliche than vérité, but if it's not genuine in intent and moving in its realization, then the Velvet Underground was only the soundtrack to Andy Warhol's pop/commercial sensibility. In the liner notes and track transitions Reed states that the recording's fourteen selections constitute a single concept that's "meant to be listened to in one fifty-eight-minute setting, as though it were a movie or a book." Reed's concerns burn through this impassioned material with palpable commitment. Even though some critics carped about *New York*'s failure to provide solutions to obvious problems, sometimes the artist's role is simply to enhance awareness, and in that he succeeds admirably. The all-digital recording offers an effective blend of clarity and intimacy.

## Lou Reed/John Cale
## Songs for Drella—A Fiction (1990)
Sire/Warner Bros. 26205-2 (54:55)   **[A]**
Time is the truest critic. In the relatively short history of rock & roll, time has burnished the work of Reed and Cale's first collaboration, the Velvet Underground, more than that of most of their sixties peers. A catalyst in the success of the Underground was Andy Warhol. So it is fitting that a musical elegy to Warhol's life and influence would provide the basis for a collaboration by Lou Reed and John Cale almost a quarter of a century after their original, groundbreaking efforts. Elegiac and bittersweet, *Songs for Drella* succeeds as a pure musical statement and as an evocation of a strange, shrouded man whose vision shaped much of modern pop culture. This is music of quiet intensity and mature understanding. Reed's guitar, Cale's keyboards, and occasional viola are the sole, simple instruments that support their haunting compositions and resonant vocals. *Songs for Drella* won't get radio or MTV airplay; it won't surface at the local dance club, or provide material for lesser talents to cover. It will, however, illuminate, reverberate, and confirm the enduring power of music and song to soothe and celebrate the joy, sadness, and complexity of life. The CD's sound is warm, natural, and consistent with its content.

# R.E.M.
Formed 1982–83—Athens, Georgia
Clearly, one of the most influential and important of America's eighties rock bands. Their sound is built upon the chiming guitars pioneered by the Byrds almost two decades before, but R.E.M.'s sensibility clearly looks forward.

## Murmur (1983)
IRS CD70014 (44:09)  [A–]

The band's first recording was an EP (now included as a part of their 1987 compilation release, *Dead Letter Office*, IRS CD70054), but this is the album that began the accolades that helped this band rise above cult status in the latter half of the eighties. Their sound has a timeless, atmospheric quality about it that defies literal explanation, but it is nonetheless palpably real. While they work in a rather narrow spectrum, and Michael Stipe's ambivalent, hidden vocals lend little "explanation" to it all, there is, at the core of it, a coiled energy that ultimately proves irresistible. The sound on this disc is equivalent to LP quality, compressed with constant hiss.

## Reckoning (1984)
IRS CD70044 (38:13)  [A+]

More of the same muffled intensity and atmospheric energy. This time around, the individual tracks have a more defined separateness which ultimately sustains greater interest. The album produced the "hit" "(Don't Go Back To) Rockville" which is excellent, but so are the rest of the selections. R.E.M. has taken some of the best of the music's glorious past and made it current in a manner that preserves, yet validly updates its antecedents. The sound is an improvement over *Murmur* in terms of both clarity and dynamics, but it still suffers from some compression and hiss.

## Fables of the Reconstruction (1985)
IRS IRSD-5592 (39:46)  [B+]

With this release, there is a subtle change in the subtle music—it remains enigmatic as ever, but *Fables of the Reconstruction* is, if anything, more dense and obtuse than its less than transparent predecessors. The sound is

roughly equivalent to that on *Reckoning,* but the content isn't as good.

## Lifes Rich Pageant (1985)
IRS IRSD5783 (38:33)  [B+]

A brighter, more dynamic version of the band. A bid for more commercial acceptance? Perhaps one can till the same narrow field only so many times. This time, there's more variety in the rhythms and instrumental textures, not to mention near-clarity in the lyrics. The sound is appreciably cleaner and more dynamic than on their earlier recordings, as well as brighter and more defined.

## Eponymous (1981–1987)
I.R.S. IRSD-6262 (43:10)  [A]

This ersatz greatest-hits compilation from a band without hits actually turns out to be one of their more listenable albums. Spanning their entire career, *Eponymous* displays this arresting band's strengths as they have evolved. The best of R.E.M.'s music has an ability to exist in its own space and time. They create individual musical moments, illuminated with intense energy. So while Michael Stipe's lyrics move from mumbled obscurity to understandable statements, the Mike Mills and Bill Berry-driven bottom maintains throughout. The only obvious criticism is that *Eponymous* draws heavily from *Document,* but as source material that's pretty astute. The sound varies from track to track, gaining clarity with time, but it's always more than adequate.

## Dead Letter Office (1987)
IRS CD70054 (63:51)  [B+]

A compilation of outtakes and "B" sides that includes several of their Velvet Underground covers which are the highlights, along with the inclusion of their outstanding debut EP, *Chronic Town.* You have to respect any group that will hang this much personal laundry on one line. Obviously the sound is all over the place, some distortion, some muddiness, and lots of hiss.

### Document (1987)
IRS IRSD-42059 (39:51)   **[A + ]**
This amazingly prolific band has previously maintained a murky, dense, chameleon-like persona which made them many things for many fans. *Document,* while a studio effort, is really their first recording that communicates their live energetic intensity—it's also the first that clearly communicates the words. Both elements prove to be a plus, resulting in their strongest release since *Reckoning,* and, perhaps, their best ever. Described by David Fricke, writing in *Rolling Stone,* as "A clench-fist manifesto of rebel bravado," *Document* is a searingly haunting experience that conjures up rock's classic moments, but, ultimately echoes nothing but itself, again and again. The CD's sound is perfectly mated to the material: clearer than ever before, yet still possessed of felt, but unheard, energies.

### Green (1988)
Warner Bros. 25795-2 (41:03)   **[A–]**
One of only a handful of original, memorable eighties rock bands, R.E.M. moves into the mainstream with *Green,* their first major-label release. This beautifully recorded effort reflects some changes from the band's earlier work—notably less atmosphere, and more clarity in Michael Stipe's vocals. The eleven selections cover a broad range of topics, from politics to pain, with surprisingly personal perspectives from Stipe, greater variety in Peter Buck's always-impressive guitar work, and overall, more of a group effort. "Turn You Inside Out" ranks with the best work this first-rate group has released. *Green* is a departure

for R.E.M., but an effective, provocative one. The songs and production lack the subtle simplicity of the band's early work, but a sense of intense involvement in the material persists.

# The Replacements
Formed 1980—Minneapolis, Minnesota
### The Replacements (1982)
Sire 9 25330-2 (37:06)   **[B + ]**
Bright, brash, highly energetic punk product from one of the many exciting young groups to come out of Minneapolis in the eighties. Punk though they may be, you can't take them too seriously, since they don't allow themselves that treacherous luxury. This is goodtime music that works. The sound is very bright.

### Tim (1985)
Sire 925330-2 (37:06)   **[B + ]**
The major-label debut of a great Minneapolis band who labeled themselves "power trash." The Replacements enjoy their reputation of latter day wild men, particularly in live performance. Their high-speed energy drives vocalist Paul Westerberg's insightful irreverance. There's more here than meets the ear, enough more that some knowledgable critics have placed them among the elite of current American rock bands. These guys understand the original essence of rock & roll—you may not find yourself singing along, but you'll remember the songs. The sound is OK, punchy and bright, but it's noticeably lacking in bottom.

### Don't Tell a Soul (1989)
Sire 25831-2 (39:20)   **[A]**
A leap in the evolution of one of the few eighties bands whose heart beats to the ragged rhythms of rock & roll, as opposed to the ringing of cash registers.

Die-hard followers of this protopunk quartet may be put off by the pop sensibilities added to the thrash attack (along with a propensity for sheer madness in performance) that was once their clarion call. But time, proximity to success, and critical adulation have taken their toll and are examined by Paul Westerberg and crew on this enduring release. The textural varieties added through these pop touches only emphasize the underlying power and density of the Replacements' attack. In a time when MTV, demographics, radio programmers, and carnivorous record companies turn art into product, the Replacements continue to prove that the music and its message can still matter: "Man, I'm dressin' sharp and feelin' dull." The sound, while occasionally a bit thin, is clear, crisp, and dynamic.

# The Residents

Formed 1970s—San Francisco, California
**The King and I (1989)**
Enigma 73547-2 (52:25)   **[C–]**
Another minimalist dose of satiric deconstruction by this Bay Area band. They have managed to maintain personal anonymity (they perform in eyeball masks, which may be the result of either self-preservation or general lack of interest) over a career that dates back to the seventies. Sixteen of the King's gold records, "Blue Suede Shoes," "Heartbreak Hotel," "All Shook Up" among them, make up this strange, yet sometimes affecting, dark "tribute." Interwoven between some tracks is a narrator telling the story of a mythical king that makes about as much sense as everything else, and ends on a truly poignant note. The sound quality is fine.

# Stan Ridgeway

Founding member (1977) of L.A.'s short-lived, synth-driven Wall of Voodoo.

**The Big Heat (1985)**
I.R.S. CDILP 26874 (45:29)   **[B + ]**
The cinematic vignette as rock song, delivered by Ridgeway in a flat narrative voice over moody, synthesized instrumentation, leading into a world that owes more to Raymond Chandler than to Elvis Presley. Ridgeway has an eye for detail and a writer's way with a lyric, creating a nice, edgy sense of menace, which isn't an easy feat in pop song. Tales of our times, intelligent echoes of tabloid headlines—it doesn't always ring true, but it has style, notably "Walkin' Home Alone." The CD has a clear, tight sound appropriate for the message.

**Mosquitos (1989)**
Geffen 24216-2 (41:06)   **[A–]**
Ridgeway carves his own wry space in the diverse realm of modern pop. Within his private, heavily synthesized, harrowing theater of the absurd, he deadpans his way through a *film noir* recording of peculiar stance and sound. This is not to suggest that Ridgeway is a downer; rather, the man has the ability to churn out dance-floor rockers like "Goin' Southbound" that echo with his very different point of view: "Can't complain, my landlord's a cop/ My neighbor's insane, but I guess I can't complain." Ridgeway's cool, rhythmic musical setting embroidered with sitars, accordions, and horns delivers a heady musical mix. The sound fits the material—cool, precise, with a lingering, haunting echo.

# The Righteous Brothers
Formed 1962—Los Angeles
## (Bill Medley)
b. September 19, 1940—Santa Ana, California
## (Bobby Hatfield)
b. August 10, 1940—Beaver Dam, Wisconsin
### Anthology (1962–1974)
Rhino R2 71488 (95:52—two discs)   [A–]
According to Dave Marsh, "Anyone who likes Hall and Oates should faint when they hear *this* stuff." He ain't wrong. This unlikely twosome, Bill Medley (the tall one with the deep voice) and Bobby Hatfield (the short one with the soaring tenor/falsetto), pretty much invented blue-eyed soul, and when, in 1964, Phil Spector got behind the controls, they patented it with one of the greatest pop songs ever laid down, "You've Lost That Lovin' Feelin'." During the dozen years covered by this excellent Rhino compilation, the Brothers charted twenty-one hits, and all of them (except 1966's "He Will Break Your Heart") are included. From their earlier, strongly R&B-influenced singles, to their later ballads, it's all here. As usual, Rhino's Bill Inglot has done a first-rate job on the digital remastering, but the age of the source material imposes some limitations: heavy compression and some distortion on the earliest tracks, and some tape hiss on the later tracks, but given Spector's multitrack overdubs, that's probably inevitable.

# The Robert Cray Band
b. August 1, 1953—Columbus, Georgia
Formed first band in Tacoma, Washington.

### Bad Influence (1983)
Hightone HCD 8001 (42:46)   [A–]
Almost singlehandedly, Robert Cray spearheaded the late-eighties American blues resurgence. His work is dependent upon a smooth singing style and terse, but effective, guitar work, frequently employed in the service of his eighties style-sensitive, somewhat self-effacing blues originals. Competent, quality work, the best selections are "Phone Booth," "So Many Women, So Little Time," and "Share What You've Got and Keep What You Need." This may well be Cray's finest outing. The sound is afflicted with some slight hiss and compression, but it is detailed with nice separation.

### False Accusations (1985)
Hightone HCD 8005 (38:13)   [B]
More modern, melodic upbeat blues material that is very much of a piece with its predecessor, providing clean playing and songs reflective of the moods of the modern world. The material is not quite as strong as that on *Bad Influence,* but, the sound is cleaner and more dynamic; in other words, excellent.

### Strong Persuader (1986)
Polygram 830 568-2 M-1 (39:26)   [A]
Riding the strength of a major label and resultant hit single, "Smoking Gun," this 1986 release brought Cray's economical, current sounds to the American mass audience. The record showcases all of his substantial strengths and features a more assured, emotive singing style with some fuller R&B sounding strains overlaid on the basic blues foundations. Again, the principal strength may be the material which features consistently excellent writing. Bright and appealing, the CD's sound is extremely dynamic, intimate, and well-separated; although, it exhibits a slight tendency to shrillness in its highs.

### Don't Be Afraid of the Dark (1988)
Hightone Mercury 834923-2 (45:10)   [A–]
*Strong Persuader* was a tough act to follow, and Cray gets close, if not all the way, on *Don't Be Afraid of the Dark*. Simply, the man can sing and play—no shit! In fact, his singing and guitar playing are the equal of his performance on the prior release, but the songs this time just don't reach *Persuader's* extraordinarily high levels. Cray, of course, has been the subject of countless comparisons (e.g., B.B. King, Al Green), but this monster is his own man with his own plan—he has the tension and the tools to pull it off. You can call it soul, blues, or R&B; in fact it's the updating of several traditions into some of the most resonant music currently being made. The title track, "Night Patrol," and "Across the Line" stand out from the rest. This CD has a hot, urgent sound that will penetrate the darkest recesses of any good smoke-filled Saturday night joint.

### Featuring the Memphis Horns
### Midnight Stroll (1990)
Mercury 846652-2 (50:08)   [A]
Prior to recording *Midnight Stroll,* Cray toured with Eric Clapton, whose band included the Memphis Horns. Cray has worked with them to produce one of the best recordings of an already impressive career. Often touted as a rare blues crossover artist, this time it's the great sounds of sixties soul that echo throughout. While Cray's intense, smoldering guitar still punctuates the strong instrumentation, his wondrous voice ignites this first-rate collection of sophisticated soul. On his earlier work Cray has sometimes seemed to be a half-step removed from the emotional core of his material, but not on *Midnight Stroll*—from aching blues to grinding soul struts, this is the work of a man in full control of his sub-

stantial talent. Add to this some right-on lyrics: "Not a day goes by that a man doesn't have to choose/Between what he wants, what he's afraid to lose" ("Consequences"), or "Love can be easy but trust is hard to find/And all I need is some walk around time" ("Walk Around Time"), and you've got a real keeper. The sound is smooth as butter; it doesn't call attention to itself, it conveys the music with near perfection.

# Robbie Robertson
# (James Robbie Robertson)
b. July 5, 1944—Toronto, Ontario, Canada
**Robbie Robertson (1987)**
Geffen 24160-2 (44:26)   [A + ]
Now that some of rock's early icons have survived careers spanning two or three decades, their audience has seen the impact of maturation on their music—not an inherently unique process, but in the newly forged medium of rock & roll, remember that the essential currency was youth. And unfortunately, with rare exception, the greater the distance from the artist's initial youthful impact, the lesser the quality of his or her later work. Perhaps this is definitional: rock & roll is first and foremost the music of adolescent rebellion, or perhaps it is the corrosive nature of the very success that prohibits career longevity. It is probably both. All of this makes Robertson's first album effort in more than a decade (since The Band) fascinating in both a personal and historical context. Happily, that's beside the point, because the music itself is so overwhelmingly good—*Robbie Robertson* is a record that reverberates with a deep vital energy, the eighties expression of the man who took the new music of the sixties back a hundred years with classics like "The Weight," "The Night They Drove Old

Dixie Down," and "Cripple Creek." Robertson wasn't a solo artist with The Band, it being one of the most multi-talented musical groups in sixties rock. While he does take vocal leads on the new release, he is ably assisted by some talented current performers, among them, U2, Peter Gabriel, and Maria McKee, as well as stalwart Garth Hudson. The nine songs show great musical textural variety, but all are anchored by Robertson's superbly crafted lyrics and hauntingly appropriate voice. This is an extraordinary release highlighted by "Somewhere Down the Crazy River," "Broken Arrow," and "Fallen Angel." The sound of the CD is absolutely first-rate in all respects.

# Smokey Robinson and the Miracles
Formed 1957—Detroit
After Berry Gordy, Robinson was the most important musical factor in the creation of the marvelous Motown sound.

### 18 Greatest Hits (1960–1981)
Motown 6071-2 TD (58:34)   **[A]**
Smokey and the Miracles were primarily, if not exclusively, a singles band; thus, compilation albums were the norm for this group. "Shop Around" (12/12/60) was Motown's first hit record, the cut that put the company on the map. Throughout the sixties, Smokey and the Miracles were the musical pinnacle of Motown's gifted raft of artists, and the songs that proved that are all right here. In addition to Robinson's consummate sense of pop musicality, which shapes both the content and the form of the material, his soaring, silky voice is simply without peer. The sound is typical Motown, generally uneven, but, overall, an improvement over prior reproductions.

**The Great Songs Written by Smokey Robinson (Various Artists) (1960–1981)**
Motown MCD06139-2MD (48:27)   **[A–]**
If there ever was any doubt why William "Smokey" Robinson was No. 2 two man at Motown, one listen to this compilation featuring sixteen of his more popular compositions will extinguish it forever. Supposedly, Bob Dylan has called him one of the great poets of contemporary pop music (and if he didn't, he should have). The sound varies—different artists, different recording dates, and it's far from perfect—but it still beats the vinyl versions all to hell. Included are Smokey's great hits for the Miracles ("Tracks of My Tears," "Shop Around"), the Temptations ("My Girl"), Mary Wells ("My Guy"), and Marvin Gaye ("Ain't That Peculiar").

# Rockpile
Formed 1976—London
**Seconds of Pleasure (1980)**
Columbia CK36886 (44:04)   **[C + ]**
Dave Edmunds and Nick Lowe have made a happy livelihood for more than a decade recycling fifties vintage rock licks, and as Rockpile they enjoyed a reputation as a live barn burner, but differing recording commitments kept the group off record until 1980's *Seconds of Pleasure*. It's a competent disappointment—it sounds like a group of seasoned pros going through the motions rather than the recorded testament of a kickin' roots-rock band. It'll get you up on the dance floor, but you won't be sweating when you leave. The CD version includes a couple of Everly Brothers classics, "When Will I Be Loved" and "Take a Message to Mary" (which were included on a seven-inch LP as a part of the original English vinyl release), plus "Cryin' in the Rain" and "Poor Jenny," both basically pleasant

impromptu acoustic covers. The originals are markedly superior. The sound has a somewhat flat, compressed quality about it.

# The Rolling Stones
Formed July, 1962—London
After more than a quarter century of constant exposure, the Rolling Stones remain one of the most enigmatic bands in the history of rock & roll. Unlike a majority of their contemporaries who turned to the music to express their rebellion or as an avenue out of an undesirable lifestyle, the Stones' approach always appeared somewhat more calculated.

As the self-appointed princes of darkness in the Beatles' magic kingdom of British sixties pop, their cynical, blues-postured stance enabled them to survive the death of the dream (Altamont) and to slide apparently effortlessly into supremacy with the advent of the self-indulgent, cynical seventies (the world's greatest rock & roll band). But their stature was obviously not only a matter of stance or attitude—musically these calculating ruffians brought a first-rate set of chops to the party—Wyman and Watts representing the best "bottom" ever; supporting Richards's classic, slashing Chuck Berry style primal guitar licks and Jones's enlightened, eclectic private madness.

They made seminal work in the seminal sixties and have continued a steady stream of material of widely varying quality for over twenty years. Their truly great contributions began with *Now* (1965) and ended with *Exile on Main Street* (1972). While the passing years have sapped the Stones' musical creativity, they have remained one of rock's cultural avatars for an impossibly long time. Until recently they seemed attuned to the cultural crosscurrents of their times more acutely than any of their peers.

### The Rolling Stones (England's Newest Hitmakers) (1964)
abco 73752 (31:12)   [B + ]
Obviously a first album, one on which Jagger, most notably, was groping for his vocal persona; but, on some cuts ("I'm a King Bee") the most famous mouth in rock & roll was beginning to find his unique sound. If Jagger was groping, the rest of the boys had found their niche—hard-assed white blues/rock, and they performed it far better than any of the many who have sought that pulsing path to musical salvation. This is determinedly hard music, played as hard as they could. The sound on most of the abco Rolling Stones digital remasters is truly revelatory. The story at the time of their release was that great care had been taken to go back to the true master tapes and eliminate a lot of the "contouring" that had been done on the analog releases. Whatever technique was employed, it works. It must be remembered that on the earliest releases, this one being from 1964, there is still a primitive, compressed quality to the markedly improved sound.

### 12 X 5 (1965)
abco 74022 (31:20)   [B]
Released in 1965, a clear successor to the '64 debut release *England's Newest Hitmakers,* this one bounces from the sublime, ("Time Is on My Side") to the ridiculous ("Under the Board Walk"). The rest of the heavily blues-oriented material is generally strong instrumentally, but somehow misses with Jagger's vocals. The sound is slightly more dynamic than that of the first recording, but is marred by occasional distortion.

## December's Children (And Everybody's) (1965)

abco 74512 (29:52)  **[C]**

"Get Off of My Cloud" and "I'm Free" rank with the best Stones singles of this period, but get them on a greatest hits collection, because the rest of this recording is lacking in both material and intensity. The sound, while generally an improvement over the record, is unlistenable on the live version of "Route 66" and varies from there.

## Now (1965)

abco 74202 (38:18)  **[A−]**

Also released in '65, but here Jagger has found his "voice," which insinuates through the thick aggressive blues-based rock that the band played better and better. The material is pretty much of a piece with its two predecessor album releases, with "Mona" and "Everybody Needs Somebody To Love" clearly the class of the outing. The sound is more uneven than on the earlier releases, and while some muddy moments occur, it remains a real improvement over the LP.

## Out of Our Heads (1965)

abco 74292 (33:59)  **[B +]**

Actually, one of their most uneven early efforts, a quality that frequently mars this great band's recorded output. Cuts like "The Last Time," "That's How Strong My Love Is," "Satisfaction," "The Under Assistant West Coast Promotion Man," and "Play With Fire" still hold their power after years of exposure, but much of the rest simply disappears. Too often the sound is murky, particularly the bass/drum track which is often distorted. It must be remembered that this wasn't supposed to be *Tubular Bells*. The garage band syndrome is, by now, endemic to the form, but the sound could be better.

## Aftermath (1966)

abco 74762 (43:46)  **[A +]**

This is the landmark statement. With *Aftermath,* the Stones staked out their own territory, reflective of their sources, but dependent upon no one. Jagger's lascivious vocal style holds its center and the best rock band in the world begins to feel its awesome authority. The texture of their sound is enhanced by Brian Jones's use of offbeat instrumentation, and, while the lyrics seem a bit calculated, the end result is a clear and identifiable posture. The sound simply leaves the LP in the Dark Ages.

## Big Hits (High Tides and Green Grass) (1966)

abco 8001-2 (36:14)  **[A]**

A powerful compilation that essentially, if not completely, sums up this legendary group's formative years, 1964–66. Not for the faint-hearted, but as honest a testimonial to the true spirit of rock & roll as any group made during this golden period of rock music. The sound varies, as expected, but this is a collection one would want in the permanent CD format.

## Between the Buttons (1967)

abco 74992 (38:36)  **[B +]**

Another change in the band's direction, marked by a quick, but inevitable withdrawal from the misogynistic lyrical posturing (and "down" sound) of *Aftermath.* It is not the musical equal of its predecessor, but contains some lesser known treasures, "Connection," "My Possession," "Complicated" as well as a couple of hits. The sound quality is more than satisfactory.

## Flowers (1967)

abco 75092 (37:49)  **[B−]**

At this point the band's album history gets somewhat confusing since most of the LP releases of this period were primarily singles compilations that included duplications. Thus, "Ruby Tuesday," "Let's Spend The Night Together," and "Lady Jane" appear on earlier albums. When these cuts, plus the filler items are eliminated, the only selections included here worthy of much attention are "Mother's Little Helper," "Right On, Baby," "Sittin' on a Fence," and "Have You Seen Your Mother Standin' in the Shadow" which are all strong sixties Stones' singles. The sound is noticeably different from cut to cut, but almost always preferable to the LP.

### Beggar's Banquet (1968)
abco 75392 (40:37)  [A + ]
While most of the rest of the pop world was lovin' through the apocalypse, the Stones told it like it was (or soon would be), and it wasn't pretty—but, God, it's frighteningly strong. One of rock & roll's true masterpiece recordings, produced by a band whose mask was evil and whose reality wasn't far behind—only the Rolling Stones could have played Altamont. If you didn't know the dream was dead, or maybe never was, then you just weren't listening. Glyn Johns, the album's engineer, called it "the Stones coming of age." The CD chisels the sound in space with a clarity that enhances an already great album.

### Let It Bleed (1969)
abco 80042 (43:00)  [A]
And the Stones adjust their stance yet again. But they were still working at the height of their dark powers and the end result is another enduring, if not a perfect, effort. While it lacks the consistency and espoused brutality of its predecessor, it nonetheless achieves an equally sublime potency on a number of cuts. The sound, while far from crystalline, throbs with all the pelvic potency intended.

### Through the Past Darkly (Big Hits Vol. 2) (1969—compilation release date)
abco 80032 (39:31)  [C]
Here we go again with the overlapping inclusions on compilation releases. Everything here is on other album releases except "She's A Rainbow," "Jumpin' Jack Flash," and "Honky Tonk Women" (both of which reappear on *Hot Rocks*); even a sampling from *Their Satanic Majesties* which was the Stones' first travesty album. The sound varies, but is generally very acceptable.

### Get Yer Ya-Yas Out! (1970)
abco 852 (47:54)  [B + ]
It was Madison Square Garden. The playlist is perfect. They were the greatest rock & roll band in the world. They were playing hot and nasty—scurrilous, biting, blues-based rock & roll. Yet somehow the recording never really ignites; there's not a definitive Stones version of any of this material. That said, it's still easily the best concert recording made by a great rock band. One of the reasons that *Get Yer Ya-Yas Out!* never fully realized its obvious potential was its sound quality, which was poor on record and isn't much improved on disc. Jagger's vocals are almost lost in the mix and the guitar sound is dirty, while the bottom succumbs to murkiness. There's also some dropout and distortion.

### Sticky Fingers (1971)
Rolling Stones Records CK40488 (46:26)  [A]
This is unrepentant, unregenerate, arrogant Stones' style rock & roll at it's best (well, maybe not "Wild Horses"). From "Brown Sugar" to "Moonlight Milc" with eight soulful, nasty numbers in between, this is the music that made them the kings (or at least the Dark Princes) of early seventies rock & roll. With this release, the Stones changed labels to Columbia for scandalous sums

of money and their own label. This is mentioned because the digital conversions of this label's material are generally not of the audio quality of the previously reviewed London (abco) earlier releases. The sound on *Sticky Fingers* is reed-thin and overbright. But it provides more clarity and detail than are available on the LP.

### Hot Rocks (1964–1971)

abco 2CD606/7 (86:42—two discs) **[B + ]**
If you're looking for a sampler, here it is; a little bit of everything. But work of the magnitude done by the Stones during the period covered by this compilation has too much richness and complexity to be properly served in a listeners' digest rendering. The sound varies, but is generally several cuts above the LP version.

### The Singles Collection: The London Years (1963–71)

abco 1218-2 (185:20-three discs) **[A + ]**
As Anthony DeCurtis points out in his excellent liner notes (part of a seventy-two-page book included in this boxed three-CD package), in the early sixties when the Stones first began to insinuate their radically cynical message, pop music was still primarily created as singles. All that power compressed into three minutes or less—potent doses when done right. A good argument can be made that the Stones (whose American counterpart would have been Credence Clearwater Revival) were essentially a singles band. When they got sucked into the concept album behind the vortex of 1967's *Sgt. Pepper,* they made their first really uninspired music of a long, lurching career. *The Singles Collection* includes fifty-seven tracks recorded between 1963 and 1971. This set, *Exile on Main Street,* and *Beg-*

*gar's Banquet* are probably the essential Stones' CDs. The digital remixes for this wonderfully comprehensive collection were partially overseen by the Stones' original producer, Andrew Loog Oldham, who heard it all as it originally was put down. Thus the earliest material is reproduced in its original mono; the original master tapes were used for all tracks, resulting in over three hours of great rock & roll. Thick as stew and brimming with the vitality of life lived earnestly for the moment, the music of the Stones is as integral to the soundtrack of the golden age of rock as any group's, and more prescient and enduring than most. The large, well-produced accompanying booklet is both insightful and informative.

### Exile on Main Street (1972)

Rolling Stone Records CGK40489
(66:35) **[A + ]**
Rock vérité—basement rock & roll, call it what you will—it is the scuzziest, dirtiest, most chaotic album release of a great rock band at the height of its powers, driving home ironically detached cynicism with undiminishing arrogance. It is one of the ten greatest rock records of all time (*Rolling Stone* ranked it third in its August 27, 1987, critics' survey of the best recorded releases of 1967–87). Literally recorded in a basement with a mobile unit, it may have been another calculated statement, but like most of the Stones' messages at the time, this one rang true on many levels. *Exile on Main Street* is tough, dense music which pertains to its times and to the continuing spirit of rock & roll. The CD improves the clarity of the sound (which some may find equivalent to colorizing a black-and-white movie), but the murky power persists, pulsing with its carnal rhythms. All that, and it's got "Tumbling Dice," too.

## Some Girls (1978)

Rolling Stones Records CK40449 (40:46)   **[B]**
Probably the last gasp of a once great band. They were playing tighter than ever, particularly Watts (drums) and Wyman (bass), but with this band that's not necessarily a virtue. This is stripped-down, straight-ahead Stones' rock & roll, and it still resonates with the echoes of their former dark grandeur (it was the group's best selling album ever), but the intensity has been replaced with something more commercially akin to the disco sensibility of the time. The sound is punchy, crisp, and terribly overbright.

## Emotional Rescue (1980)

Rolling Stones Records/CBS CK40500 (41:18)   **[D]**
A little look backward, a little grungy, a little going through the motions. Yet, when you've got a contract, you've got to deliver, but does this really count? Eminently forgettable, if not forgiveable. The sound is a bit brighter than the LP, otherwise it's a toss-up.

## Tattoo You (1981)

Rolling Stones Records/CBS CK40502 (43:00)   **[B–]**
This may prove to be ultimately the last viable gasp by a once nonpareil rock band. The fans loved it anyway; it's probably the all-time best-selling Stones' release (topping *Some Girls*). It's not a bad Stones album by their standards of the last fifteen years, but who can forget what once was? Clearly, its one truly outstanding moment is "Waiting on a Friend," both because of its mature lyrical stance and, especially, because of Sonny Rollins's sax solos. While it evidences some compression and hiss, the disc does have a cutting dynamic edge to its open sound, which is an enhancement.

## Dirty Work (1986)

Rolling Stones Records/CBS CK40250 (40:05)   **[C]**
This 1986 release is primarily a Keith Richards/Ron Wood guitar record, but the real punch comes from Wyman's bass and Watts's drums that just seem to improve with age. Clearly, the emphasis here is more on the instrumental than vocal attributes of the group. Measured by the stature this once great band had attained, *Dirty Work* is an obvious disappointment (eighties pop in the guise of rock & roll). Measured by the standards of its current competition, it just ain't that bad. Besides, it might be the final chapter (but don't bet on it). The sound is open, driving, and clean, with a slight edge to the upper mid-range.

## Steel Wheels (1989)

Rolling Stones/Columbia CK 45333 (53:58)   **[B–]**
With the release of *Steel Wheels* and their worldwide tour, the Rolling Stones reaffirmed their presence at the end of the eighties. Clearly their best work since *Some Girls, Steel Wheels* includes all the elements that have established the Stones' unique and enduring career, the duration of which defies explanation. On *Steel Wheels* the Stones are in first-rate instrumental and vocal condition; they're tight as a whip. This all-digital recording's dynamics amply suit the driving sound that has propelled this band over three decades. What is lacking is the tightrope over the sinister edge over which, in their glory years, they strutted with wicked cunning and madcap glee. Commercial reward, vastly realized, not enduring hooks or relevant lyrics, was the motivation behind this recording. Upon repeated listenings, this shows. Highlighted by "Hearts for Sale" and the wistful "Slipping Away," *Steel Wheels* is a testament to tenacity, but

fails to yield any single cut that can stand alongside this band's many classics.

## Linda Ronstadt
b. July 15, 1946—Tucson, Arizona
**Heart Like a Wheel (1974)**
Capitol CDP7 46073-2 (31:45)   **[D]**
Her strength is her achingly pure, perfect pitched voice which is truly a remarkable instrument. Her devastating weakness is an inability to convey, or worse, comprehend the meaning of the lyrics she performs. *Heart Like a Wheel*, which was the initial move away from the more country sounds of her prior records, is probably her strongest recorded outing—good song selection, excellent musicianship, and more vitality in her lyrical interpretations than she's displayed before or since. Sadly, this one shining recorded moment has been butchered in its conversion to disc; the mix is muddy, thick, distorted, and generally inexcusable.

## Roxy Music
**Avalon (1982)**
Polydor/EG800 032-2 (37:25)   **[C + ]**
The spark and intensity that made Roxy Music the great British seventies art-rock band had passed. In its place appeared a sleek, sophisticated sound that, while utterly listenable (preferably as background music), offered little in the way of substance or meaningful intent. It is a lovely sound, precisely produced and packaged. The CD provides an excellent complement to the sound of the music—very open, relatively clean, and nicely defined with excellent separation.

## Todd Rundgren
June 22, 1948—Philadelphia, Pennsylvania
Original group The Nazz (named after a Lord Buckley rap)

**Nearly Human (1989)**
Warner Bros. 25881-2 (53:36)   **[A–]**
A live, recorded-in-the-studio romp into the joy of pop music that echoes with a love of Philly soul and pure gospel voicings. Rundgren creates a Spectorian wall of sound against which he bounces some of his best singing in years. Conceived as a statement about the dry, studio-manufactured sound that leaches the life from much of pop music, this all-digital recording is a bit thin in the mid- and upper ranges, with a tendency toward harshness at the top, but it has dynamics and vitality to burn. Rundgren's acknowledged mastery of the form is not diminished by this noble, largely successful experiment—more pure pop from a man who's made a career out of hooks and happiness.

## Leon Russell
b. April 2, 1941—Lawton, Oklahoma
**Leon Russell (1970)**
DCC Shelter SRZ 8001 (42:33)   **[B–]**
This was the debut album from "the master of space and time" and the first release on the Shelter label founded by Russell and Kenny Cordell. While Russell had initially built his reputation as another sixties unknown L.A. studio stalwart, his celebrity was rising at the time of this release because of his highly visible role in Joe Cocker's *Mad Dogs and Englishmen* tour and film. *Leon Russell* provided the composer's own visions of his quasi-classic material: "A Song For You," "Hummingbird," and "Delta Lady," along with eight other tracks. The CD adds two bonus selections: "Masters of War (Old Masters)," a Bob Dylan politi-

cal chestnut, here sung to the tune of "The Star Spangled Banner," which was deleted from the vinyl version, and a solo version of "Shoot Out on the Plantation," which received a fuller working as one of the album's original tracks. Even with the talented Glyn Johns doing the mix, the disc's sound is somewhat thin, compressed, and a little harsh in the high midrange.

### And the Shelter People (1971)
Shelter/DCC SRZ-8005 (53:57)  **[B]**
Jam session rock & roll roaring like a tornado across the flatlands of Oklahoma, *Leon Russell and the Shelter People* will liven up any party and bring back memories of hairier times. This was Russell's second solo outing following his associations with Joe Cocker and George Harrison. Several of the strong musicians who make up the Shelter People were alums from the Mad Dogs and Englishmen gang who worked behind Cocker. The fourteen cuts include eight Russell originals—the best of which, "Stranger in a Strange Land" and "Home Sweet Oklahoma," are first-rate—plus Harrison's "Beware of Darkness," and "A Hard Rain's a-Gonna Fall" among five Bob Dylan covers. Russell's twangy, twisted voice and piano pyrotechnics keep things moving, but twenty years betray the fact that, talented though he is, Russell is a slick stylist who lacks substance. The sound also betrays its age with some hiss, compression, and muddiness.

# Mitch Ryder and the Detroit Wheels
Formed 1965—Detroit
### Rev Up—The Best Of (1962–1966)
Rhino R270941 (62-67) (64:39)  **[A]**
Twenty-five years after the fact, most people think Motown when they think of great Motor City sounds. That groundbreaking company was born out of a large black urban community with an active and vital R&B heritage. But some of the homeboys weren't black, yet they experienced that same R&B sound as a part of their lives. One of them, Mitch Ryder, used it to fashion some of the all-time great party music of the sixties. As wonderfully served up on this, another great Rhino collection, it still pounds with unrelenting intensity. Ryder's rough, raucous vocals backed with Johnny Badanjek's extraordinary drumming and Jim McCarty's always-right guitar licks riding through classics ("Jenny Take a Ride!," "Little Latin Lupe Lu," "Devil With a Blue Dress On," and "Good Golly, Miss Molly") to lesser-known gems ("Shake a Tail Feather") will still ignite a dance floor or a rock & roll heart. The sound retains the bottom-heavy, rough vocal raunch that made it great originally. Don Snowden's liner notes provide thorough biographical augmentation.

### Greatest Hits (1965–1967)
Roulette RCD59020 (34:12)  **[B]**
Detroit has been a major contributor to American rock & roll, and one of its premier contributions was Mitch Ryder and the Detroit Wheels (among the music's true anthems, Ryder's "Devil With a Blue Dress/Good Golly Miss Molly" and "Jenny Take a Ride" still ring loud and clear). This is rock & roll. The sound varies all over the place, but overall it adds a dynamic punch and highlights the raucous noise which was Ryder's pure rock voice.

## Doug Sahm
b. November 6, 1942—San Antonio, Texas
**Juke Box Music (1989)**
Antones Ant0008CD (42:16)  **[C–]**
Back in the late sixties, when Sahm masqueraded as Sir Douglas and brought his native Tex-Mex roots and Augie Meyers's Farfisa organ to such barroom classics as "Mendocino" and "She's About a Mover," he was inspired. Two decades later, Sahm seems to have settled into an easy Texas-roadhouse R&B groove working with a tight, horn-driven traveling band. A visit to the studio by this group resulted in *Juke Box Music.* It's good, not great, beer-drinking, Saturday night music. The sound is OK, a bit compressed, and lacking any special distinction.

## Santana
Formed 1967—San Francisco
**Caravanserai (1970)**
Columbia CK31610 (51:23)  **[C–]**
What had begun in the late sixties as an improvisational Latin rock band became, with this release, a Latin jazz/rock fusion experiment. *Caravanserai* has its moments, but it's mostly ambling, formless, and lacking in central theme or meaning. The recording is plagued with hiss and, overall, has roughly the same sound characteristics as its LP predecessor.

## Boz Scaggs (William Royce Scaggs)
b. June 8, 1944—Ohio
Boz got his start as the singer in the Steve Miller Band and ultimately migrated with Miller from Texas to San Francisco in 1967. Over the next decade or so, Scaggs developed into one of the smoothest white soul singers around. In recent years, he has quit recording and now owns the Blue Light Cafe and Slim's in the City by the Bay.

**Slow Dancer (1974)**
Columbia CK32760 (36:38)  **[B–]**
Working with former Motown producer, Johnny Bristol, Scaggs lends his smooth voicings to ten soul selections, largely written by the artist and Bristol. This is slick, listenable, ballad-to-medium-tempo white soul music performed by one of the better practitioners of the form. The sound is generally very good; nice separation among the instruments and slightly enhanced dynamics, with some compression and occasional distortion on a few vocals.

**Silk Degrees (1976)**
CBS CK33920 (41:33)  **[B +]**

**Silk Degrees (1976)**
Mobile Fidelity UDCD 535 (41:28)  **[A–]**
Still the best available example of Boz's cool, smooth white soul sound—one of

the better Bay-Area lackluster-seventies sounds. Lush, sophisticated pop performed with detached professionalism, it still manages to evoke genuine feeling. The ballads are meant for firelit midnights, the uptempo numbers for ballroom dance floors, and all fit comfortably into their intended niches. The whole affair has a sort of deco elegance about it, but it never displays affectation. It's hard to imagine anyone resisting the pleasures of "Georgia," "Lido Shuffle," or "We're All Alone." The CBS disc sounds compressed, afflicted by a muddiness in the instrumentation. Mobile Fidelity's gold ultradisc is a marked sonic improvement, much more open and dynamic, but with a tendency to bury the lead vocal.

**Hits! (1980—compilation release date)**
Columbia CK36841 (43:13)  **[B + ]**
First-rate compilation of some of the smoothest white soul music to come along in the seventies. Scaggs is both a fine, easy vocalist and an excellent soul/pop writer, both of which are amply illustrated on this ten-selection package which includes "Lowdown," "You Make It So Hard (To Say No)," "Lido Shuffle," and "Dinah Flo." Given the differences in the age and source of the included recordings, the sound is a model of consistency. It's smooth, detailed, open and well-defined with excellent separation.

**Other Roads (1989)**
Columbia CK 40463 (45:09)  **[D + ]**
The sound is sumptuous, but Boz has been away a long time between recordings and, sadly, it shows. The voice is slick and urbane as always, but the ten tunes never rise above the mediocre; Scaggs sings as if, in his heart, he knows it. A production effort for late-eighties formulized radio programmers, and

that has yet to prove a basis for real inspiration.

# Bob Seger
b. May 6, 1945—Ann Arbor, Michigan
It's almost un-American not to like Bob Seger. The blue-collar, truckin', hard-rockin', hard-workin' rock & roller who just kept bringing it to the people; working the toughest gig in the biz—the road—more days than not, year in and year out. He ain't what he used to be, but, then, who is?

**And the Silver Bullet Band**
**Night Moves (1976)**
Capitol CDP7 46075 2 (36:59)  **[A + ]**
There's nothing new here, just the best of the fifties and sixties rock & roll and soul music restated with honest currency and sung by one of rock's best voices. The years of dues behind *Night Moves* cling to it like grime on flesh. Dave Marsh described it best: "That wonderful chronicle of moments when age becomes irrelevant and innocence gains experience." There really isn't a bad cut on the album. The sound is a joy, not perfect, but a joy—bright, full, detailed, clean, and very dynamic (it does have some compression and occasional distortion in the vocals).

**And the Silver Bullet Band**
**Live Bullet (1976)**
Capitol CDP7 46085 2 (71:24)  **[B + ]**
Seger took his raspy-voiced blue-collar rock & roll to superstar status in the mid-seventies on the strength and endurance of his constant touring schedule. As concert recordings go, this one does a credible job of capturing the edgy intensity that Bob and the boys were able to generate live—particularly on the "Travelin' Man/Beautiful Loser" medley. The release contains most of his obligatory

material: "Turn the Page," "Ramblin' Gamblin' Man," and "Katmandu." The band is in fine fettle; Seger (as always) sings his ass off, and the hometown Detroit audience is appropriately appreciative. The sound, while overbright and edgy at its most intense moments, is generally first-rate for a live recording.

# The Sex Pistols
Formed 1975—London
The epitome of Britain's 1960's rock bands, the Beatles and the Stones, have both been identified with a Svengali who guided them to greatness. As Brian Epstein packaged the Beatles and Andrew Loog Oldham the Stones, Malcolm McLaren provided that service and much more to the Sex Pistols. The idea was simple enough. Create a band that would be the turd in the palace of smug success-smothered music that was then impersonating rock & roll. McLaren's genius was in finding the right turd.

### Never Mind the Bollocks Here's the Sex Pistols (1977)
Virgin CDV 2086 (38:54)   [A+]
It's an assault. A remembrance of things past and of a spirit almost lost. You feel the Sex Pistols. The hearing is almost irrelevant. This is dissolute, daring music that isn't easy in any way, but it is one of those rare recordings that somehow affects the way everything after it is heard. *Never Mind the Bollocks* was the one unchallenged rock & roll album of the seventies. Nihilistic, nasty, neurotic, and pneumatic, it was/is the spirit incarnate. The sound is tight, driving, and abrasive, just as was intended.

# The Shirelles
Formed 1958—Passaic, New Jersey
**Anthology (1959–1964)**
Rhino RNCD 75897 (40:10)   [A]
The late fifties through the early sixties was the time of Phil Spector and the great "girl group" sounds (the Crystals, Ronettes, etc.), but the Shirelles may have started it all and were probably the best of the bunch, the "wall of sound" notwithstanding. In addition to their abilities as vocalists, the Shirelles wrote much of their own material and, in 1963, the Beatles covered a couple of their songs, "Baby It's You" and "Boys" on their first English album. This almost comprehensive package, another sonic gem by Bill Inglot, combines fine music with wondrous production values to deliver digital magic in its truest form.

# Michelle Shocked
b. circa 1962—Texas
**Short Sharp Shocked (1988)**
Mercury 834-924-2 (36:33)   [B+]
From *The Texas Campfire Tapes,* literally recorded outdoors on a Walkman, the politically motivated Shocked garnered enough attention to make it into an honest-to-God recording studio. She makes the trip with ease. Except for Jean Ritchie's "The L&N Don't Stop Here Anymore," she provides ten fresh originals (the last one isn't listed on the back cover and provides a wild change of pace), that reflect her activist stance and her recollections of growing up in simpler, rural times. Pete Anderson's acoustic/country production provides fine, sympathetic backing for this contemporary folk fest. However, it is Shocked's keen, askance lyrics and committed vocals that make *Short Sharp Shocked* a treat, not to mention some first-rate songs: "Anchorage," "When I

Grow Up," and "If Love was a Train."
The sound quality of this disc is
impressive, with clean, well-defined
voicings.

**Captain Swing (1989)**
Mercury/Polygram 838 878-2 (31:55) **[A]**
Who would have ever expected the
gentle folk persona behind *The Texas
Campfire Tapes* to joyously explode into
barroom wailer holding her own amidst
a hot horn-driven band? Michelle
Shocked does—she damn well does.
Her first studio release, *Short Sharp
Shocked,* was a strong statement from a
writer capable of razor-sharp satire
buoyed by a happy sense of pure musicality. *Captain Swing* is another major
step forward—it's got body, spirit, and
guts, and as the album notes advise,
"Swing is a feeling—everything else is
just style." Michelle's surely got the feeling and on *Captain Swing,* she shares it.
An undisputed winner with sound quality to match the material, production
and performance.

**The Silos**
Formed 1980's—Florida
**The Silos (1990)**
RCA 2051-2-R (41:01) **[B+]**
Subtlety is not an ingredient for pop success, which may explain why this gently
intense recording will probably vanish
without much trace. This is the third
release by the group fronted by Walter
Salas Humera and Bob Rupe. It focuses
on the simple details of daily life to
evoke lasting imagery. Their acoustic guitar-driven sound draws heavily
from the crosscurrents of American regional music with generally good effect.
While it lacks any hook-laden potential
hits, the recording breathes musical sincerity that rewards repeated listenings.
Highlights include "I'm Over You," "The

Only Story I Tell," and "Take My Country
Back/(We'll Go) Out of Town." Coproduced and recorded by Peter Moore (the
man behind the Cowboy Junkies' *Trinity
Sessions* sound), it sacrifices some clarity
for a slightly reverent sound that nicely
fits the material.

**Simon & Garfunkel**
Formed 1957/1964—New York City
This immensely popular duo really was
more folk or pop-oriented than true purveyors of pure rock & roll; however,
their pioneering efforts, marked by
Simon's musical craftsmanship and
creativity, broadened the rock audience
throughout their highly successful
career.

**Parsley, Sage, Rosemary and Thyme
(1966)**
Columbia CK9363 (28:34) **[B+]**
The master of sardonic eclecticism in
his collegiate folk phase, Simon's sense
of musicianship and compositional craft,
combined with Garfunkel's truly lovely
voice, has resulted in music of lasting
quality. Additionally, ever since producer Tom Wilson made the duo stars by
investing their acoustic "Sounds of
Silence" with some "after the fact" studio
electric guitar magic, they always handled their production with meticulous
care, thanks largely to the engineering
precision of Roy Halee. That care pays
off on the digital conversion. The sound
has a purity to it, particularly in the
glorious harmonies.

**Bookends (1968)**
Columbia CK9529 (29:49) **[A+]**
It was the year after *Sgt. Pepper*—it was
the time of "concept albums." Most who
undertook this format failed, either by
comparison or by simple lack of talent.
Simon & Garfunkel were the exception.

*Bookends* is an essential musical picture of its time and place. "America" is one of the great pop/rock songs. You're gonna love how this CD sounds.

### Bridge Over Troubled Water (1970)
Columbia CK9914 (37:29)  [B + ]
Well-crafted as they are, the lyrics haven't worn all that well; perhaps because of overexposure due to the tremendous popularity the album initially enjoyed in 1970 and its continued playability. What endures are the lush melodies, superbly produced. Overall, the CD's sound revitalizes this old chestnut providing a precise, yet warm, dynamic rendering of the craftsmanship displayed by the duo and their wonderful producer/engineer, Roy Halee, in the recording studio. The sound is sadly afflicted with consistently audible hiss and some distortion and/or muddiness in its loudest passages. Yet, on balance, the digital conversion is a substantial improvement; in fact, it offers several truly stunning moments.

### Greatest Hits (1972—compilation release date)
Columbia CK31350 (44:32)  [D–]
You certainly can't fault the song selection on this first-rate compilation. But on most cuts the sound is incredibly poor, thin and shrill with some distortion thrown in for good measure. This is one disc where the record wins hands down.

# Paul Simon
b. October 13, 1942—Newark, New Jersey
While his body of work is impressive for both its innate quality and its popular acceptance, his ultimate legacy may be as a bridge between the indigenous music of the world's divergent cultures.

### Paul Simon (1972)
Warner Bros. 25588-2 (34:36)  [A + ]
Probably his least guarded recording. Simon's sense of joy and exhilaration at being unleashed from the personal and musical constraints of *the* sixties folk/rock duo, Simon & Garfunkel, is palpable in the eleven selections that make up *Paul Simon*. From its better-known cuts, "Mother and Child Reunion," "Duncan," and "Me and Julio Down by the Schoolyard," to lesser-known classics like "Peace Like a River," the CD's enhanced dynamics and openness give this release an appealing intimacy its vinyl predecessor lacked. As the first chapter of a solo career notable for its high quality and duration, this remains one of the highlights of a body of recordings that now spans three decades. It also presaged Simon's involvement with World Beat, as it was one of the first U.S. mainstream recordings to use Jamaican reggae. The CD's sound does betray its analog roots, evidencing slight hiss and some compression, but it is a marked improvement over the LP.

### There Goes Rhymin' Simon (1973)
Warner Bros. 25589-2 (35:49)  [A]
Simon's eclecticism shifts from blues to gospel to Dixieland, and in the process embraces what may be his finest song, "American Tune." Among those who have taken the Tin Pan Alley strain of American pop music into the rock era, Simon simply has no peer. What his music lacks in depth of soul is more than compensated for by his musical and lyrical craft, intelligence, and wit. This is first-rate Simon and that translates into some of the best pop/rock music of the seventies. Simon's meticulousness also extends to production, resulting in consistent sonic excellence, and this CD only confirms it. Given its age, the CD's sound is extraordinary.

### In Concert/Live Rhymin' (1974)
Warner Bros. 25590-2 (51:57)  **[C]**
Released in 1974, this concert recording
underscores the fact that Simon, the
consummate pop craftsman, functions
most effectively in a studio setting. The
selections include hits from his high-fly-
ing days with Art Garfunkel as well as
highlights from Simon's subsequent solo
career. It does have its moments—the
Jesse Dixon Singers' work on "Bridge
Over Troubled Water"—but in every
case the originals are better than these
live reworkings. The CD's sound is that
of an enhanced LP—a decent concert
recording; nothing special. The package
is marred by pathetic liner information.

### Still Crazy After All These Years (1975)
Warner Bros. 25591-2 (35:14)  **[B]**
The wonderful production values are
still evident, as is the compositional
craftsmanship—but melancholy is one
thing, lugubriousness another. There
are some fine moments—"Still Crazy
After All These Years" and "50 Ways To
Leave Your Lover"—but too much of
the rest is either a bit facile or a bit too
afflicted with emotional malaise. For
an analog source, the sound is nicely
dynamic, clean, and suitably warm.

### Greatest Hits, Etc. (1977)
Columbia CK35032 (51:53)  **[A + ]**
Just as Garfunkel's musical career
plummeted following the duo's breakup,
Simon's sharply ascended. As his eclectic craftsmanship became more pronounced, his musical product became
more diverse, but always professionally
and precisely presented. Simon has
managed to extend the Brill Building
pop ethic into a valid contemporary popular idiom. Faulting this collection has to
be simply a matter of personal idio-
syncrasy: "Slip Slidin' Away," "Still Crazy
After All These Years," "An American

Tune," "Mother And Child Reunion,"
"Take Me to the Mardi Gras," plus eight
other wonderful pop songs. At his best
("An American Tune"), Paul Simon is one
of the finest writers of popular music the
form has known. If all that weren't
enough, the CD is pure sonic joy. This
is the best of seventies pop product
heard through the best of the eighties
sound technology.

### One Trick Pony (1980)
Warner Bros. 3472-2 (38:18)  **[B–]**
The soundtrack to the movie of the
same name that Simon wrote and in
which he starred. This isn't vintage
Simon by any stretch of the imagination,
but he's too fine a craftsman for it to be
without merit; however, most of the
material is fairly forgettable. "Late in the
Evening" became a bit of a hit in 1980,
but the highlight is "Ace in the Hole,"
one of the best songs ever written by
one of America's best contemporary
song writers. The sound is generally
impressive: dynamic, very open, and
detailed, but it does have a less than
clear background, and occasional distortion. However, in this case these are
minor complaints.

### Hearts and Bones (1983)
Warner Bros. 9 23942-2 (40:45)  **[A–]**
Simon's 1983 release, which was probably the least commercially successful
recording of his long career. This was
the case even though it contains all the
elements common to his well-received
work: fine songs sensitively performed
set against the best pop production values. The obvious answer is that it lacked
the hit song necessary to make the
album a success. Yet, there are some
great songs included here: the autobiographical title cut that chronicles his
marriage to and divorce from Carrie
Fisher, as well as the more obvious

potential hit, "The Late, Great Johnny Ace." Perhaps it's all just too grown-up for pop success; *Hearts and Bones* again demonstrates pop craftsmanship of the highest order as well as ingenious lyrics sung with genuine feeling. As is usually the case with Simon's work, the sound quality is a major addition to the proceedings and so it is with this CD.

### Graceland (1986)
Warner Bros. 9 25447-2 (43:10)   **[A + ]**
Throughout his lengthy career, Simon has been an eclectic craftsman. Prior to this release, his pop music incorporated sounds from South America and Jamaica as well as American blues and gospel material. In late 1985 and early 1986, Paul Simon discovered the current popular music of South Africa and it inspired this truly wondrous recording. Working with a number of native musicians whose roots-oriented material represents the best of South Africa current pop sounds, Simon has grafted his fine melodic sense to the extraordinary harmonies and complex rhythms which in the truest sense represent the source material for much of American popular music. Perhaps because of its political aspects, *Graceland* represents a rock & roll album in the truest sense. Beyond these political considerations, musically it is simply perhaps the finest pop album to be released in the decade of the eighties. Consistent with its moving, meaningful, melodic contents, the sound quality of the compact disc is excellent.

### The Rhythm of the Saints (1990)
Warner Bros. 26098-2 (44:41)   **[A]**
His 1987 *Graceland* exploded with the addictive, melodic rhythms of South African township jive—*The Rhythm of the Saints* ebbs and flows with the sinuous rhythms of Brazil and West Africa.

What sets both of these World Beat–based recordings apart is the consummate pop craftsmanship of Paul Simon, one of pop/rock's best lyricists. Hypnotic, impressionistic, *The Rhythm of the Saints* is the work of a mature artist grappling with the crimes of omission and commission that bedevil life's potential paradise. Yet at its core, the shifting shadow rhythms and often oblique lyrical imagery lead to a statement of faith and redemption. *Rhythm* is less an assemblage of songs and styles (like *Graceland*) and more an interwoven song cycle, lilting with interior monologs and floating in a gently percussive crosscurrent. The best art, regardless of its form, is like a wellspring affording a source of continual renewal and insight over the passage of time. *The Rhythm of the Saints* is unlikely to capture the casual listener on first hearing, but it possesses those elements that will reward and replenish with repeated experience. This recording possesses a unique dynamic—a powerful subtlety based on the tension between its strong rhythm foundations and its languid melodic structure. Working again with engineer Roy Halee, Simon has produced a recording of remarkable sound characteristics and reverberating bass overlaid with subtle, clean voicings blended with a warm, natural sound.

## Simple Minds
Formed 1977—Scotland
### Once Upon a Time (1985)
A&M CD5092 (40:17)   **[B]**
A big eighties anthemic rock sound, musically derived from Roxy Music's fine seventies work, but which has now reached a point where the message is almost lost in the grandeur of the sonics. *Once Upon a Time* remains a prime example of eighties arena rock with sub-

stance in addition to waves of pounding sound. Jim Kerr is a passionate performer with the ability to communicate his obviously sincere humanistic messages. The sound quality on this disc is excellent: extremely dynamic, vastly open, and also providing excellent clarity and detail.

# Simply Red
Formed 1985—Manchester, England
**Picture Book (1986)**
Elektra 9 60452-2 (44:30)  **[C–]**
*New Musical Express* summed this one up, ". . . soul-by-the-numbers is as cliché-ridden as the ugliest offspring of gothic interbreeding." The sound, however, is first-rate.

# The Sir Douglas Quintet
Formed 1964—California
**The Collection (1980–1981)**
Castle CCSCD 133 (55:26)  **[A–]**
Texas has been a major contributor to the rock movement almost from its inception (Buddy Holly was born in Lubbock on September 7, 1938). In large part, this arises because that state's music is, in many ways, a microcosm of rock itself; i.e., the ultimate amalgamation of all forms of pop music. From Tex-Mex through Western Swing to rockabilly, Doug Sahm and his trusty sidekick, Augie Meyer (on the Farfisa organ) make music that incorporates all these elements into what is great roadhouse Saturday night listening. Yet, this is no homage to the past; the Quintet's music, made primarily in the late sixties to early seventies, was very much of its time and held its own at a time when the overall quality of rock music was substantially higher than it has ever been since. This is loose (sloppy?) good-time sound enhanced by a heritage and com-

mitted performance. The seventeen selections cover essentially all of the group's vintage efforts. The sound is dynamic and fairly open, but suffers from some heavy hiss and compression from time to time.

**"Live" (1983)**
Takoma TAKCD7095 (41:14)  **[B +]**
Doug Sahm is another of the many Texas musicians who moved to California in the early 1960s. His music reflects his "roots," incorporating country, Tex-Mex, jazz, blues, and Western Swing into a unique "rock" sound that was notable for the introduction of the Vox (Farfisa) organ sound which Augie Meyer brought to the original Sir Douglas group. The result was a distinctive sound that propelled the band to its two most memorable hits, "Mendocino" and "She's About a Mover" (both included here). This '86 release captures the band doing ten selections recorded "live" in Austin and Los Angeles. Something of the grungy sixties charm may be missing, but Doug's got a great rock voice and there is an honesty of intent about it that remains compelling. Given the source locales, the sound is pretty impressive; a bit compressed and subject to constant hiss, but otherwise, it's clear and dynamic with a nice open spacious feel.

# The Skyliners
Formed late 1950s—Pittsburgh, Pennsylvania
**Greatest Hits (1958–1961)**
Original Sound Entertainment OSCD 8873 (47:24)  **[C]**
1959's "Since I Don't Have You" by the Skyliners is one of prerock pop's more compelling ballads, enhanced by very sophisticated production for the era. On the whole, this late fifties, early sixties quintet made predictable but appealing

music—if you know and love it, this disc is a must; if it is uncharted territory, stay clear and look for the bigger hits on comprehensive oldies collections particularly from the Original Sound Entertainment label. The digital mix employed by Original Sound on all their releases is specially enhanced (FDS), which results in a clear dynamic sound, albeit very slightly overbright and mechanical.

# Percy Sledge
b. 1941—Leighton, Alabama
**The Ultimate Collection (When a Man Loves a Woman) (1966–1968)**
Atlantic 780212-2 (57:59)   **[C + ]**
Soul for the soap opera set—Sledge sludged through some of the most tear-stained lyrics to be found in sixties soul music. He did it pretty well, often overblown productions notwithstanding. His popularity reached its zenith in April of 1966 when his "When a Man Loves a Woman" reached the No. 1 position on the charts; it was his first release. As is too often the case with Atlantic's vintage material, the sound is comparable to a clean LP; not bad, but not what it might be.

# Sly and the Family Stone
Formed 1966/1967—San Francisco
Sly is one of the most underrated major contributors to the history of rock & roll. In addition to his innovative rock/funk sounds, Sly was the first to physically present a band reflective of the ideals of his time in that it included performers both male and female, black and white.

**Stand! (1969)**
Epic EK26456 (41:31)   **[A]**
A positive, intelligent expression of the upheaval that energized the sixties, by

a band that broke all the rules and produced some of the best and most innovatively exciting music of the time. This is music that seethes with vitality—it makes you happy—it speaks the vernacular of its day. The sound is strong and clean, but, occasionally, a bit edgy.

**Greatest Hits (1968–1970)**
Epic EK30325 (40:04)   **[A + ]**
This recording coalesces the upbeat sounds and sentiments of the Woodstock era through the exuberant, innovative, creative genius of Sly and his "family" that was a real embodiment of the ideals of which they sang. Because Stone had a tendency to try to do it all in each song, too often his reach exceeded his grasp; and, because his mood and music change radically with his next release (*There's A Riot Goin' On*), this recording, which literally includes every Sly single that successfully achieved his vision, is one of the best compilation rock/pop/funk recordings ever issued. It will make you dance and smile and maybe remind you of what it might have been. It's chock full of brilliant, influential, and too-often-overlooked pop greatness. The sound, while varying a little, is bright, crisp, clean, clear, detailed, and dynamic—you can't ask for much more.

**There's a Riot Goin' On (1971)**
Epic EK30986 (47:40)   **[A + ]**
Nihilistic and nasty, this tough, abrasive slice of community hopes and shattered dreams remains one of the most disturbing recordings ever released by a commercially successful pop band. A couple of the songs charted: "Family Affair" reached No. 1 and "Runnin' Away" got some airplay, but you ain't gonna dance to this music for long—not if the messages are coming through the lyrics. This is Sly's last great album statement—its rhythms are extraordinary, its

message brutally honest. *There's a Riot Goin' On* and *Greatest Hits* are the two ends of the spectrum of one of the least-appreciated, most influential musicians of the soul/rock era, and both recordings are genuine classics. The CD's excellent sonics are hard, bright, and completely appropriate.

**Anthology (1973)**
Epic EGK 37071 (74:02)   **[A]**
This compilation includes all twelve tracks from *Greatest Hits,* plus three from *Riot* (including "Family Affair"). There's also the caustic "Don't Call Me Nigger, Whitey," a sampling from *Fresh,* and a downright chilling reading of Doris Day's hit, "Que Sera, Sera." If you're looking for the most complete Sly compilation, this has to be it. The polarity between their wondrous early "up" material (covered in *Greatest Hits*) and the harsh early seventies cuts in this package somehow diminishes both when served on the same platter. The CD's sound is generally excellent.

# Sly & Robbie
Formed 1974—Kingston, Jamaica
**Silent Assassin (1989)**
Island 91277-2 (59:17)   **[D + ]**
Some things that look good on paper just don't pan out. Given rap's direct lineage to reggae, the idea of bringing the latter's best-known rhythm section together with some righteous raps dealing with current social concerns makes a lot of sense—it just doesn't work on *Silent Assassin.* Too much rap, not enough Sly & Robbie. The sound's OK by current standards, but this ain't no demo record.

# The Smithereens
Formed late 1980's—Georgia
**11 (1989)**
Enigma/Capitol 91194 (34:27)   **[C–]**
High-tech garage sounds from an eighties Georgia band with solid roots but little originality, either musically or lyrically. Competence alone doesn't cut it in a creative enterprise, and this well-intentioned quartet shows little sign of lasting beyond the moment, critical acclaim (which they've had) notwithstanding. The sound, like the music, is above average, but not much.

# The Smiths
Formed 1982—Manchester, England
**Rank (1988)**
Sire 25786-2 (56:08)   **[B]**
While the rhythm section is too often ignored given its undeniable strong contribution to the Smiths' sound and success, it is the polarities between Stephen Morrissey's puerile lyrics and vocals and Johnny Marr's wondrous music/guitar that distinguished this now-defunct band. *The Trouser Press Record Guide* summed them up: "Morrissey and company stand for traditional values of selfishness, self-pity, and the unbearable anguish of love. His melancholy, romantic sensibility makes Elizabeth Barrett Browning sound like Nelson Algren." *Rank,* a live concert recording, turned out to be the group's final release and covers many of their standout cuts. While sonically suffering from live recording limitations (the band is too far back, lost in the mix, and the bottom is a bit muddy), it does afford both Morrissey and Marr a chance to loosen up, resulting in less self-absorbed vocals and the reaffirmation of Marr's stature as one of the eighties best punk/rock guitarists.

# Phoebe Snow
## (Phoebe Laub)
b. July 17, 1952—Teaneck, New Jersey
**Phoebe Snow (1974)**
Shelter SRZ-8004 (39:50)   **[B]**
1974 was smack dab in the middle of the
singer/songwriter era in American pop
music. It was the era that brought the
solo female performer to the fore, principally through the fine work of Joni
Mitchell and Carole King. This recording, Snow's debut, brought a jazz
sensibility and a husky, resonant voice
to the party. Riding on the strength of
her Top Five hit, "Poetry Man" (1975),
and simple, acoustic instrumentation
by jazz veterans Zoot Sims, Ralph
McDonald, and Bob James, *Phoebe
Snow* is an intimate, pleasant outing
which, with the passage of time, still
offers a pleasant listen, albeit a bit on the
cocktail/jazz side. The CD is enhanced
by wonderfully remastered sound;
Snow's voice is full, intimate, and warm,
while the sparse instrumental backing is
precise and dynamic. A bonus track is
included, "Easy Street," which was originally the B side to the hit single that
came from the same sessions.

# Spike & Co.
**do it a cappella (1990)**
Elektra 9 60953-2 (44:45)   **[B]**
This soundtrack to the PBS special is,
like much of public broadcasting, a
grand idea flawed in its execution. From
both a historical and a musical perspective exposing the pure, unaccompanied
sound of the human voice raised in song
is a worthy idea, long overdue. The participants are among the elite within the
small world of a cappella groups:
Ladysmith Black Mambazo, the Persuasions, Take 6, and the Mint Juleps,
among others. The live audience, which

is heard applauding some cuts, is attentive and appreciative. So why isn't this
review a rave? Perhaps because the
whole thing seems too much like a
sampler. But the biggest problem is the
all-digital sound, which is too often dry
and thin; in the case of some female
leads, too edgy and bright. This said,
there are resplendent moments: everything by Ladysmith, the Persuasions,
"Up on the Roof," and "Pass On the
Love" (but the recently deceased Herbert "Tubo" Rhoad, to whom the TV
special was dedicated, is sorely missed),
and "Higher and Higher" by the Mint
Juleps, will be more than enough to satisfy any a cappella fan who doesn't
approach the entire recording with
inflated expectations.

# The Spinners
Formed 1957—Detroit
**The Best Of (1973—compilation release
date)**
Motown MCD09008MD (30:03)   **[C–]**
This collection, originally released in
1973, covers this fine singing group's
early seventies Motown material but
does not include any of the smooth soul
hits produced by Thom Bell after the
group moved to Atlantic (e.g., "One of a
Kind [Love Affair]" or "Mighty Love").
While their appealing vocal skills are
evident on some of these brief selections, the whole affair is just too much
Motown production-line pop, allowing
little of the Spinners' unique appeal to
shine through. The CD's sound is bright,
clean, and dynamic with some harshness in the upper mid-range vocal tracks.

# Bruce Springsteen
b. September 23, 1949—Freehold, New Jersey
In the early seventies, the word leaked
out that Columbia Records late famed

talent scout, John Hammond (who had been responsible for bringing Billie Holliday, Count Basie, Pete Seeger, Aretha Franklin, the Four Tops, and Bob Dylan to that label's roster) had made another major discovery, Bruce Springsteen. His first release, *Greetings From Asbury Park, N.J.*, came out in 1973 and his greatest, *Born To Run,* was released in 1975 which resulted in Bruce making the covers of both *Time* and *Newsweek,* still a unique event in rock's brief history. Springsteen represents the reincarnation of rock & roll's basic tenets: escapism and rebellion as product for mass consumption. These attributes, combined with his highly acclaimed personal values which, in many instances, amounted to an endorsement of America's traditional values; as well as a deep concern about this nation's loss thereof, make up the elements out of which he has carved incredible stardom. Devoid of rock star trappings, Bruce was the blue-collar rock & roller working concerts that generally started on schedule and often ran for more than five breathtaking hours; leaving his audiences sated with the power of the music to redeem the moment and to create a truly meaningful experience. To see "The Boss" in a small venue was as close as most fans ever got to the true power of the music, and it was an unforgettable experience, made palpable by Springsteen's repeatedly proven desire to reach each and every soul who came to hear. The payoff, in a literal sense, didn't come until the 1980s when Bruce reached true superstardom, inevitably sacrificing some of his intimacy, but preserving the best of it all through sheer will, awesome energy, and a genuine, caring talent.

**Greetings from Asbury Park, N.J. (1973)**
Columbia CK31903 (37:14)   **[B]**
His original 1972 release is divided between acoustic cuts focusing on his then-wordy (Dylanesque) lyrics, and the R&B inflected power-rock upon which his Jersey reputation had been built. While the record never received the acceptance suggested by the hype, it does contain some classic cuts, "Blinded by the Light," "Growin' Up," "Spirit in the Night," and "It's Hard to Be a Saint in the City," which bespoke the teen vision of the times with an intimacy and immediacy that parallels that attained by the first rock & rollers twenty years before. The recording somehow lacked continuity and suffered from generally crude production values, which ultimately undermined the poignancy of the message. On CD, the vocals become more intimate and the instrumental separation is enhanced, but there is also audible hiss; thin, somewhat compressed sound; and a frequent edginess to the stronger vocals.

**The Wild, the Innocent, and the E Street Shuffle (1973)**
Columbia CK324232 (46:56)   **[A–]**
A clear transition from the individually focused *Greetings from Asbury Park, N.J.,* to the ensemble power of *Born to Run,* this fascinating recording shows the artist groping toward the potent, ultimately romantic sounds which would come to epitomize rock & roll for many young Americans. It is here, also, that his narrative lyrics, studded with quick, canny, compelling characters supported by truly adventurous song structures is first exposed; all to celebrate the glories and the grotesqueries of youth. Included are some transcendant moments: "4th of July, Asbury Park (Sandy)" and "Rosalita (Come Out Tonight)" being the obvious highlights. While the sound

stage is a bit constricted and the vocal tracks more mixed into the instrumentals, the sound is very good, devoid of hiss; dynamic and nicely defined.

### Born to Run (1975)
Columbia CK33795 (39:38) **[A + ]**
It all comes together here—the E Street Band, the drama, the romance, the grandiose vision for the common fan. This is a concept recording—which owes a strong production nod to Phil Spector—that distills down to some of the best rock songs of the decade (the title cut, "Thunder Road," "Jungleland," "Backstreets," and "Tenth Ave. Freezeout," among them). It all amounts to a territorial imperative by a man whose vision encompasses all things American. Both the CD and LP suffer from very noticeable compression and some muddiness, but the CD is a bit brighter, with slightly enhanced detail. Considering what has been done with much older, and assumably more primitive master material (e.g., almost anything Bill Inglott has reworked at Rhino), it is a crime that something sonically better couldn't have been done with the first CD release of this true seventies classic recording; the heroic nature of which would nicely mesh with more heroic sound. Columbia remastered the digital conversion in late 1987, so more current copies of the CD sound appreciably better than the first disc releases. This was a very difficult, daring recorded statement which Springsteen has called "the most intense experience I ever had."

### Darkness on the Edge of Town (1978)
Columbia CK35318 (43:02) **[A]**
From the cover photos to the contents, it's clear that this is the statement of a changed man; the boyish beliefs have been supplanted by hard won knowledge of the "real" world. (Obviously, a

reflection of two years of court battles with his first opportunistic manager which kept him out of the recording studio where he might have capitalized on the resounding acclamation accorded *Born to Run*.) *Darkness on the Edge of Town* echoes with the honed down grittiness of material that reflects more the reality than the romance of his beloved road. Highlighted by Bruce's painfully potent vocal outpourings and his slashing guitar, it includes some of his strongest material, "Promised Land," "Badlands," "Adam Raised a Cain" and the title cut. The CD sound is uneven, admittedly dynamic and crisp most of the time, it is impaired by occasional harshness and audible hiss on the quieter sections. Overall, the sound is an improvement over the LP, but would be substantially better if there were clearer separations among the various voicings.

### The River (1980)
Columbia CK36854 (83:50—two discs) **[A + ]**
This sprawling summation of his seventies work finally brought Springsteen the mass audience he had deservedly been seeking for almost a decade with the hit single, "Hungry Heart." While a majority of the cuts are up-tempo rockers of the first order, included in the twenty selections on this release are a number of Springsteen's personal, moving ballad statements. *The River* is filled with great rock & roll: "The Ties That Bind," "Cadillac Ranch," "You Can Look (But You Better Not Touch)," "I'm a Rocker," and "Ramrod," as well as an excellent sampling of his meaningful narrative ballads: "Independence Day," "The River," "Fade Away," "The Price You Pay," and "Wreck on the Highway." All in all, *The River* is a world unto itself, a world of intense feeling and driving rock & roll. The sound is an improvement over the LP, particularly in the detail

afforded Springsteen's vocals; however, at volume the overall brightness leans toward harshness, which impairs the clarity otherwise found on the discs.

**Nebraska (1982)**
CBS CK38358 (40:26)   [A + ]
In 1982, Bruce Springsteen released this, his most unique and perhaps, ultimately, his most enduring recording. Actually, the release is made up of the demo tapes that Springsteen had done on his four-track home machine utilizing only his acoustic guitar, harmonica, and voice to capture the desolation and despair that he perceived at the heart of America's heartland. This is a portrait of the underside of the American Dream presented in a stark, highly personal style. There are a number of true classics among the ten included cuts, "Atlantic City" (which garnered some airplay), "Highway Patrolman," and "Nebraska" among them. The sound of the CD is defined by the sound of the source material, which means that if you are looking for sonic perfection, this is one to pass by. It's constantly filled with the tape hiss arising out of overdubs, and is fuzzy and murky much of the time. Yet, somehow, the sound seems totally appropriate for the content, making this disc an excellent addition to the 1980s library of American rock & roll.

**Born in the U.S.A. (1984)**
CBS CK38653 (46:58)   [A + ]
This is the one that did it. *Born in the U.S.A.* is the classic rock & roll album that elevated Springsteen above the rest of the musical crowd to the status of living legend. Energetic, mature, and featuring the E Street Band playing tighter than ever, it is an album composed of consistently outstanding compositions, the title, "My Home Town," "No Surrender," "Glory Days,"

and "Dancin' in the Dark" (its first major hit) being merely illustrative of the overall quality to be found here. The sound quality is excellent, particularly in the detailed rendering of the vocals, and impressive separation. However, there is a bit of upper mid-range edge to it, as well as occasional muddiness in the instrumentation, notably the drum track on occasion.

**Bruce Springsteen and the E Street Band Live/1975–85 (1985)**
CBS 40558 (216:16—three discs)   [A + ]
From the outset of his historic career, Springsteen's been first and foremost a live performer. To understand this artist's truly awesome power, one just has to experience him live, to feel the energy, to know that it is his honest desire to make every member of every audience feel that they have known the very best that he and the E Street Band have to deliver. Thus, over his lengthening career, his ever-growing audience has craved a live recording in the hopes of catching those magic concert moments once again. Bootleg copies of various concerts and live radio broadcasts have surreptitiously circulated since the mid-seventies. Finally, in 1986, Bruce set out to remedy this situation with the ultimate concert recording. This compilation is the equivalent of a real Springsteen concert because the total playing time runs over three and a half hours and covers forty selections, a few that are offered here for the first time on record. Musically, the package is uneven. Too many of his older classics are included as they were presented post-1985. This may be a concession to the availability of better recordings in later years, but often results in less than impassioned performances. That said, the set does contain some magnificently inspired moments such as the 1975 bal-

lad rendition of "Thunder Road," several songs from *Nebraska* performed with the band for the first time on record, as well as some smashing rock & roll ("Cadillac Ranch") and the closer, a cover version of Tom Waits's "Jersey Girl." The real greatness of Bruce Springsteen is his strong sense of personal honesty and commitment behind a very humanistic concern. These attributes come through, in part, on this live release; but, unfortunately, the principal thing that echoes through the music is a sense of "event" rather than the substance of the its message. Given the fact that these are live recordings, the overall quality of the CD sound will simply blow you away. It is almost as if one were sitting with the band given the degree of detail and the intimacy afforded by this release.

### Tunnel of Love (1987)
Columbia CK40999 (46:27)   **[A + ]**
There had been much speculation about how Springsteen would follow up *Born in the U.S.A.,* the album that led to his deification. There had been concern expressed about how his mega-stardom would impact on the man and his work. The answer lies in *Tunnel of Love,* in which Springsteen turns to his greatest resource, his honest artlessness, now deepened with understanding and acceptance born out of survival. Somewhat akin to *Nebraska* in its intimacy, though very different in stance and coloration, *Tunnel of Love* is a subtle triumph in the face of incredible odds— a testament to the traits and talents that have placed Springsteen in the unique company where the only standards are self-defined. *Tunnel of Love* is ultimately about survival on all levels, and Springsteen provides both truth and poetry, augmented by spare but effective instrumentation to help us along the way.

Various members of the E Street Band add effective, but relatively minimal tints to Springsteen's songs and stories— Max Weinberg, Bruce's longtime drummer, appears on almost all the cuts, again demonstrating his ultimate tastefulness. The all-digital sound is beautifully natural, open, and clear, essentially flawless.

# Squeeze
Formed 1974—London
**Eastside Story (1981)**
A&M CD3253 (48:39)   **[A]**
Once again, Dave Marsh summed it up best, this '81 release ". . . is a near perfect pop-rock album of pithy vignettes that fuse Beatlesesque lyricism with new wave wit." The sound, while slightly compressed, is spatially open, crisp, dynamic, and well-defined.

### Singles—45's & Under (1983—compilation release date)
A&M CD-4922 (43:44)   **[B + ]**
The principal writer/composers behind Squeeze (Chris Difford and Glenn Tilbrook) were often critically anointed as the punk Lennon/McCartney of British seventies new wave rock & roll. While their well-crafted hook-filled pop vignettes certainly adhere to many of the tenets established by their illustrious sixties English pop predecessors, Squeeze's songs certainly remain a far cry from the Beatles in either originality or execution. That said, the band remains one of the most elegantly crafted proponents of the post-punk power-pop sound of the era. Their work is sharp, lustrous, and instantly appealing. This relatively brief compilation, which focuses primarily on their seventies successes, but includes early eighties material as well, works both as an overview of a fine pop band and

an introduction to the eighties pop slickness that was to become a principal element of the once vital English music scene. The sound, of course, improves with the advancing date of recording, but overall, while it is more dynamic and spacious than the LP, it is afflicted with noticeable compression and hiss.

## Lisa Stansfield
**Affection (1990)**
Arista ARCD-8554 (63:26)   **[C + ]**
Philly soul filtered through the wondrous voice of a young white English woman and flavored with a melange of current styles (hip-hop, house, new jack swing, and Latino). Support is provided by producers/instrumentalists Ian Devaney and Andy Morris, and it's real slick—almost slick enough to mask the lack of substance or originality in the material, but not quite. Simply, Stansfield can sing, and with a few years and some substantial songs, she could make some enduring recordings. She hasn't this time, but *Affection* is an impressive debut that is enhanced by first-rate, clear, open sound.

## The Staple Singers
Formed 1953—Chicago
A true family group who produced first-rate gospel sounds in the mid-fifties and early sixties. Founded upon Roebuck "Pop" Staples's simple, effective guitar lines and the expressive, unique lead vocals of daughter, Mavis. In the early 1970's, the Staples succeeded in grafting secular "message" lyrics to their infectious pop/gospel sound with appreciable commercial success. (Mavis's voice may be an acquired taste, but once acquired, it's addictive [although her crossover pure pop efforts in recent years have lacked major acceptance]).

**Be Attitude: Respect Yourself (1972)**
Mobile Fidelity Sound Lab MFCD832
(41:49)   **[B]**
The two highlights, "I'll Take You There" and "Respect Yourself" are prime examples of this seventies pop/gospel sound. The remaining eight selections all sound great, but they all sound too much alike—as well as suffering from less than average lyrics. Spare, minimalistic production sensibility underscores the rhythmic foundation and the vocal interplay that are the strengths of the Staple sound. The sound of this disc is impressive, dynamic, propulsive, with beautiful spacing and clarity. The mix is a bit strange in that the vocals are often behind the instruments and there is a suggestion of vocal harshness at high volume, but these are minor criticisms.

**The Best of the Staple Singers (1970–1974)**
Stax FCD60-007 (61:14)   **[A–]**
A reasonable argument can be made for gospel as the principal ingredient of that heady mix: rock & roll. What the Staples provide in addition to Pop's purefyin' guitar and vocals, is a lightly bleached gospel sound built on honest roots and Mavis Staples's wondrous voice. What they also provide is a truly joyous listening experience for everyone. This sixteen song compilation, originally released in 1975, includes: "Heavy Makes You Happy," "Respect Yourself," "I'll Take You There," "If You're Ready," and "City in the Sky." The sound is generally impressive: crisp, detailed, and dynamic with excellent separation. It does evidence some hiss and a tendency to excessive brightness at high volume.

# Ringo Starr
## (Richard Starkey)
b. July 7, 1940—Liverpool, England
**Ringo Starr and His All-Starr Band (1990)**
Rykodisc RCD 10190 (56:02)   **[C]**
A trot down memory lane with Mr. Starr and a pack of legitimate all-stars—Dr. John, Levon Helm, Joe Walsh, Billy Preston, Rick Danko, Nils Lofgren, Jim Keltner, and Clarence Clemons. This live recording was made on the final stop of their thirty-one-city tour at the Greek Theatre in L.A. From the performance, it's obvious that both the band and the audience were having a grand time, but its value for at home/in car listening is questionable. Astutely, Ringo allows many of his bandmates a turn at the mike—Dr. John does "Iko Iko," Levon Helm sings "The Weight," and Joe Walsh sings "Life in the Fast Lane," but their signifance is mostly nostalgic. Ryko, as always, delivers fine sounding product and this live recording is no exception.

# Steely Dan
Formed 1972—Los Angeles
**A Decade of Steely Dan (The Best Of) (1982—compilation release date)**
MCA MCAD5570 (68:11)   **[D–]**
Muzak for the pseudo-set. I'll bet Horace Silver's still pissed, not to mention the Bird. Pompous, pilfered pap. The sound isn't bad, but noticeably compressed and occasionally muddy. (This may be the most aptly named band in rock.)

# Cat Stevens
## (Steven Georgiou)
b. July 21, 1947—London
**Greatest Hits (1975—compilation release date)**
A&M CD4519 (39:21)   **[C+]**
The material sounds dated, but the sound quality remains impressive. Singer, songwriter, seventies success, Stevens left the business disillusioned (after a half-dozen gold albums). The melodies and production are both first rate, the lyrics tend to be either silly or a downer, with far too much of the latter. The CD sounds great.

# Rod Stewart
b. January 10, 1945—London
Once upon a time (a long time ago) before "blond ambition" took its continuing toll, he was the forefront of rock vocalists.

**Gasoline Alley (1970)**
Mercury 824 881-2 M-1 (41:57)   **[B+]**
From compositions by Dylan, to Elton John/Bernie Taupin and Bobby Womack (plus his own fine additions), Stewart mixes folk and pure rock & roll for a heady blend that very much follows the formula of his critically acclaimed first release. This time around, the highlights aren't as bright, but for overall quality, it is an excellent package. Also, like the first release, the sound is obviously compressed, but generally clear.

**Every Picture Tells a Story (1971)**
Mercury 822 385-2 M-1 (40:43)   **[A]**
One of the truly great rock & roll albums; in part, because here is where it all came together for Stewart, and, in part, because of Mickey Waller's stupendous drumming. This is the essence of what once made Rod Stewart great. His

compositions (the title cut, "Maggie May" and "Mandolin Wind") are the highlights; his singing is sublime, and his production, utilizing both pedal steel and mandolin to augment a basic rock & roll lineup created an English country rock classic that easily withstands the test of time. It never was this good again for Rod, but then there are very, very few who achieve a creative pinnacle equal to *Every Picture Tells a Story*. (But, oh, how the mighty have fallen). Thankfully, the sound on CD maintains the same high standards as the material: clean, crisp, dynamic with decent separation, it does exhibit some compression (particularly on the drums) but it isn't that bad, and what distortion there is is minimal. This one is a must.

**Every Picture Tells a Story (1971)**
Mobile Fidelity UDCD 532 (40:52)  **[A + ]**
Once again Mobile Fidelity has issued a gold disc of certified classic material and made it better—not perfect (perfection wouldn't fit the attitude of the material), but appreciably better, particularly in cleaning up the overall sound and improving the spatial definition. Worth the extra tariff.

**Never a Dull Moment (1972)**
Mercury 826 263-2 (33:11)  **[B + ]**
The package comes pretty close to *Every Picture Tells a Story*, minus the mandolin, and it results in fine listening, but its predecessor was so damn great! Still, "You Wear It Well" and his cover of Sam Cooke's "Twistin the Night Away" would hold up anywhere. This, to date, sadly also represents his last real quality recorded effort. The sound has an overall muffled, dirty quality to it, that still reflects greater dynamic enhancement than the LP, but it's not much improvement over the vinyl.

**Storyteller: The Complete Anthology (1964–1990)**
Warner Bros. 4/2-25987 (297:37—four discs)
**[B]**
Greg Geller, the highly knowledgeable A&R man behind this compilation, has provided more than ample proof of Stewart's undeniable talent and musical longevity. The sound and the music criss-cross from acceptable to great; the early material (particularly from his first solo album through *Every Picture Tells a Story*) is clearly Rod's most creative and powerful statement, though the sound quality is a bit uneven. The selections from later years sound great, but his musical approach had become trendy and formulaic. Yet it's undeniable that Stewart can rock, and he has done so since 1964. The set closes with 1989 studio recordings, including "I Don't Want to Talk About It" and "Downtown Train," which are among his strongest releases in years. If you're a fan, this is a comprehensive collection with few desirable selections omitted. Unfortunately, the set is hampered by its poor packaging. Robert Palmer's notes are neither informative nor insightful, but Rod's brief comments on each selection have a pleasant irreverence.

# Sting (Gordon Sumner)
b. October 2, 1951—Wallsend, Northumberland, England
**Nothing Like the Sun (1987)**
A&M CD6402/DX2163 (55:11)  **[D + ]**
Pseudo rock/jazz from a pseudo artist. The all-digital sound is state-of-the-art.

# Syd Straw
**Surprise (1989)**
Virgin 70177-2 (52:40)   **[C]**
A genuine talent—check out her work
with the Golden Palominos—in search
of an identity. Straw's assembled an
impressive array of production talent
(Van Dyke Parks and Daniel Lanois) and
able players (Richard Thompson, Marshall Crenshaw, Don Was, Benmont
Tench, Dave Alvin, John Doe, Ry
Cooder, Jim Keltner, Anton Fier, David
Grissom, Michael Stipe, and Brian Eno)
who combine for a polished, fragmented, ultimately empty compendium
of styles and moods, which, for lack of a
central vision or concept, ends up as
pretty much a waste of time. It's a
shame, because this woman can sing.
The sound quality, while not obtrusive,
is mediocre overall.

# The Subdudes
Formed 1980—Colorado
**The Subdudes (1989)**
Atlantic 782015-2 (41:22)   **[A–]**
Beneath the slick surface that was the
benchmark of most successful pop of
America's great material decade, there
remain a few groups whose roots and
love of playing still produced enduring
music. The Subdudes' roots are in the
fertile delta of New Orleans, their
home in the clarity of Colorado's crystalline air, and their ears in the sweet
soulful harmonics generally associated
with seventies Philly sound. Relying
on well-recorded acoustic backings,
fine harmony singing, and bassist
Johnny Ray Allen's fine writing, they
deliver a listenable release that may lack
any single standout selection, but compensates with an easy, honest, heartfelt
quality that imbues every cut with a
ringing simplicity that is more than just

durable. The sound on this disc is generally first rate.

# Donna Summer
# (Donna Gaines)
b. December 31, 1948—Boston
The crowned queen of disco, who survived to build a successful seventies pop
career.

**The Summer Collection (Greatest Hits)
(1985—compilation release date)**
Mercury 826 144-2 M-1 (40:23)   **[C+]**
Bright, brash, and brassy—Summer
brought an appropriately cool persona
and hot voice to the disco demimonde
that signaled the nadir of seventies pop
music. Obviously, it wasn't Donna's
fault; she was, and is, just a fine pop
singer looking for an audience. There's
not much here in the way of soul or
intent, it's just glossy pop product
designed to accompany the Me Decade's
dance to artificial decadence. Formula
material worked by talented professionals who end up with sleekly
packaged instant fun—for somebody
somewhere? The CD's sound is reflective
of the overall production sensibility;
bright, punchy, and spacious.

# Supertramp
Formed 1969—London
**Breakfast in America (1979)**
Mobile Fidelity UDCD 534 (46:01)   **[B–]**
Somewhat histrionic, late-seventies British pop that just about makes up in
sonic exuberance what it lacks in musi-
cal/lyrical substance. Age hasn't been
kind to even its most popular cuts, "The
Logical Song," "Goodbye Stranger," and
"Take the Long Way Home," but if you
want to impress your friends and neigh-
bors with the wonders of your CD stereo

rig, the pure sound quality of this release is up to the task. The original "standard" CD release, like the LP before it, sounded pretty damn good; this gold disc is an improvement, principally in enhanced dynamics.

# The Supremes
Formed 1960—Detroit
**Diana Ross and the Supremes 20 Greatest Hits (1963–1971)**
Motown MCD06073 MD (58:34)   **[A + ]**
The greatest creation of Berry Gordy, the man who finally, effectively marketed the great black pop product to the white audience—and market it, he did. In the case of the Supremes, all the way to the No. 1 on the pop chart twelve times, which is little short of amazing; particularly in the sixties, the richest musical decade ever known. One listen to this disc is all the explanation needed—it's still perfect pop music. The sound, which has its weak moments, is, overall, markedly superior to the low-end vinyl that originally conveyed this joyous product.

# Talking Heads
Formed 1975—New York City
Dance music for the mind. Or, as England's *Record Mirror* said of this extraordinarily influential American punk/new wave quartet: "After all these years, someone can still take the five basic components of rock—a singer, a song, a guitar, bass, and drums—and come up with something totally fresh."

### Talking Heads: 77 (1977)
Sire 6036-2 (39:02)   **[A]**
One of the most original debut albums of the decade, if not in the history of rock & roll. Providing civilized techno-tension that is palpably real, the Heads firmly affix themselves to the classic traditions of the form while giving it a contemporary vernacular. Truly the music of its times. On *Talking Heads: 77,* David Byrne utilizes his performance and conceptual genius to create simple melodic underpinnings that reverberate with the tension of his petrified, edgy vocals. The sound is bright, crisp, dynamic, and clear; nicely enhancing Byrne's quavering vocal inflections.

### More Songs About Buildings and Food (1978)
Sire 6058-2 (41:48)   **[A–]**
The experimentation begins. Brian Eno becomes the fifth Head, at least for a while. The textures and tonalities of the band's sound expand, but the stance (modernism, minimalism) and central musical element (the tension between Byrne's vocals and the music) remain a constant. *More Songs About Buildings and Food* also introduced an R&B aspect to the Heads' sound that would endure. The album also produced their first hit, a cover version of Al Green's "Take Me to the River." The CD's sound is, again, an enhancement: beautifully spaced and defined with a slight tendency to some overbrightness.

### Fear of Music (1979)
Sire 6076-2 (40:43)   **[B]**
As the musical values move forward and become more edgy and rhythmically propulsive, the tension between the music and Byrne's uniquely fascinating vocals has diminished. There are moments when everything coalesces ("Life During Wartime") and rises to the level of the band's best, and that's a fairly potent level. While this is still a fascinating and effective musical statement by one of the few original groups creating in the late seventies, too much of the material doesn't quite measure up and too much of the production is intrusive. The sound is first-rate, with great separation and clarity.

### Remain in Light (1980)
Sire 6095-2 (40:10)   **[A]**
New wave meets African polyrhythms and performance techniques. In a sense,

*Remain in Light* is single continuum of song, a fact which the complete playability of the CD enhances. A fascinating recording, which reflects the conceptual genius of the band as well as its impressive musicality. Its rhythmic appeal is totally seductive, and the recognizable, fragmented phrases which make up the floating lyrics create a strange reality. The sound isn't wonderful, far too much hiss and obvious compression.

**Speaking in Tongues (1983)**
Sire 9 23883-2 (41:16)   **[A + ]**
The Heads' most fully realized album. It retains the potent, rhythmic underpinnings that had been the essence of *Remain in Light* and overlays them with the best set of songs the band ever performed. Melodically pop-oriented with more narrative congruity to the lyrics, this is a more accessible release than its predecessors. A great album of eighties new wave techno-pop music. The sound quality of the CD is almost flawless.

**Stop Making Sense (1984)**
Sire 25186-2 (46:33)   **[A]**
The soundtrack to what is probably the best rock concert film ever made. The academic background of all the band members was in the visual and architectural arts; thus, the concert setting with its audio/visual aspects seems to bring out their best. In addition, by 1984, Byrne had grown comfortable with his uncomfortable performance persona, and his vocal confidence and weird expressiveness are a highlight of one the best live albums released. The nine selections cut across the entirety of the band's recorded history, making this an excellent career overview, as well as providing new insights into the older material. The sound is extraordinary with excellent imaging.

**Little Creatures (1985)**
Sire 25305-2 (38:46)   **[B + ]**
The band returns to basics this time around—a more direct rock & roll approach, albeit tempered with an intended pop consciousness, still echoing with rhythmic drive. The result is a good, but not brilliant, Heads recording. It has its moments, notably "Walk it Down" and "Road to Nowhere," and their trademark sound still sets them above most of their creative contemporaries. The line between art and artifice grows more blurred with time (and David Byrne's outside interests). The sonics on this recording are excellent.

**True Stories (1986)**
Sire 25512-2 (46:35)   **[A–]**
The soundtrack to Byrne's bizarre motion picture. Musically, it marks a return to the less pop-oriented, more frenetic new wave sounds upon which their original work was based. This band seems incapable of making boring music; and while *True Stories* may not represent the change or growth that has been reflected on each of their previous releases, it still rewards repeated listening. The sound, while not quite as impressive as *Little Creatures,* is still almost flawless.

**Naked (1988)**
Fly/Sire 9 25654-2 (52:51)   **[B + ]**
As time and careers pass, it gets to feeling more and more like this may be the last outing by one of America's premiere bands. Energetic and eclectic, *Naked* was recorded in Paris under the aegis of Stone Hilly White utilizing the talents of many international players (Eric Weissberg, Johnny Marr, and Kirsty McColl among them). Perhaps because of his identification with World Beat or because of the band's evolution, *Naked* somehow feels more like a David Byrne

album than a Talking Heads collaboration. With its various rhythms and
textures, strong horn arrangements,
and Byrne's fragmented lyrics, it functions on several levels ("Nothing But
Flowers," "Mr. Jones"), but it lacks individual standout tracks. It ranks as one
of the more interesting and successful
recordings of 1988, but fails to measure
up to some of the Heads' earlier outings.
Given the overdubbing and complexity
of the recording, the sound, with the
exception of some buried vocal passages, is excellent.

# James Taylor
b. March 12, 1948—Boston
Taylor has proved to be one of the most
talented, genuine (though troubled), and
enduring members of the early seventies
singer/songwriter movement.

### Sweet Baby James (1970)
Warner Bros. 1843-2 (31:54)   **[B]**
Taylor's second album release, this is
the recording that garnered his first real
commercial success, based principally
on the popularity of the confessional
"Fire and Rain." Also included on this
enduring release are the fine title cut
and "Steamroller." Taylor expresses
some intense emotions here, but always
with the surface control that, at its best,
heightens the impact of his harrowing
messages; but, too often, drains meaning from the lyrics. The recording
remains a seminal example of the male
singer/songwriter school. Sadly, the
sound is consistently accompanied by
some of the most audible hiss available
on disc. On the positive side, the CD
provides amazing vocal intimacy (with a
slight tendency to overbrightness) as
well as good dynamics, openness, and
precision of detail.

### Greatest Hits (1970–1976)
Warner Bros. 3113-2 (43:49)   **[A–]**
The consummate collection from the
consummate male of the singer/song-
writer subgenre of rock. And he's a
curious, class act—subtle in his blatant
self-exposure. His easy, convincing vocal
style and fine melodic sense draw heavily on earlier American musical traditions. His writing ability is such that one
wonders why he messes with cover material, since that's generally the weakest
part of his recordings, which is definitely
the case here. While these dozen selections are the product of seven different
recording sessions, Taylor and his producers have always been sensitive to the
sound of his recordings, a sensitivity
that results in almost uniform, excellent
sound quality on this disc.

### JT (1977)
CBS CK34811 (38:01)   **[A]**
The culmination of Taylor's recorded
output, featuring fine compositions and
restrained but expressive vocal readings. His folk/jazz/R&B derived pop
productions perfectly showcase the
direct appeal and strength of the material and are beautifully rendered. While
every cut offers quality, the highlights
include the hit, "Handy Man," as well as
"Another Grey Morning," "Bartender's
Blues," "Traffic Jam," "Terra Nova," and
the simple but inordinately valid "Secret
of Life." The sound of it all is little short
of revelatory: remarkably clean, spacious, warm, intimate, and detailed.
This is one of the best sounding pop
discs available.

## The Temptations
Formed 1962—Detroit
**17 Greatest Hits (1964–1973)**
Gordy GCD06125 GD (58:04)  **[B + ]**
For all of Berry Gordy's assembly line
precision, Motown remained a producer's studio and the Temptations' most
inventive producer was Norman Whitfield (the man who brought us, "I Heard
it Through the Grapevine" by both
Gladys Knight and Marvin Gaye). The
original Temptations lineup, which featured two of the era's better soul lead
voices, tenor Eddie Kendricks, and bari-
tone David Ruffin, was a perfect vehicle
for Whitfield's creative production which
ultimately helped to open up and sustain the Motown magic as well as
employing the medium for something
more than just the financial rewards
("Poppa Was a Rolling Stone"). It's all
here, and it all sounds better than you
ever heard it before.

## 10,000 Maniacs
Formed 1981—Jamestown, New York
Named after a B-movie.

**In My Tribe (1987)**
Elektra 9 60738-2 (46:58)  **[B]**
This release represents the coming of
age of an excellent pop/folk/rock
eighties band, and particularly its lyricist
and lead singer, Natalie Merchant, who
is one of the most fascinating female
leads to come along in recent years—
although she really needs to be seen to
be fully appreciated. This is very listenable, intelligently accessible modern pop
music which promises an interesting
future. Credit should be given to Peter
Asher for his immaculately direct production which brings the band clearly
into focus. This focus is also reflected in
nearly flawless all-digital sound.

## Texas Tornados
**Texas Tornados (1990)**
Reprise 926251-2 (31:36)  **[A–]**
One of the quality refuges amid the
arid mainstream of early nineties pop
can be found in regional recordings. The
title tells the region, and Doug Sahm,
Augie Meyer (formerly of the Sir Douglas
Quintet), Flaco Jiminez, and Freddie
Fender are all charter members. This is
their first recording together, and given
the rich and varied musical heritage
from which they draw, it is shocking that
the disc contains barely thirty minutes
of music—but what a potent half-hour it
is. Highlighted by Sahm's "Adios Mexico," Fender's "A Man Can Cry," and
Butch Hancock's fine "She Never Spoke
Spanish to Me," this is all-star cantina
dance music guaranteed to lead feet to
the floor. Add a longneck and some chili
rellenos and baby, you're home. The
sound is perhaps a little distant and
maybe a little too clean, but it's really
hard to fault.

## Richard Thompson
b. April 3, 1949—London
## Linda Thompson
## (Linda Peters)
Born out of the traditional English folk
roots of Fairport Convention and shaped
by their Sufi beliefs, Richard and Linda
Thompson's modal folk/rock may well
be the single greatest undiscovered joy
of seventies pop music. There are many
who believe Richard is the finest living
electric guitarist. He writes some of the
most intelligent, compelling (and frequently witty) music around. Linda, who
has now divorced him and attempted a
currently aborted solo career (although
it did yield one wonderful, but largely
ignored album, *One Clear Moment,*

Warner Bros. 25164-1, LP only), has a haunting, full, expressive voice that perfectly compliments Richard's lyrics and musical textures.

**First Light (1978)**
Chrysalis CCD1177 (43:22)   **[C + ]**
All the elements that made the Thompsons one of the decade's most compelling but least acknowledged performers are included here, but, in what appears to be a rare nod to commercial appeal, the background musicians and instrumentals are more American than English. The end result is a substantial diminution in the potency of the product. It's not a bad collection, and it does have some fine moments, "Restless Highway," "Layla," and the haunting "Strange Affair," but somehow, their unique magic is never really expressed; probably, in no small part, because Richard's amazing guitar work is submerged in weaker ensemble playing. The sound on the CD is clean and clear, but noticeably compressed, resulting in sound analagous to that of a slightly enhanced, good quality LP.

**Shoot out the Lights (1982)**
Hannibal HNCD 1303 (40:55)   **[A + ]**
Simply the great undiscovered rock masterpiece. Music of power the equal of anything recorded in the last fifteen years. Linda's vocals are majestically beautiful, Richard's guitar uniquely eloquent. At its best, it has moments of terrifyingly magical potency ("The Wall of Death" and "Shoot out the Lights"), as well as transcendental beauty ("Just the Motion"). Conceived and recorded during the final death throes of their marriage, the music vibrates with incredible tension and energy. The sound is excellent; while slight hiss and minor compression are occasionally evident, the clarity and spatial definition

are a perfect enhancement. (As an added plus, the CD contains a track not included on the LP, "Living in Luxury," which isn't bad, but isn't necessary, either.)

# Richard Thompson
**Hand of Kindness (1983)**
Hannibal HNCD1313 (41:23)   **[A + ]**
From the rocking opening chords of "Tear Stained Letter" (a great rock number by any standards) to the polka-driven craziness of "Two Left Feet" that closes *Hand of Kindness,* Thompson delivers music of power, integrity, and majestic intensity. "How I Wanted To" may be one of the most intimately searing laments on record. Throughout it all, Thompson's incredible, modal guitar playing and John Kirkpatrick's buoyant accordion, keynote music of variety, texture, and tension. The sound is warm, clean, and adequately dynamic.

**Across a Crowded Room (1985)**
Polydor 825 421-2 (41:49)   **[A]**
In 1982, Richard and Linda Thompson released *Shoot out the Lights,* one of the most powerful recordings in rock history. Part of its potency arose out of the final tensions of the destruction of their marital relationship. *Across a Crowded Room* is Richard's first recording preoccupied with their divorce. Thompson is one of the largely undiscovered giants of the current rock scene, and, perhaps, the best guitarist working, a fact which this release doesn't belie. But it must be remembered that much of this album concerns itself with the pain of separation ("Ghosts in the Wind") and the bitterness, too ("When The Spell is Broken" and "She Twists the Knife Again"). It also includes some strong, driven rock & roll ("Fire in the Engine Room"). *Across a Crowded Room* is not neces-

sarily an easy or pleasant listening experience, but it is a potent one. The sound, while a shade thin, is clear, open, defined, and extraordinarily precise.

**Daring Adventures (1986)**
Polydor 829 728-2 (47:15)  **[A + ]**
The fact that this guy isn't a major star is eloquent testimony to the sickness in today's pop music industry. Although, in Thompson's case, lack of mass recognition may in large part be self-inflicted. He doesn't care enough to play the game. Instead, that energy goes into making some of the best music being played in the eighties. "Valerie" is the great rock single that no one ever heard. The rest of the material on this stellar 1986 release is as inventive, creative, and downright beautiful as anything you're likely to hear. Oh well, you can only lead a horse to water. The sound is all you can ask for, as well.

**Amnesia (1988)**
Capital CDP7 488452 (43:47)  **[A]**
Simply another great recording by the single most unjustly overlooked talent in rock. Thompson continues to do it all—writing intelligent, biting lyrics; creating music of subtlety and substance; and playing some of the most amazing guitar around. Yet, as far as mass popularity is concerned, he remains a virtual unknown. A favorite of critics, supported by a small number of the enlightened, Richard Thompson makes music that, at its best, has the ability to suspend time. From politics to jaundiced love songs, Thompson's insights and passions are exposed with frightening directness. Mitchell Froom's production has a certain pop bent, but ultimately resolves itself into a fairly natural approach, and his instrumental contributions add body to Thompson's spirit. *Amnesia* is first-rate Thompson, though a little less per-

sonal than his earlier eighties releases, which may account for a little less heat. But the end result still offers more pleasures than most artists ever achieve. The sound of the CD is excellent—natural, open, balanced with clarity and dynamics.

# Timbuk 3
**Greetings from Timbuk 3 (1986)**
IRS 5739 (37:04)  **[A–]**
A guy (Pat McDonald) plus a gal (Barbara K nee Kooyman) plus a boombox equal Timbuk 3. And Timbuk 3 equals some of the wittiest, most attractive new pop product of the last few years. McDonald, whose prior classics include the unknown, but unforgettable "Assholes on Parade," writes some of the most perceptively entertaining lyrics you are likely to hear, and it's all packaged in simple, basically guitar and rhythm sounds that provide a fitting setting for his jaundiced eye. The sound is impressive: clean, immaculately detailed, and dynamically precise. For a good time, try Timbuk 3.

# Toots and the Maytals
Formed 1962—Kingston, Jamaica
**Funky Kingston (1965)**
Mango CCD 9330 (38:21)  **[A]**
Among reggae's pioneer artists Toots Hibbert stands as the best singer the form has known—with a sound that does more than evoke memories of Otis Redding. *Funky Kingston* is a collection of Toots and the Maytals' early-to-mid-sixties pop-influenced, highly melodic brand of danceable reggae sunshine singles. It includes a couple of American pop covers, "Louie Louie," and the best version of John Denver's (yes, *that* John Denver) "Country Roads" ever released; but it really shines when Toots hits the

purer strains of "Time Tough," "Funky Kingston," "Pomp and Pride" and the wondrous "Pressure Drop." If you like your reggae light on the politics and heavy on the lilt, *Funky Kingston* is your island punch. Unfortunately, the sound quality is much like that of a clean LP, and is, at times, muddy at best.

# Peter Tosh
# (Winston Hubert MacIntosh)
b. October 9, 1944—Westmoreland, Jamaica
d. 1987—Jamaica
**The Toughest (1978–1987)**
Capital CDP7 90201 2 (52:06)   **[B]**
This posthumous compilation (Tosh was brutally murdered in 1987) covers a rather strange array from the solo career of one of the Wailers' founding members. It captures the ambivalence between his infatuation with mass crossover stardom (the Mick Jagger duet on the Temptations' "Don't Look Back") and his militant political stance ("Bush Doctor," "Equal Rights/Downpressure Man"). Unfortunately, it reprises nothing from his strong first albums *Equal Rights* and *Legalize It,* and brings back the putrid "Mystic Man." It does include some fine work by Sly and Robbie. Tosh was neither the writing nor singing equal of his cohort, Bob Marley, but his roots and political stance were valid, his persona both fascinating and ultimately fatally problematic. While the sound quality varies depending on source recording, overall, it's pretty impressive.

# Pete Townshend
b. May 19, 1945—London
**Pete Townshend & Ronnie Lane**
**Rough Mix (1977)**
Atlantic/Atco 90097-2 (41:30)   **[A]**
Perhaps the CD reissue of *Rough Mix* will elevate this forgotten gem to the

classic status it deserves. Described by Robert Christgau as "Meher Baba–inspired psalmody so plain and sharply observed (that) maybe he was all reet after all," and by a thankfully forgotten critic as "the great lost Who album," it is a recording of simple charms. Heavily influenced by Lane's folkishness, it shimmers with the pleasure of two artists and friends expressing the open joy of shared musical experience. With the likes of Eric Clapton, John Entwistle, Charlie Watts, and Ian Stewart along to lend a hand, Townshend and Lane's unpretentious compositions rest gently on the ear and mind—the sole exception being Townshend's "Street in the City," which reflects his highbrow pretentiousness; yet even it is better than much of his better-known solo work, although it doesn't quite fit in this recording's overall context. The whole wonderful experience is enhanced by Glyn Johns's warm, immaculate production, which has never sounded better than in this digital remix.

**White City (1985)**
Atco 90473-2 (38:42)   **[D–]**
"Almost as if he's learned how to avoid enjoying himself. . ."—*New Musical Express.* Aside from that, the sound is absolutely first-rate.

# Traffic
Formed 1967—England
**Mr. Fantasy (1968)**
Island 7 90060-2 (34:15)   **[B–]**
An impressive, but dated, debut from this undeniably talented quartet. There's too much echo of the Beatles' *Sgt. Pepper* aesthetic, which may be inevitable, given the time and the place. Traffic's heady blend of diverse musical forms and their strong playing set them apart from most of the later wave of the British

Invasion, and Steve Winwood's singing was at times luminescent ("No Face, No Name and No Number"). Soundwise, *Mr. Fantasy* is barely adequate—the spectrum is narrow, there's some tape hiss, and the vocals tend to be overbright and edgy.

### Traffic (1968)
Island 7 90059-2 (40:51)   **[B+]**
Clearly the band's best release, with Dave Mason assuming the lion's share of the writing, including his classic "Feelin' Alright." "Who Knows What Tomorrow May Bring," written by the other group members, holds up equally well. Given the versatility and breadth of their talents, it's arguable that none of the recordings ever fully captured them, but *Traffic*, with its above-average songs, fine singing, and excellent keyboards, is about as good as it ever got. Badly afflicted with tape hiss, the sound on this CD is more dynamic and clear than that on *Mr. Fantasy.*

### John Barleycorn Must Die (1970)
Island 7 90058-2 (34:35)   **[C]**
With the departure of Dave Mason, who went solo because of artistic differences with Steve Winwood, the remaining trio sounds a bit adrift in a backlog of old English folk mannerisms. Heavily instrumental in the wake of Mason's departure, the whole affair seems rather pointless, but if you like Chaucerian jams. . . . While the mix tends to get a bit murky on "Every Mother's Son," and there's a trace of hiss here and there, the sound of this CD isn't half bad.

### The Low Spark of High Heeled Boys (1971)
Island 7 90026-2 (39:55)   **[B–]**
Maybe it's the addition of more percussion, or the more focused singing of Winwood, this time there is a sustaining structure to the material, resulting in

their most effective work post Mason. The overly long title track is almost as good as the title itself, and Jim Capaldi's Dave Mason sound alike "Light Up or Leave Me Alone" sustains itself with an honest energy. With the exception of "Rainmaker," the sound quality of this disc is quite impressive, with good clarity and impressive dynamics.

# Traveling Wilburys
Formed 1988—Southern California
### Volume I (1988)
Wilbury/Warner Bros. 25796-2 (36:20)   **[A]**
Get Bob Dylan, George Harrison, Roy Orbison, Tom Petty, and Jeff Lynne together, give them two weeks to come up with ten songs, and hope that lightning stikes. It does. *Volume 1* echoes of simpler, happier times, when the music was everything. Nothing heavy here—just five vets displaying the basic love of ragged rock & roll that has kept each of them at or near the top for decades. Sometimes Lynne's heavy production techniques take their toll, but this is a warm and generous treat that includes at least one classic: "End of the Line." The sound has a natural, warm ambience that fits the material to perfection.

### Volume 3 (1990)
Wilbury/Warner Bros. 26324 (36:13)   **[B]**
More of a piece than its startling predecessor, *Volume 1,* the Wilburys' second release is more laid-back, good-time, well-produced classic rock & roll. If you loved the first one, you'll probably like the second. While the "brothers" sound more integrated on *Volume 3,* the absence of Roy Orbison's soaring voice, weaker material, and too much of Jeff Lynne's pop production touches blurs the entire project. On the positive side, the music's tight, the beat infectious, and

Bob Dylan sounds more natural and relaxed than he has in years. His is the predominate voice this time around—he even sings lead on the doo-wop sendup "Seven Deadly Sins." The sound's OK by nineties standards, but somewhat lacking in depth and articulation.

# Trip Shakespeare
## Across the Universe (1990)
A&M 7502-15294-2 (40:58)   **[B–]**
This weird pop confection really shouldn't work, but it does. Assisted by Fred Mahren's sure production and crystalline sound, this group delivers quasimystical messages and oblique romantic sentiments in overblown arrangements that are just weird enough to reverberate in some offbeat way. Not for everyone, but vastly interesting if only for the comfortable uniqueness of it all.

# Ike and Tina Turner
Formed 1957/58—St. Louis
## River Deep—Mountain High (1966)
A&M 393 179-2 (37:14)   **[B +]**
One of the strangest pairings in rock history—Phil Spector's Wagnerian production with Ike and Tina's spare, hard-edged R&B attack. This is also the recording that temporarily moved Tom Woolfe's "Tycoon of Teen" (Spector) out of the industry that he had conquered only a few years earlier. The story is that Phil's high-handed airs caused the industry to sabotage the title selection, which Spector had dubbed his consummate studio effort. Thus, while *River Deep* surged in Britain, it sank in the U.S. This album is a bit of a hodgepodge, veering between Phil's grandiose, echo-laden effects and Ike's reworking of earlier classic material; it remains fascinating, if flawed. The sound, while far

from ideal, is a great improvement over the LP and substantially cleaner than that on the *Best Of* collection.

## Greatest Hits (1960–1973)
Curb 22-77332 (33:37)   **[B]**
Ike and Tina Turner brought the sweaty, sexy sound of fifties and sixties R&B to a major audience and this brief, budget collection covers their tracks, including their original 1960 hit "A Fool in Love," and their biggest smashes: "Proud Mary," "I Want to Take You Higher," "Come Together," and "River Deep, Mountain High" (not the wondrous Spector version). The other inclusions are more dubious, although both "Poor Fool" and "Nutbush City Limits" enjoyed decent chart action, but the exclusion of "I Idolize You" is unforgivable. The sound varies markedly from track to track: "A Fool in Love" sounds dated, and too often others sound muddy, thin, and harsh—but the two gems, "Proud Mary" and "Come Together," sound great.

## The Best Of (1960–1974)
EMI America CDP7-46599-2 (46:08)   **[C +]**
The music is great, the sound quality is, unfortunately, best described as abrasive, particularly on the classic early material (the disc covers work from the early 1960s through the early 1970s). This is primarily noticeable with Tina's voice, which tends to stridency in the first place, a quality which CDs do not readily accommodate. But Ike ran one of the tightest, most explosive soul revues of the sixties, so the music is almost strong enough to overcome the sonic limitations, and the later cuts are less diminished by distortion. Unfortunately, it is the stronger, earlier selections ("I Idolize You") which sound the worst. Even at its best, the sound on this disc is thin.

# Tina Turner (Annie Mae Bullock)
b. November 26, 1938—Nutbush, Tennessee
**Foreign Affair (1989)**
Capitol CDP7-918732 (52:25) **[D +]**
The sound is fine, the content is another matter. We all know the formula—*Private Dancer* left an indelible, and now too familiar, imprint on Tina's eighties recordings. But she is still a fine soul shouter, and given the right material, such as "Steamy Windows," she delivers with polished emotion. But overall, it's too little too late, because the rest is rapidly forgettable.

# The Turtles
Formed 1963—Inglewood, California
**20 Greatest Hits (1965–1970)**
Rhino RNCD5160 (52:26) **[A–]**
Properly conceived and packaged, the compact disc provides the current ideal for musical information. Rhino Records, which has carved out a profitable niche in the music market by realizing the value of preserving material from earlier eras, has extended their sensitivity to the CD format and Rhino's combination of vintage works on CD mesh like the proverbial "hand in glove." This disc is a prime example of how a little care and intelligence can result in an invaluable package. The Turtles, a mid-sixties L.A. folk/rock group (with appropriate New York roots), scored one No. 1 hit, "Happy Together" (2/11/67) and a number of other Top Ten singles that captured the innocent, joyous side of the sixties with precision. While not great innovators, they made very polished, very popular music through a five-year career (1965–70), and, basically, it's all here. Enhanced by informative liner notes and excellent production of twenty-year-old material, this is a disc that will sustain.

# 2 Live Crew
**As Nasty as They Wanna Be (1989)**
Luke Records CDXR107 (79:44) **[F]**
Along with Michael Milliken's prison sentence and Milli Vanilli's pathetic exposure, 2 Live Crew's *As Nasty as They Wanna Be* represents the morally bankrupt nadir of the junk-dominated eighties. Luther Campbell, the maven behind 2 Live Crew, has mastered the art of using the media to his advantage. It could be said that this CD is nothing more than a symptom of a sick society, but it is more than that—it is blatant pandering in the most juvenile, tasteless, and vicious form. There's worse tripe out there, but thankfully it has been spared the media spotlight. So while I'll defend to the rooftops the right of Campbell and company to market their crap, which demeans every person who purchases it, I believe it to be pure shit. Soundwise, you can understand the words—which is all there is.

# UB40
Formed 1978—Birmingham, England
**Labour of Love (1983)**
Dep CD5 (40:05)  **[C]**
The most successful American release for this black/white English reggae band, *Labour of Love* is a set of the group's updated cover versions of earlier hits of many of reggae's original stars. If you don't take it too seriously, or are unfamiliar with the originals, it's a pleasant listen, but little more. The sound quality is fairly ordinary: slightly more dynamic and clean than the LP, but obviously compressed and a little muddy.

# U2
Formed 1978—Dublin, Ireland
Considered by many to be the finest rock & roll band in the world today (1987), which says more about the artistic level of the era than that of the group.

**War (1982)**
Island 90067-2 (42:21)  **[A–]**
It was with this release that U2's blend of punk, piety, sincerity, and heavy metal caught commercial fire. Fueled by wonderfully dramatic performance dynamics (á la Led Zeppelin), this anti-war protest release rings with the power of true commitment. U2 is a band that has captured its moment in time. The sound quality, while slightly compressed and occasionally a bit instrumentally muddy, still remains impressive.

**The Joshua Tree (1988)**
Island 90581 (50:16)  **[A + ]**
This is the fifth release since 1980 by an Irish band many consider to be the best in rock today. This record will do nothing to diminish that belief. U2 has a palpable vision and they don't sell out. They may get a little too strident or naive at times, but they don't sell out, and this time around, they avoid both the naivete and stridency as well: the best of a mature rock sound. The spirit of rebellion is still there, but tempered with the wisdom of age and experience. It's not that they want to change the world, just shift its course a little. *The Joshua Tree* is a powerful album filled with sadness, serenity, and hope. It is about the reality of faith. It is easily the strongest recording in an already brilliant career—probably because the band plays more within itself than on earlier work. In addition to Bono's compelling vocals and the searing minimalism of Edge's guitar, *The Joshua Tree* also showcases the potent bass work of Adam Clayton over Larry Mullen, Jr.'s, pulsing drums. This is music with sufficient depth to endure. This is also one of those rare recordings where there isn't any filler to be found; "Running to Stand Still" is one of the best songs in years. The sound is simply flawless.

## Rattle and Hum (1988)
Island 91003-2 (72:29)   **[B–]**

The rock audience points the direction of American pop culture. At the end of the eighties that audience was waiting to prick the bubble of the mighty who had grown too successful, too rich, and too popular. The film for which this release is the soundtrack was U2's Waterloo. Sure, they set their sights too high and their sincerety doesn't convey comfortably in 10,000-seat-plus arenas; it's a noble failure, if a failure at all. U2 is a band of limited but undeniable power—built on the strength of Adam Clayton's and Larry Mullen, Jr.'s, insistent, driving bottom and The Edge's incendiary guitar. With *Rattle and Hum* they attempt to take a huge bite out of American musical and political history, and it is to their credit that they don't choke on it, but it's not totally nourishing either. Too often their "tributes" miss the mark ("All Along the Watchtower"), but when they succeed ("I Still Haven't Found What I'm Looking For," "When Love Comes to Town," "Bullet the Blue Sky") they manage to stoke the glorious fires of real rock & roll. On average there are two misses for each hit—not a great ratio for a band that aspires to greatness, and has frequently displayed it. The sound varies because of the different locations and conditions used in the recording; overall, it is somewhat boxy and compressed, with occasional annoying hiss.

## Frankie Valli & the Four Seasons
Formed 1961—Newark, New Jersey
**25th Anniversary Collection (1962–1978)**
Rhino RNRD 72998-2 (163:45—three discs)
**[A+]**
Gloryoski, Frankie! Was it really that great back at the start of the sixties? Damn right—you betcha! And here's hearing proof—Italian-American East Coast doo-wop/R&B produced and performed the way good ol' American rock & roll was supposed to be. Music that moves with some of the most creative percussion dynamics ever laid down. Music subtly rich in naive social insight. Music sung in soaring voices and heavenly harmonies. Beginning with their debut "Sherry" (1962), The Four Seasons placed forty-one songs on *Billboard*'s Top 100, with fifteen making it into the Top Ten and five reaching No. 1. All but five of their most minor charters, as well as Frankie Valli's four solo Top Ten entries, are here: "Can't Take My Eyes Off You," "My Eyes Adored You," "Swearin' to God," and "Grease," are included—a wondrous collection. In its direct, deceptively simple way, this is some of the greatest pop music released, and this is *the* comprehensive CD collection. It comes with an eighteen-page book providing informative liner notes by Gene Sculatti, with release dates, labels, and original catalog numbers for each of the singles. Bob Crewe's production perfection was a major element in the Seasons' success, and Bill Inglot and the digital wizards at Rhino drew only on first-generation tapes to provide sound quality that's stunning overall, occasionally affected by minor tape hiss—but that is a negligible complaint.

## Stevie Ray Vaughan and Double Trouble
b. 1956—Dallas, Texas
d. 1990—Alpine Valley, Wisconsin
**Soul to Soul (1985)**
Epic EK40036 (40:09)   **[C+]**
Reheated Allman Brothers. Vaughan was a fine guitarist, but that's about it. The sound is above average, not real clean, but dynamic and fairly open.

**In Step (1989)**
Epic EK45024 (41:13)   **[A]**
In what sadly proved to be his last studio recording with his tight, driving touring band, Stevie Ray amply demonstrates those qualities that helped him, along with Robert Cray and others, bring the blues back into American mainstream music. His singing is adequate, his intensity enveloping, and his guitar technique already legendary. Combining B.B. King, Jimi Hendrix, and jazz, he serves up a mighty brew of fire and soul. Vaughan had cleaned up his personal demons prior to this recording, and while he deals with it lyrically, this ain't

no sermon—it's kick-ass Saturday night music, played the way it's supposed to be played. The closer, "Riviera Paradise," is Sandy Bull–haunted light jazz/blues that's genuinely affecting. The sound quality of this CD is uniformly excellent.

# The Vaughan Brothers
**Family Style (1990)**
Epic/Associated ZK46225 (40:49)  **[B–]**
The idea of getting Stevie Ray Vaughan and older brother Jimmie Lee Vaughan (formerly of the Fabulous Thunderbirds) together on record has immediate appeal, sadly enhanced in this instance by the untimely death of Stevie Ray, blues guitarist extraordinaire. *Family Style* was recorded just before his death, and was his first release after his Grammy Award-winning *In Step.* So maybe expectations were just too high, or maybe these two brothers were a little too concerned about each others feelings to get down to the competitive fire that might have sparked a truly memorable matchup. As a result, *Family Style* is easily listenable and instantly appealing, but with the exception of the Hendrix-influenced "Telephone Song," the crackling energy that made Stevie Ray the idol of his fans and his peers is sadly lacking. Part of the problem could well be producer Nile Rodgers's pop sensibilities, clearly evidenced in the vapid single, "Tick Tock." Soundwise, there's little to criticize; the clarity of this digital recording is first-rate, and the analog mastering may explain the warmth of the final product.

# Suzanne Vega
b. circa 1960—New York City
**Suzanne Vega (1985)**
A&M CD5072 (35:54)  **[A–]**
Sometimes labeled the savior of contemporary folk music after this 1985 release

remarkably received mass market acceptance. It's a fine debut, highlighted by, "Marlene on the Wall," "Undertow," and "Small Blue Thing." This is intelligent, contemporary folk material directly presented, ultimately affecting. The sound is marvelous.

**Solitude Standing (1987)**
A&M CD5136 (44:24)  **[B +]**
The material gets a little thinner and the arrangements a little thicker. Somehow it just doesn't balance out. The sound is even better than on her debut release: true demonstration quality.

**Days of Open Hand (1990)**
A&M 7502-15293-2 (45:51)  **[A–]**
Images, both verbal and musical, float like dreams or clouds through *Days of Open Hand.* Personal, poetic, minimalist, and consummately affecting, Vega's third release continues charting this artist's shadowy, intimate vision. Folk music for the Philip Glass set, poetry for all who will listen. The musical scrims fashioned by Anton Lanko enhance the mood and moment. The sound on this CD is almost flawless.

# The Velvet Underground
Formed 1965—New York City
One of the most succinctly accurate observations of rock criticisms ever made was, "The Velvet Underground didn't have a lot of fans, but every one of them formed their own rock band." The influence of this amazing group on the music of the seventies and eighties has been both pervasive and potent.

**The Velvet Underground & Nico (1967)**
Verve 823 290-2 (48:26)  **[A +]**
The testament to the Velvet's greatness is all right here. It's not pretty music. But it's real music, made at a time when the

mass audience was less than beguiled with reality. *The Velvet Underground & Nico* is one of the most important recordings in the history of rock & roll. This is one of those rare records where it all cosmically came together, or, as John Cale later said of the experience, "We just started playing and held it to the wall." The sound is both intentionally and unintentionally scuzzy (the original recording costs for this album supposedly totaled $1,500). This CD brings you the scuzz with new clarity, which is perfect.

### White Light/White Heat (1968)
Verve 825 119-2 (40:01)   **[B + ]**
Dissonance, both lyrical and musical, was always a part of the Velvet's sound. Well, this is their paean to the electronically discordant. While it is not pleasant listening, it is serious music. The sound is more open than the LP, but it's far from clean—it wasn't recorded clean.

### The Velvet Underground (1969)
Verve 815 45402 (43:00)   **[A]**
This is as laid-back as this cruelly prophetic band got. The recording is very well-crafted and listenable. Unfortunately, it followed *White Light/White Heat,* the dissonance of which alienated a substantial number of their already less than substantial following of fans. That's too bad. Hopefully the disc release will awaken more listeners to the edge of truth which echoes through these recordings. The sound, while far from perfect, is a discernible improvement over the LP, and adds a warm intimacy to the preponderance of valid material included.

### Velvet Underground Live Vol. 1 (1969)
Mercury 834 823-2 (59:06)   **[A–]**

### Velvet Underground Live Vol. 2 (1969)
Mercury 834 824-2 (60:48)   **[A–]**
Given the tremendous influence they had on the music that followed, the Velvet Underground's paucity of recordings is little short of amazing. The original band, plus Nico, appeared only on their debut, *The Velvet Underground and Nico.* Then John Cale was replaced by Doug Yule, who was with the group in 1969 when these recordings were made. Crude, honest, and deadpan, the nineteen selections on these two CDs were recorded at live gigs in Texas and San Francisco, and in their appropriately primitive way provide new insights into much of the group's classic material ("Waiting for My Man," two versions of "Heroin," "Sweet Jane," "Femme Fatale," and "Rock and Roll") and four then-unreleased tracks. Based on the crowd response (or lack thereof), it sounds as though the audience numbered less than a dozen, which, given the period and recording locations, is not inconceivable. In his liner essay, Elliott Murphy says that this kind of rock & roll (the only *real* rock & roll) is about new, honest, on-the-edge experience, and that's a fair description of what sets the Underground apart—and that's what you'll find on this pair of CDs. Unfortunately, these historic recordings are afflicted with hideous sound quality, not as bad as *Live at Max's Kansas City* (among the worst-sounding commercial recordings ever released), but bad enough to adversely affect my ratings (offset by good material); they may be unlistenable to true audiophiles. There are times when tape hiss is the most prominent sound, and there is no dynamic range in the ghostly thin sound.

**Loaded (1970)**
Warner Special Products 9-27613-2 (39:20)   **[A]**
Easily the band's most accessible and
"musical" record; it, of course, wasn't
released until after Lou Reed, the center
of it all, had abandoned the group. This
is not the abrasive, seamy sound with
which the band first lashed its miniscule
but devoted audience; hell, this is almost
gentle, yet made special by Reed's lyrical
character studies of some fascinating fictional creations. Perhaps if *Loaded* had
been the Velvet's first, instead of final,
release, their audience would have
achieved its deserved dimension; but,
by the time this album hit the racks
(with the band itself in final disarray),
the abrasive power and sonic experimentation of their earlier work had
pretty much alienated most of their not-
too-numerous original following. That's
a shame. As it is, *Loaded* has become an
enduring final testament to the work of
one of the most influential and important bands in the history of rock & roll.
The CD sound, while not revelatory, is
both a dynamic and spatial improvement over the LP, but is afflicted with
occasional distortion and frequently
heavy hiss.

**The Best of (Words and Music of Lou Reed)
(1966–1970)**
Polygram 841 1642 (62:18)   **[A]**
The passage of time only reaffirms the
influence and importance of this great
late-sixties New York band. The fifteen
selections effectively cover the emotional and musical terrain the Velvet
Underground pioneered. If you can live
with only one Underground item in your
collection (not recommended, by the
way), this would probably have to be the
one. The sound is just OK, but sonic
clarity was never intended to be part of
this package.

# Violent Femmes
Formed circa 1980—Milwaukee, Wisconsin
**3 (1988)**
Slash/Warner Bros. 25819-2 (36:15)   **[B]**
The Femmes are one of those quirky
bands whose work and appeal are so
personal they almost defy description—
they can be simultaneously disturbing,
consoling, and provocative. Ira Robbins
said it best: "Resembling a punk version
of the Modern Lovers." Their stripped-
down, acoustic instrumentation supports the intimate, open vocal confes-
sions of leader Gordon Gano's complex
naivete. Their influences are diverse;
their spirit embodies everything from
gospel to the profane—from fragile to
frightening. *3* is the best thing they've
done since their self-titled 1983 debut,
although it is flawed by some jarring
changes in attitude ("See My Ships"), but
overall has a naked intensity and heartfelt feeling. The sound quality is first-
rate.

# Tom Waits
b. December 7, 1949—Pomona, California
Rock's Kerouac with a cough.

**Nighthawks at the Diner (1975)**
Asylum 2008-2  **[B–]**
This live performance at L.A.'s late
Record Plant fairly captures a man who
is as much performance artist as singer/
songwriter. It sounds just like an imagi-
nary fifties blues/jazz beatnik dive is
supposed to. The responsive crowd
lends credibility and requisite responses
to the often lengthy, always humorous
spoken interludes between songs. The
jazz-influenced backdrop is consistently
tasty and Waits is consistently without
voice—it all works just fine if you have a
taste for this offbeat scene—it's the way
hip night people were supposed to
sound when Kerouac was chronicling it
all. The overall approach works, and the
live sound is appropriately clean and
intimate; its failure is a lack of the first-
rate songs, the kind that set Waits's better work apart from this arduously
constructed milieu.

**Rain Dogs (1985)**
Island CID131 (54:08)  **[A+]**
Waits is a true original with a voice
out of *The Exorcist* and a vision out of
Bukowski. He is also one of the most
original and affecting artists working
today. A reincarnation of the cool-jazz,
beat-generation fifties, he's a breath of

fresh air in the techno-eighties. This is
one of his best efforts, but for a little too
much filler, it might be his very best.
The sound isn't as clean as it could be,
but it's well-defined, detailed, and
dynamic.

# Jerry Jeff Walker
# (Paul Crosby)
b. March 16, 1942—Oneonta, New York
Well shucks!

**Gypsy Songman (1988)**
Rykodisc RCD 20071 (71:23)  **[C+]**
Walker's weary, laconic songs and delivery really haven't changed that much.
There ain't no "Bojangles" here, but his
ghost hovers over the proceedings. Die-
hard fans won't be disappointed; new-
comers would probably be happier with
a greatest-hits collection. The sound is
open and clean, consistent with Ryko's
fine reputation.

# Jennifer Warnes
b. circa 1940—Seattle, Washington
**Famous Blue Raincoat (1986)**
Cypress 661 111 2 (41:38)  **[A+]**
Leonard Cohen wrote some of the most
poetic and affecting material of any of
the singer/songwriters, but the monotonal delivery he utilized failed to attract
much of an audience beyond sincere
seventies college girls. Jennifer Warnes
has been a fan as well as a musical con-

tributor to Cohen's recent recordings, and she has one of the finest pop voices around. Thus, this recording of Warnes doing essentially all Cohen material is a perfect match. Cohen himself joins in on "Joan of Ark," but the show belongs to Jennifer, the vocalist and coproducer with Roscoe Beck, as well as with Van Dyke Parks and Bill Ginn for the perfect arrangements. This one is a sleeper. It's not rock & roll, but it's great pop/folk product. The sound is absolutely awesome—this is the one to play to demonstrate what CD sound is capable of delivering.

# Was (Not Was)
Formed circa 1980—Detroit, Michigan
**Born to Laugh at Tornados (1983)**
Geffen 9 24251-2 (35:46)  **[B + ]**
Contemporary Motor City madmen, the Was brothers sprung their off-the-wall white funk on an unsuspecting world in 1983 (actually it was their second recording, but the first self-titled release (1981) caused barely a ripple). An irresistible mix of Don Was's dance-floor production and David Was's twisted narratives, *Born to Laugh at Tornados* skirts the edges, but never strays too far from its pop motivations. To add to the strangeness, they employ a bizarre mix of guest vocalists: Doug Fieger (former Knack vocalist), Mitch Ryder, Ozzy Osbourne, and Mel Torme. The clarity of their vision (bizarre though it may be) and command of the recording studio somehow tie it all together into a listenable, danceable recording that was a breath of fresh air in a record market where freshness had lost out to packaging. The sound is crisp, percussive, and clear, but has a tendency toward overbrightness.

**What Up, Dog? (1988)**
Chrysalis VK41664 (57:09)  **[A]**
*What Up, Dog?* is where weirdly literate dance-hall funk and Philly soul smoothness came together to produce a surprise hit for these self-declared iconoclasts. Was (Not Was) will move your feet and wrinkle your brain with a contagious offhand ease. The soul is served with sass and class by R&B veterans Sweet Pea Atkinson and Sir Harry Bowens. The intraterrestial madness emanates from David Was, with leash by Don Was, and vocal support on "Wedding Vows in Vegas" from Frank Sinatra, Jr. The Was brothers wrote all tracks except Otis Redding's "I Can't Turn You Loose," running the gamut from promiscuity through presidential assassinations, with dinosaurs and robots tossed in for texture. It all adds up to one of the more humorous, thought-provoking releases to come along, one of the best of 1988. Don's production wizardry is reflected in the CD's sound quality, which is open, crisp, and appropriately dynamic.

**Are You Okay? (1990)**
Chrysalis F2 21778 (50:13)  **[A]**
Another soulful concoction of dance-floor dynamics overlaid with absurdist lyrics of nineties trivia/media–induced madness presented in state-of-the-art sonic purity. The beats may be universal; the lyrical stance remains anything but. *Are You Okay?* runs the gamut from the extremely soulful singing of Sweet Pea Atkinson, Sir Harry Bowens, and Donald Ray Mitchell, to rap refrains, to guest Leonard Cohen's resonant monotonal musings. The result is a danceable, upbeat, off-the-wall collection that induces joy and disbelief equally. Their remake of the Temptations' classic "Papa Was a Rollin' Stone" garnered some airplay, but it's their own gloriously twisted

creations ("Are You Okay?," "I Feel Better Than James Brown," "How the Heart Behaves," "Maria Navarro," and "Elvis's Rolls Royce") that make this a worthy successor to 1988's great *What Up Dog?* While their sources are diverse, the end result is a unique musical vision, perhaps best described by Chris Willman: "The hip-hop once again hits the fan and comes back in shards of danceably disconnected Dada." As is usually the case with these production-fixated popsters, the sound is bright, crisp, and first-rate.

# Rob Wasserman
**Duets (1988)**
MCA MCAD 42131 (47:21)   **[A]**
Moody, evocative, haunting—more jazz/pop than rock. *Duets* is fascinating both in concept and execution. Building on a simple idea, bassist Rob Wasserman has recorded ten duets with a variety of major talents. Aaron Neville shares "Stardust," Rickie Lee Jones, "The Moon is Made of Gold" and "Autumn Leaves," Lou Reed, "One for My Baby (And One More for the Road)," Stephane Grappelli, "Over the Rainbow." Jennifer Warnes proves that she owns Leonard Cohen's songs, with a time-stopping version of his "Ballad of the Runaway Horse." Bobby McFerrin, Dan Hicks, and Cheryl Bentyne also appear. Wasserman, whose work varies with each artist and song, displays an awesome jazz sensibility as well as fine rock licks (actually displayed to much better advantage on Lou Reed's classic *New York*). Bass players are generally the unsung heroes of pop music, and perceptive listeners know that there have been few, if any, great rock bands that lacked a great bass player—who provides the rhythmic and chordal foundation on which all else is built. Wasserman is a great bass player—

a sensitive, imaginative musician—which *Duets* amply demonstrates. The sound quality of this disc is simply superb—a class effort in all respects.

# The Waterboys
**Room to Roam (1990)**
Chrysalis F2 21768 (42:42)   **[C +]**
Mike Scott is in love—with a woman and a place—Ireland. His joy is sweetly innocent and infectious, there just isn't much of insight or substance involved, which probably wasn't intended. Imbued heavily with the raucous sounds of electrified Irish folk, *Room to Roam* is a happy listen, but not an enduring one. The CD's sound is as open and bright as the lyrics.

# Muddy Waters (McKinley Morganfield)
b. April 4, 1915—Rolling Fork, Mississippi
d. April 30, 1983—Chicago
One of the first, and probably the best, of the fifties Chicago electric-urban blues purveyors whose influence on rock & roll (particularly the members of the original British Invasion) is incalculable.

**Hard Again (1977)**
Blue Sky ZK34449 (45:40)   **[A]**
Produced by Texas albino blues-guitar great Johnny Winter, this is the blues: urban and hard. Waters's singing is majestically powerful, painful, and expressive, and Winter's guitar burns while James Cotton's harp defines the sound. One listen and it's easy to understand what made the Rolling Stones do what they did. The CD adds punch, clarity, and some separation to the sound, which is also a bit compressed, with a tendency to muddiness in the band's sound. There's also an occasional harsh

edge on some of Waters's definitive vocals.

## The Chess Box (1947–1954)
MCA CHD3-80002 (216:01—three discs)   **[A +]**
It's urban, electrified, delta blues by the master—it's possibly the taproot of rock & roll—it's the passion, the power, and the glory of a man who impacted music like a force of nature. McKinley Morganfield, son of a delta sharecropper, working with Leonard Chess in the Chicago studios that also birthed Chuck Berry, Bo Diddley, and Willie Dixon, made a sound that ignited much of the British Invasion which, in turn, created the music of the sixties, the most potent decade in the long history of popular music. This is the music of a group of blues greats who have influenced most of the blues tradition that followed. The seventy-two cuts include every classic in Waters's Chess catalog: "I Just Want to Make Love to You" (1954), "Mannish Boy" (1955), "Got My Mojo Workin'" (1956), "Rolling Stone" (1950), "Hoochie Coochie Man" (1954), as well as a treasure of lesser-known killers: "My Home is the Delta" (1963), "Black Night" (1966); but also previously unreleased and alternate versions—consistently throbbing, aching, touching music. Waters's work has endured for almost half a century, and still grows in stature with the passing of time. Combine all this with the best possible sound quality (acknowledging the technical studio limitations of the times), as well as a high-quality thirty-page booklet featuring excellent biographical commentary by Mary Katherine Aldin and critical commentary by Robert Palmer, and you have a package that is nothing less than essential.

# John "Guitar" Watson
b. 1935—Houston
## I Heard That! (1953–1961)
Charly CD Charly 48 (44:15)   **[B–]**
Watson's recording began when he was eighteen, in 1953, and continued at least into the mid-seventies. The sixteen cuts cover his work from 1953 to 1963. These are the urban electrified blues sounds that have found a steady audience in America since the forties, and provided a nurturing ground for both the music and the musicians who are elemental to rock & roll. Watson has been credited as an early Hendrix influence. What's for sure is that he writes some fun blues material, "Gangster of Love" and "Cuttin' In," being two included here, and performs it with tight aplomb. The sound is very clean, but compressed; certainly far superior to vinyl versions.

# The Who
Formed 1964—London
## Meaty Beaty Big and Bouncy (1971)
MCA MCAD37001 (42:18)   **[A–]**
The Who were the garage rock singles band of the British Invasion, making this compilation of those singles almost an essential rock album. "I Can't Explain," "Pictures of Lily," "My Generation," "Pinball Wizard," "Magic Bus," "I Can See for Miles," "Substitute," and "Anyway, Anyhow, Anywhere" rank with the best releases of their era. Townshend has called it "the greatest of Who albums" noting that "it reminds . . . [the band] . . . who we really are." Sadly, the sound is inconsistent, but is generally very compressed, often abrasive, and distorted, muddy, and afflicted with constant, noticeable hiss. It's still wonderful.

## Who's Next (1971)
MCA MCAD 37217 (43:15)   **[A + ]**
*Tommy* was the Who album that garnered all the hype (rock opera!) and
became a motion picture; but *Who's
Next* is their classic—the recording by
which this powerful band will be measured and remembered. This effort
represents the best that each member
had to offer, but in the end, it is Daltrey's
triumph. His vocals soar over and slice
through the dense driven sound of a
first-rate rock band at the peak of its
power, ultimately capturing the pure animal ecstasy at the heart of great rock &
roll. "Baba O'Riley," "Bargain," "My
Wife," "Goin' Mobile," "Behind Blue
Eyes," and one of rock's all-time great
anthems "Won't Get Fooled Again" are
the highlights, but there's not a selection
on the album which isn't first-rate. The
sound is as close to a perfect fit to the
material as is likely to be captured—
powerfully dynamic, with wonderful
separation and openness, as well as precise individual detailing. Yes, there is
occasional audible hiss, but let's not be
nitpicking in the face of great rock & roll.

## The Singles (1966–1981)
Polydor 815 965-2 (58:17)   **[B + ]**
This disc covers sixteen cuts from 1966
to 1981 (some of the earliest in mono)
and seven of them are from the group's
sixties glory years. One of the era's more
self-conscious concept bands, thanks to
Townshend's intellectual pretensions,
the enduring work they did was the
songs treasured by their fans—the
garage band singles comprehensively
included here. Driven by Keith Moon,
probably the finest drummer in the history of rock—the man was a veritable
war back there—their great singles captured the teenage spirit of rebellion—
which knows no decade—as well as any
group around. It was their core strength,

and when their music sought to be
"more," it generally overreached. The
sound doesn't provide a lot of surprises;
it varies markedly from cut to cut and
decade to decade. But the early material
particularly suffers from compressed
reproduction and most of it is a bit on
the harsh side. Still, probably a worthwhile addition to the comprehensive
rock CD library.

# Jackie Wilson
b. June 9, 1934—Detroit
d. January 21, 1984
## The Jackie Wilson Story (1983—compilation release date)
Epic EGK38623 (64:46)   **[B + ]**
This collection, released in 1983, covers
material from Wilson's earliest recorded
efforts (Berry Gordy's "Reet Petite" from
1957 and his first real hit "Lonely Tear
Drops" in 1959) to his mediocre, limited
seventies output. During the sixties,
Wilson was a genuine star on the R&B
circuit, combining a first-rate singing
voice with an athlete's performing
pyrotechnics. Too often, his material was
sabotaged by overbearing arrangements
and the artist's tendencies to show off his
vocal prowess. It's all here on this extensive package: the good, the bad, and the
ugly. This is one of those CDs which,
thanks to thoughtful song selection and
comprehensive, intelligent liner notes,
provides a fine encapsulation of a total
career. The sound, of course, varies
from cut to cut and a few sound awful,
but, all in all, it's clean and an improvement over the corresponding LPs.

# Stevie Wonder (Steveland Judkins or Morris)
b. May 13, 1950—Saginaw, Michigan
A true musical genius whose career
began as a Motown child star, but whose

real influence dates to his mature work done in the early seventies when he made the synthesizer and the studio his personal instruments. Wonder created a funk-based pop sound that enjoyed strong popular acceptance, widespread critical acclaim, and immense influence on the pop product that followed. His strength is in the sound and structure of his music; his lyrics often tending to veer off into some personal, flaky never-never-land.

**Talking Book (1972)**
Tamla TCD06151TD (43:30)   **[A–]**
With this release, Wonder not only forever established his independence from Motown's traditional hit-making formula, he also entered the first rank of popular recording artists on the strength of its two major hits, "You Are the Sunshine of My Life" and "Superstition." Unfortunately, a part of the legacy he created was an excessive reliance on synthesizers in pop/rock music (thereafter generally used by those who lacked either Wonder's genius or vision with expectedly dire results). The sound on this disc is pretty clean, somewhat dynamically enhanced, but lacking spatial benefits because overall compression keeps it from escaping the bounds of LP sound.

**Innervisions (1973)**
Tamla MCD09052MD (44:12)   **[A+]**
This recording represents the pinnacle of a very important artist's career, and of his physically blind, but nonetheless extraordinarily humane vision. For all intents and purposes, and for all of its richness and variety of texture, it is essentially *all* Stevie Wonder. He personally created and arranged every sound heard. His canvas stretches from the

tough realities of ghetto streets to the transcendent joy of spiritual acceptance, each rendered with an original, unique musical palette. The feel is a little more jazz than funk, the result is simply glorious pop music—uplifting in sound and message. The CD sound is a marked improvement over the LP, with greater clarity, definition, and dynamics; although hiss remains fairly evident throughout.

**Musiquarium (1982)**
Motown 6114TD (84:04—two discs)   **[A+]**
An excellent compilation of the seventies and early eighties work of one of the most influential artists of the time. All the goodies are here: "Superstition," "Boogie on Reggae Woman," "You Are the Sunshine of My Life," "Livin' for the City," "You Haven't Done Nothin'," "Masterblaster," and ten others (four of which are new to this release and digitally recorded). They're all here in truly excellent sound.

# World Party
**Goodbye Jumbo (1990)**
Chrysalis/Ensign F2 21654 (54:26)   **[B]**
This is Karl Wallinger's party, and Wallinger is an immensely talented pop performer who wears his influences (Bob Dylan, the Rolling Stones) proudly. His synth-driven efforts are immediately appealing, and at their best ("Is It Too Late" and "Way Down Now") are first-rate examples of what constitutes contemporary pop. In other words, *Goodbye Jumbo* is a good listen, but not necessarily something to return to tomorrow or the day after. The overall sound quality is fine, but the production is a bit confused, sometimes resulting in muddy mixes.

# X

Formed 1977—Los Angeles
After the Ramones, X was America's most important (country) punk band—but few outside of Southern California ever knew it.

### Under the Big Black Sun (1982)
Elektra 9 60150-2 (34:09)  **[B + ]**
The first major label release by this critically anointed L.A. country/punk outfit. In Dave Marsh's opinion, however, their music was "directionless and abrasively unemotional." But the listeners have rightfully applauded their raw energy, biting vocal harmonies, and sometimes incisive lyrics. The power of drummer D.J. Bonebrake is undeniable, and Billy Zoom's guitar is electric slash-out-Chuck-Berry-thunder. The mood isn't up and the music isn't melodic, but "Dancing With Tears in My Eyes" just ain't abrasive—to the contrary. The sound *is* often abrasive—raw, ragged, and consistent.

### More Fun in the New World (1983)
Elektra 9 60283-2 (41:32)  **[A]**
The band's most consistent statement to date. As usual, this is mostly attributable to stronger material but is also aided mightily by Zoom's soaring, searing guitar. Sure, there's still ambivalence in direction and too much involvement in role definition (as chronicled in the appealing "True Love Pt. 2"), but they're tighter and more self-assured. As things have progressed, it is likely that this may be their definitive album statement, with all its flawed power ("Let the Music Go Bang"), and it does have Exene's killer cover of Jerry Lee Lewis's "Breathless." The sound echoes the distorted roar of performance, albeit with noticeable compression.

### See How We Are (1987)
Elektra 60492-2 (37:46)  **[A + ]**
In the eighties, in the name of "classic" rock, radio suppressed the spirit of rock itself with its silent boycott of anything remotely connected to the punk (translate: new rock & roll) movement of the seventies. X, which was born in L.A. in 1977, certainly traces its roots to that city's second-wave punk scene. However, a decade later, it is clear that this is one of the great American rock bands of the eighties, whether they get airplay or not. With their incisive lyrics, haunting country-tinged harmonies, and energetic drive, X is one of the few current bands tending to the essential spirit of the music. This is their first release without founding lead guitarist Billy Zoom, and the remaining trio (John Doe, Exene, and Don Bonebrake) are here augmented by Dave Alvin and Tony Gilkyson on guitars and vocals. The result is one of the best recordings from a band whose musical standards have always been exceedingly high. The

sound isn't clean, but it seems purposeful and is thickly potent.

## Live At the Whisky A Go-Go (1988)
Elektra 960788-2 (72:38)   [B + ]

Before an enthusiastic audience at the L.A. club where they built their local fame, X matches and merits that enthusiasm with over twenty-one selections covering their recorded history from 1981. You'd think that coming from the music capital of the world, and recording on a major label, a band of this variety and potency would have garnered more fan attention to go with its critical acclaim, but you'd be wrong. The punk-tinged spirit of rock & roll lives in this great American band, and *Live* offers an energetic overview. The performance sound is adequate, but overall it's muddy, a bit removed, and too often the vocals are buried in the mix.

# The Yardbirds
Formed 1963—London
**The Best of British Rock (1964–1965)**
Pair SPCD2-1151 (49:03)  **[A]**
The English link between American
R&B and international heavy metal, the
Yardbirds' mid-sixties music, covered on
this sixteen-track release, has had an
extensive and enduring influence on
the rock music that followed. This arose
out of the group's succession of lead
guitarists, Eric Clapton, Jeff Beck, and
Jimmy Page, each possessed of technical dexterity, emotive purity, and a feel
for the blues. These three expanded the
vocabulary of electric guitar with their
use of fuzztones, feedback, and other
innovative techniques to accommodate
a creative fusion of their blues roots with
the psychedelic posture of their times.
Of course, the end result was Led Zeppelin, who opened the gates for the
unwashed horde that followed. But that
doesn't detract from the quality or innovation that was evidenced in the best of
the Yardbirds' music. The selections on
this CD were all recorded in 1964 and
1965, and included all their best known
cuts; the lead guitars on all tracks being
either Eric Clapton or Jeff Beck, and
their licks are lively. The sound varies
but is never anything real special;
though still far superior to LP versions.

# Neil Young
b. November 12, 1945—Toronto, Canada
Rock's most sophisticated primitive. A
loner, despite numerous career affilia-
tions; e.g., Buffalo Springfield, Crazy
Horse, and Crosby, Stills, Nash & Young.
An artist whose oblique persona may be
as much a factor in his commercial success as his musical talent. Called a
visionary by some, he has managed to
sustain a sometimes brilliant, sometimes
banal, but always interesting career for
more than two decades.

**With Crazy Horse**
**Everybody Knows This is Nowhere (1969)**
Reprise 2282-2 (40:31)  **[A]**
Reams have been written about how
Young has diluted his talent by his need
to play out his various musical personas.
Yet a good argument can be made that
this diversity has been the source of his
continually renewing career. Upon the
release of his 1989 masterpiece, *Freedom*, *Rolling Stone*'s reviewer accurately
noted that it was the third time in which
Young had issued a major recording in
the final year of a decade. *Everybody
Knows This is Nowhere* was the first
of these decade-ending recordings,
released in the spring of 1969, and
it remained on the charts for almost
two years. *Everybody Knows This is
Nowhere* is his second album, and the
first with Crazy Horse; it captures his
lonesome, brash, electrified folk/coun-

try sound. With "Cinnamon Girl," the title song, "Round & Round (It Won't Be Long)," and "Down by the River," it contains some of Young's best writing since his Buffalo Springfield days. Admittedly, the ten-and-a-half-minute closer "Cowgirl in the Sand" is extremely overindulgent at best, but Young has brought us a lot of exceptional music, which is a valid reason to grant him some leeway. The sound is big, dynamic, and bright—that's the good news. It is afflicted with excessive tape hiss and metallic edginess in some of the vocals and instrumental highs, which may be exactly the way Young believes it should sound.

### After the Goldrush (1970)
Reprise 2283-2 (35:15)   [A–]
The eccentric rock & roller in the guise of singer/songwriter. This is a recording which was intended as the soundtrack to a movie that was never made, which, in retrospect, somehow seems totally appropriate. It is at once dense and simple, prophetic and mundane. What really matters is that after more than two decades, it retains a uniqueness of vision and sound that still holds interest. It is also the record which, probably more than any other, established Young's star status. The disc has dynamics and clarity which are markedly superior to the LP, but it is afflicted with excessive and pervasive hiss.

### Harvest (1972)
Reprise 2277-2 (37:38)   [D + ]
This difficult artist's most popular album, probably alienated the listening/buying public from the rock record reviewers more than any other major release. The former loved it, the latter were cool to or disdainful of it ("puerile, precious, and self indulgent, not to mention musically insipid," John Mendelsohn said). The critics may have over-

stated the negative, but they were on the right track. The CD sound adds nothing to that of the LP; very compressed, dirty, and lacking in articulation.

### Tonight's the Night (1975)
Reprise 2221-2 (45:01)   [A + ]
Young is an acquired taste, primarily because of the nasal whine that he uses for a voice; also because of his propensity for employing distortion as an element of his sound tapestry. His vision and wide roving intensity, however, cannot be doubted. Written in part as a response to the drug-related deaths of two members of his musical touring aggregation, *Tonight's the Night* is a dark, rough, less than pleasant experience which Young's record company held for two years before offering it to the market. With this release, Young may have been motivated by very personal losses, but the end result is a conceptual elegy to the youth and dreams that buoyed the great sixties myths. This isn't easy music to listen to, but it is redemptive—it is pure rock & roll in the fullest sense. Or, as Young himself has said of it, "I probably *feel* this more than anything else I've ever done." The sound, which features continuous, obvious hiss, is a bit more dynamic and defined than the LP, but the digital conversion is murky, dirty and distorted which may, in this case, represent perfect reproduction.

### With Crazy Horse
### Zuma (1975)
Reprise 2242-2 (36:34)   [B + ]
This is the closest thing to a traditional Neil Young recording—complete with a gentle, acoustic love song, "Pardon My Heart," some failed country/hippie tripe, "Lookin' for a Love," and some rough, hard, guitar-driven rock & roll, "Danger Bird." It also proves Young's consistent inconsistency in delivering one classic,

"Cortez the Killer," but closes with a treacly bit of Crosby, Stills, Nash & Young harmonizing on "Through My Sails." Not a bad recording, but surely not a great one, either. The sound of *Zuma* is as good or better than anything Young released in the seventies.

### Decade (1966–1976)
Reprise 2257-2 (144:33—two discs)   **[A + ]**
Young's panoramic career would seem a natural for ten-year retrospectives, and *Decade*, which spans 1966 (Buffalo Springfield) through 1976 (duet with Stephen Stills), verifies it. The thirty-five songs, five of which were previously unreleased, cover essentially all of his best work of that decade, and their quality is among the most impressive produced during a strong era. Of all his contemporaries, Neil Young has remained the most vital—perceptive and expressive—still producing meaningful work twenty-five years after the earliest material included here. This fact adds resonance to the foundation work included in this well-chosen compilation. Young's awareness of his artistic persona and production has always been a major consideration in his work. This is somewhat borne out in the handwritten comments he includes for each song, some of which are wonderfully informative (he *was* suffering from a high fever when he was possessed by "Cowgirl in the Sand"). As expected, the sound quality is all over the map, some cuts are afflicted with too much hiss, some are too compressed, some a bit shrill, but it is still a dynamic improvement over the original three-LP compilation.

### Comes a Time (1978)
Reprise 2266-2 (37:16)   **[B + ]**
Young, effectively immersed in his country/folk mode, with a little help from

Crazy Horse and some less-than-successful harmony vocals from Nicolette Larson. Replete with pleasant melodies, quietly intense performances, and hardbitten homilies about love's losses, *Comes a Time* has an easy, loping, country tinged listenability, even if it lacks any really great Young compositions ("Goin' Back" gets close). It closes with a strong cover of Ian Tyson's classic "Four Strong Winds"—after all roots is roots. The sound quality is equivalent to that of a clean LP.

### With Crazy Horse
### Rust Never Sleeps (1979)
Reprise 2295-2 (38:29)   **[A + ]**
As has been noted elsewhere, the final year of each decade seems to be Young's ultimate inspiration, and *Rust Never Sleeps* is a major tenet for that theory. Arguably his most successful noncompilation release, it is imbued with rock poetry, anguished performance, and insightful vision. For all his celebrity and success, Neil Young still maintains the hungry, vigilant stance that gave such an electrifying edge to the music in the two preceding decades. "It's better to burn out than to fade away"—"Down the timeless gorge of changes where sleeplessness awaits"—"Then I saw black and my face splashed in the sky"—"Welfare mothers make better lovers"—"I'm makin' another delivery of chemicals and sacred roots"—"Hey, hey, my, my/ Rock & roll will never die/There's more to the picture/Than meets the eye"—he may say it offhandedly, but he *says* it. More than just an essential Neil Young recording, this is an essential rock & roll record, and there aren't as many of those around. While sadly a bit compressed, the sound moves from bright, appropriately edgy acoustic, to raw, harsh rasps of electronic assault—it fits.

## With Crazy Horse
## Live Rust (1979)
Reprise 2296-2 (74:01)   **[B]**
This double-LP live release inspired diverse critical commentary: David Marsh, who is no fan of Young's, trashed it; Greil Marcus, who *is* a fan, took a similar position, and Robert Christgau, with reservation, was generally positive. These sixteen songs have all been previously released and these garage-band live versions add more heat than light. Even the heat suffers from too much slashing guitar indulgence. Young remains a somewhat problematic artist, albeit one who proudly carries his musical baggage with little apparent regard for the weight of the ever-growing load. *Live Rust,* which was released as a concert film, closes with a driving, incendiary trio of Young classics: "Like A Hurricane," "Hey Hey, My My," and "Tonight's the Night" that turn today's heavy metal to tinfoil. The sound is a bit boxy, but for a live recording of this vintage, it packs a fair amount of impact.

## And the Bluenotes
## This Note's For You (1988)
Reprise 25719-2 (39:24)   **[B–]**
I suppose in some perverse way it was inevitable—after all, he's sampled about every other North American roots (and futurist) musical format, so why not a horn-driven R&B outing? It's just that—Neil Young, a *blues singer?* Never was, never will be. Too often he seems to be working too hard, maybe to overcome the horns, which are obviously working too hard. But then there's the wonderful irony of the title song winning an MTV (that's right, *MTV*) award for best video of 1989—after having banned it—the ultimate irony for any time other than the cynical eighties, which makes it perfect somehow. Actually, "Coupe de Ville" has a haunting quality, nicely colored

with minimal horn background, and Young does get some tasty jazz/blues licks off his guitar throughout. The recording has a warm, bright, dynamic sonic quality.

## Freedom (1989)
Reprise 25899-2 (61:04)   **[A + ]**
As *Rolling Stone* accurately noted in its glowing review of *Freedom,* this is the third end-of-a-decade release by Young that confirms his immense stature as a rock artist. If honesty, integrity, and purpose are the criteria for great rock performance, Young's place is more than assured. In a career marked by unique eclecticism and constant deviation from any single direction, Young's best work echoes with the country/rock sounds that made Buffalo Springfield's sound indelible. On *Freedom,* Young maintains a strong political stance, addressing America's end-of-the-eighties problems, both domestic and foreign. As he has done in the past, Young bookends this album with live (acoustic) and studio (electric) versions of the same anthem, "Rocking in the Free World," the prescience of which is eerie considering the turn of world events within weeks after *Freedom*'s release. (This is not to suggest any direct causal relationship, only that Young's awareness that good ol' rock & roll would prove more potent than tanks in the final resolution of forty-five years of Cold War tensions. The tanks probably also played a role.) The recording, which ranges from searing rock to gentle ballads, and from country lilt to bombastic bitterness, reveals one gem after another. Both versions of "Rocking in the Free World" as well as "Crime in the City (Sixty to Zero Part 1)," "Hanging On a Limb," "Too Far Gone," "Wrecking Ball," and a dolefully dissonant reading of the Drifters' classic "On Broadway" (which says more about the erosion of

urban America than any other song I can think of) are the highlights among a dozen selections, but there's nothing mediocre in the bunch. On *Freedom,* Young proves resoundingly that great rock & roll is not simply the product of youthful genius and energy, rather, that a truly inspired artist can walk the walk and talk the talk well into middle age. The dynamic all-digital recording is the froth on an already heady brew. May be the best record of the eighties.

### Ragged Glory (1990)
Reprise 9 26315-2 (62:44)   **[A + ]**
A grunge-guitar symphony by a preeminate sixties artist still making valid, vital music in the nineties. Young's power and passion are undiminished by the passage of decades. His intensity has grown as the world he perceives around him has diminished. Aptly titled, *Ragged Glory* is an electrified guitar/vocal scream, a redemptive reminder of what makes real rock & roll the most emo-

tionally compelling music of our times (rare though it may now be). *Ragged Glory* reunites Young on record for the first time since the late seventies with Crazy Horse, his wholly empathetic garage band, resulting, in Kurt Loder's words, in "a monument to the garage— to the pursuit of passion over percussion, to raw power, and unvarnished soul." Lyrically *Ragged Glory* reprises Young's themes: love/disillusionment, politics/disillusionment, relationships/ disillusionment, leavened with hope, faith, and an almost crushing belief in the power and responsibility of each struggling soul. It echoes the past and grasps volcanically toward the future. Its heart and soul resides in Young's guitar—a slashing, abrasive, feedback ridden cry of anguish and ragged glory. The sound is obliterating, raw, and perfect—not in the audiophile sense, but in the musical sense. Lock the doors, shut the windows, and crank it up—Neil Young has!

## Frank Zappa
b. December 21, 1940—Baltimore
Rock's reigning intellectual; and in the eighties, perhaps its most eloquent spokesman. His absurdist, satiric, sophisticated work encompasses both rock/jazz/symphonic aspirations as well as the crassest forms of apparent scatalogical pandering. He has created a body of work unique in the annals of popular music and which has attracted and held a substantial hardcore audience for over two decades.

### We're Only In It For the Money/Lumpy Gravy (1967)
Rykodisc RCD40024 (70:54)   [A–]
A two-fer for the twisted. *We're Only In It For the Money,* Zappa's satirical response to *Sgt. Pepper,* the Summer of Love, San Francisco, and anything else that would stick to the ceiling. Sound/music/montage/collage—ultimately an homage to the art of tape editing. *Lumpy Gravy* (his first solo release) presents his weirdness leading the fifty-person Abnuceals Emuukha Electric Symphony Orchestra and Chorus—'nuff said? The sound is truly outstanding, crystal clear, beautifully spaced, and absolutely insane.

## Warren Zevon
b. January 24, 1947—Chicago
The enfant terrible of the seventies L.A. music scene, whose lyrical occupations run from British werewolves to headless mercenaries, while his music is based upon the rock format, often inflected with symphonic colorations. A prodigious talent whose promise has never been fully realized.

### Excitable Boy (1978)
Elektra/Asylum 118-2 (31:51)   [A]
The excitable boy at his macabre best—macho madness exposed, well-coiffed monsters resuscitated, and another vote of confidence for the legal profession. Zevon's demons were obviously in proper orbit when this mad minor masterpiece was hatched. And, oblique or not, there is a compelling tenacity to "Accidentally Like a Martyr." As always, the instrumentation and production are fresh and effective; what Warren lacks in vocal flexibility he compensates for with a nicely nuanced delivery and damn fine lyrics. The overall quality of the songs is excellent, the wonderful "Werewolves of London" being the closest Zevon's come to a hit single (No. 21). The sound, while spacious, has a slightly muffled quality to it, which is too bad.

### The Best of Warren Zevon—A Quiet Normal Life (1976–1982)
Asylum 9 60503-2 (47:34)   [A]
Zevon's personal vision reveals a style more akin to pulp detective fiction than pop lyrics, redeemed by a bizarre, literate sense of humor. Additionally, he has

captured the sun/smog-drenched seamy decadence of lotus land more effectively than any other L.A. habitué. This four-teen-song collection, which opens with his one quasi-hit, "Werewolves of London," is an excellent overview of a promising, flawed career that has pro-duced more than a few brilliant and beautiful moments ("Desperados Under the Eaves" and "Accidently Like A Mar-tyr"). The compilation also includes the original version of Zevon's composition, "Poor, Poor, Pitiful Me" which, in itself, should be enough to keep Linda Ronstadt in Gilbert & Sullivan for the rest of her natural life. The sound varies, but overall, is somewhat compressed, roughly equivalent to that of a dynamic LP.

### Transverse City (1989)
Virgin 91060-2 (41:40)   **[C + ]**
Zevon has a rep for chasing his demons with booze, but in recent years he's sup-posedly escaped the habit, and that may be so, but the demons have taken over in *Transverse City.* These are the over-technical, overchemically dependent societies' demons, and Zevon brings them to throbbing reality. Unfortunately, this time he has little to add to previous indictments of our homogenized, self-indulgent society. The twisted lyrical bent that makes much of his earlier work memorable is sadly missing from *Transverse City.* There's a lush grunge to the instrumental backing, but even that lacks the melodic and textural variety that enhanced his better outings. This is a bit surprising, given his all-star sup-porting lineup: Jerry Garcia, David Gilmour, Chick Corea, Neil Young, Jorma Kaukoren, Jack Casady, and Ben-mont Tench. Zevon has not totally lost his mordant charm, and "Run Straight Down" almost realizes its dire vision, but there's a lot of talent just going through the motions here. The sound is adequate by current commercial stan-dards, but is nothing extraordinary.

# COLLECTIONS

**Alligator Stomp (Cajuns Zydeco Classics)**
**(1990 compilation release date)**
Rhino R2 70946 (48:45)  **[B + ]**
Cajun music traces its country romance
to the transplanted French, who originally settled in Canada only to be driven
by the British to Louisiana. Once in
bayou country, it rapidly assimilated
black/Creole influences with their Afro-
Caribbean rhythmic underpinnings, ultimately to evolve into zydeco. As heard
today, the stately waltz tempos are often
supplanted with inflections of R&B,
swamp rock, and basic blues. The heady
result is nonpareil party music nicely
captured on this, another first-rate
Rhino compilation disc. Its eighteen
selections include the hit "My Toot-Toot"
by Rockin' Sidney, and proceed through
a fairly comprehensive roster of stalwarts, old and new, including Queen
Ida, Cleveland Crochet, Jo-El Sonnier,
Beausoliel, and the father of it all, Clifton
Chenier. Given the various vintages of
the recordings, Rhino, as always, distin-
guishes its product with quality sound,
although the age and technological limitations of the older material remain
evident in sometimes compressed, occasionally harsh moments. Overall, a fine
addition to the collection of anyone
interested in a cross-section of American
pop music. As the liner notes say: "Put
this CD on, turn it up loud, and let the
good times roll—*bon ton roulet*!"

**Atlantic Rhythm & Blues**
Other than Motown, which literally created the form of music it recorded and so
effectively marketed, no other major
American record company was more
closely associated with a specific seg-
ment of American popular music than
was Atlantic Records in the R&B field
from the end of World War II to the early
seventies. Each of the CDs in this series
essentially covers a double-volume LP
that constituted a seven-volume landmark release by this company in 1985.

**Atlantic Rhythm & Blues (1947–1952)**
47–74 Volume 1; Atlantic 781293-2
(73:27)  **[B + ]**
We're talking prehistoric roots material
here, but up the tempo and electrify the
instrumentation and it wouldn't sound
alien to any true rock fan. As has to be
expected with material of this vintage,
the sound, while unexpectedly clean,
certainly reflects its age in its limited
dynamic range. If you're interested in
where it all began, this is a large part of
the story.

**Atlantic Rhythm & Blues (1952–1955)**
47–74 Volume 2; Atlantic 781294-2 (73:37)  **[A]**
Rarities and classics by the artists and
groups who were dominating black pop
music when it was serving as an inspiration to those who would explode the
musical world (and pop culture) with

rock & roll. Contains first-rate works by giants like Joe Turner, Laverne Baker, Clyde McPhatter, and Ray Charles, among others. The sound is generally clean and clear, but obviously compressed.

### Atlantic Rhythm & Blues (1955–1958)
47–74 Volume 3; Atlantic 781295-2
(71:27)   [A–]
Black musical history just pours out of these compact discs. Included are the Coasters' influential classics (the masterworks of Leiber and Stoller, two of rock's largely unsung writing and production pioneers), along with Chuck Willis, who receives merited attention, and later works by artists whose earlier efforts are chronicled on the preceding volume of this essential series. As these recordings move forward in time, there is a notable improvement in the dynamic range on these well-produced vintage efforts.

### Atlantic Rhythm & Blues (1956–1962)
47–74 Volume 4; Atlantic 81296-2
(71:25)   [A+]
With this volume, Atlantic enters its golden decade. This was the vintage era for groups like the Coasters, whose musical vignettes remain among the most enduring and influential sounds of the times; and the Drifters, and their smooth soul lead, Ben E. King (whose "Young Boy Blues" is one of the many highlights on this recording). The sound, which has a few noticeable glitches, generally is done with quality and ever-improving dynamic enhancement.

### Atlantic Rhythm and Blues (1962–1966)
47–74 Volume 5; Atlantic 7 81297-2
(72:45)   [A]
Volume 5 of this essential series covers R&B hits of such well-known acts as the Drifters, Otis Redding, Sam & Dave, Percy Sledge, and Wilson Pickett, as well as gems by lesser-knowns: Barbara

Lewis, Chris Kenner, and Don Covay. It adds up to twenty-six classic selections representative of the best of this type of material from an era when it was a vibrant musical form. The sound, while varying, is generally clean, but is clearly reflective of the limitations inherent in masters of this age, including some too-apparent hiss on certain cuts. Unfortunately, Atlantic did not extend the same concern for recording qualities as they did on artists and repertoire. It's still a wonderful package, superior soundwise to the LP counterparts.

### Atlantic Rhythm and Blues (1966–1969)
47–74 Volume 6; Atlantic 7 81298-2
(73:15)   [A+]
The twenty-five selections provide a fair sampling of Aretha "Lady Soul" Franklin's most popular recordings, as well as hits by Sam & Dave, Wilson Pickett, Joe Tex, and Otis Redding, among others. This is the cream of the great soul music explosion of the late sixties. The sound, which is similar to that described on Volume 5 of this series, is a bit more dynamic and spacious than that heard on the earlier volumes.

### Atlantic Soul Classics (1954–1968)
Warner Special Products 9-27601-2 (44:41)   [A]
A curious fifteen-selection sampling from the great Atlantic R&B catalog which is fairly comprehensively covered in the multivolume *Atlantic Rhythm & Blues (1947–74)* series reviewed earlier. You really can't complain about the included selections, which encompass many of the greats: Aretha, Otis, Sam & Dave, the Coasters, the Drifters, Ray Charles, Wilson Pickett, and other less successful but nonetheless talented artists from what was once known as the chitlin' circuit. While care has been taken to clean up the sound, which varies with each cut, overall, it does reflect

the compression inherent in most analog source material from this era.

## Beach Classics (1961–1965)

Dunhill Compact Classics D2S030 (46:01)  **[B]**
Surfing has been a sustaining American subculture for some time, and God knows that in these homogenous times we need as many subcultures as we can find. Besides that, everyone needs at least one CD version of Minneapolis's own surf band, the Trashmans' classic "Surfin' Bird" (with apologies to the Rivingtons). Seriously, if the surf sound has any appeal (or if you just happen to like somewhat monotonous bass-heavy, sax-voiced instrumentals), this is a fun collection of some offbeat classics. From Dick Dale (the granddaddy of it all) to the Beach Boys, with a lot of one-hit wonders along the way, this is a nice overview of some of pop's more mindlessly appealing California sounds, but sadly without Jan & Dean. Dunhill has come up with a clean, warm digital sound that doesn't overwhelm the listener with its dynamics, but clearly reflects the benefits of CD technology.

## The Best of Doo-Wop Ballads (1954–1961)

Rhino R2 75763 (51:38)  **[A + ]**
These seminal recordings of the classic doo-wop groups of the fifties and early sixties (Dion & the Belmonts, the Dells, the Moonglows, the Crests, and the Penguins, among others) simply have never sounded better. This quasi-a cappella approach to R&B was a major force in roots-rock sounds, and interpreted by these talents it delights even after repeated listenings. Rhino sets the standards by which reissue packages must be measured, from Bill Liebowitz's brief but informative liner notes to Bill Inglot's and Ken Perry's sonic miracles, this disc allows you to hold an era in your hands.

## The Best of Doo-Wop Uptempo (1954–1963)

Rhino R275764 (43:51)  **[B + ]**
A continuation of Rhino's *Best of Doo-Wop Ballads,* so my comments on that compilation generally apply. The major difference is a decline in the quality of the selections overall, but *Uptempo* is not without its indispensables: the Silhouettes' "Get a Job," the Crows' "Gee," and the Marcels' "Blue Moon," among them. If *Ballads* didn't quite satisfy your appetite for these joyous sounds, you won't be disappointed with this follow-up. Again, the sound on the eighteen tracks, many of which can be found on other compilations, is consistently the best available.

## The Best of Sun Rockabilly (1953–1959)

CD Charly 16 (50:33)  **[A]**
Further proof of Sun Studios' claim as the birthplace of rock & roll. There is a sampling by the Studios' acknowledged giants, Jerry Lee Lewis, Carl Perkins, and Roy Orbison, but the contributions of such lesser-knowns as Billy Riley, Warren Smith, the Miller Sisters, Onie Wheeler, and Malcolm Yelvington equal or exceed much of Sun's better-known output. This was the music that didn't make it to New York or Los Angeles—you had to drop by a roadside tavern on a Saturday night for a couple of cold ones to really appreciate how much it comprised an integral part of the fabric of the lives of small-town America. If the sounds weren't enough, which they are, the liner notes are comprehensive, adding to the quality of the overall package. The sound varies among the cuts, as expected, but with two or three noticeable exceptions, the overall quality is extremely strong for material of this vintage.

## Soundtrack: The Big Chill (1983)
Motown MCD06120 MD (43:40)  **[B +]**
Obviously, this material, encompassing numerous Motown classics plus other familiar sixties hits—Three Dog Night's "Joy to the World" and Procol Harum's "Whiter Shade of Pale"—is marvelously appealing. The movie and its soundtrack are credited with much of the sixties musical revival that has ultimately resulted in classic rock formats on many FM stations. The sound is not the equal of the music, and it varies from selection to selection. While some cuts are well recorded, others, like Marvin Gaye's signature "I Heard it Through the Grapevine," are plagued by excessive hiss. Overall, the sound of the disc is thin and compressed, however, excessive distortion is generally avoided.

## Billboard Top R&B Hits 1971 (1971)
Rhino R2 70659 (34:36)  **[B +]**
This series is a safe bet if a majority of the included selections strike your fancy. This year's edition is highlighted by Marvin Gaye's "What's Going On" (the best-sounding version besides the one on Motown's *The Marvin Gaye Collection*), Aretha Franklin's hot version of "Spanish Harlem," and Betty Wright's workin' "Clean Up Woman." The rest is given over to the syrupy, confessional ballads that charted that year.

## Billboard Top R&B Hits 1972 (1972)
Rhino R270660 (35:34)  **[A]**
Bargain-priced music presented with better sonics than you've ever heard—another prime example of Rhino's savvy catalog marketing. This disc boasts Al Green's "Let's Stay Together," the Staples' "I'll Take You There," Harold Melvin and the Blue Notes' "If You Don't Know Me By Now," James Brown's "Get Out the Good Foot (Part 1)," and the only currently available CD version (to my knowledge) of Billy Paul's classic "Me and Mrs. Jones"—that's reason enough to own it.

## The British Invasion—The History of British Rock
**Vol. 1 (1963–1965)**
Rhino R2 70319 (47:22)  **[B]**
**Vol. 2 (1964–1965)**
Rhino R2 70320 (50:13)  **[C]**
**Vol. 3 (1964–1966)**
Rhino R2 70321 (51:01)  **[C +]**
The beachhead was established on February 9, 1964, the night the Beatles conquered America on "The Ed Sullivan Show." They opened a musical door to an audience that had largely forgotten the energy of the birth of rock & roll less than a decade before—an America that was still struggling with the void of JFK's recent assassination. And the bands of Britain came pouring in—regurgitating America's music but capturing the ears of a turbulent decade. While not comprehensive, this series maintains the very high standards Rhino has brought to their outstanding CD catalog—terrific sound and informative packaging. A large sampling of first-rate material has been assembled, performed by the Kinks, the Zombies, the Searchers, Gerry & the Pacemakers, Freddie & the Dreamers, Peter & Gordon, Manfred Mann, the Yardbirds, Donovan, Chad & Jeremy, the Hollies, the Troggs, Billy J. Kramer and the Dakotas, the Swinging Blue Jeans, and others. The sound is uniformly improved over the vinyl originals.

## Class of '55 (Carl Perkins, Jerry Lee Lewis, Roy Orbison, Johnny Cash)
## Memphis Rock & Roll Home Coming (1986)
Polygram 830 002-2 M-1 (37:12)  **[B]**
Legendary is the operative word for this Chips Moman-inspired recorded gathering, thirty years after the fact, of four of

the original Sun artists that helped begin it all in the first place. They all take a turn (singly and together) at some new compositions and some classics (Jerry Lee Lewis's rendition of "Sixteen Candles" being the most successful), all with a deep bow to the King departed, and often with obvious feeling. The spark has not gone out, but the fire has been banked now for a few years. All in all, *Class Of '55* offers more than just nostalgia, and it was obviously a meaningful moment for all involved (and that included John Fogerty and Dave Edmunds). The sound is clear and clean, though lacking somewhat in separation and evidencing some minimal compression.

**Elvis Classics (1955–1965)**
P-Vine PCD-2517 (71:07)   **[C]**
The idea behind this Japanese import was first-rate—compile the original performances of the King's earliest and strongest material. The twenty-six selections include Arthur Big Boy Crudrup's "That's All Right" (Elvis's first release), Kokomo Arnold's "Milk Cow Blues," Arthur Gunter's "Baby Let's Play House," and almost all the important others. Sadly, as is the case with too many Japanese compilations of older American material, the CD sounds like it was mastered from original well-worn 45s. It is that very poor sound quality that diminishes this collection, because the performances are often powerful and it is fascinating to see how closely Presley often adhered to the nuances of original vocals.

**Every Day is a Holly Day (1989)**
Emerg EMD 9465 (42:43)   **[B–]**
Seventeen regional, lesser-known artists provide covers of Buddy Holly classics as well as songs about this highly influential early original. They succeed in

proving the enduring quality of Holly's deceptively simple art, but that's about it. Probably aimed at the devout Holly fan, who shouldn't be offended, but won't be enlightened, either. The sound quality varies from cut to cut; none are extraordinary and none are regrettable. If you're looking for something by Tav Falco's Panther Burns, your search is over.

**Folkways: A Vision Shared (A Tribute to Woody Guthrie and Leadbelly) (1988)**
Columbia CK44034 (46:30)   **[A–]**
Among the generation of artists who preceded the rock era, Woody Guthrie and Leadbelly, in terms of their political stance and popular appeal, were among the most influential. Their work became influential in large part through their recordings on the infamous Folkways label. So it was perfectly natural that some of rock's and country's current legends—Bob Dylan, Little Richard, Bruce Springsteen, Willie Nelson, and Emmylou Harris, among others—would come forward for this project to raise funds for the Smithsonian to acquire the Folkways catalog. Whether it's the music, the sentiment, or both, it inspired some classic performances, notably Dylan's throwback version of "Pretty Boy Floyd" and Taj Mahal's powerful "The Bourgeois Blues." Actually, with the exception of Brian Wilson's weird "Goodnight Irene," all the remaining tracks have something to recommend them. Meaningful music with intensity, feeling, and respect—it all adds up to a worthwhile package. Adding to it is generally first-quality sound.

**Great Songs Written by Holland-Dozier-Holland (mid/late sixties)**
Motown MCD06138MD (60:08)   **[A+]**
Motown has been as creative as any record company in the repackaging of their classic hits for the CD market (they

pioneered the two-fer concept—two albums on one disc). The Composer Series, out of which this package arises, rightfully focuses on the men and women behind the scenes who had so much to do with the label's success. Holland-Dozier-Holland, working with the Supremes, the Four Tops, Marvin Gaye, and Martha Reeves, were the sonic architects of many of Motown's contributions to the sixties Hit Parade, and these twenty cuts are representative of the best pop music of the times, highlighted by the big multi-instrumental productions for which this team was duly noted. The sound is pretty clean (especially for Motown), but has a tendency toward overbrightness, particularly on the female vocals.

### Groove'n'Grind—'50s and '60s Dance Hits (1957–1967)
Rhino R2 70992 (45:54)   **[B +]**
The perfect party disc for the over-forty crowd, it includes "The Stroll" from 1957, "Funky Broadway-Part 1" from 1967, and sixteen dance hits from the ten years between—there's Little Eva's "Locomotion," Chubby Checker's "Twist," plus "The Monkey Time," "Cool Jerk," and "The Madison," all in their original versions and all in Rhino's much better-than-average digital sound. This one's not for listenin', it's about shakin' your money maker—and shake it does.

### Heartbeat Reggae (seventies/eighties)
Ryko RCD219 (64:14)   **[B +]**
A first-rate compilation of seventies and eighties reggae and dub material from a variety of reputable practitioners of Jamaica's principal cultural export to the modern Third World. Among the artists included: Big Youth, Black Uhuru, Burning Spear, Gregory Isaacs, the Mighty Diamonds, Mutabaruka, and Lee

"Scratch" Perry, all rendered in Ryko's generally first-quality digital sound.

### Highs of the '60s
Warner Special Products 9-27607-2 (53:52)   **[B]**
With the advent of the sixties, the democratic roots of rock & roll resulted in the emergence of bands from all over the place—after all, this was everyman's music; so, theoretically, every man and every woman could make it. All of this resulted in a number of regional acts that became one-hit wonders, often generically described as psychedelic garage-band music. This strange assemblage of material includes a number of genuine classics of the form by such enduring artists as the Kingsmen, Count Five, Shadows of Knight, Blue Cheer, and the Seeds. Actually, the "hits" by these groups were often classic rock & roll imbued with raw, driving energy, and many are included here. Strangely, also included are the Association, the Knickerbockers, the Beau Brummels, and surf music from the Marketts whose selections add nothing, and really dilute the rough edge that gives the other cuts stature. The sound is not as bad as one might expect considering the primitive sources and this label's generally poor attention to digital conversions.

### Hits From the Legendary Vee Jay Records (1953–1966)
Motown MCD06215MD (68:04)   **[B +]**
Probably a majority of record buyers pay scant attention to the label on which a recording is released—the only practical question being, is it readily available? If that is an accurate assumption, it's regrettable, because the great independent record companies of the fifties and sixties were truly as responsible for the creation of rock & roll as the performers whose work they merchandised and popularized. Sun, Atlantic, Chess, Stax,

Vee Jay—these names belong in the Rock & Roll Hall of Fame along with Presley, Berry, etc. Vee Jay lasted thirteen years, from its founding in 1953 in Gary, Indiana, to its bankruptcy in 1966. Originally conceived as a black gospel label, it ultimately provided some of the fifties' best black doo-wop sounds, plus several name black artists (Jerry Butler and Betty Everett), not to mention blues greats John Lee Hooker and Jimmy Reed. All this fine material (exclusive of gospel recordings) is effectively sampled on this historic release. As usual, production values vary markedly from cut to cut, but overall, these recordings are sonically the best renditions available of this fine material. The package is enhanced by strong liner information, making this a wholly worthwhile compilation.

**The Indestructable Beat of Soweto (1981–1984)**
Shanachie SH43033 (45:54)  **[A + ]**
This compilation of South African township jive leaves no doubt as to Paul Simon's acknowledged inspiration for his classic *Graceland.* A dozen cuts by the exuberant musicians who make some of the most joyously compelling music being played anywhere. It's irresistible. The sound, while a bit compressed, is still consistently first-rate.

**Soundtrack: La Bamba (Los Lobos, Bo Diddley, Howard Huntsberry, Brian Setzer, and Marshall Crenshaw) (1987)**
Slash/Warner Bros. 25605 2 (31:26)  **[A]**
Almost thirty years ago, seventeen-year-old Ritchie Valens came out of the large Los Angeles Mexican-American community to achieve national celebrity in the second wave of fifties rock & roll. "La Bamba," "Come On, Let's Go," and "Donna" rocketed him to fame—a small plane, Buddy Holly, The Big Bopper, and

a snowy night in Iowa established his epitaph: "The day the music died." 1987 brought the movie version of this tragically brief story with Los Lobos paying musical homage to an acknowledged inspiration with intensity and integrity. While the eight cuts performed by Los Lobos are the core of the recording, the remainder isn't filler by any means. Bo Diddley's "Who Do You Love" by itself is almost worth the price of admission, and the Crenshaw, Setzer, and Huntsberry covers, particularly the latter doing Jackie Wilson's "Lonely Teardrops," maintain the excellent musical standards established by Los Lobos. The sound on this all-digital disc is a major plus: clean, dynamic, and spacious.

**More Reggae Music (sixties/eighties)**
Sound REG CD5 (59:30)  **[C + ]**
Aptly titled, this sixteen-song set includes efforts by Bob Marley and the Wailers, UB40, Jimmy Cliff, Desmond Dekker, Peter Tosh, and Yellowman. Both the sound and musical quality vary substantially. Of the included classics, Dekker's "Israelites" and "You Can Get It if You Really Want It" both suffer from excessive hiss and bad distortion, as does Cliff's "Many Rivers to Cross;" the sound quality of the remainder is pretty good, given some compression and fairly frequent hiss.

**Nuggets (A Classic Collection from the Psychedelic Sixties) (1964–1969)**
Rhino RNCD 75892 (50:20)  **[A]**
Call them one-hit wonders. Their music has been labeled trash rock, garage band, and sixties psychedelia, but under any name, it's indispensable to rock's indispensable decade. When the music rose to supremacy in the sixties, it brought with it literally hordes of local bands effecting the image and lifestyle of the era's musical heroes. Some of them

had their cosmic moments, which is what this disc is all about. If the Troggs, the Seeds, "Psychotic Reaction," the Nazz, or "Journey to the Center of the Mind" strike any responsive chords, then this is a must CD; if all of the above sounds like a foreign tongue and you want to check out some of the sixties' sleazier successes, climb aboard; it's a worthwhile trip. Again, Bill Inglot's meticulous production values result in a wondrous revitalization of original Chevy recordings. It all works—works because it's infused with the joyous spirit of rock & roll.

**Oldies But Goodies Volume 3 (1956–1975)**
OSCD8853 (45:35)
**Volume 4 (1955–1969)**
OSCD8854 (44:12)
**Volume 5 (1951–1971)**
OSCD8855 (43:24)
**Volume 6 (1956–1965)**
OSCD8856 (36:46)
**Volume 9 (1958–1967)**
OSCD8859 (39:54)
**Volume 10 (1955–1973)**
OSCD8860 (44:53)
**Volume 11 (1957–1974)**
OSCD8861 (43:54)
**Volume 14 (1955–1978)**
OSCD8864 (49:59)
**Volume 15 (1963–1980)**
OSCD8865 (45:13)   **[B–]**
This series almost defies description in terms of the crazy quilt admixture of selections, the sequencing of the same, and the issuing sequence of the volumes themselves (*Oldies But Goodies* have been available as LP compilations for years). The material covered runs the gamut from the fifties through the seventies, but a majority of the work included is from the sixties. The collection is the brainchild of Art Laboe, "a disc jockey from L.A. who shares your special memories," and maybe that's all the explanation required. Laboe provides liner notes including release dates of each cut and chart position attained, if the cut ever charted. But most of the material is familiar, at least to those over thirty-five or forty. Other than idiosyncrasies evidenced in the juxtaposition of eras and artists, what sets this series apart is the sound. A part of the digital conversion process on this series involves a patented enhancement process dubbed FDS that adds heightened dynamics to much of the material. Frequently, the versions of popular cuts included on the *Oldies But Goodies* CDs represent the best sonic examples of the material available from any CD source. It's difficult to compare the volumes. Suffice it to say that the material covered on any given disc is generally appealing, so if you like the included songs, you won't be disappointed with the recording.

**The Original Rock & Roll Hits of the '50s Volume 1**
Roulette RCD 58001 (40:49)   **[B]**
Included are the Crows, Orioles, Little Anthony and the Imperials, the Flamingos, and Frankie Lyman and the Teenagers—primarily one-or two-hit doo-wop wonders who left a legacy of music based on black street corner harmonies—simple and accessible. Perhaps it's pure nostalgia, yet these songs remain attractive to this day. Given that many of these sixteen recordings were essentially one-shot efforts done on less than state-of-the-art equipment, this compilation's sound qualities are impressive, if subject to certain limitations.

**The Original Rock & Roll Hits of the '50s Volume 2**
Roulette RCD 58002 (40:24)   **[B +]**
Doo-wop was an essential ingredient in the heady fifties musical mix that was distilled into rock & roll. This compila-

tion features first-rate examples by some fine purveyors of those street-corner harmonies that have proved so enduring. In addition, included are some offbeat classics like Wilbur Harrison's "Kansas City." The sound, while frequently obviously compressed and occasionally flawed, is pretty good, given the original sources. The total value of this package would be enhanced with decent liner notes.

### Out of the Blue
Ryko RCD20003 (62:19)   [A–]
A little zydeco, a lot of blues and R&B; it all boils down to over an hour of good times/bad times Saturday night roadhouse music in first-quality digital sound. The seventeen selections include works by Buckwheat Zydeco, the Night Hawks, Roomfull of Blues, George Thorogood, John Hammond, Duke Robillard & the Pleasure Kings, Clarence Gatemouth Brown, Johnny Copeland, and Solomon Burke.

### Soundtrack: Pump Up the Volume (1990)
MCA MCAD8039 (47:15)   [A–]
With *Pump Up the Volume* writer-director Allen Moyle and star Christian Slater have created the first great teenage cult-classic film of the nineties. One of the reasons for the movie's potent impact is its soundtrack. While the film uses abbreviated versions of the soundtrack material, the music often provides the focus rather than the background. These eleven songs provide an excellent overview of current alternative rock. Among the included participants are Concrete Blonde, whose chilling version of Leonard Cohen's "Everybody Knows" is one of the highlights, Ivan Neville, the Pixies, Sonic Youth, Cowboy Junkies, and Above the Law, whose "Freedom of Speech" captures one of the film's central tenets with brutal directness. The sound quality is generally consistent

and first-rate. If you liked the movie, you'll love the soundtrack, and if you missed the movie, catch up—rent it.

### Red Hot & Blue (1990)
Chrysalis F2-21799 (77:55)   [A]
This fascinating compilation by twenty-four contemporary artists performing twenty-two Cole Porter songs was assembled to benefit AIDS research and care through heightened awareness and financial support. Conceptually intriguing, the performances range from the sublime (Lisa Stansfield's "Down in the Depths") to the ridiculous (Tom Waits's "It's All Right With Me"). As might be expected with ballad material, the generally straighter interpretations by the female artists—Sinead O'Connor, Annie Lennox, and k.d. lang, among others—set the tone of the recording. But it is the revisionism of Neneh Cherry's "I've Got You Under My Skin" that sets off real sparks, capturing the essence of the project with chilling effectiveness. The Jungle Brothers provide a rap reading of "I Get a Kick" that is as direct in its message as Porter was subtle with his. The Neville Brothers employ Aaron's ballad prowess for a great rendition of "In the Still of the Night," while Fine Young Cannibals update "Love For Sale." Not all is balladry; David Byrne brings his current World Beat preoccupations to bear on "Don't Fence Me In" to humorous effect, and Erasure's version of "Too Darn Hot" leaves that chestnut mostly intact but freshly minted. In a time when pop/rock/rap music is being dragged through legislatures and courtrooms by the forces of suppression, it may be too easy to overenthusiastically embrace each effort of good citizenship the industry makes. Yet the fact remains that no other current art form has as consistently and effectively dealt with real human concerns—even in the face

of its public vilification. Happily, *Red Hot & Blue* succeeds on more than ideological levels. By publicly verifying Porter's homosexuality, it may also cause some more mature listeners, for whom his lyrics have for so long accurately expressed feelings of love and romance, to gain a more compassionate insight into the gay experience. While it is doubtful you'll like every one of the covers, the majority should appeal to anyone with a fondness for great pop music lovingly performed. The sound quality is first-rate throughout, and is extraordinary in the intimacy of O'Connor's "You Do Something To Me" and the dynamism of Aztec Camera's "Do I Love You."

### Red Hot & Blue (1990)
Mobile Fidelity UDCD 542 (77:57)   [A]
This gold ultradisc version of the Cole Porter-based AIDS benefit recording is overall a sonic improvement on the standard issue release, adding richness and clarity, but is a microscope of sorts, revealing flaws along with enhancing the positive. Thus, the tape hiss on "Every Time We Say Goodbye" is more evident, and the uneven production qualities among the tracks are emphasized.

### Rhythm & Blues House Party (1952–1960)
Ace CDCH 179 (44:20)   [B]
If you ever wondered why the young Jerry Lee Lewis and other wilder Southern prerockers of the fifties spent their Saturday nights in the "off limits" black clubs on the wrong side of town, give this disc a spin. The sounds are a little rough and harsh, but the energy and message are clear—this ain't no sock hop.

### Rhythm Come Forward (sixties/seventies)
Columbia CK39472 (39:40)   [C+]
The nine reggae selections include works from Bob Marley and Peter Tosh to Aswad and Jimmy Cliff, although none of them are the best material from these artists. The Marley cuts are marred by overly bright sound, and the rest of it varies from LP quality to fairly impressive sound (if not content). A decent, but far from outstanding, collection.

### Rock & Roll The Early Days (early/mid-fifties)
RCA PCD1-5463 (29:33)   [A+]
The quality of the production and the innate power, not to mention historic importance, of its musical contents overcome the embarrassingly short playing time (about forty percent of the CD's capacity) of this essential disc. Real roots, presented as effectively as the medium and the source material will allow. These are the folks that flipped the switch and turned the lights on for everybody! (Another Greg Geller milestone.)

### The Soul of New Orleans (fifties/sixties)
CD Charly 14 (61:15)   [A+]
From Fats Domino to Little Richard, the musical heritage of the Crescent City (a heady mixture of African, Caribbean, and Cajun influences) has provided the source of some of this country's best pop music of the last thirty years. This excellent collection, featuring some of the City's premier sixties local stars (Lee Dorsey, Robert Parker, Aaron Neville, the Meters, the Dixie Cups, and Hughie "Piano" Smith, among others) is a wonderful summary of the upbeat, polyrhythmic sound clearly identifiable with New Orleans. This is music that inspired a lot of rock hits. While the age of the source material is apparent on the CD,

this is one of the better sixties compilations in terms of sound quality.

### Soul Shots: A Collection of Sixties Soul Classics (1962–1969)
Rhino R2 75774 (53:36)   **[A]**
Rhino has built a sizable industry through the creative repackaging of vintage material. *Soul Shots* is a great example of why the concept has been so effective. The sixties were soul's golden age and these eighteen tracks are evidence of what made it so: James Brown's "I Got You (I Feel Good)," Fontella Bass's "Rescue Me" (with its wondrous bass line), Billy Stewart's, "Summertime," James & Bobby Purify's "I'm Your Puppet," J.J. Jackson's "But It's Alright," and the Intruders' "Cowboys to Girls." While there are some pretty esoteric inclusions (Larry Williams's and Johnny Watson's "Two For the Price of One"), the overall quality is first-rate. As always, the care Rhino takes in its digital remastering shines through, bringing consistently excellent sonics to vintage material.

### Soul Shots, Volume 2 (1961–1969)
Rhino R2-75770 (52:28)   **[B + ]**
The material is a little slicker and more ballad-oriented (more strings) than the first volume of this excellent series, because it was drawn primarily from the last half of the decade when Motown influences were, frankly, unavoidable. But any package remastered by Bill Inglott and Ken Perry that provides historic, insightful liner notes and goodies like Johnnie Taylor's "Who's Making Love," The Dells' "Oh, What a Night," Booker T & the MG's "Time Is Tight," Brenton Woods's "The Ooogum Boogum Song," and Major Lance's "The Monkey Time" can't be ignored. As is generally the case with Rhino, the sound can't be beat.

### Soul Shots: A Collection of Sixties Soul Classics, Vol. 3 (1989)
Rhino R2 75757 (48:04)   **[B + ]**
By the time you get to the third volume of this well-chosen Rhino compilation, the tracks become more obscure. Even though the overall material lacks the strength and consistency of Volumes 1 and 2, the performances, overall, still reflect the dynamic drive and diversity of the classic R&B sounds of a classic decade. Highlights include the Capitols' "Cool Jerk," Brenton Wood's "Gimme Little Sign," the Sweet Inspirations' "Sweet Inspiration," James and Bobbie Purify's "Let Love Come Between Us," and the breathtaking "I'm So Proud" by Curtis Mayfield and the Impressions. Begin with the first volume in the series, and if you still want more, Volume 3 won't disappoint; in fact, you'll probably discover some new favorites. The sound reflects its analog origins, but Rhino does well with it; for the most part, everything sounds better than ever.

### Soundtrack: Stand By Me (1986)
Atlantic 781677-2 (23:36)   **[C + ]**
Ten brief examples of classic fifties pop performed by Jerry Lee, Buddy Holly, the Del Vikings, Silhouettes, etc. The tunes are first-rate, the sound quality generally the same, but twenty-three minutes of music when the disc can deliver three times that amount simply amounts to a rip-off.

### Stax Greatest Hits (1968–1974)
Special Import (Fantasy) JCD-702-1110 (65:20)   **[B]**
In the late sixties and the early seventies—slightly pre-disco times—black popular music began to soften as the raw power of the earlier R&B influence began to give way to a sleeker, more urban pop sound that mirrored changes in the black listening audience. Stax led

the move with the sounds captured here—the Dramatics, Isaac Hayes, and Johnny Taylor epitomized the later Stax product. Today, its primary relevance is historical, but it still provides pleasant listening. Included on this compilation are some cuts that retain the drive of prior mainstream black music—the Staple Singers' "Respect Yourself," Rufus Thomas's wonderful "Do the Funky Chicken," and Little Milton's "That's What Love Will Make You Do." It should be noted that this disc is a Japanese import and the sound it provides is first-rate—clean, crisp, and dynamic.

### Storytellers: Singers & Songwriters (late sixties/early seventies)
Warner Special Products 9-27615-2 (69:28) **[B]**
Despite the corny title, this is a pretty tolerable collection; eighteen songs by the likes of Joni Mitchell, James Taylor, Arlo Guthrie, Tom Waits, John Prine, Randy Newman, Judy Collins, John Sebastian, Tom Rush, Steve Goodman, Tom Paxton, Jerry Jeff Walker, Phil Ochs, and various and sundry others. In most cases, the song performed by each is familiar and representative. As was inevitable, the sound quality is erratic; the nadir being the hiss afflicting Prine's "Sandstone," and (sadly) Newman's "I Think It's Going to Rain Today," while Tom Rush's "Circle Game" is a sonic wonder. The rest of the cuts sound OK; not great, not awful, more like lightly compressed, relatively clean LPs. A fair sampler of contemporary folkish sounds.

### The Sun Story (1953–1959)
Rhino RNCD75884 (47:29) **[A+]**
Combine the Sun Studios' soundtrack of hits (and classic near-misses) recorded between 1953 and 1959 by the likes of Elvis, Jerry Lee, Carl Perkins, and Johnny Cash among others, with the digital artistry of Rhino's Bill Inglot, and

the magic with which caring, meticulous digital reproduction can imbue historical material is little short of amazing. This disc is essential to any comprehensive rock & roll collection.

### Toga Rock (1962–1968)
Dunhill DZ5029 (42:48) **[A+]**
Despite the insultingly silly title and cover, this turns out to be one of the better sixties compilation CDs (and it is all still great party music). A first-rate collection of elbow-bending, hip-shaking "standards" ("Louie, Louie," "Woolly Bully," "Mony, Mony," "Devil With a Blue Dress" . . . you get the idea) with high-quality sound. Dunhill has been a company that has respected the permanent nature of the disc by taking the time to do careful digital conversions from the cleanest, least manipulated masters available, and the audio payoff comes through loud and clear.

### 20 Party Classics (1960s)
Warner Special Products 9-27602-2 (49:26) **[D]**
Whoever chose the twenty included selections deserves a pat on the back— whoever did the digital mastering deserves a kick in the ass. 'Nuff said.

### More Party Classics (1960s)
Warner Special Products 9-27670-2 (43:20) **[C+]**
This time out the material is not as consistently strong. The sound quality is generally improved, although still far from what it might be. Overall, a slightly better package, but there are much better sixties collections.

### 20 Rockabilly Classics (1956–1960)
MCA 5935 (44:37) **[B]**
Rockabilly, rock & roll's first form, is very pure, very simple music both in terms of its instrumentation and lyrical content. By adhering to a highly defined format, this music maintains its purity,

but at the expense of its scope. This fascinating collection, which includes Dale Hawkin's "Suzie-Q," as well as work by Buddy Holly, Brenda Lee, Webb Pierce, Johnny Burnette, and Billy Lee Riley, is made up of obscure offerings by unknowns whose fame was primarily regional, at best. But names or not, these artists all possess a naive intensity that infuses their music with an energy that endures a quarter of a century later. The sound is generally surprisingly clean and clear, without a great deal of dynamic or spatial enhancement. The notes, though brief, are factual and informative.

### Vintage Music Volumes I & II (1955–1959)
MCA MCAD 5777 JVC509 (52:47)   [B + ]
From Chuck Berry's "Maybellene" to Pat Boone's "Love Letters in the Sand," this well-produced collection is an excellent sonic window on fifties rock radio—it's a little bit of doo-wop, some Buddy Holly, and other and sundry classics. While the admixture of selections is a bit random, the material covered generally highlights well-known hits from this era, and MCA's usual attention to the sound quality of its digital transfers makes this one of the better fifties rock & roll collections.

### Vintage Music Volumes III & IV (1954–1959)
MCA MCAD5778 JVC510 (49:27)   [B–]
The above comments regarding the first disc in this series (Volumes I & II) are generally applicable here, except that the material included (aside from the Buddy Holly and Chuck Berry cuts, all available on artist's collection) is generally weaker than that included on the first disc.

### The Vocal Group Collection (The Platters, the Penguins, Del Vikings, Dan Leers) (1950s)
Mercury 830283-2 M-1 (69:22)   [D]
Second-rate material from first-rate groups combined with the best work of second-best groups still adds up to a pretty boring outing. The sound quality, which varies, is generally clean, but compressed.

### Wonderwomen (History of the Girl Group Sound) (late fifties/early sixties)
Rhino RNCD 75891 (41:16)   [B + ]
During the early-to-mid sixties, a strain of pop/rock was established that has garnered the tacky title "girl group sound." It is, however, descriptive. Probably founded by the Shirelles (included here), the form was popularized by Phil "Wall of Sound" Spector with his grandiose productions behind the likes of the Crystals and Ronettes (*not* included here). Actually, these sounds represent an interesting bridge between a standard pop form that dominated the charts before the advent of rock & roll and the music of the sixties rock revolution. Like the standard pop, this was music usually created by committee—a writer, an artist, a producer, and an arranger. But, like rock, it was dominated by propulsive rhythms and a teenage lyrical stance. This compilation, especially the true "girl group" cuts, is consistently first-rate. As is the usual case with Rhino, the sound, while reflecting its age from time to time, is a solid improvement over any other versions of hits made at a time when women vocalists enjoyed their greatest popular success. Excellent album notes complete a fine package.

**Soundtrack: Woodstock/Woodstock II
(1969)**
Mobile Fidelity Sound MFCD41816 (226:09—
four discs)   **[B]**
More aural history than concert recording. To say that it's all here would obviously be a literal overstatement—the festival ran for over three days (and these
selections were drawn from seventy-two
hours of recorded tape). But after listening to the three hours and forty-six
minutes of music as well as the now-
infamous stage announcements, it's as
close as one is going to get two decades
after the fact. It's worthwhile to remember that the 400,000 who were a part of
this event were representatives of the
last real people's revolution this nation
has experienced. Impossible as it now
seems, they and countless others like
them really did stop the Vietnam War.
Woodstock was the first great sixties
event, the first mega-be-in, and no one
was prepared for the human outpouring
to which it bore musical witness. Soundwise, what you get is the magic moment
with all its warts intact—the feedback
and the hums, the flat performances and
the faux pas that make this more concert
verité than musical pinnacle—it was
really a question of who was there and
why, rather than what they played or
heard. This CD package captures that as
well as it can now be done, but you
won't play this one for its sound quality.

# THE TOP

## ROCK COMPACT DISCS
### (listed alphabetically by artist)

| | |
|---|---|
| **The Band** | MUSIC FROM BIG PINK (Mobile Fidelity ultradisc) |
| | THE BAND |
| **Beach Boys** | PET SOUNDS |
| **The Beatles** | ABBEY ROAD |
| | RUBBER SOUL |
| | SGT. PEPPER'S LONELY HEARTS CLUB BAND |
| | THE BEATLES (THE WHITE ALBUM) |
| **Chuck Berry** | THE CHESS BOX |
| | THE GREAT 28 |
| **James Brown** | LIVE AT THE APOLLO (1962) |
| | THE CD OF JB (SEX MACHINE AND OTHER |
| | SOUL CLASSICS) |
| **Jackson Browne** | THE PRETENDER |
| **Buffalo Springfield** | AGAIN |
| **The Byrds** | SWEETHEART OF THE RODEO |
| **Ray Charles** | ANTHOLOGY |
| | GREATEST COUNTRY & WESTERN HITS |
| **Eric Clapton** | CROSSROADS |
| **The Clash** | THE CLASH |
| **Collections** | ATLANTIC RHYTHM AND BLUES 1947–74 VOLUME 6 |
| | (1966–69) |
| | THE BEST OF DOO-WOP BALLADS |
| | GREAT SONGS WRITTEN BY HOLLAND-DOZIER- |
| | HOLLAND |
| | ROCK & ROLL THE EARLY DAYS |
| | THE SOUL OF NEW ORLEANS |
| | TOGA ROCK |

| | |
|---|---|
| **Sam Cooke** | THE MAN AND HIS MUSIC |
| **Elvis Costello** | MY AIM IS TRUE |
| | SPIKE |
| **Creedence Clearwater Revival** | CHRONICLE (20 GREATEST HITS) |
| **Nick Drake** | BRYTER LAYTER |
| **Bob Dylan** | BLONDE ON BLONDE |
| | BLOOD ON THE TRACKS |
| | BRINGING IT ALL BACK HOME |
| | HIGHWAY 61 REVISITED |
| **The Everly Brothers** | CADENCE CLASSICS (THEIR 20 GREATEST HITS) |
| **Bryan Ferry** | THESE FOOLISH THINGS |
| **Aretha Franklin** | 30 GREATEST HITS |
| **Marvin Gaye** | WHAT'S GOING ON/LET'S GET IT ON |
| **The Jimi Hendrix Experience** | ARE YOU EXPERIENCED? |
| | ELECTRIC LADYLAND |
| **John Hiatt** | BRING THE FAMILY |
| **Buddy Holly** | FROM THE ORIGINAL MASTER TAPES |
| **Elton John** | TO BE CONTINUED |
| **Led Zeppelin** | LED ZEPPELIN (1969–1979) |
| **John Lennon** | PLASTIC ONO BAND |
| **Jerry Lee Lewis** | FERRIDAY FIREBALL |
| **Little Richard** | 18 GREATEST HITS |
| **Bob Marley & the Wailers** | LIVE! |
| | UPRISING |
| **Joni Mitchell** | COURT AND SPARK |
| **Van Morrison** | ASTRAL WEEKS |
| | MOONDANCE |
| | IT'S TOO LATE TO STOP NOW |
| | INTO THE MUSIC |
| **Randy Newman** | 12 SONGS |
| **Sinead O'Connor** | I DO NOT WANT WHAT I HAVEN'T GOT |
| **Roy Orbison** | FOR THE LONELY: 18 GREATEST HITS |
| **Graham Parker & the Rumour** | HOWLING WIND |
| | SQUEEZING OUT SPARKS |
| **Pink Floyd** | DARK SIDE OF THE MOON (Mobile Fidelity ultradisc) |
| **Elvis Presley** | ELVIS |
| | THE MEMPHIS RECORD |
| | ELVIS PRESLEY |
| | THE SUN SESSIONS |

| | |
|---|---|
| **The Pretenders** | THE PRETENDERS |
| **Prince** | 1999 |
| **Prince and the Revolution** | PURPLE RAIN |
| **R.E.M.** | RECKONING |
| **The Rolling Stones** | AFTERMATH<br>BEGGAR'S BANQUET<br>EXILE ON MAIN STREET<br>THE SINGLES |
| **Otis Redding** | THE OTIS REDDING STORY |
| **Lou Reed** | NEW YORK |
| **Diana Ross and the Supremes** | 20 GREATEST HITS |
| **The Sex Pistols** | NEVER MIND THE BOLLOCKS HERE'S THE SEX PISTOLS |
| **Paul Simon** | GRACELAND<br>PAUL SIMON |
| **Simon & Garfunkel** | BOOKENDS |
| **Sly and the Family Stone** | GREATEST HITS<br>THERE'S A RIOT GOING ON |
| **Bruce Springsteen** | BORN TO RUN<br>BORN IN THE USA<br>NEBRASKA<br>TUNNEL OF LOVE |
| **Rod Stewart** | EVERY PICTURE TELLS A STORY (Mobile Fidelity) |
| **Talking Heads** | REMAIN IN LIGHT<br>SPEAKING IN TONGUES |
| **James Taylor** | JT |
| **Richard Thompson** | HAND OF KINDNESS |
| **Richard and Linda Thompson** | SHOOT OUT THE LIGHTS |
| **U2** | THE JOSHUA TREE |
| **Frankie Valli & the Four Seasons** | THE TWENTY-FIFTH ANNIVERSARY COLLECTION |
| **Velvet Underground** | THE VELVET UNDERGROUND AND NICO |
| **Jennifer Warnes** | FAMOUS BLUE RAINCOAT |
| **The Who** | WHO'S NEXT |
| **Stevie Wonder** | INNERVISIONS<br>MUSIQARIUM |
| **Neil Young** | DECADE<br>FREEDOM<br>RUST NEVER SLEEPS |

(In compiling this list the intention was to provide a basic library of rock & roll available on compact disc that would be representative of the major strains, influences, and acknowledged "classics" that have shaped popular music since 1955, generally conceded to be the year it all officially began. In a few instances, the sound quality is not necessarily state-of-the-art, but the musical content or historical import more than outweigh the sonic deficiencies.)

# BIBLIOGRAPHY

Aftell, Mandy. *Death of a Rolling Stone: The Brian Jones Story.* New York: Delilah Books, 1982.

Anson, Robert Sam. *Gone Crazy and Back Again (The Rise and Fall of the Rolling Stone Generation).* New York: Doubleday, 1981.

Aquila, Richard. *That Old Time Rock & Roll.* New York: Schirmer Books, 1989.


Bacon, Tony, ed. *Rock Hardware: The Instruments, Equipment and Technology of Rock.* New York: Harmony Books, 1981.

Baker, Glenn A., and Stuart Coups. *The New Music.* New York: Harmony Books, 1980.

Balfour, Victoria. *Rock Wives.* New York: William Morrow & Co., 1986.

Bane, Michael. *White Boys Singin' the Blues: The Black Roots of White Rock.* New York: Charles Scribner's Sons, 1982.

Bangs, Lester. *Blondie.* New York: Delilah, 1983.

Bangs, Lester. *Psychotic Reactions and Carburetor Dung.* New York: Knopf, 1987.

Bebey, Francis. *African Music: A Peoples Art.* Translated by Josephine Bennett. Westport, Conn.: Lawrence Hill & Co., 1975.

Belsito, Peter, and Bob Davis. *Hard Core California: A History of Punk and New Wave.* Berkeley, California: Last Gasp of San Francisco, 1983.

Berry, Chuck. *The Autobiography.* New York: Harmony Books, 1987.

Bockris, Victor, and Gerard Malanga. *Uptight: The Velvet Underground Story.* New York: Quill, 1983.

Boot, Adrian, and Michael Thomas. *Jamaica: Babylon on a Thin Wire.* New York: Schocken Books, Inc., 1977.

Bronson, Fred. *The Billboard Book of Number 1 Hits.* New York: Billboard Publications, Inc., 1985.

Brooks, Elston. *I've Heard Those Songs Before.* New York: Quill, 1981.

Brown, James, with Bruce Tucker. *James Brown: The Godfather of Soul.* New York: Macmillan Publishing Co., 1986.

Butler, Dougal, and others. *Full Moon: The Amazing Rock & Roll Life of Keith Moon.* New York: Quill, 1981.

Byrne, David. *True Stories.* New York: Penguin Books, 1986.


Carr, Roy, Brian Case and Fred Dellar. *The Hipsters, Jazz and the Beat Generation.* London: Faber & Faber, Inc., 1986.

Castleman, Harry, and Walter Podrazik. *All Together Now (The First Complete Beatles Discography 1961–75)*. New York: Ballantine Books, 1975.

Charone, Barbara. *Keith Richards Life as a Rolling Stone*. New York: Dolphin Books, 1982.

Christgau, Robert. *Any Old Way You Choose It (Rock and Other Pop Music, 1967–73)*. New York: Penguin Books, 1973.

Christgau, Robert. *Christgau's Record Guide*. New York: Ticknor & Fields, 1981.

Christgau, Robert. *Christgau's Record Guide: Rock Albums of the 80s*. New York: Pantheon Books, 1990.

Cianci, Bob. *Great Rock Drummers of the 60s*. Milwaukee, Wisconsin: Hal Leonard Publishing Corporation, 1989.

Clarke, Donald, ed. *The Penguin Encyclopedia of Popular Music*. New York: Viking, 1989.

Clifford, Mike, consultant. *The Illustrated Encyclopedia of Black Music*. New York: Harmony Books, 1982.

Clifford, Mike. *The Harmony Illustrated Encyclopedia of Rock and Roll*. New York: Harmony Books, 1983.

Coleman, Stuart. *They Kept on Rockin'.* New York: Blandford Press Ltd., 1982.

Cott, Jonathan. *Dylan*. New York: Rolling Stone Press/Doubleday, 1984.

Coupe, Stuart, and Glenn A. Baker. *The New Rock'N'Roll: The A–Z of Rock in the 80s*. New York: St. Martin's Press, 1983.


Dalton, David. *The Rolling Stones: The First 25 Years*. New York: Alfred A. Knopf Inc., 1981.

Davis, Miles, with Quincy Troupe. *Miles—The Autobiography*. New York: Simon & Schuster, 1989.

Davis, Stephen. *Bob Marley.* New York: Doubleday, 1985.

Davis, Stephen. *Hammer of the Gods: The Led Zeppelin Saga*. New York: William Morrow & Co., 1985.

Davis, Stephen, and Peter Simon. *Reggae Bloodlines: In Search of the Music and Culture of Jamaica*. New York: Anchor Books Press, 1977.

Davis, Stephen, and Peter Simon. *Reggae International*. New York: R&B, 1982.

Denisoff, R. Serge. *Solid Gold: The Popular Record Industry.* New Brunswick, N.J.: Transaction Books, 1975.

Doerschuk, Bob, ed. *Rock Keyboard*. New York: Quill, 1985.

Duncan, Robert. *The Noise (Notes From Rock'N'Roll Era)*. New York: Ticknor & Fields, 1984.

Duncan, Robert. *Only the Good Die Young*. New York: Harmony Books, 1986.

Dylan, Bob. *Bob Dylan Writings and Drawings*. St. Albans, England: Panther, 1974.

Dylan, Bob. *Bob Dylan Lyrics 1962–85*. New York: Alfred A. Knopf, Inc., 1985.

Dylan, Bob. *Tarantula*. St. Albans, England: Panther, 1966.


Eisen, Jonathan, ed. *The Age of Rock (Sounds of the American Cultural Revolution)*. New York: Vintage, 1969.

Eisen, Jonathan, ed. *The Age of Rock 2 (Sights and Sounds of the American Cultural Revolution)*. New York: Vintage, 1970.

Eliot, Marc. *Rockonomics . . . The Money Behind the Music*. New York: Franklin Watts, 1989.

Elliott, Martin. *The Rolling Stones Complete Recording Sessions 1963–1989*. New York: Blandford/Sterling Publishing Co. Inc., 1990.

Elson, Howard, and John Burnton. *Whatever Happened To . . . ?* New York: Proteus, 1981.

Escott, Colin, and Martin Hawkins. *Sun Records*. New York: Quick Fox, 1975.

Fawcett, Anthony, *California Rock/California Sound*. Los Angeles: Reed Books, 1978.

Fawcett, Anthony. *John Lennon: One Day at a Time*. New York: Grove Press Inc., 1976.

Flanagan, Bill. *Written in My Soul*. Chicago: Contemporary Books Inc., 1986.

Flippo, Chet. *On the Road with the Rolling Stones*. New York: Dolphin Books, 1985.

Fong-Torres, Ben, ed. *The Rolling Stone Rock'N'Roll Reader*. New York: Bantam, 1974.

Fox, Ted. *In the Groove*. New York: St. Martin's Press, 1986.

Frame, Pete. *The Complete Rock Family Trees, Volumes 1 and 2*. Port Chester, N.Y.: Omnibus Press, 1980.

Friedman, Myra. *Buried Alive: The Biography of Janis Joplin*. New York: Bantam, 1974.

Frith, Simon, ed. *Facing the Music*. New York: Pantheon Books, 1988.

Frith, Simon. *Music for Pleasure*. New York: Routledge, Chapman & Hall, 1988.

Frith, Simon and Andrew Goodwin, eds. *On Record*. New York: Pantheon Books, 1990.

Frith, Simon. *Sound Effects (Youth, Leisure and the Politics of Rock'N'Roll)*. New York: Pantheon, 1981.

Gaines, Steven. *Heroes and Villains: The True Story of the Beach Boys*. New York: New American Library, 1986.

Gambaccini, Paul. *Critics Choice: The Top 100 Rock'N'Roll Albums of All Time*. New York: Harmony Books, 1987.

Gans, David. *Talking Heads*. New York: Avon, 1985.

George, Nelson. *The Death of Rhythm and Blues*. New York: Pantheon Books, 1988.

George, Nelson. *Where Did Our Love Go? (The Rise and Fall of the Motown Sound)*. New York: St. Martin's Press, 1985.

Gilbert, Bob, and Gary Therou. *The Top 10 1956–Present*. New York: Simon & Schuster, 1982.

Gillette, Charlie. *Making Tracks: Atlantic Records and the Growth of a Multi-Billion-Dollar Industry*. New York: E.P. Dutton, 1974.

Gillette, Charlie. *The Sound of the City (The Rise of Rock & Roll)*. New York: Pantheon Books, 1970. Revised and updated, 1983.

Gleason, Ralph J. *The Jefferson Airplane and The San Francisco Sound*. New York: Ballantine Books, 1969.

Goldrosen, John. *The Buddy Holly Story*. New York: Quick Fox, 1975.

Goldrosen, John, and John Beecher. *Remembering Buddy*. New York: Penguin Books, 1987.

Gouldstone, David. *Elvis Costello: God's Comic.* New York: St. Martin's Press, 1989.

Greenberg, Allan. *Love In Vain (The Life and Legend of Robert Johnson).* New York: Doubleday & Co., 1983.

Greene, Bob. *Billion Dollar Baby.* New York: Signet, 1974.

Greig, Charlotte. *Will You Still Love Me Tomorrow: Girl Groups from the 50s On. . . .* London: Virago Press, 1989.

Guralnick, Peter. *Feel Like Goin' Home: Portraits in Blues and Rock'N'Roll.* New York: Vintage Books, 1971.

Guralnick, Peter. *Lost Highway.* New York: Vintage Books, 1982.

Guralnick, Peter. *Searching for Robert Johnson.* New York: E.P. Dutton, 1989.

Guralnick, Peter. *Sweet Soul Music (Rhythm & Blues and the Southern Dream of Freedom).* New York: Harper & Row, 1986.

Guthrie, Woody. *Bound for Glory.* New York: Plume, 1943. (Autobiography)

Hammond, John, with Irving Townsend. *John Hammond On Record.* New York: Penguin Books, 1977.

Haralambos, Michael. *Soul Music: The Birth of a Sound in Black America.* New York: Da Capo Press, 1974.

Heilbut, Anthony. *The Gospel Sound: Good News and Bad Times.* New York: Limelight Editions, 1985.

Helander, Brock. *The Rock Who's Who.* New York: Schirmer Books, 1982.

Henderson, David. *Jimi Hendrix: Voodoo Child of the Aquarian Age.* New York: Doubleday & Co., 1978.

Herman, Gary. *Rock'N'Roll Babylon.* New York: Perigee Books, 1982.

Hill, Dave. *Prince, a Pop Life.* New York: Harmony Books, 1989.

Hirshey, Gerri. *Nowhere to Run: The Story of Soul Music.* New York: Times Books, 1984.

Holliday, Billie, with William Duffy. *Lady Sings the Blues.* New York: Penguin Books, 1956.

Hopkins, Jerry. *Hit & Run—The Jimi Hendrix Story.* New York: Perigee Books, 1983.

Humphries, Patrick, and Chris Hunt. *Springsteen: Blinded by the Light.* New York: Henry Holt & Co., 1985.

Johnson, Howard, and Jim Pines. *Reggae: Deep Roots Music.* New York: Proteus Books, 1982.

Jones, LeRoy. *Blues People.* New York: William Morrow Co., Inc. 1963.

Joynson, Vernon. *The Acid Trip: A Complete Guide to Psychedelic Music.* London: Babylon Books, 1984.

Kooper, Al, with Ben Edmonds. *Backstage Passes.* Briarcliff Manor, N.Y.: Stein & Day, 1977.

Kozak, Roman. *This Ain't No Disco: The Story of CBGB.* London: Faber & Faber, Inc., 1988.

Landau, Jon. *It's Too Late to Stop Now: A Rock & Roll Journal.* San Francisco: Straight Arrow Books, 1972.

Lazell, Barry, with Dafydd Rees and Luke Crampton. *Rock Movers & Shakers: An A to Z of the People Who Made Rock Happen*. New York: Billboard Publications, 1989.

Lennon, John. *Skywriting by Word of Mouth*. New York: Harper & Row, 1986.

Lewisohn, Mark. *The Beatles Lives*. New York: Henry Holt & Co., 1986.

Lewisohn, Mark. *The Beatles Recording Sessions*. New York: Harmony Books, 1988.

Lydon, Michael. *Rock Folk*. New York: Citadel Press, 1990.

Macken, Bob, and others. *The Rock Music Source Book*. New York: Anchor Press, 1980.

Marcus, Greil. *Lipstick Traces*. Cambridge, Massachusetts: Harvard University Press, 1989.

Marcus, Greil. *Mystery Train (Images of America in Rock'N'Roll Music)* 3d ed. New York: E.P. Dutton, 1990.

Marcus, Greil. *Stranded (Rock & Roll for a Desert Island)*. New York: Alfred A. Knopf Inc., 1979.

Marre, Jeremy, and Hannah Charlton. *Beats of the Heart*. New York: Pantheon Books, 1985.

Marsh, Dave. *Before I Get Old: The Story of the Who*. New York: St. Martin's Press, 1983.

Marsh, Dave. *The Book of Rock Lists*. New York: Dell/Rolling Stone Press, 1981.

Marsh, Dave. *Born to Run: The Bruce Springsteen Story*. New York: Delilah, 1979.

Marsh, Dave. *The First Rock & Roll Confidential Report*. New York: Pantheon Books, 1985.

Marsh, Dave. *Fortunate Son: The Best of Dave Marsh*. New York: Random House, 1985.

Marsh, Dave. *The Heart of Rock & Soul: The 1001 Greatest Singles Ever Made*. New York: New American Library, 1989.

Marsh, Dave, and John Swenson. *The New Rolling Stone Record Guide*. New York: Random House/Rolling Stone Press, 1979, rev. 1983.

Marsh, Dave, and others. *Rock Topicon*. Chicago: Contemporary Books Inc., 1984.

Martin, George, with Jeremy Hornsby. *All You Need Is Ears*. New York: St. Martin's Press, 1979.

McDonough, Jack. *San Francisco Rock 1965/1985: The Illustrated History of San Francisco Rock Music*. San Francisco: Chronicle Books, 1985.

Meltzer, Richard. *The Aesthetics of Rock*. New York: Da Capo Press, 1970.

Mendelssohn, John. *Kinks Kronikles*. New York: Quill, 1985.

Miller, Jim, ed. *The Rolling Stone Illustrated History of Rock and Roll*. New York: Random House/Rolling Stone Press, 1976.

Millers, Wilfrid. *A Darker Shade of Pale (A Backdrop to Bob Dylan)*. New York: Oxford University Press, 1985.

Morse, David. *Motown*. New York: Collier, 1971.

Morthland, John. *The Best of Country Music*. New York: Doubleday/Dolphin, 1984.

Muirhead, Bert. *The Record Producers File: A Directory of Rock Album Producers 1962/1984*. New York: Blandford Press Ltd., 1984.

Muirhead, Bert. *Stiff: The Story of a Record Label* New York: Blandford Press Ltd. 1983.

Murray, Charles Shaar. *Crosstown Traffic*. New York: St. Martin's Press, 1989.

Murrells, Joseph, compiled by. *The Book of Golden Discs: The Records That Sold a Million.* n.p.: Barrie & Jenkins, 1974.
Murrells, Joseph. *Million Selling Records from the 1900s to the 1980s: An Illustrated Directory.* New York: Arco Publishing Co., 1984.

Naha, Ed, compiled by. *Lillian Roxson's Rock Encyclopedia.* New York: Grosset & Dunlap, 1978.
Nite, Norm N. *Rock On Almanac.* New York: Harper & Row, 1986.
Nite, Norm N. *Rock On (The Illustrated Encyclopedia of Rock & Roll—The Solid Gold Years, Volume I).* New York: Thomas Y. Crowell, 1974.
Nite, Norm N. *Rock On (The Illustrated Encyclopedia of Rock & Roll—The Modern Years, 1964–Present Volume II).* New York: Thomas Y. Crowell, 1978.
Nite, Norm N. *Rock On Volume III (The Illustrated Encyclopedia of Rock & Roll—The Video Revolution 1978–Present).* New York: Harper & Row, 1985.
Noble, Peter L. *Future Pop: Music for the 80s.* New York: Delilah, 1983.
Norman, Philip. *The Road Goes On Forever.* New York: Simon & Schuster, 1982.
Norman, Philip. *Shout! The Beatles and Their Generation.* New York: Simon & Schuster, 1981.
Norman, Philip. *Sympathy for the Devil: The Rolling Stones Story.* New York: Linden Press/Simon & Schuster, 1984.

Palmer, Robert. *Deep Blues.* New York: Penguin Books, 1981.
Palmer, Tony. *All You Need Is Love: The Story of Popular Music.* New York: Penguin Books, 1977.
Pareles, John, and Patricia Romanowski. *The Rolling Stone Encyclopedia of Rock & Roll.* New York: Rolling Stone Press/Summit Books, 1983.
Partridge, Marianne. *The Motown Album.* New York: St. Martin's Press, 1990.
Pattison, Robert. *The Triumph of Vulgarity.* New York: Oxford University Press, 1967.
Pearlman, Jill. *Elvis for Beginners.* London: Unwin Paperbacks, 1986.
Peellaert, Guy, and Nick Cohn. *Rock Dreams.* New York: R&B, 1982.
Pichaske, David. *A Generation in Motion: Popular Music and Culture in the 60s.* Granite Falls, Minnesota: Ellis Press, 1989.
Pickering, Stephen. *Bob Dylan Approximately.* New York: David McKay Co. Inc., 1975.
Pleasants, Henry. *The Great American Popular Singers.* New York: Simon & Schuster, Inc., 1974.
Pollock, Bruce, *When Rock Was Young.* New York: Holt, Rinehart & Winston, 1981.
Pollock, Bruce. *When the Music Mattered: Rock in the Sixties.* New York: Holt, Rinehart & Winston, 1983.
Porter, Cole. *The Complete Lyrics of Cole Porter.* New York: Vintage Books, 1984.

Raker, Muck. *Rockbottom.* New York: Proteus, 1981.
Reese, Krista. *Chuck Berry: Mr. Rock'N'Roll.* New York: Proteus, 1982.
Reese, Krista. *Elvis Costello.* New York: Proteus, 1981.
Reese, Krista. *The Name of This Book Is Talking Heads.* New York: Proteus, 1982.
Reich, Charles, and Jann Wenner with Jerry Garcia and others. "Garcia: A Signpost to New Space." *Rolling Stone* interview. San Francisco: Straight Arrow Books, 1972.

Riley, Tim. *Tell Me Why*. New York: Alfred Knopf, 1988.
Rinzler, Allan. *Bob Dylan: The Illustrated Record*. New York: Harmony Books, 1978.
Ritz, David. *Divided Soul: The Life of Marvin Gaye*. Toronto/New York: PaperJacks Ltd., 1986.
Rivelli, Pauline, and Robert Levin, eds. *Giants of Rock Music*. New York: Da Capo Press, 1978.
Robbins, Ira A., ed. *The New Trouser Press Record Guide*. New York: Collier Books, 1985.
Robbins, Ira A. *The Trouser Press Guide to New Wave Records*. New York: Charles Scribner's Sons, 1983.
Rockwell, John. *Sinatra: An American Classic*. New York: Random House/Rolling Stone Press, 1984.
Rogan, Johnny. *Van Morrison*. New York: Proteus, 1984.
*Rolling Stone* eds. *The Rolling Stone Interviews Volume 2*. New York: Warner Books, 1973.
*Rolling Stone* eds. *The Rolling Stone Interviews 1967–80*. New York: St. Martin's Press/Rolling Stone Press, 1981.
*Rolling Stone* eds. *The Rolling Stone Interviews: The 1980s*. New York: St. Martin's Press/Rolling Stone Press, 1989.
*Rolling Stone* eds. *The Rolling Stone Record Review*. New York: Pocket Books, 1971.
*Rolling Stone* eds. *The Rolling Stone Record Review Volume 2*. New York: Pocket Books, 1974.
Russell, Ethan A. *Dear Mr. Fantasy*. Boston: Houghton Mifflin Co., 1985.
Ryback, Timothy W. *Rock Around the Bloc*. New York: Oxford University Press, 1990.

Sanchez, Tony. *Up and Down with the Rolling Stones*. New York: William Morrow & Co., Inc., 1979.
Santelli, Robert. *Sixties Rock*. Chicago: Contemporary Books, Inc., 1985.
Saporita, Jay. *Pourin' It All Out*. Secaucus, N.J.: Citadel Press, 1980.
Sarlin, Bob. *Turn It Up (I Can't Hear the Words)*. New York: Simon & Schuster, 1973.
Scaduto, Anthony. *Bob Dylan An Intimate Biography*. New York: Grosset & Dunlap, Inc., 1971.
Scaduto, Tony. *Mick Jagger: Everybody's Lucifer*. New York: Berkley Medallion, 1974.
Schaffner, Nicholas. *The British Invasion*. New York: McGraw-Hill Inc., 1982.
Schnabel, Tom. *Stolen Moments*. Los Angeles: Acrobat Books, 1988.
Sculatti, Gene, and Davin Seay. *San Francisco Nights: The Psychedelic Music Trip 1965–68*. New York: St. Martin's Press, 1985.
Shannon, Bob, and John Javna. *Behind the Hits: Inside Stories of Classic Pop and Rock & Roll*. New York: Warner Books, 1986.
Shaw, Arnold. *Honkers and Shouters: The Golden Years of Rhythm & Blues*. New York: Macmillan Publishing Co., 1978.
Shaw, Arnold. *Dictionary of American Pop/Rock*. New York: Schirmer Books, 1982.
Shaw, Arnold. *The Rockin' 50s*. New York: Da Capo Press, Inc., 1974.
Shelton, Robert. *No Direction Home . . . The Life and Music of Bob Dylan*. New York: Beech Tree Books, 1986.
Shepard, Sam. *Rolling Thunder Log Book*. New York: Penguin, 1977.

Shore, Michael, with Dick Clark. *The History of American Bandstand.* New York: Ballantine Books, 1985.

Sklar, Rick. *Rocking America.* New York: St. Martin's Press, 1984.

Smith, Joe. *Off the Record.* New York: Warner Books, Inc., 1988.

Smith, Wes. *The Pied Pipers of Rock 'n' Roll: Radio Dee Jays of the 50s and 60s.* Marietta, Georgia: Longstreet Press, Inc., 1989.

Stallings, Penny. *Rock'N'Roll Confidential.* New York: Little, Brown & Co., 1984.

Stambler, Irwin. *Encyclopedia of Pop, Rock & Soul.* 2d ed. New York: St. Martin's Press, 1989.

Stambler, Irwin, and Grelun Landon. *The Encyclopedia of Folk, Country & Western Music.* Revised and expanded. New York: St. Martin's Press, 1984.

Stapleton, Chris, and Chris May. *African Rock.* New York: E.P. Dutton, 1987.

Street, John. *Rebel Rock.* New York: Basil Blackwell Inc., 1986.

Stokes, Geoffrey. *Starmaking Machinery (Inside the Business of Rock & Roll).* New York: Vintage Books, 1976.

Swenson, John. *Bill Haley: The Daddy of Rock and Roll.* New York: Stein & Day, 1982.

Szatsmary, David P. *Rockin' in Time: A Social History of Rock 'n' Roll.* New Jersey: Prentice Hall, Inc., 1987.

Tabler, John, and Stuart Grundy. *The Record Producers.* New York: St. Martin's Press, 1983.

Tamm, Eric. *Brian Eno: His Music and the Vertical Color of Sound.* London: Faber and Faber, Inc., 1989.

Taylor, Derek. *It Was Twenty Years Ago Today (An Anniversary Celebration of 1967).* New York: Simon & Schuster, Inc., 1987.

Thomson, Elizabeth, and David Gutman, eds. *The Lennon Companion.* New York: Schirmer Books, 1987.

Tobler, John. *The Buddy Holly Story.* New York: Beaufort Books, 1979.

Tobler, John, and Andrew Doe. *The Doors.* New York: Proteus Books, 1984.

Tobler, John, and Stuart Grundy. *The Record Producers.* New York: St. Martin's Press, 1982.

Tosches, Nick. *Country.* New York: Charles Scribner's Sons, 1977, revised 1985.

Tosches, Nick. *Hellfire: The Jerry Lee Lewis Story.* New York: Dell Books, 1982.

Tosches, Nick. *Unsung Heroes of Rock'N'Roll.* New York: Charles Scribner's Sons, 1984.

Ulsan, Michael, and Bruce Solomon. *Dick Clark's The First 25 Years of Rock and Roll.* New York: Dell Books, 1981

Various authors. *New Women in Rock.* New York: Putnam, 1982.

Waller, Don. *The Motown Story.* New York: Charles Scribner's Sons, 1985.

Ward, Ed. *Michael Bloomfield: The Rise and Fall of an American Guitar Hero.* Port Chester, N.Y.: Cherry Lane Books, 1983.

Ward, Ed, and others. *Rock of Ages: The Rolling Stone History of Rock & Roll.* New York: Rolling Stone Press/Summit Books, 1986.

Weinberg, Max, with Robert Santelli. *The Big Beat.* Chicago: Contemporary Books Inc., 1984.

Wenner, Jann. *Groupies and Other Girls.* New York: Bantam Books, 1970.

Wenner, Jann S., ed. *Twenty Years of Rolling Stone . . . What a Long, Strange Trip It's Been.* New York: Straight Arrow Publishers, Inc., 1987.

West, Red, and others, as told to Steve Dunleavy. *Elvis What Happened?* New York: Ballantine Books, 1977.

Whitburn, Joel. *The Billboard Book of Top 40 Hits 1955 to Present.* New York: Billboard Publications, Inc., 1983.

Whitburn, Joel. *The Billboard Book of Top 40 Hits.* New York: Billboard Publications, Inc., 1985.

Whitburn, Joel. *Billboard's Music Yearbook 1986.* Menomonee Falls, Wisconsin: Record Research, Inc., 1987.

Whitburn, Joel. *Billboard's Top 2,000 1955-85.* Menomonee Falls, Wisconsin: Record Research, Inc., 1985.

Whitburn, Joel. *Pop Memories.* Menomonee Falls, Wisconsin: Record Research, Inc., 1986.

Whitburn, Joel. *Top Pop 1955-82.* Menomonee Falls, Wisconsin: Record Research, Inc., 1983.

Whitburn, Joel. *Top Pop Albums 1955-88.* Menomonee Falls, Wisconsin: Record Research, Inc., 1985.

Whitburn, Joel. *Top R&B Singles (1942-1988).* Menomonee Falls, Wisconsin: Record Research, Inc., 1988.

Whitcomb, Ian. *After the Ball.* New York: Simon & Schuster, Inc., 1973.

Whitcomb, Ian. *Rock Odyssey: A Musician's Chronicle of the 60s.* New York: Dolphin Books, 1983.

White, Charles. *The Life and Times of Little Richard (The Quasar of Rock).* New York: Harmony Books, 1984.

White, Timothy. *Catch a Fire: The Life of Bob Marley.* New York: Holt, Rinehart & Winston, 1983.

White, Timothy. *Rock Stars.* New York: Stewart, Tabori & Chang, 1984.

Wicke, Peter. *Rock Music: Culture, Aesthetics, & Sociology.* New York: Cambridge University Press, 1990.

Wilder, Alec. *American Popular Song . . . The Great Innovators 1900-50.* New York: Oxford University Press, 1972.

Williams, Allan, and William Marshall. *The Man Who Gave the Beatles Away.* New York: Ballantine Books, 1975.

Williams, Don. *Bob Dylan: The Man, The Music, The Message.* New York: Fleming H. Revell Co., 1985.

Williams, Paul. *Outlaw Blues (A Book of Rock Music).* New York: E.P. Dutton, 1969.

Wilson, Mary, with Patricia Romanowski and Ahrgus Juilliard. *Dreamgirl: My Life as a Supreme.* New York: St. Martin's Press, 1987.

Woliver, Robbie. *Bringing It All Back Home (25 Years of American Music at Folk City).* New York: Pantheon Books, 1986.

Worth, Fred L. and Steve D. Tamerius. *Elvis: His Life From A to Z.* Chicago: Contemporary Books, 1988.

York, William, ed. *Who's Who in Rock Music.* New York: Charles Scribner's Sons, 1982.